4. Have you visited the ADV Manga website?
- ☐ Yes
- ☐ No

5. Have you made any Manga purchases online ..o.. .ie ADV website?
- ☐ Yes
- ☐ No

6. If you have visited the ADV Manga website, how would you rate your online experience?
- ☐ Excellent
- ☐ Good
- ☐ Average
- ☐ Poor

7. What genre of Manga do you prefer?
(*Check all that apply*)
- ☐ adventure
- ☐ romance
- ☐ detective
- ☐ action
- ☐ horror
- ☐ sci-fi/fantasy
- ☐ sports
- ☐ comedy

8. How many manga titles have you purchased in the last 6 months?
- ☐ none
- ☐ 1-4
- ☐ 5-10
- ☐ 11+

9. Where do you make your manga purchases? (*Check all that apply*)
- ☐ comic store
- ☐ bookstore
- ☐ newsstand
- ☐ online
- ☐ other:_____
- ☐ department store
- ☐ grocery store
- ☐ video store
- ☐ video game store

10. Which bookstores do you usually make your manga purchases at?
- ☐ Barnes & Noble
- ☐ Walden Books
- ☐ Suncoast
- ☐ Best Buy
- ☐ Amazon.com
- ☐ Borders
- ☐ Books-A-Million
- ☐ Toys "Я" Us
- ☐ Other bookstore:
  _____

11. What's your favorite anime/manga website?
- ☐ adv-manga.com
- ☐ advfilms.com
- ☐ rightstuf.com
- ☐ animenewsservice.com
- ☐ animenewsnetwork.com
- ☐ Other:_____
- ☐ animeondvd.com
- ☐ anipike.com
- ☐ animeonline.net
- ☐ planetanime.com
- ☐ animenation.com

 **MANGA SURVEY**

PLEASE MAIL THE COMPLETED FORM TO: EDITOR – ADV MANGA
c/o A.D. Vision, Inc. 10114 W. Sam Houston Pkwy., Suite 200 Houston, TX 77099

Name:_____

Address:_____

City, State, Zip:_____

_____

E-Mail:_____

Male ☐   Female ☐   Age:_____

☐ **CHECK HERE IF YOU WOULD LIKE TO RECEIVE OTHER INFORMATION OR FUTURE OFFERS FROM ADV.**

All information provided will be used for internal purposes only. We promise not to sell or otherwise divulge your information.

1. Annual Household Income (*Check only one*)
☐ Under $25,000
☐ $25,000 to $50,000
☐ $50,000 to $75,000
☐ Over $75,000

2. How do you hear about new Manga releases? (*Check all that apply*)
☐ Browsing in Store   ☐ Magazine Ad
☐ Internet Reviews   ☐ Online Advertising
☐ Anime News Websites   ☐ Conventions
☐ Direct Email Campaigns   ☐ TV Advertising
☐ Online forums (message boards and chat rooms)
☐ Carrier pigeon
☐ Other:_____

3. Which magazines do you read? (*Check all that apply*)
☐ Wizard   ☐ YRB
☐ SPIN   ☐ EGM
☐ Animerica   ☐ Newtype USA
☐ Rolling Stone   ☐ SciFi
☐ Maxim   ☐ Starlog
☐ DC Comics   ☐ Wired
☐ URB   ☐ Vice
☐ Polygon   ☐ BPM
☐ Original Play Station Magazine ☐ I hate reading
☐ Entertainment Weekly   ☐ Other:_____

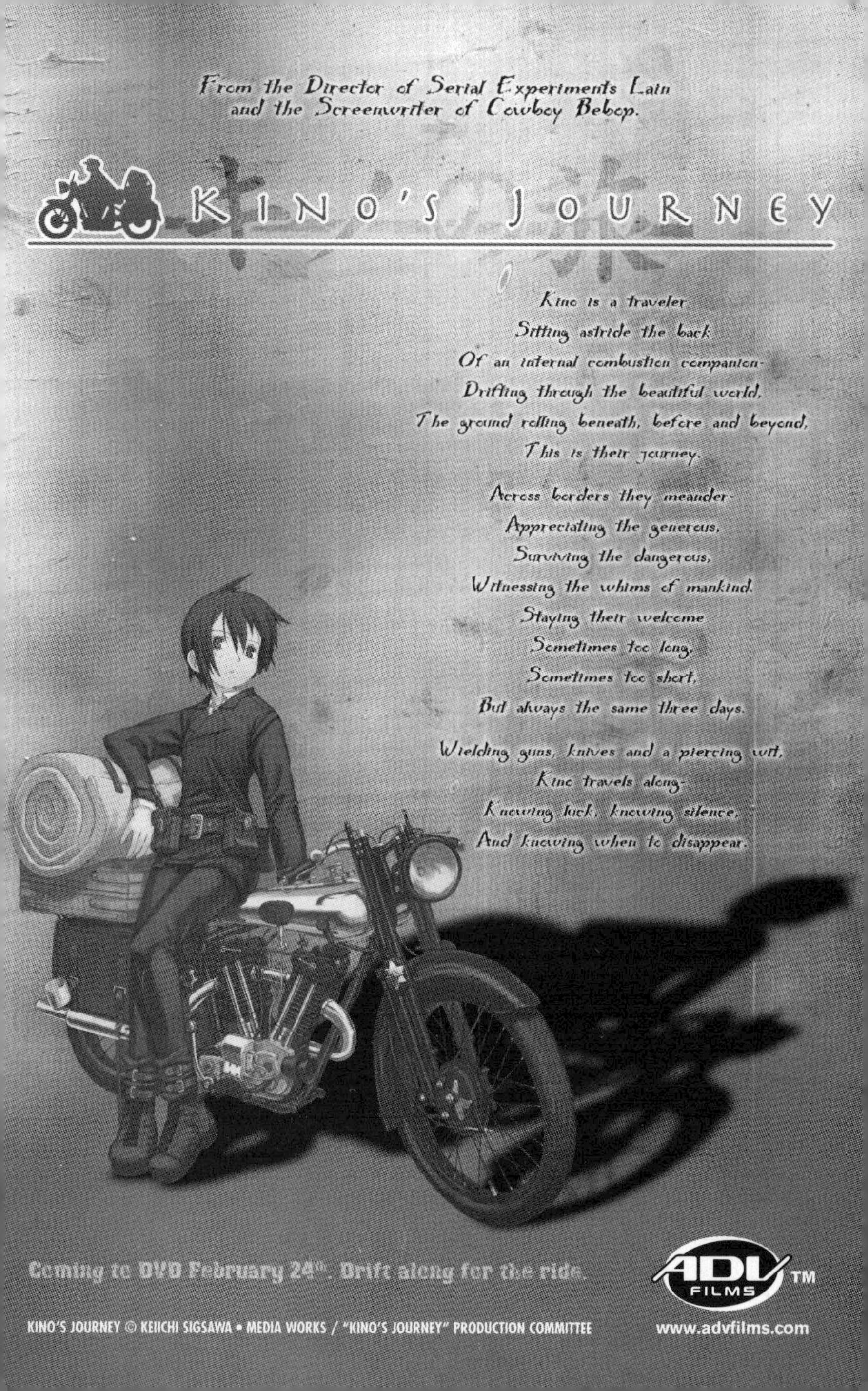
From the Director of Serial Experiments Lain
and the Screenwriter of Cowboy Bebop.
KINO'S JOURNEY
Kino is a traveler
Sitting astride the back
Of an internal combustion companion-
Drifting through the beautiful world,
The ground rolling beneath, before and beyond,
This is their journey.
Across borders they meander-
Appreciating the generous,
Surviving the dangerous,
Witnessing the whims of mankind.
Staying their welcome
Sometimes too long,
Sometimes too short,
But always the same three days.
Wielding guns, knives and a piercing wit,
Kino travels along-
Knowing luck, knowing silence,
And knowing when to disappear.
Coming to DVD February 24th. Drift along for the ride.
ADV FILMS TM
KINO'S JOURNEY © KEIICHI SIGSAWA • MEDIA WORKS / "KINO'S JOURNEY" PRODUCTION COMMITTEE
www.advfilms.com

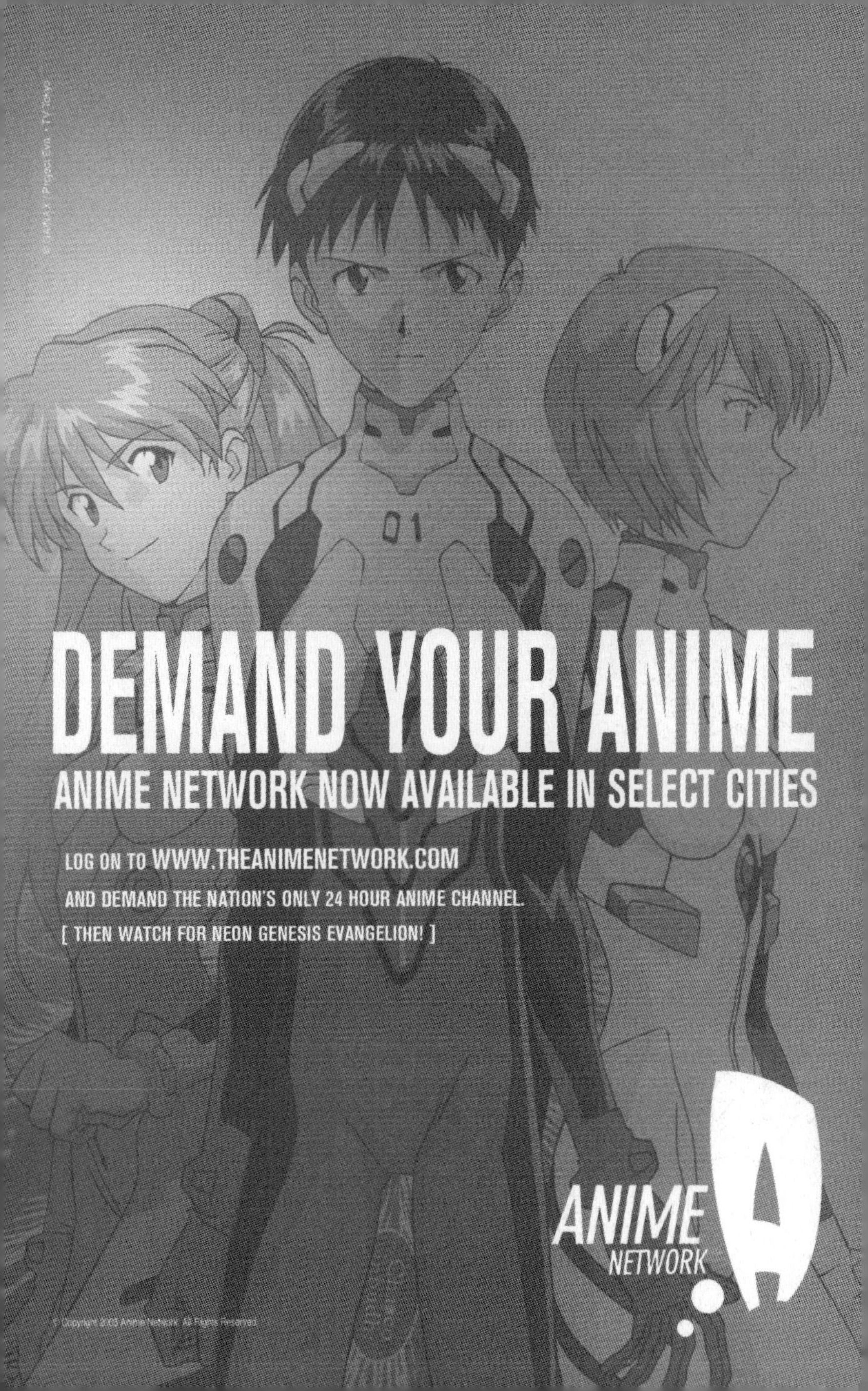
DEMAND YOUR ANIME
ANIME NETWORK NOW AVAILABLE IN SELECT CITIES
LOG ON TO WWW.THEANIMENETWORK.COM
AND DEMAND THE NATION'S ONLY 24 HOUR ANIME CHANNEL.
[THEN WATCH FOR NEON GENESIS EVANGELION!]
ANIME NETWORK
© Copyright 2003 Anime Network. All Rights Reserved.

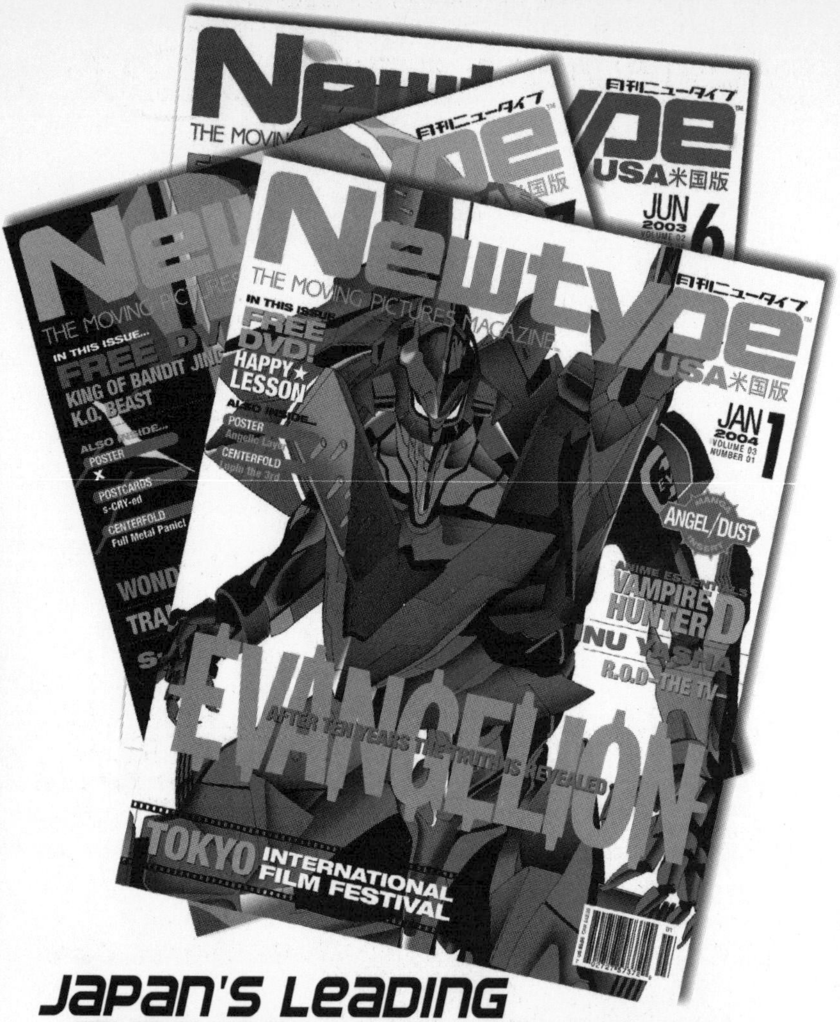
Newtype
THE MOVING PICTURES MAGAZINE
月刊ニュータイプ
USA 米国版
JUN 2003 6
IN THIS ISSUE...
FREE
KING OF BANDIT JING
K.O. BEAST
ALSO INSIDE...
POSTER
X
POSTCARDS
s-CRY-ed
CENTERFOLD
Full Metal Panic!
JAN 2004 1
VOLUME 03
NUMBER 01
FREE DVD!
HAPPY★LESSON
POSTER
CENTERFOLD
Lupin the 3rd
ANGEL/DUST
VAMPIRE HUNTER D
INU YASHA
R.O.D -THE TV-
EVANGELION
AFTER TEN YEARS THE TRUTH IS REVEALED
TOKYO INTERNATIONAL FILM FESTIVAL

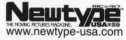

ALSO AVAILABLE FROM ADV MANGA™

Manga

Demon Palace Babylon
FULL METAL PANIC!
Azumanga Daioh
GUNSLINGER GIRL
Vol. 1

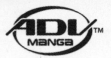

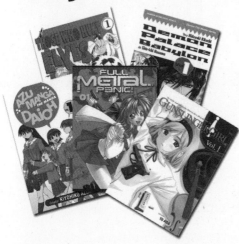

- Full Metal Panic!
- Azumanga Daioh
- Demon City Hunter
- Demon City Shinjuku
- Demon Palace Babylon
- Seven of Seven
- Gunslinger Girl
- Steel Angel Kurumi
- Those Who Hunt Elves
- Happy Lesson
- Darkside Blues

Illustration Books

ADV FILMS®

Rahxephon BIBLE
FULL METAL PANIC!
The Anime Mission

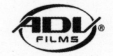

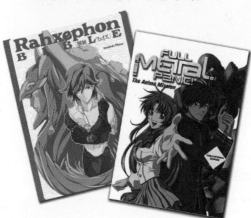

Rahxephon Bible

Full Metal Panic!

LETTER FROM THE ADV MANGA TRANSLATION STAFF

Dear Reader,

On behalf of the ADV Manga translation team, thank you for purchasing an ADV book. We are enthusiastic and committed to our work, and strive to carry our enthusiasm over into the book you hold in your hands.

Our goal is to retain the true spirit of the original Japanese book. While great care has been taken to render a true and accurate translation, some cultural or readability issues may require a line to be adapted for greater accessibility to our readers. At times, manga titles that include culturally-specific concepts will feature a "Translator's Notes" section, which explains noteworthy references to the original text.

We hope our commitment to a faithful translation is evident in every ADV book you purchase.

Sincerely,

Javier Lopez
Lead Translator

Eiko McGregor

Kay Bertrand

Brendan Frayne

Amy Forsyth

LETTTER
FROM THE
EDITOR

Dear Reader,

Thank you for purchasing an ADV Manga book. We hope you enjoyed the daring adventure of Louie.

It is our sincere commitment in reproducing Asian comics and graphic novels to retain as much of the character of the original book as possible. From the right-to-left format of the Japanese books to the meaning of the story in the original language, the ADV Manga team is working hard to publish a quality book for our fans and readers. Write to us with your questions or comments, and tell us how you liked this and other ADV books. Be sure to visit our website at www.adv-manga.com and view the list of upcoming titles, sign up for special announcements, and fill out our survey.

The ADV Manga team of translators, designers, graphic artists, production managers, traffic managers, and editors hope you will buy more ADV books —there's a lot more in store from ADV Manga!

www.adv-manga.com

Publishing Editor	Assistant Editor	Editorial Assistant
Susan B. Itin	Margaret Scharold	Varsha Bhuchar

LOUIE THE RUNE SOLDIER VOL. 1

© 2000 RYOU MIZUNO • JUN SASAMEYUKI
© 2000 MAMORU YOKOTA

Originally published in Japan in 2000 by KADOKAWA SHOTEN PUBLISHING CO., LTD., Tokyo.
English translation rights arranged with KADOKAWA SHOTEN PUBLISHING CO., LTD., Tokyo.

Translator	**BRENDAN FRAYNE**
Lead Translator/Translation Dept. Supervisor	**JAVIER LOPEZ**
ADV Manga Translation Staff	**EIKO McGREGOR, AMY FORSYTH, KAY BERTRAND**
Print Production/ Art Studio Manager	**LISA PUCKETT**
Art Production Manager	**RYAN MASON**
Sr. Designer/Creative Manager	**JORGE ALVARADO**
Graphic Designer/Group Leader	**SHANNON RASBERRY**
Graphic Designer	**KRISTINA MILESKI**
Graphic Artists	**WINDI MARTIN, NATALIA MORALES, LANCE SWARTOUT, GEORGE REYNOLDS, NANAKO TSUKIHASHI**
Graphic Intern	**IVAN CURIEL**
International Coordinators	**TORU IWAKAMI, ATSUSHI KANBAYASHI**
Publishing Editor	**SUSAN ITIN**
Assistant Editor	**MARGARET SCHAROLD**
Editorial Assistant	**VARSHA BHUCHAR**
Proofreader	**SHERIDAN JACOBS**
Research/ Traffic Coordinator	**MARSHA ARNOLD**
President, C.E.O & Publisher	**JOHN LEDFORD**

Email: editor@adv-manga.com
www.adv-manga.com
www.advfilms.com

For sales and distribution inquiries, please call 1.800.282.7202

 is a division of A.D. Vision, Inc.
10114 W. Sam Houston Parkway, Suite 200, Houston, Texas 77099

ISBN: 1-4139-0085-2
First printing, March 2004
10 9 8 7 6 5 4 3 2 1
Printed in Canada

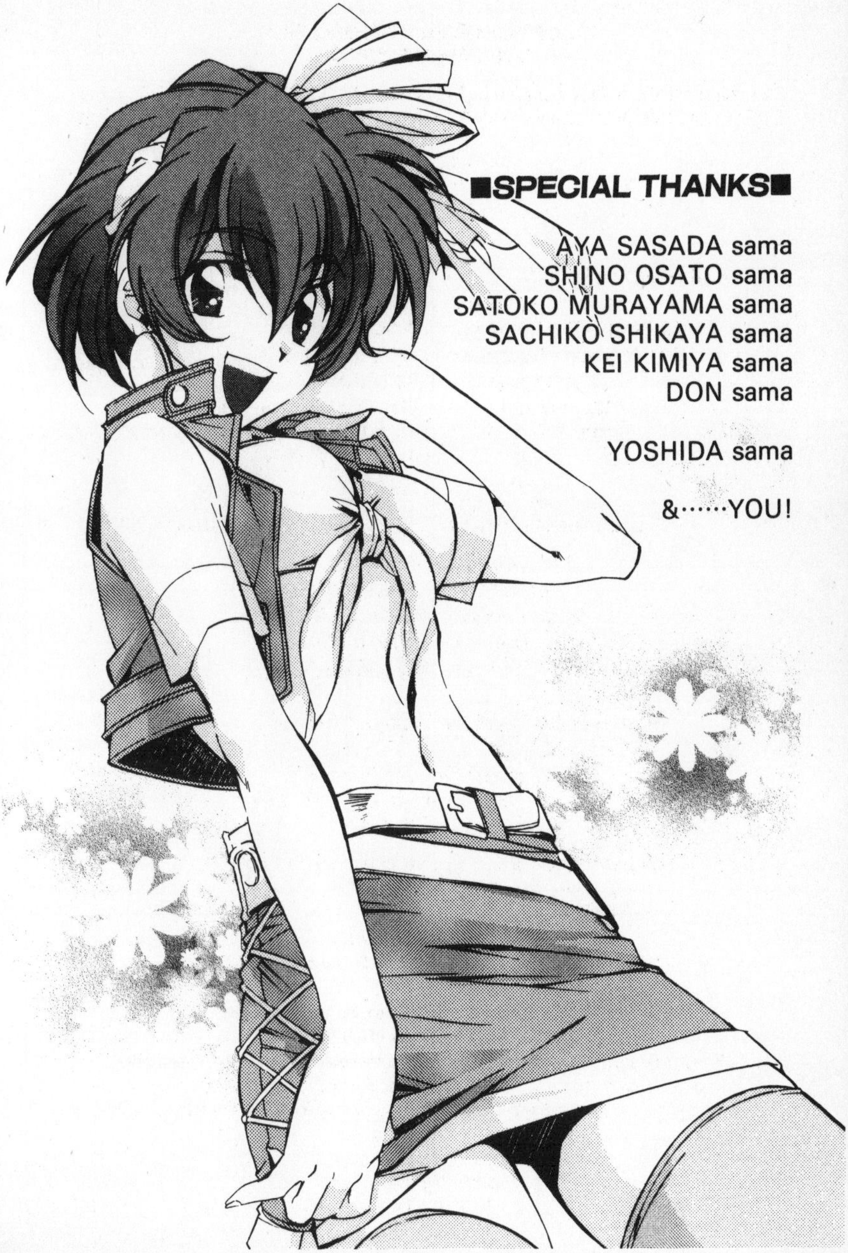

■SPECIAL THANKS■

AYA SASADA sama
SHINO OSATO sama
SATOKO MURAYAMA sama
SACHIKO SHIKAYA sama
KEI KIMIYA sama
DON sama

YOSHIDA sama

&……YOU!

AFTERWORD ♡

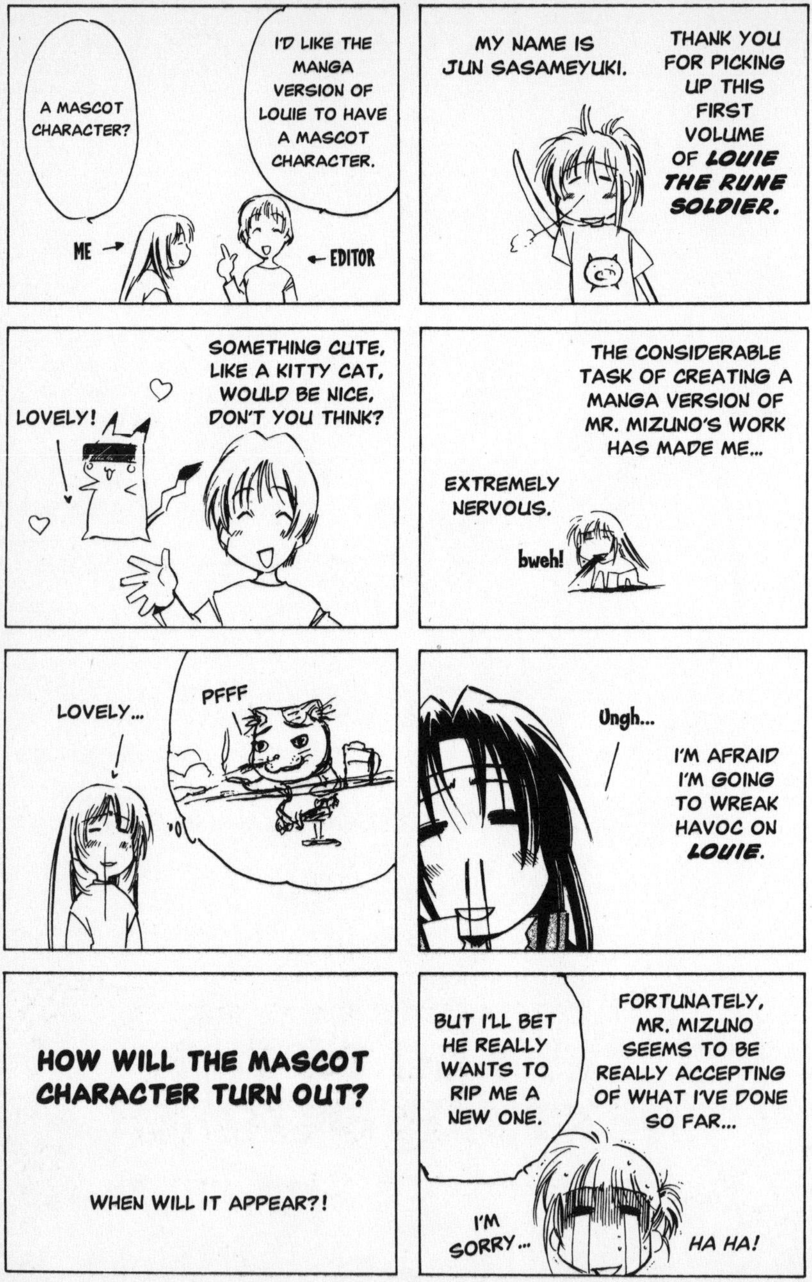
THANK YOU FOR PICKING UP THIS FIRST VOLUME OF LOUIE THE RUNE SOLDIER.
MY NAME IS JUN SASAMEYUKI.
I'D LIKE THE MANGA VERSION OF LOUIE TO HAVE A MASCOT CHARACTER.
A MASCOT CHARACTER?
EDITOR
ME
THE CONSIDERABLE TASK OF CREATING A MANGA VERSION OF MR. MIZUNO'S WORK HAS MADE ME...
EXTREMELY NERVOUS.
bweh!
SOMETHING CUTE, LIKE A KITTY CAT, WOULD BE NICE, DON'T YOU THINK?
LOVELY!
Ungh...
I'M AFRAID I'M GOING TO WREAK HAVOC ON LOUIE.
PFFF
LOVELY...
FORTUNATELY, MR. MIZUNO SEEMS TO BE REALLY ACCEPTING OF WHAT I'VE DONE SO FAR...
BUT I'LL BET HE REALLY WANTS TO RIP ME A NEW ONE.
HA HA!
I'M SORRY...
HOW WILL THE MASCOT CHARACTER TURN OUT?
WHEN WILL IT APPEAR?!

LET'S GO TO THE
NEXT ADVENTURE!!

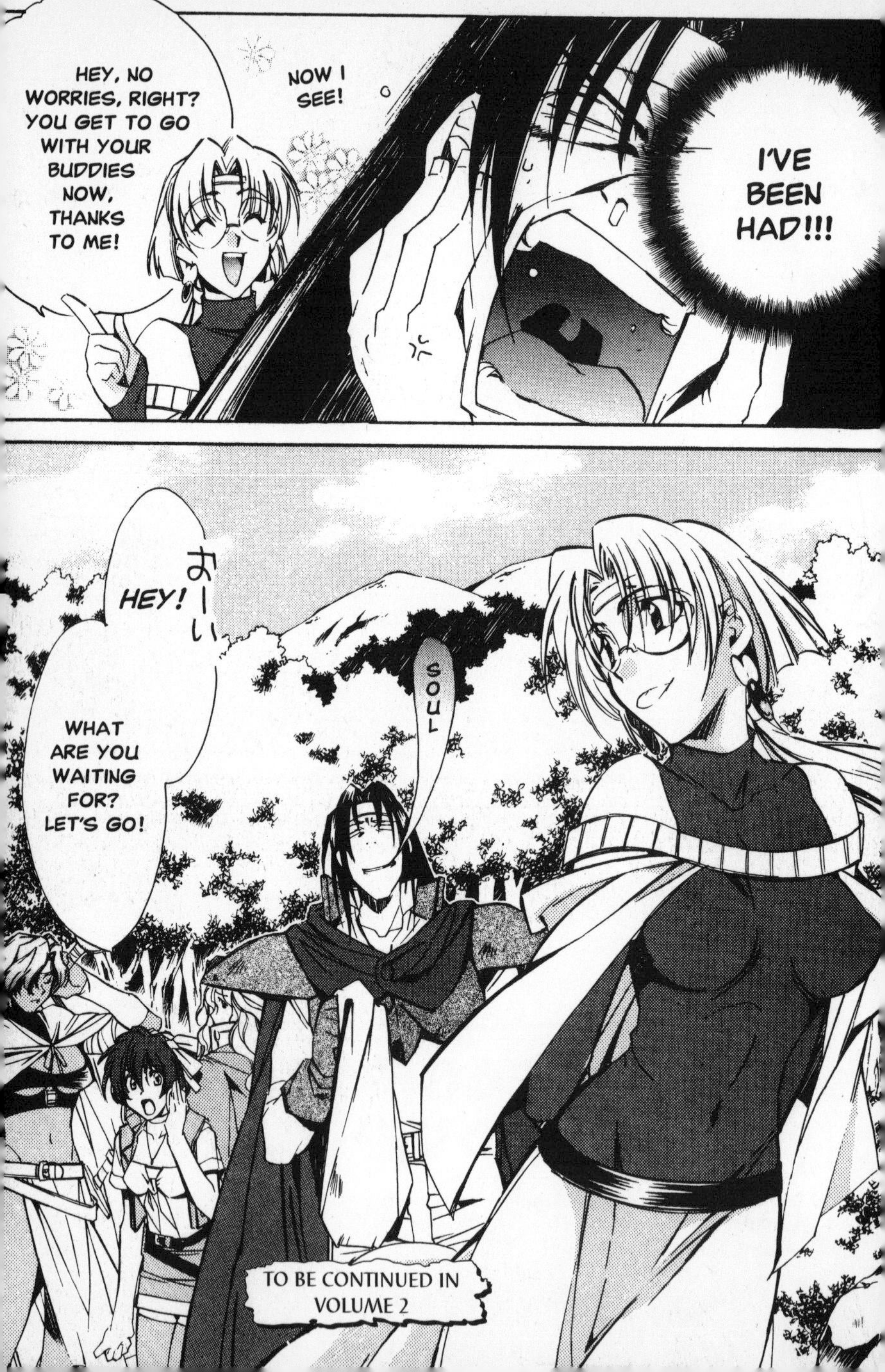
I'VE BEEN HAD!!!
NOW I SEE!
HEY, NO WORRIES, RIGHT? YOU GET TO GO WITH YOUR BUDDIES NOW, THANKS TO ME!
HEY!
おーい
WHAT ARE YOU WAITING FOR? LET'S GO!
SOUL
TO BE CONTINUED IN VOLUME 2

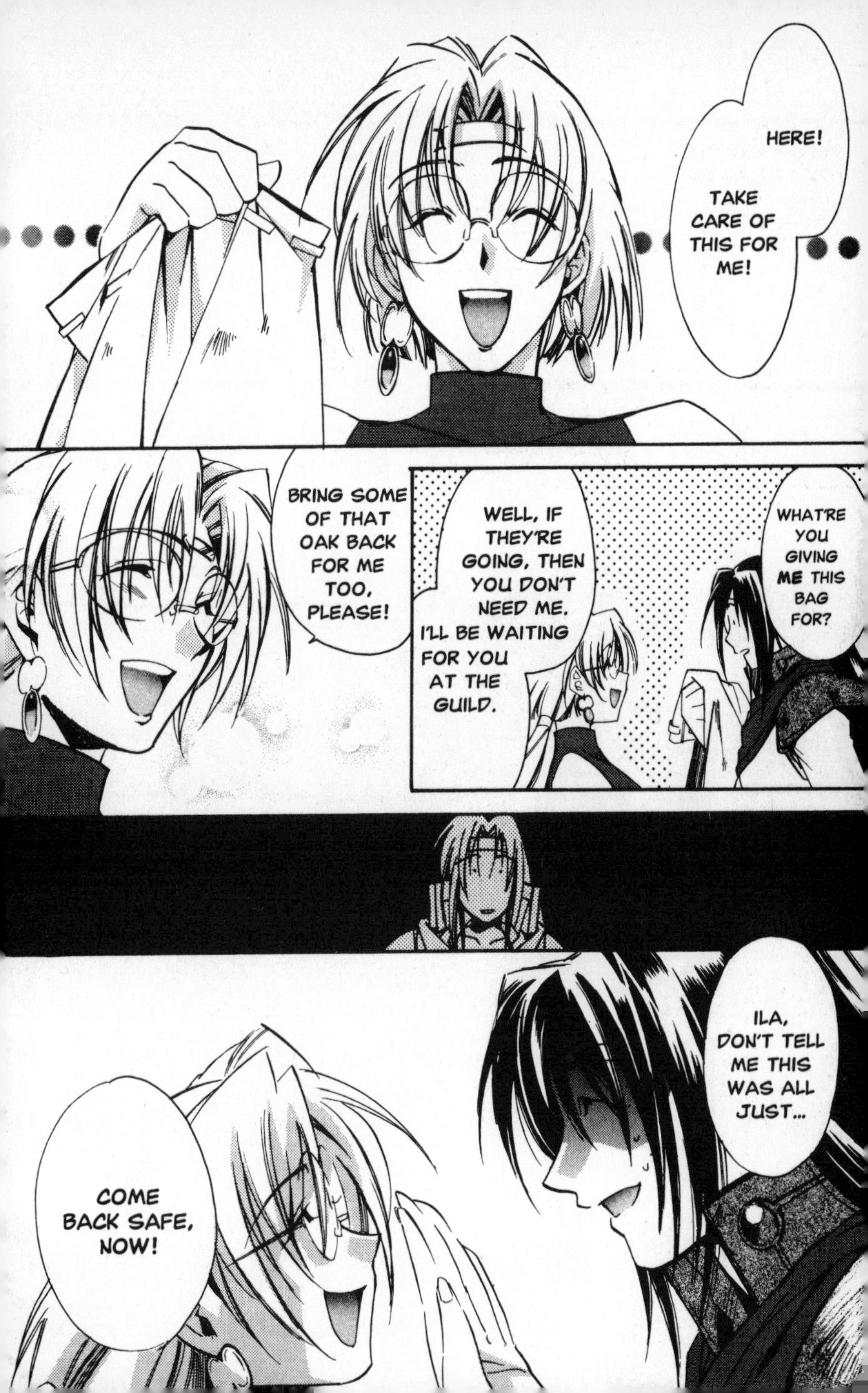
HERE!
TAKE CARE OF THIS FOR ME!
WHAT'RE YOU GIVING ME THIS BAG FOR?
WELL, IF THEY'RE GOING, THEN YOU DON'T NEED ME. I'LL BE WAITING FOR YOU AT THE GUILD.
BRING SOME OF THAT OAK BACK FOR ME TOO, PLEASE!
ILA, DON'T TELL ME THIS WAS ALL JUST...
COME BACK SAFE, NOW!

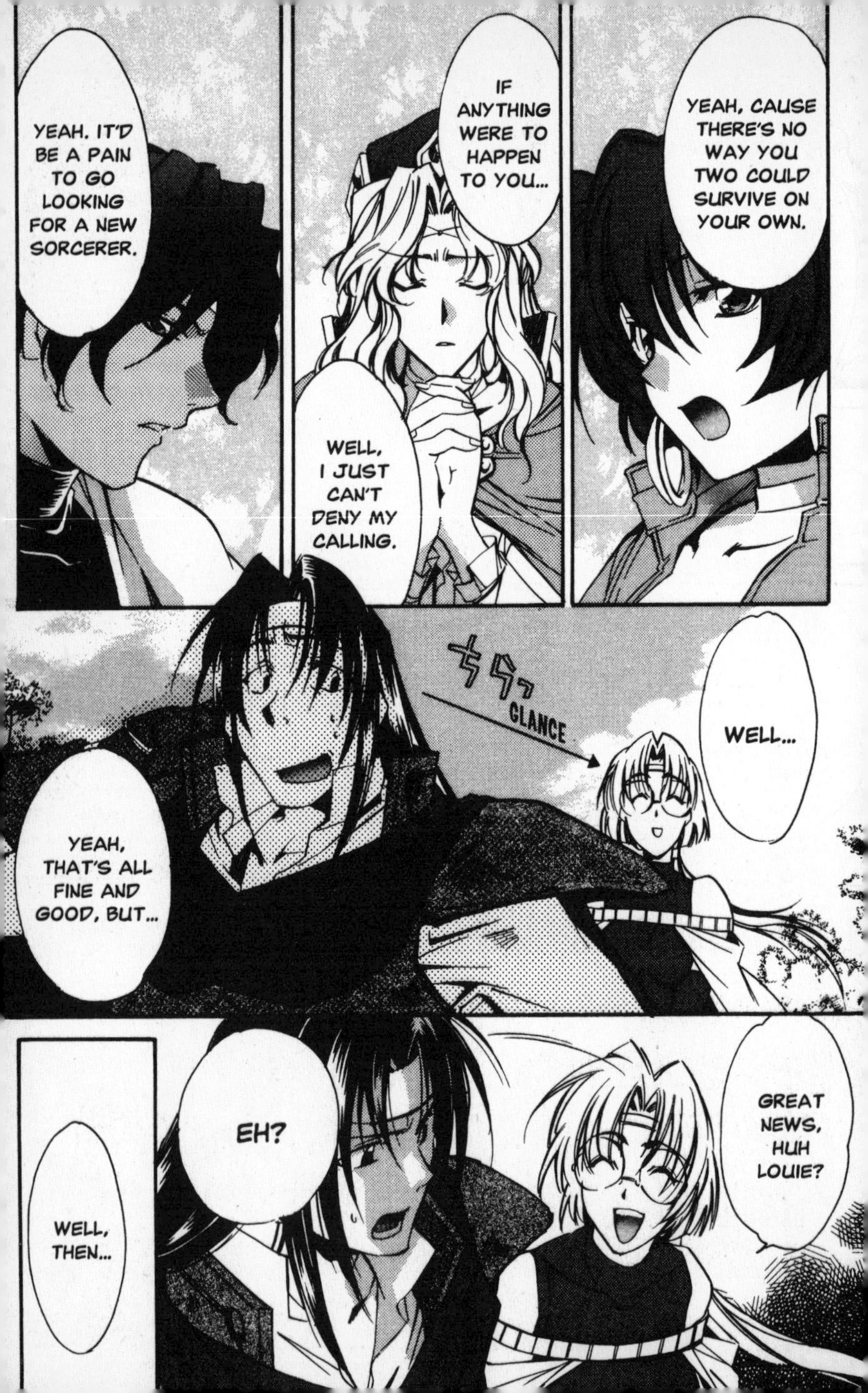
YEAH, CAUSE THERE'S NO WAY YOU TWO COULD SURVIVE ON YOUR OWN.
IF ANYTHING WERE TO HAPPEN TO YOU...
WELL, I JUST CAN'T DENY MY CALLING.
YEAH. IT'D BE A PAIN TO GO LOOKING FOR A NEW SORCERER.
WELL...
GLANCE
YEAH, THAT'S ALL FINE AND GOOD, BUT...
GREAT NEWS, HUH LOUIE?
EH?
WELL, THEN...

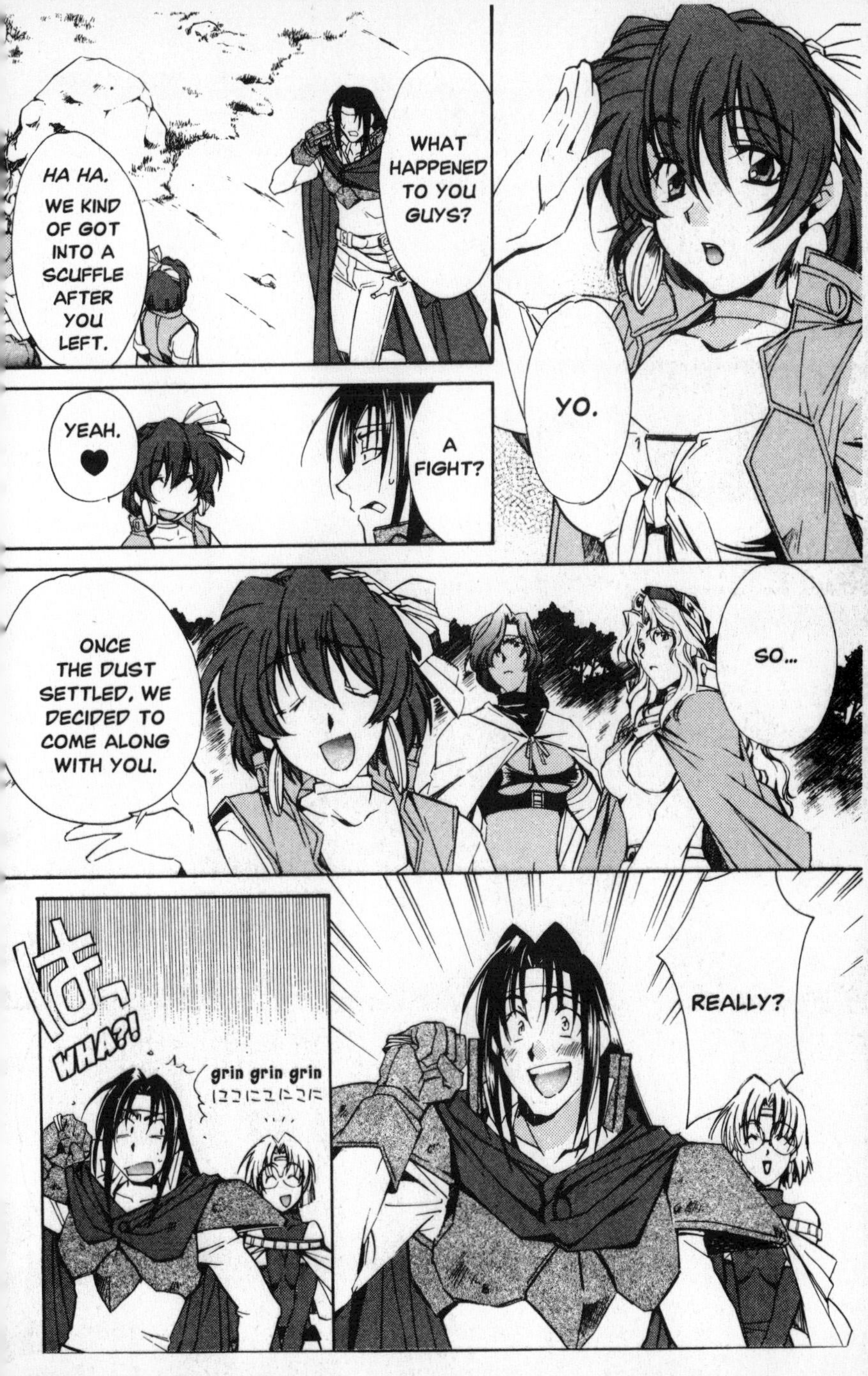
YO.
WHAT HAPPENED TO YOU GUYS?
HA HA. WE KIND OF GOT INTO A SCUFFLE AFTER YOU LEFT.
A FIGHT?
YEAH. ♥
SO...
ONCE THE DUST SETTLED, WE DECIDED TO COME ALONG WITH YOU.
REALLY?
はっ
WHA?!
grin grin grin
にこにこにこに
...

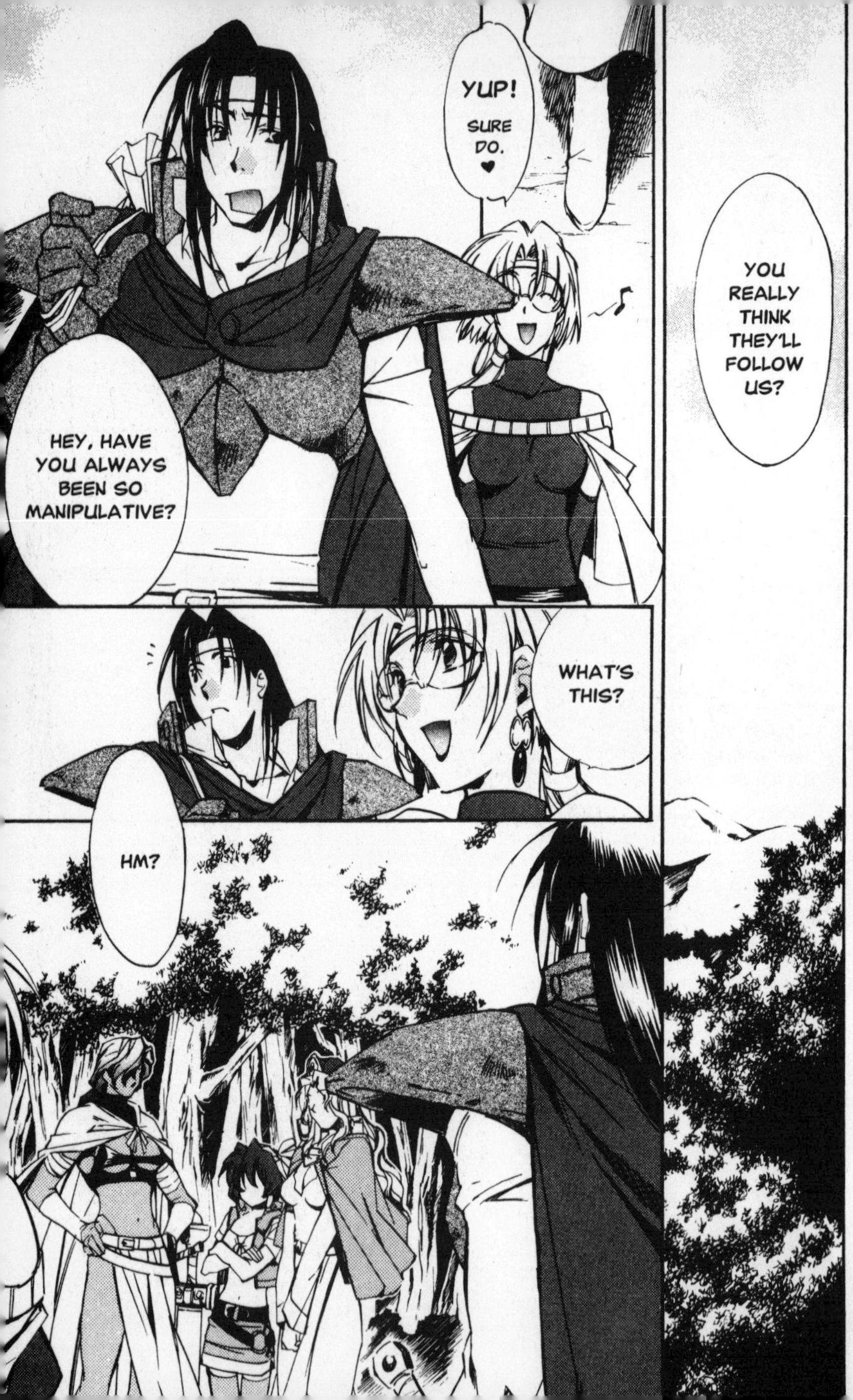
YOU REALLY THINK THEY'LL FOLLOW US?
YUP! SURE DO. ♥
HEY, HAVE YOU ALWAYS BEEN SO MANIPULATIVE?
WHAT'S THIS?
HM?

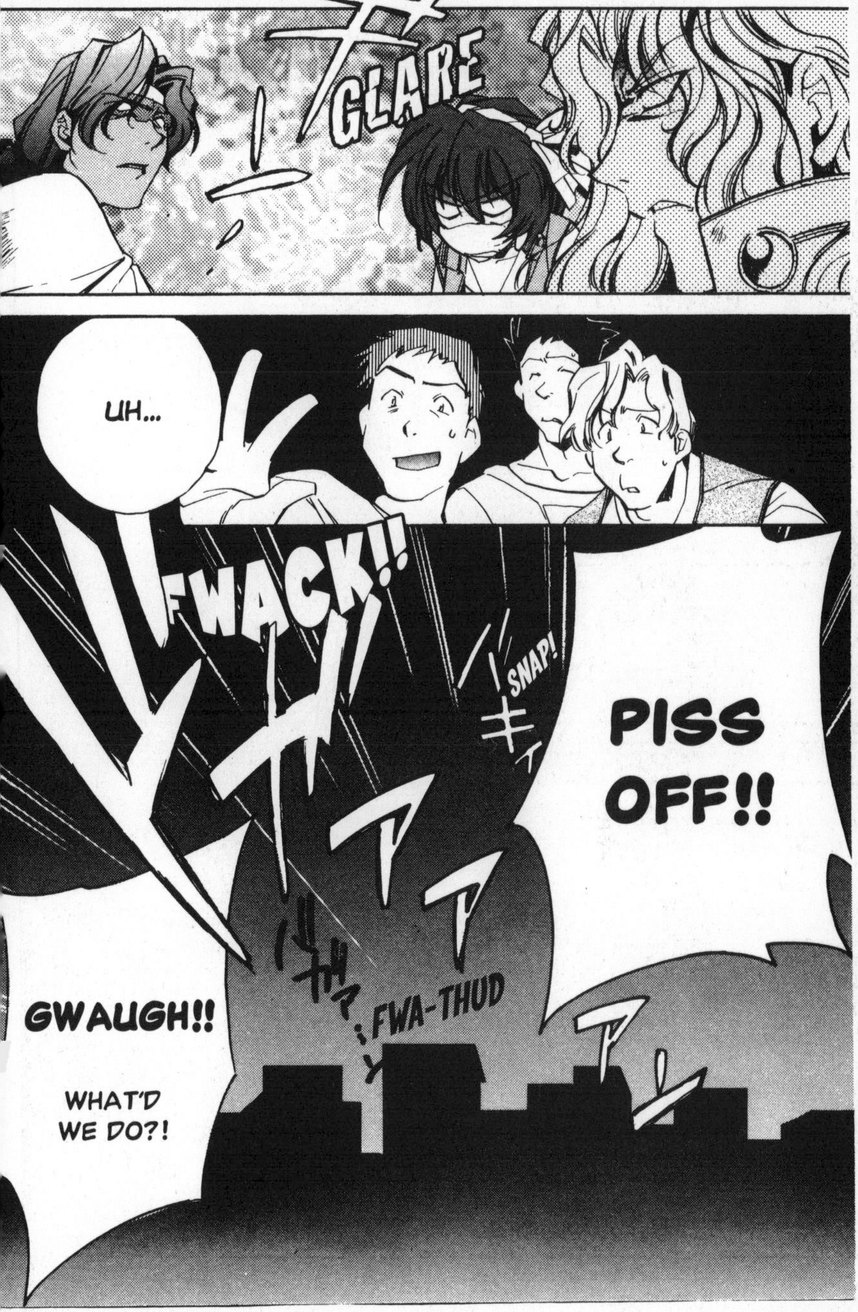
GLARE
UH...
PISS OFF!!
SNAP!
FWACK!!
FWA-THUD
GWAUGH!!
WHAT'D WE DO?!

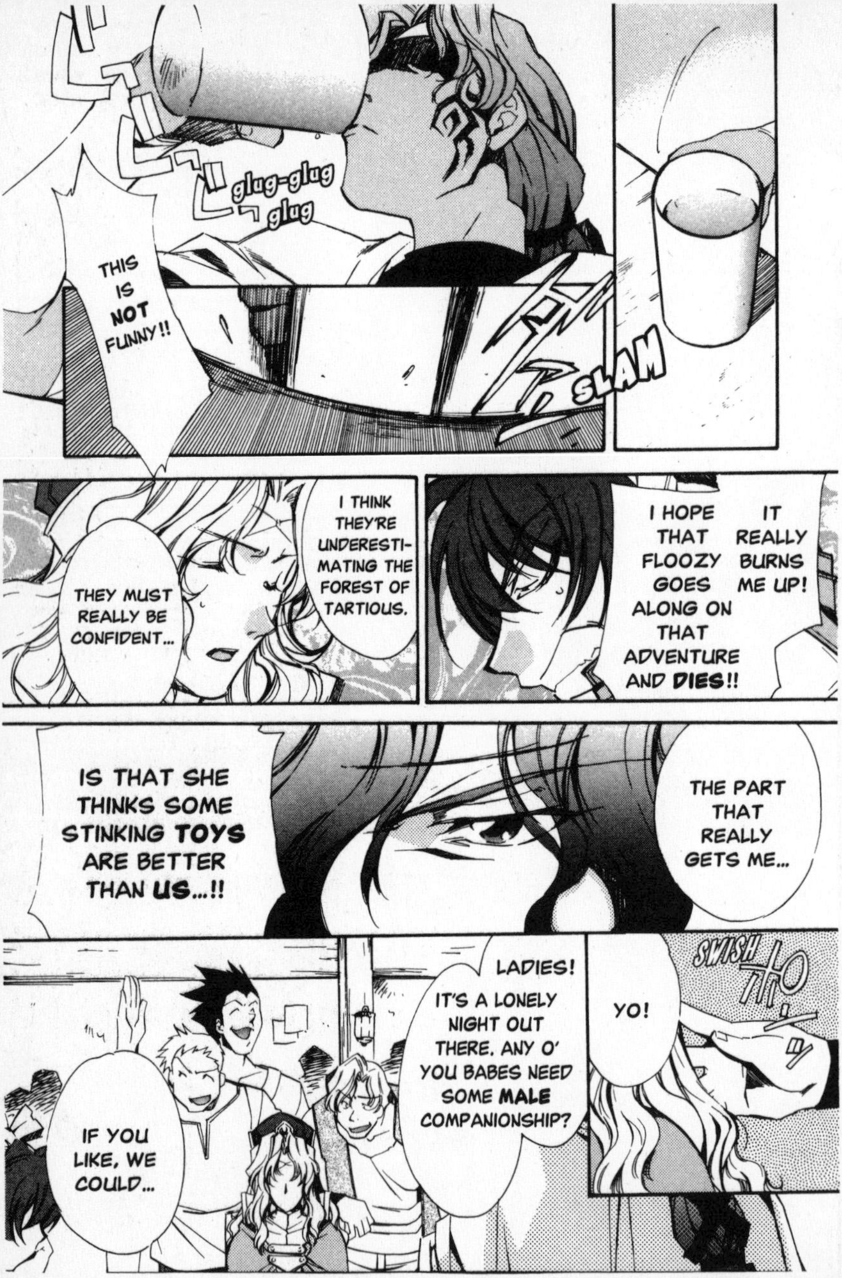
glug-glug
glug
SLAM
THIS IS NOT FUNNY!!
IT REALLY BURNS ME UP!
I HOPE THAT FLOOZY GOES ALONG ON THAT ADVENTURE AND DIES!!
I THINK THEY'RE UNDERESTI-MATING THE FOREST OF TARTIOUS.
THEY MUST REALLY BE CONFIDENT...
THE PART THAT REALLY GETS ME...
IS THAT SHE THINKS SOME STINKING TOYS ARE BETTER THAN US...!!
SWISH
YO!
LADIES! IT'S A LONELY NIGHT OUT THERE. ANY O' YOU BABES NEED SOME MALE COMPANIONSHIP?
IF YOU LIKE, WE COULD...

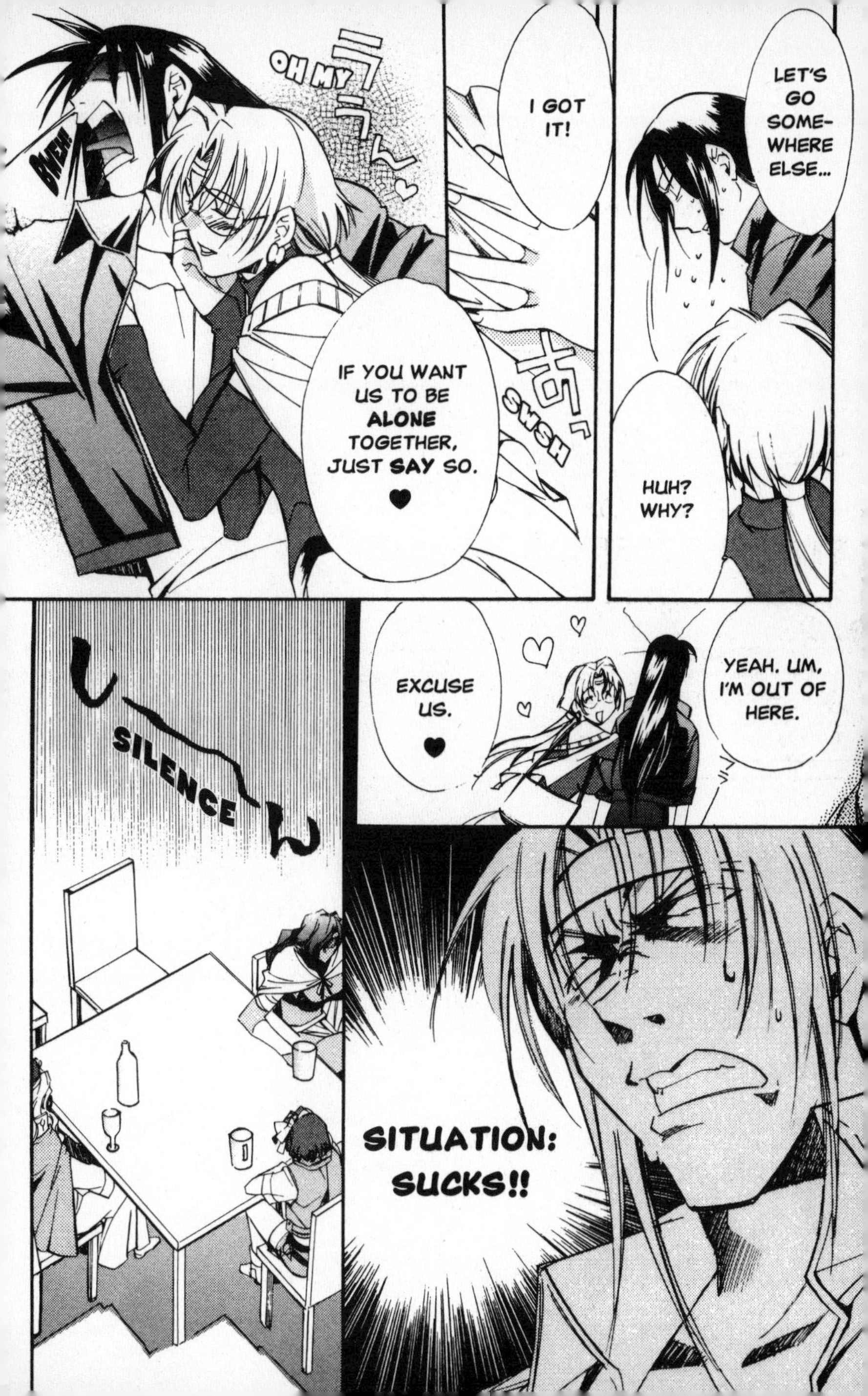
LET'S GO SOME-WHERE ELSE...
HUH? WHY?
I GOT IT!
OH MY
BWEH!
IF YOU WANT US TO BE ALONE TOGETHER, JUST SAY SO. ♥
SWSH
YEAH. UM, I'M OUT OF HERE.
EXCUSE US. ♥
SITUATION: SUCKS!!
SILENCE

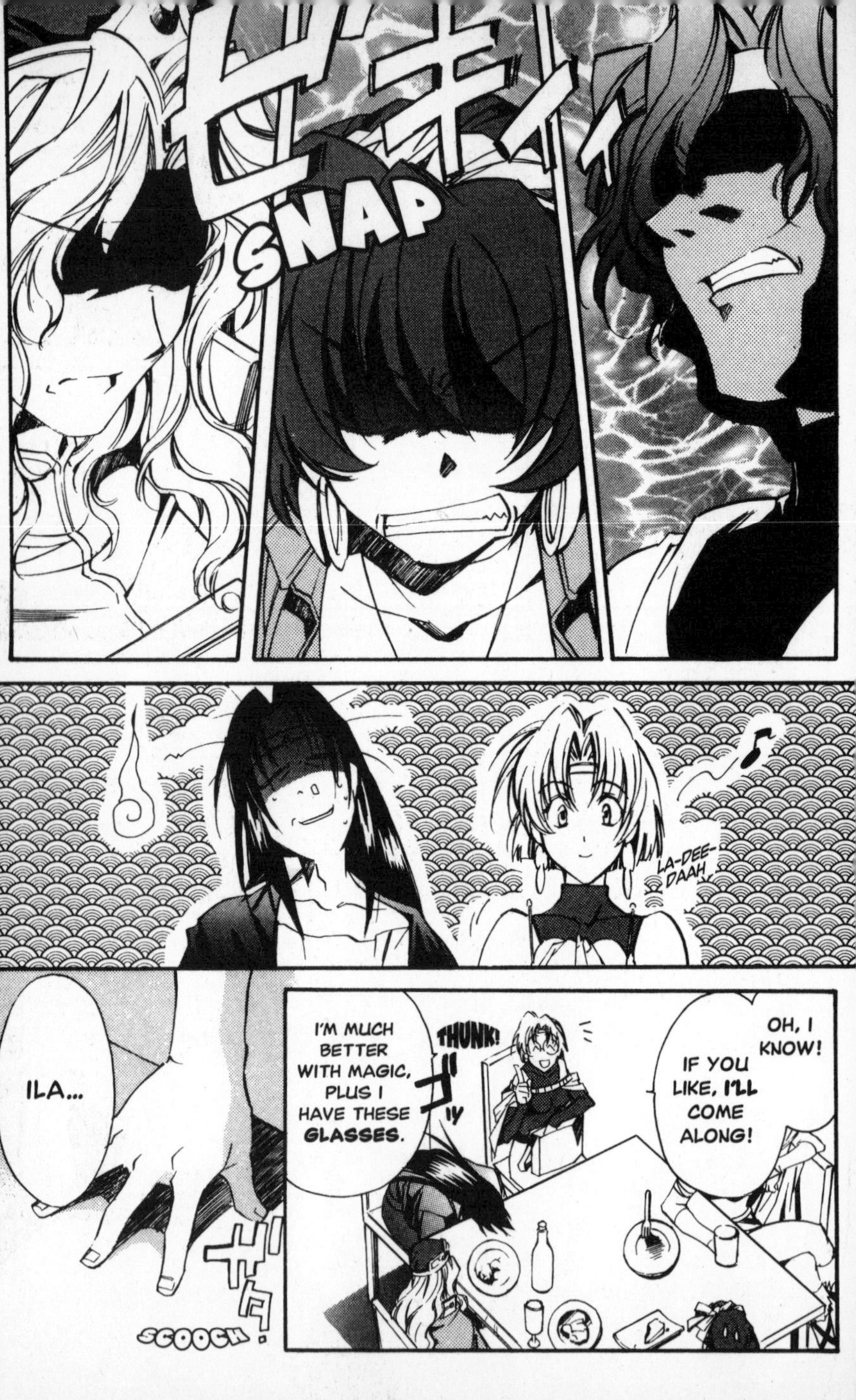
SNAP
LA-DEE-DAAH
OH, I KNOW!
IF YOU LIKE, I'LL COME ALONG!
THUNK!
I'M MUCH BETTER WITH MAGIC, PLUS I HAVE THESE GLASSES.
ILA...
SCOOCH!

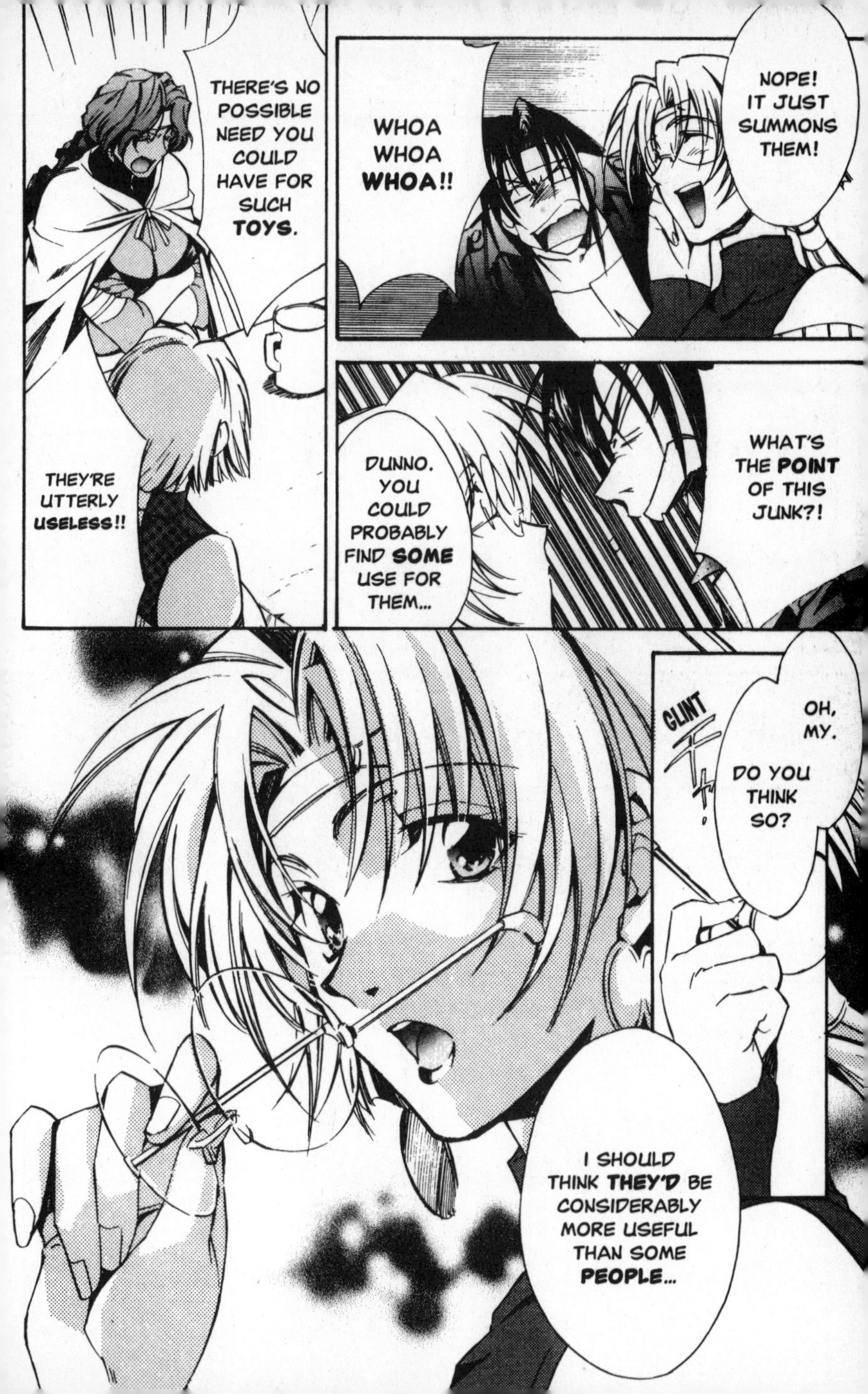
NOPE! IT JUST SUMMONS THEM!
WHOA WHOA **WHOA**!!
WHAT'S THE **POINT** OF THIS JUNK?!
DUNNO. YOU COULD PROBABLY FIND **SOME** USE FOR THEM...
THERE'S NO POSSIBLE NEED YOU COULD HAVE FOR SUCH **TOYS**.
THEY'RE UTTERLY **USELESS**!!
GLINT
OH, MY.
DO YOU THINK SO?
I SHOULD THINK **THEY'D** BE CONSIDERABLY MORE USEFUL THAN SOME **PEOPLE**...

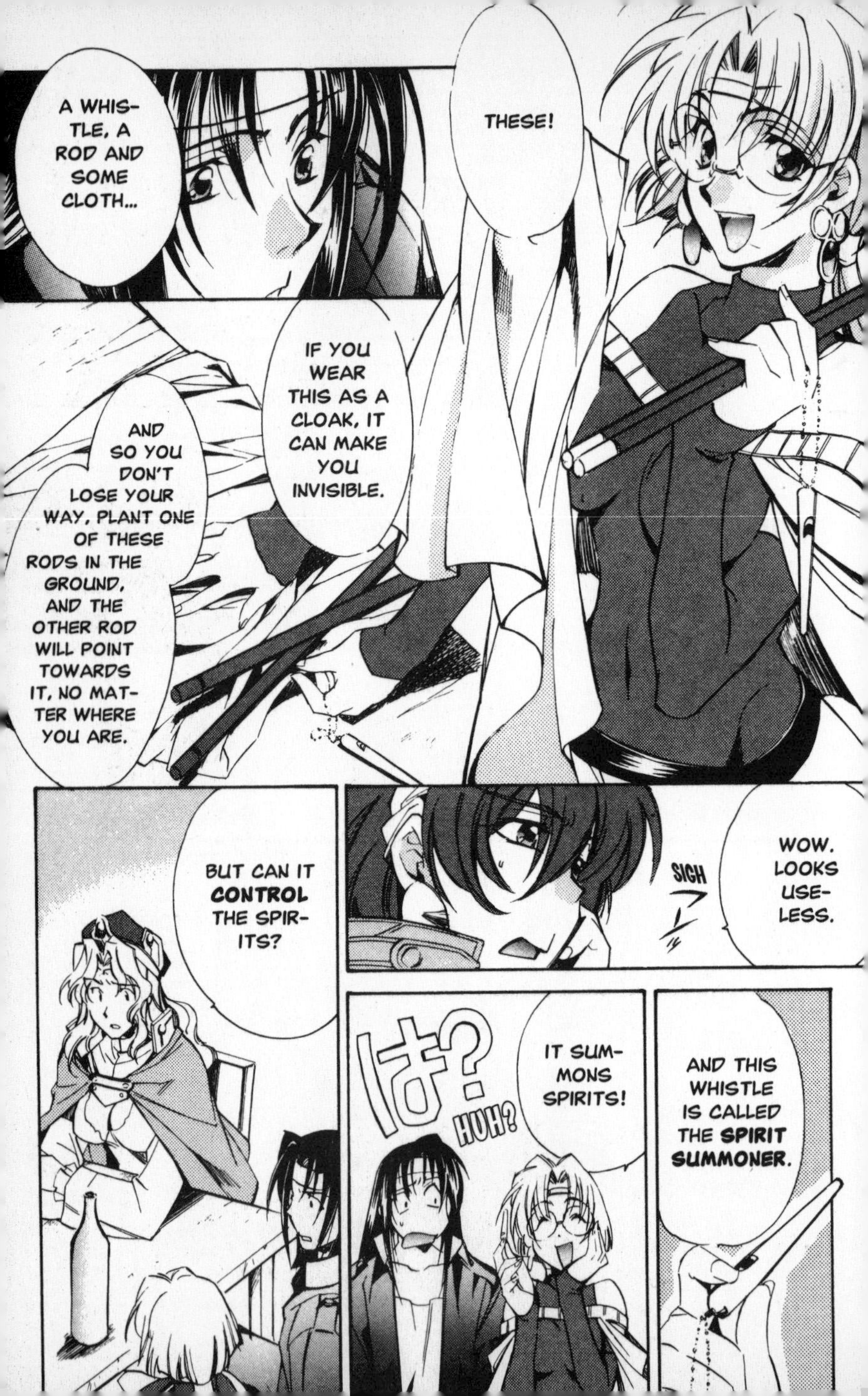
THESE!
A WHISTLE, A ROD AND SOME CLOTH...
IF YOU WEAR THIS AS A CLOAK, IT CAN MAKE YOU INVISIBLE.
AND SO YOU DON'T LOSE YOUR WAY, PLANT ONE OF THESE RODS IN THE GROUND, AND THE OTHER ROD WILL POINT TOWARDS IT, NO MATTER WHERE YOU ARE.
WOW. LOOKS USELESS.
SIGH
AND THIS WHISTLE IS CALLED THE **SPIRIT SUMMONER.**
IT SUMMONS SPIRITS!
は?
HUH?
BUT CAN IT **CONTROL** THE SPIRITS?

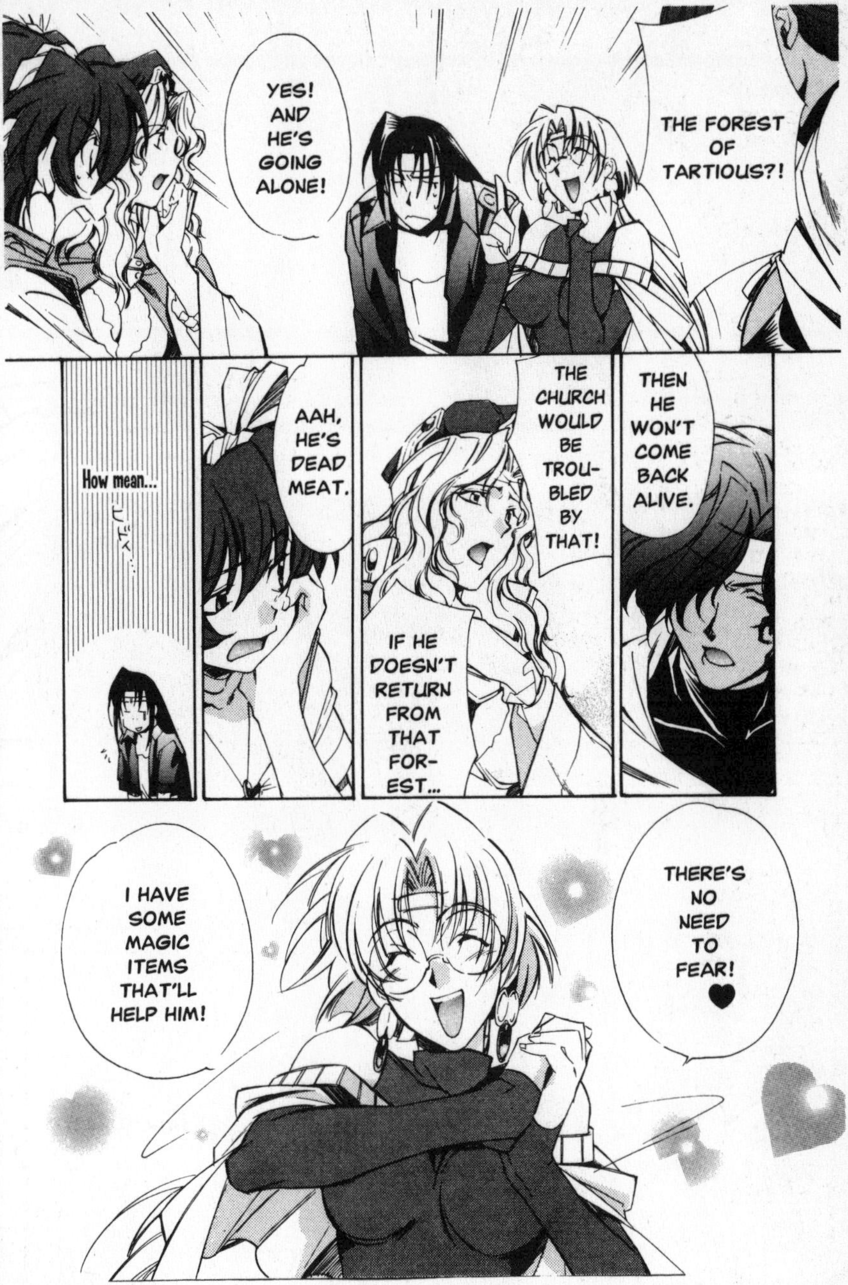
THE FOREST OF TARTIOUS?!
YES! AND HE'S GOING ALONE!
THEN HE WON'T COME BACK ALIVE.
THE CHURCH WOULD BE TROU- BLED BY THAT!
IF HE DOESN'T RETURN FROM THAT FOR- EST...
AAH, HE'S DEAD MEAT.
How mean...
THERE'S NO NEED TO FEAR! ♥
I HAVE SOME MAGIC ITEMS THAT'LL HELP HIM!

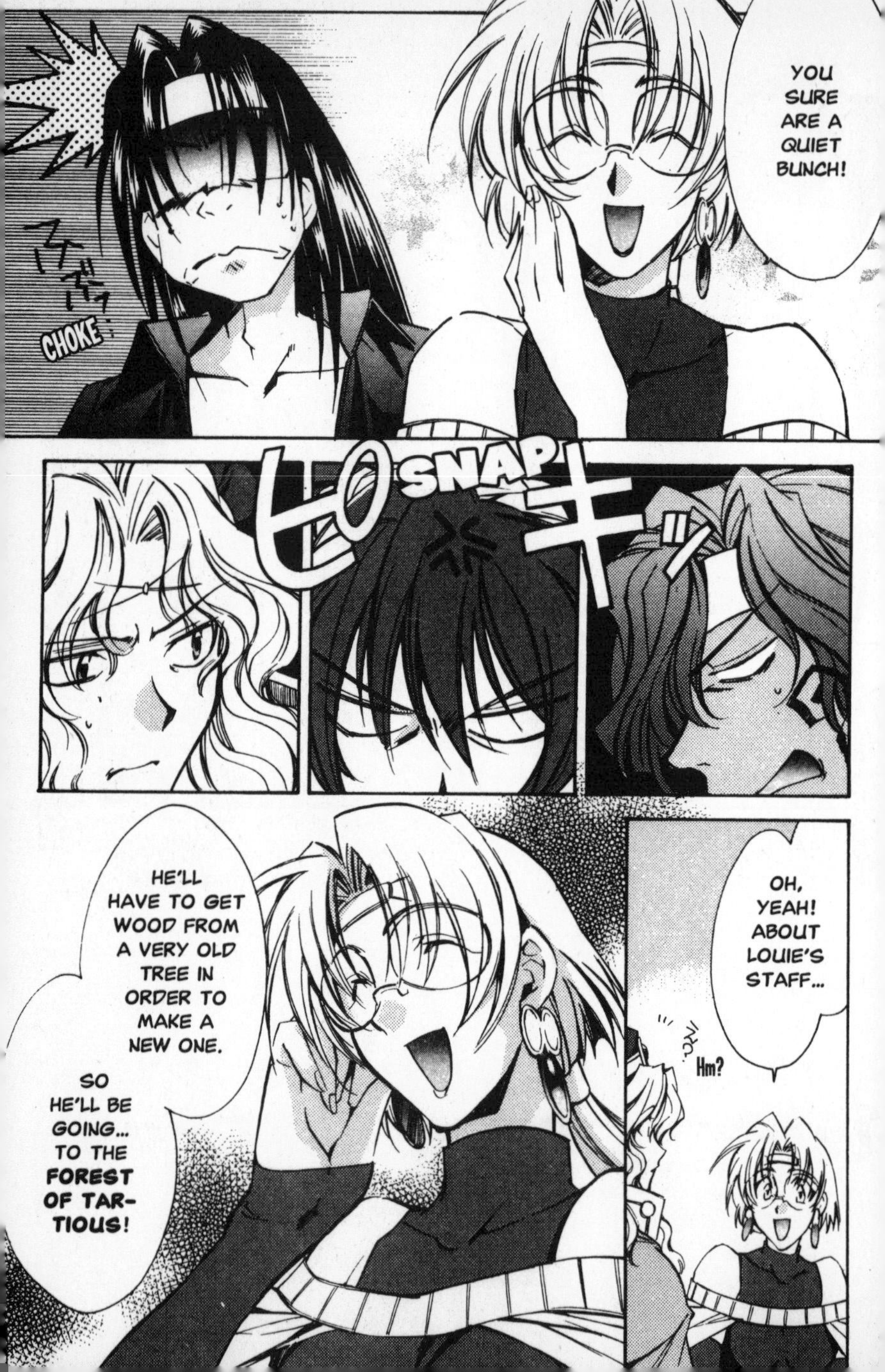
YOU SURE ARE A QUIET BUNCH!
CHOKE
SNAP
OH, YEAH! ABOUT LOUIE'S STAFF...
Hm?
HE'LL HAVE TO GET WOOD FROM A VERY OLD TREE IN ORDER TO MAKE A NEW ONE.
SO HE'LL BE GOING... TO THE FOREST OF TAR-TIOUS!

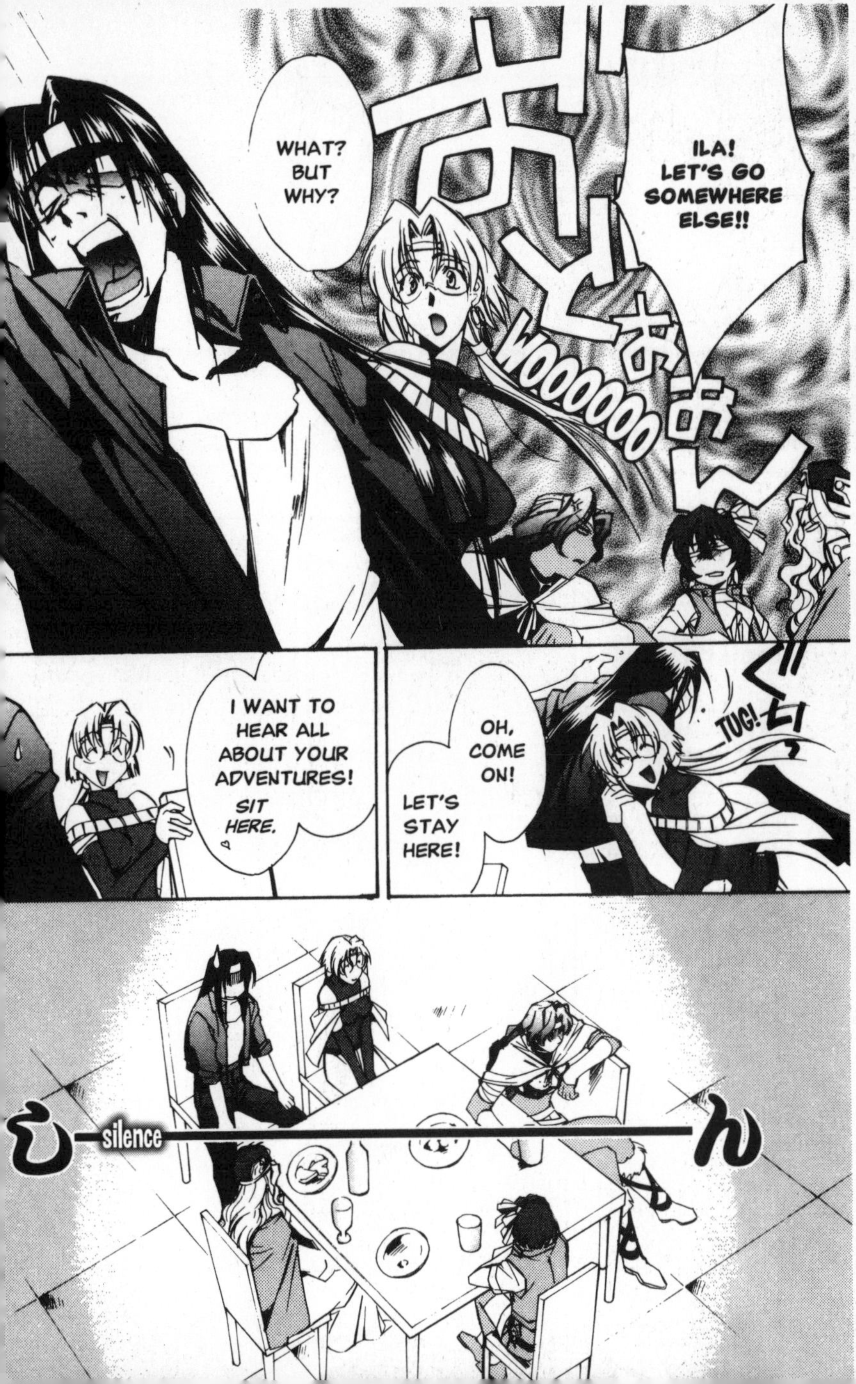
ILA! LET'S GO SOMEWHERE ELSE!!
WOOOOOOO
WHAT? BUT WHY?
OH, COME ON!
LET'S STAY HERE!
TUG!
I WANT TO HEAR ALL ABOUT YOUR ADVENTURES!
SIT HERE.
silence

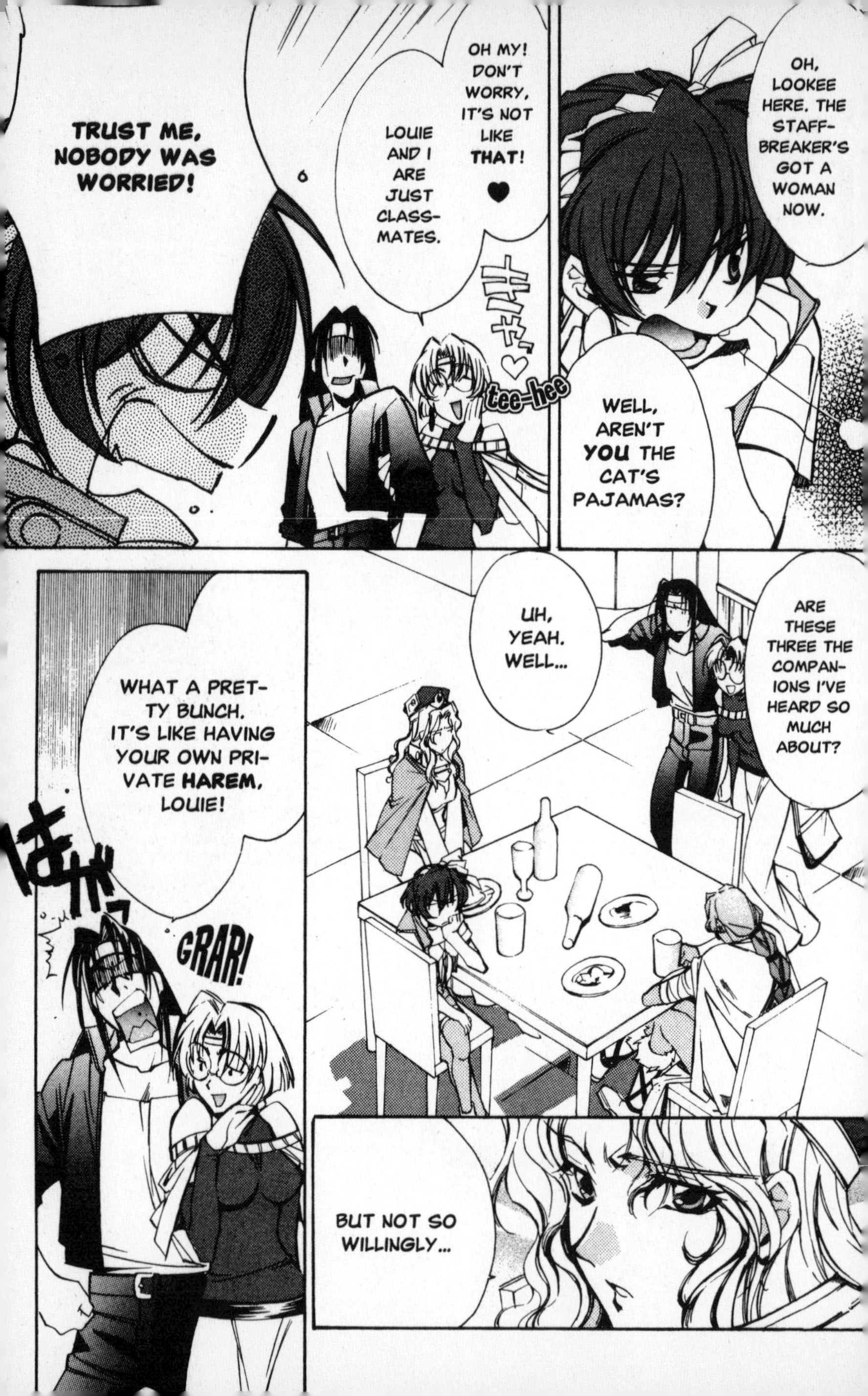
OH, LOOKEE HERE. THE STAFF-BREAKER'S GOT A WOMAN NOW.
WELL, AREN'T **YOU** THE CAT'S PAJAMAS?
OH MY! DON'T WORRY, IT'S NOT LIKE **THAT**! ♥
LOUIE AND I ARE JUST CLASS-MATES.
きゃっ ♥
tee-hee
TRUST ME, NOBODY WAS WORRIED!
ARE THESE THREE THE COMPAN-IONS I'VE HEARD SO MUCH ABOUT?
UH, YEAH. WELL...
BUT NOT SO WILLINGLY...
WHAT A PRET-TY BUNCH. IT'S LIKE HAVING YOUR OWN PRI-VATE **HAREM**, LOUIE!
はがっ
GRAR!

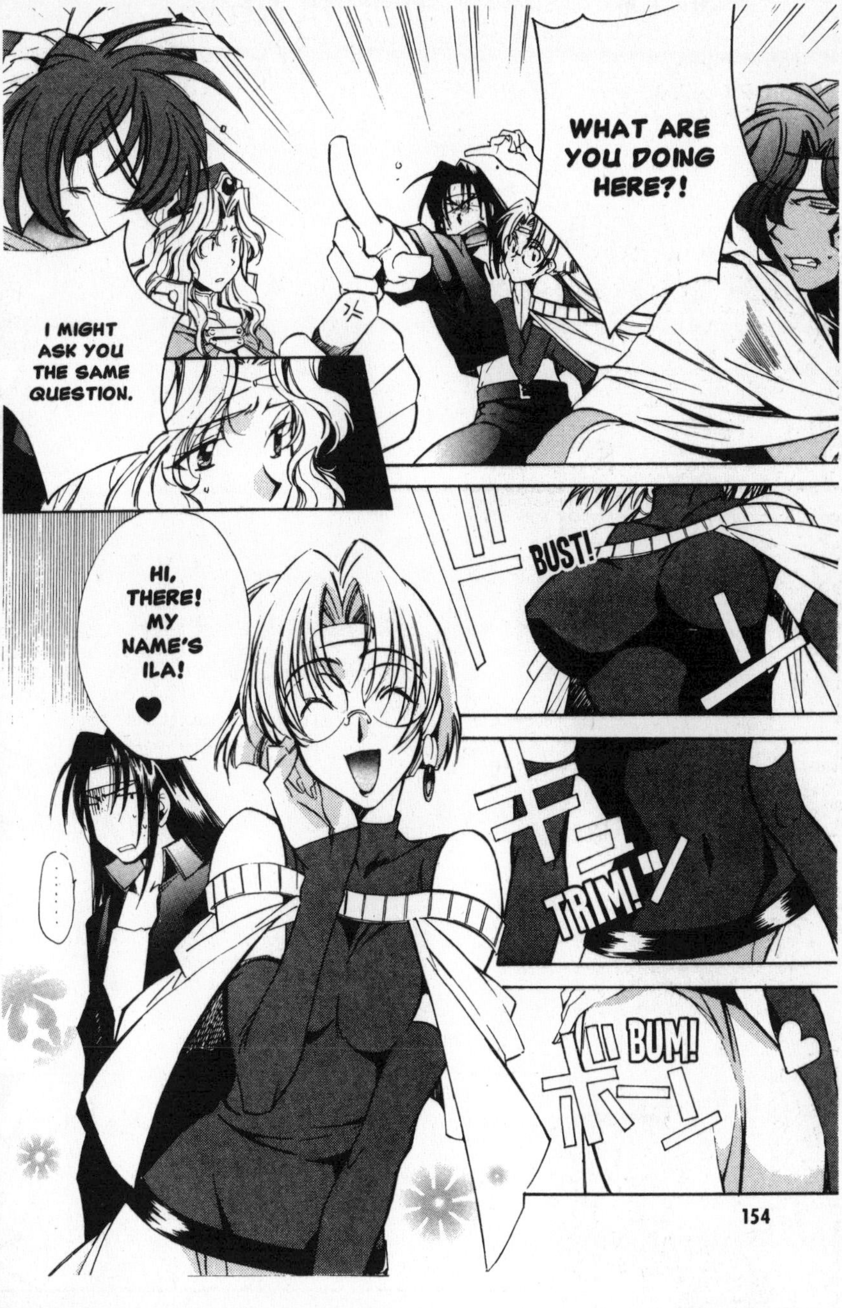
WHAT ARE YOU DOING HERE?!
I MIGHT ASK YOU THE SAME QUESTION.
BUST!
TRIM!
BUM!
HI, THERE! MY NAME'S ILA! ♥
......

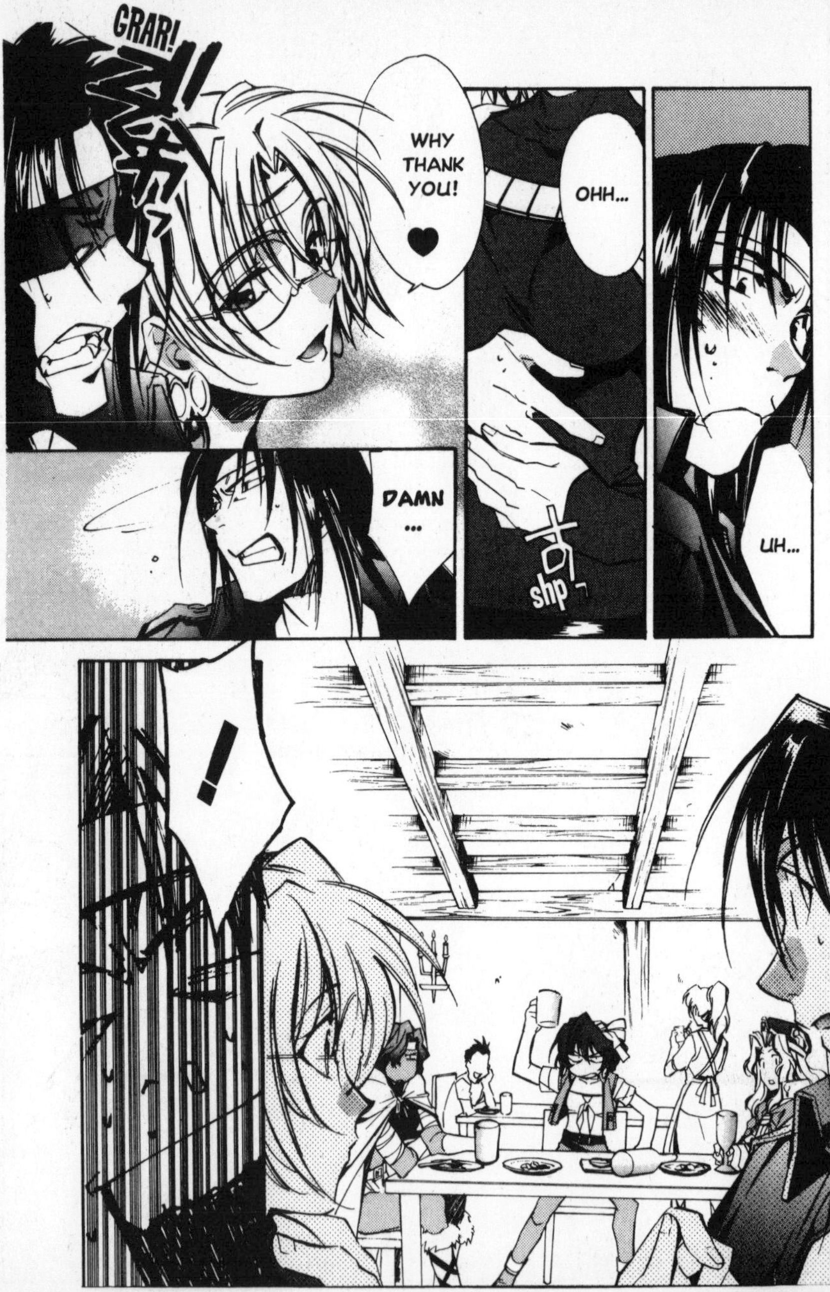
UH...
OHH...
shp
WHY THANK YOU! ♥
GRAR!
DAMN ...
!

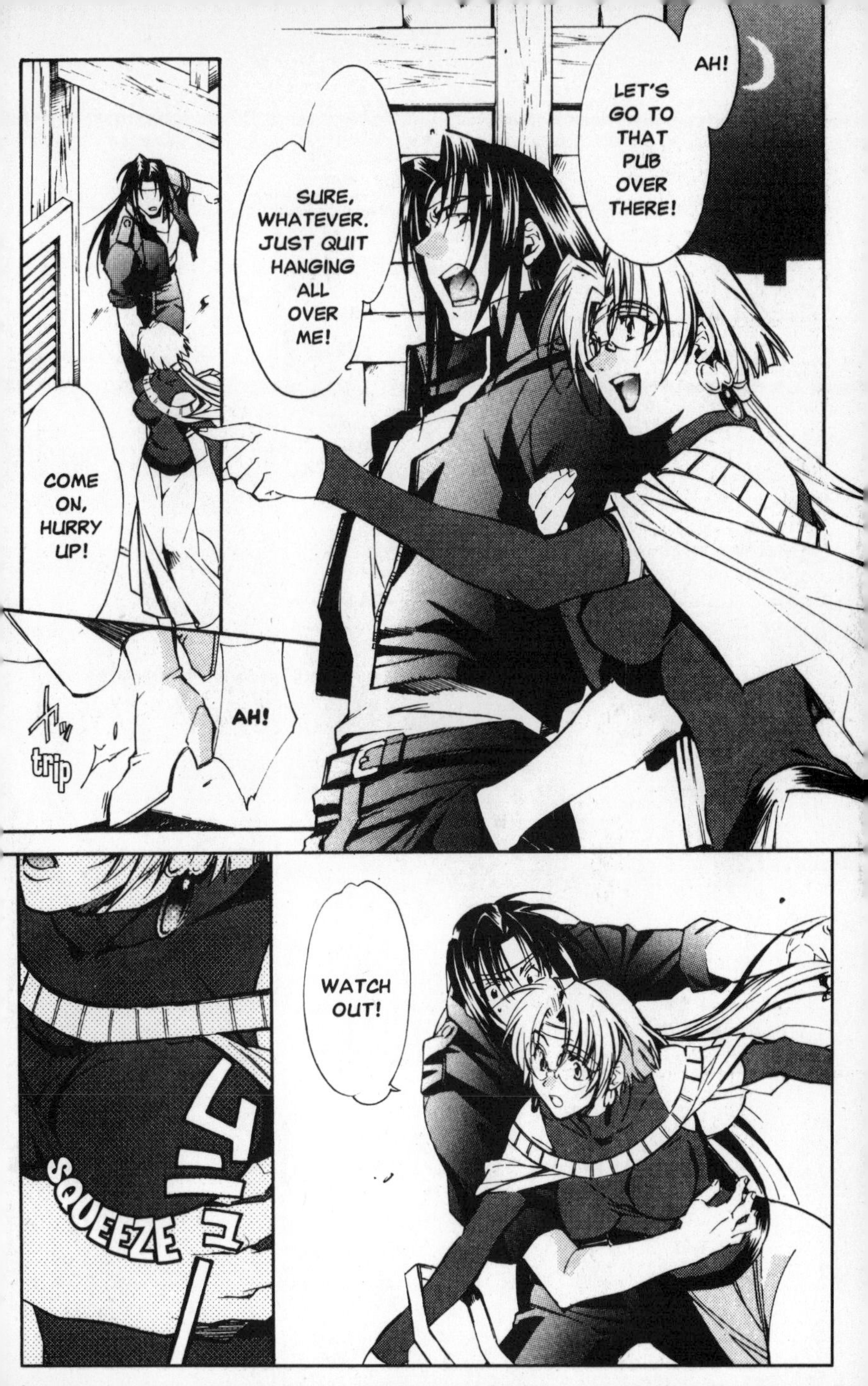
AH! LET'S GO TO THAT PUB OVER THERE!
SURE, WHATEVER. JUST QUIT HANGING ALL OVER ME!
COME ON, HURRY UP!
AH!
trip
WATCH OUT!
SQUEEZE

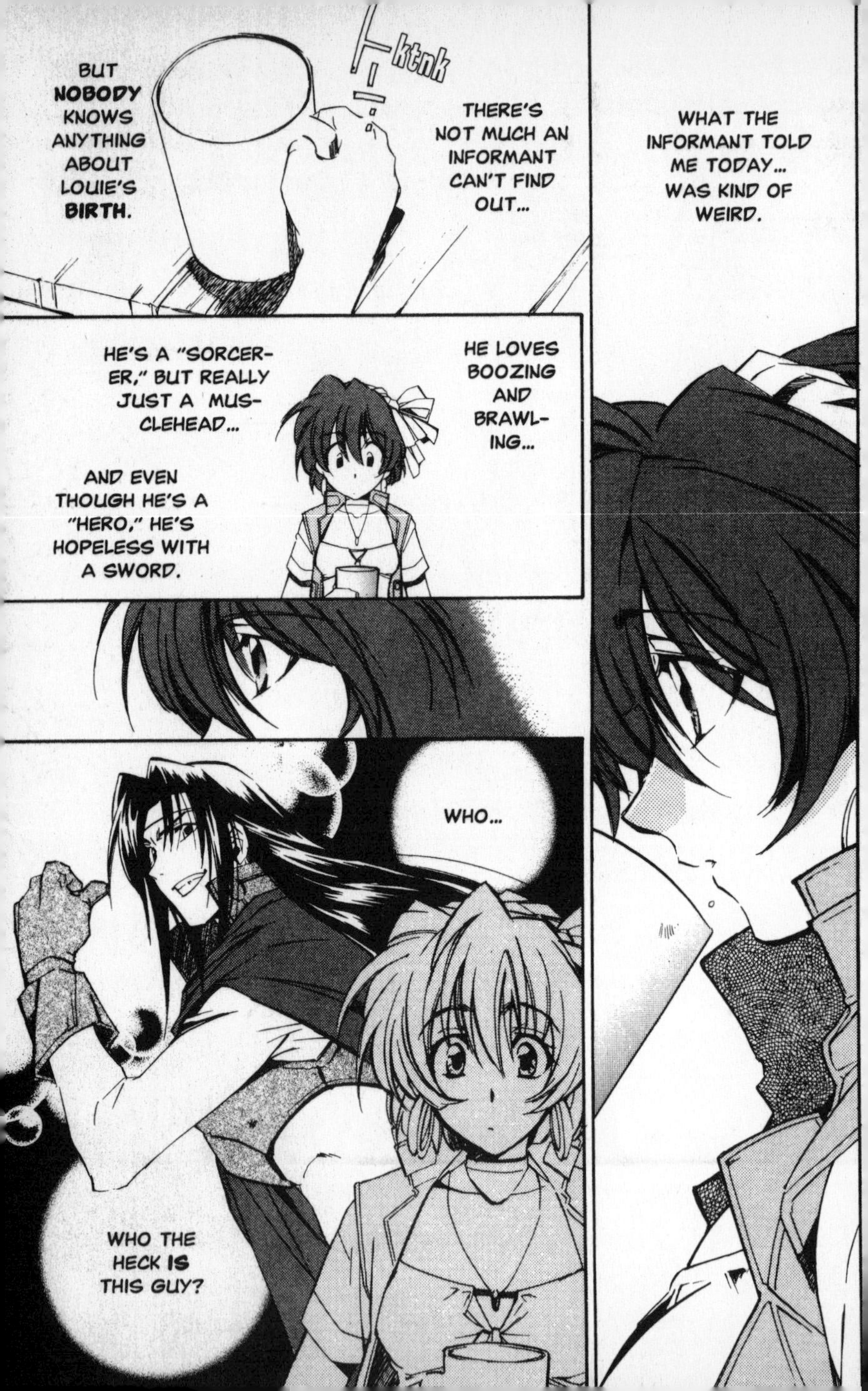

WHAT THE INFORMANT TOLD ME TODAY... WAS KIND OF WEIRD.
ktnk
THERE'S NOT MUCH AN INFORMANT CAN'T FIND OUT...
BUT NOBODY KNOWS ANYTHING ABOUT LOUIE'S BIRTH.
HE LOVES BOOZING AND BRAWLING...
HE'S A "SORCERER," BUT REALLY JUST A MUSCLEHEAD...
AND EVEN THOUGH HE'S A "HERO," HE'S HOPELESS WITH A SWORD.
WHO...
WHO THE HECK IS THIS GUY?

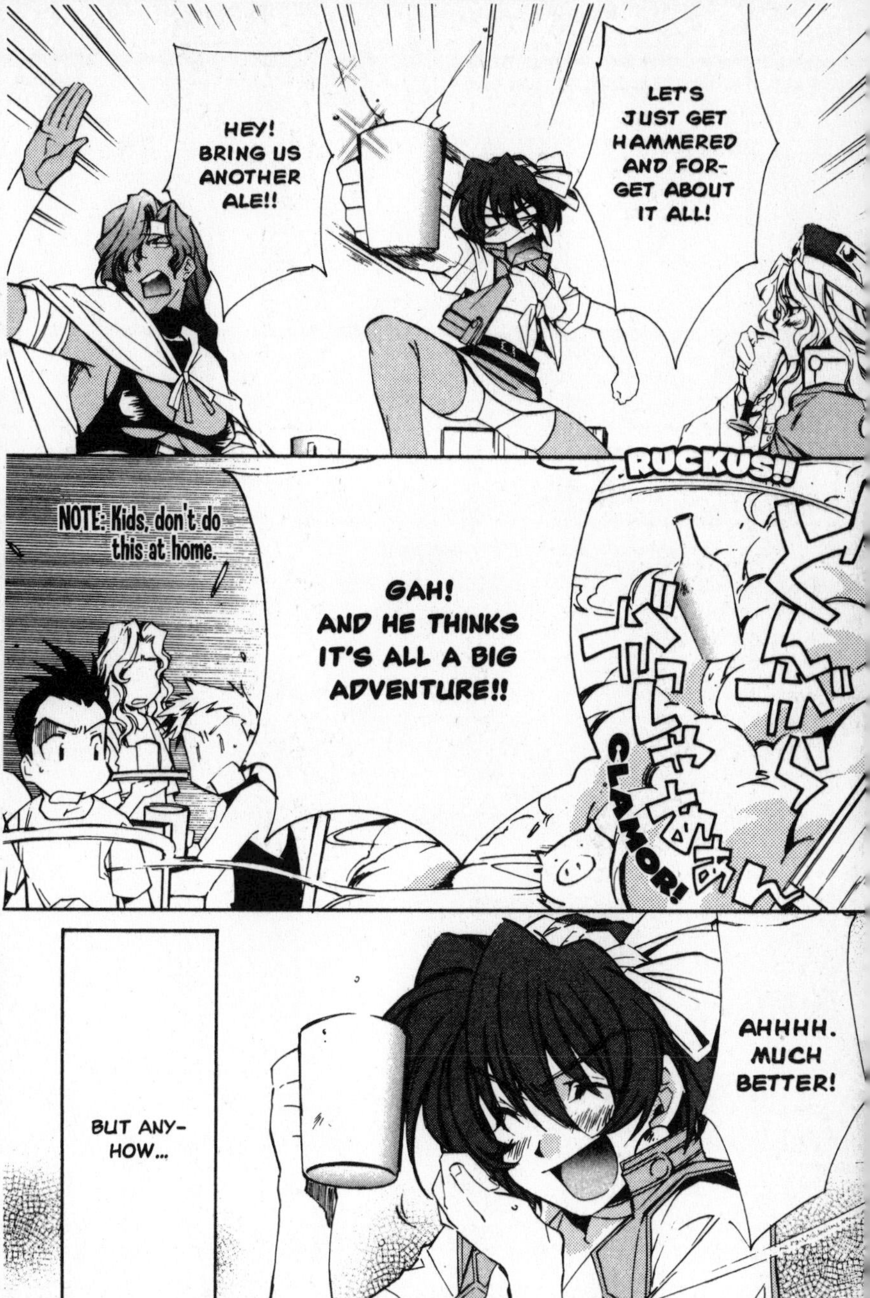
LET'S JUST GET HAMMERED AND FOR-GET ABOUT IT ALL!
HEY! BRING US ANOTHER ALE!!
RUCKUS!!
CLAMOR!
GAH! AND HE THINKS IT'S ALL A BIG ADVENTURE!!
NOTE: Kids, don't do this at home.
AHHHH. MUCH BETTER!
BUT ANY-HOW...

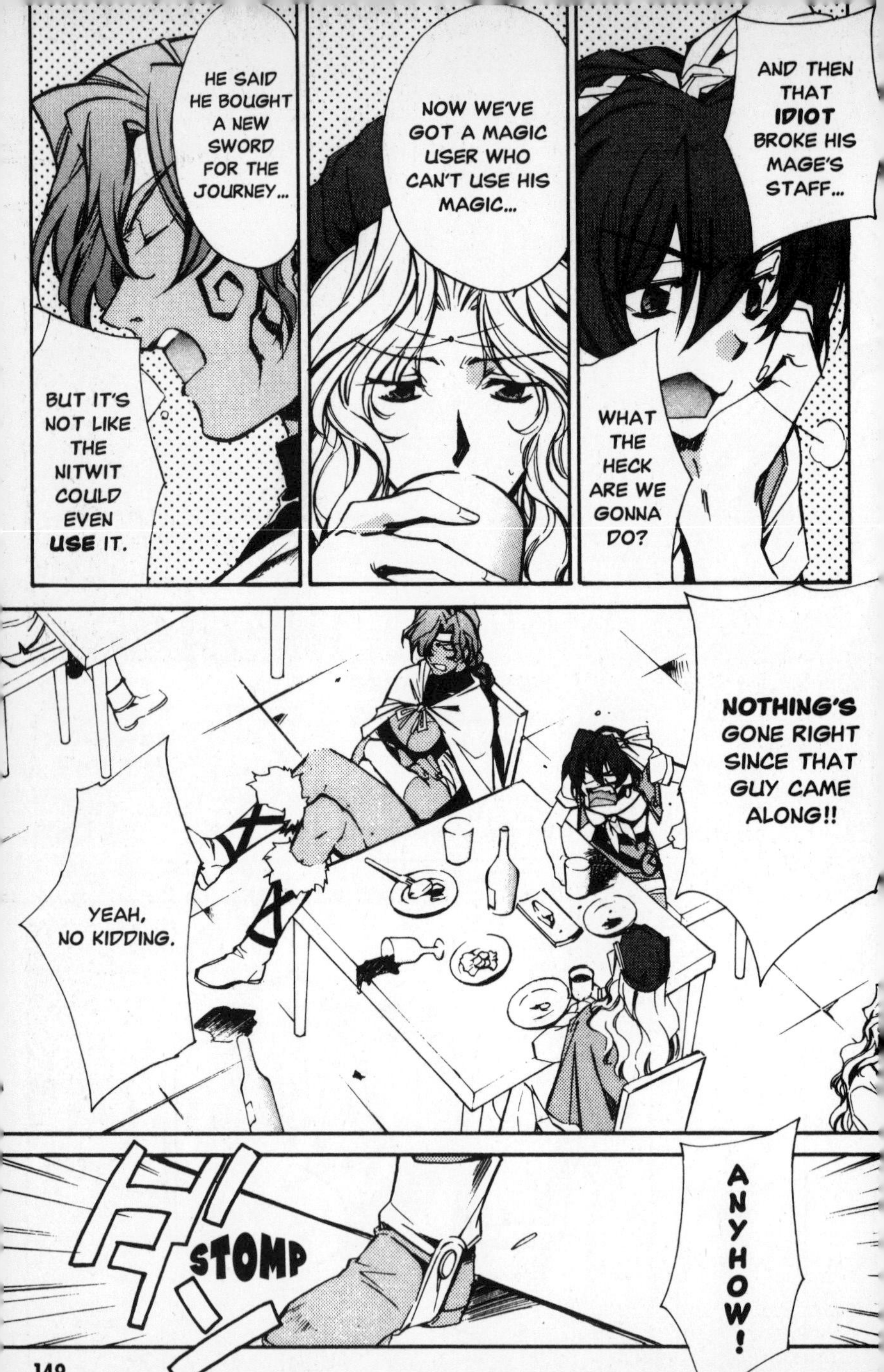
AND THEN THAT IDIOT BROKE HIS MAGE'S STAFF...
WHAT THE HECK ARE WE GONNA DO?
NOW WE'VE GOT A MAGIC USER WHO CAN'T USE HIS MAGIC...
HE SAID HE BOUGHT A NEW SWORD FOR THE JOURNEY...
BUT IT'S NOT LIKE THE NITWIT COULD EVEN USE IT.
NOTHING'S GONE RIGHT SINCE THAT GUY CAME ALONG!!
YEAH, NO KIDDING.
ANYHOW!
STOMP

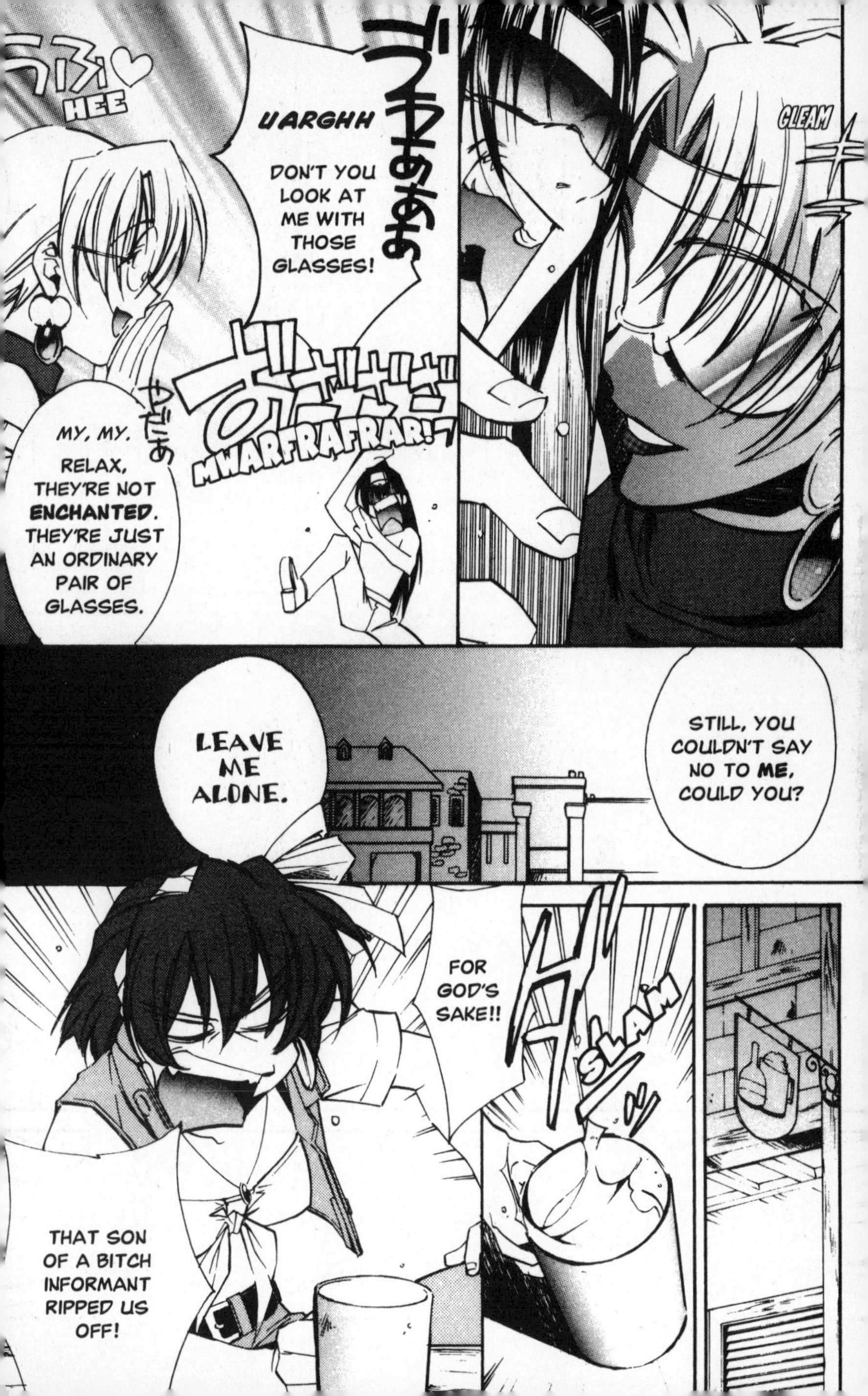
GLEAM
UARGHH
DON'T YOU LOOK AT ME WITH THOSE GLASSES!
HEE
MWARFRAFRAR!?
MY, MY.
RELAX, THEY'RE NOT **ENCHANTED**. THEY'RE JUST AN ORDINARY PAIR OF GLASSES.
STILL, YOU COULDN'T SAY NO TO **ME**, COULD YOU?
LEAVE ME ALONE.
SLAM
FOR GOD'S SAKE!!
THAT SON OF A BITCH INFORMANT RIPPED US OFF!

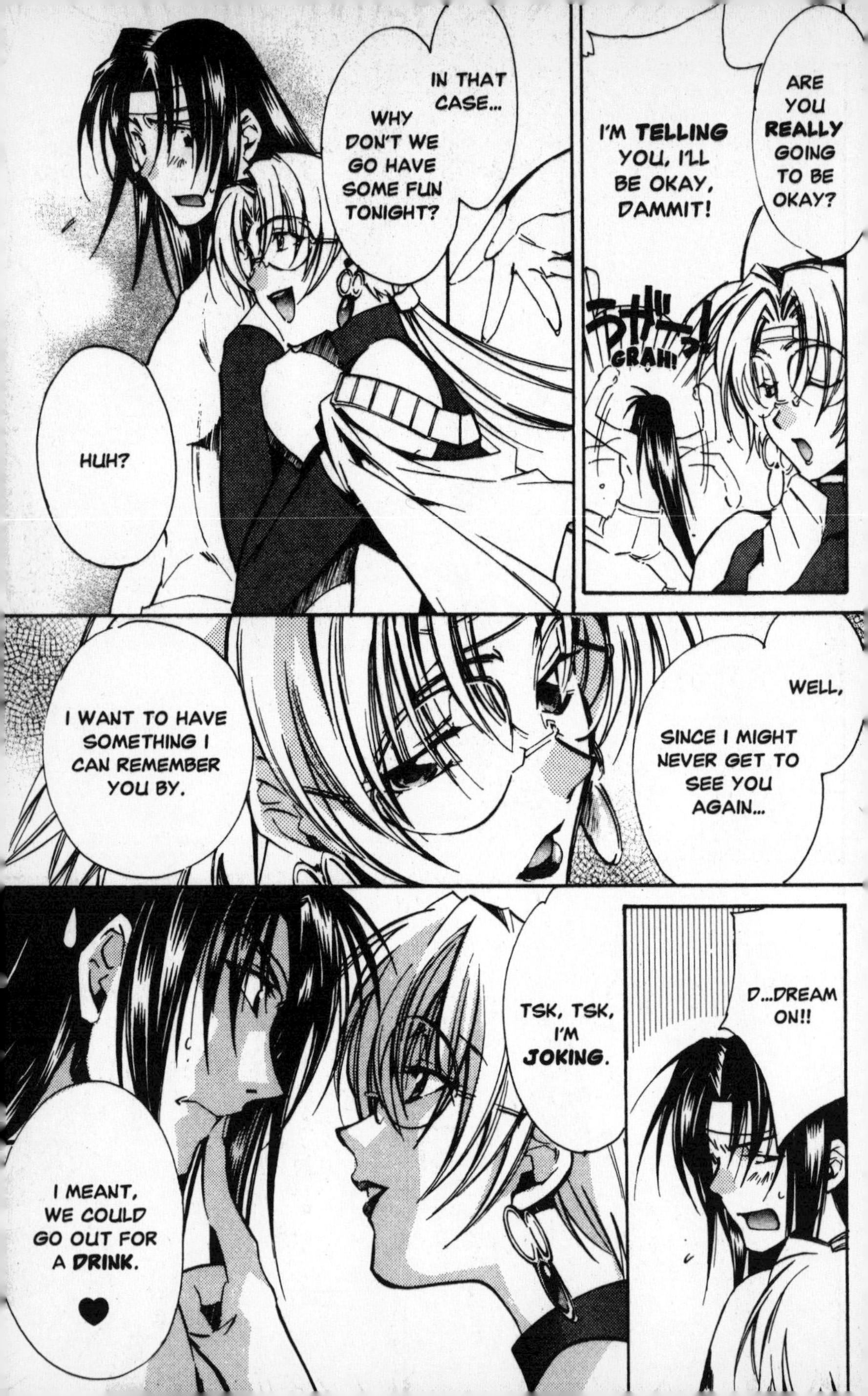

ARE YOU REALLY GOING TO BE OKAY?
I'M TELLING YOU, I'LL BE OKAY, DAMMIT!
GRAH!
IN THAT CASE...
WHY DON'T WE GO HAVE SOME FUN TONIGHT?
HUH?
WELL,
SINCE I MIGHT NEVER GET TO SEE YOU AGAIN...
I WANT TO HAVE SOMETHING I CAN REMEMBER YOU BY.
D...DREAM ON!!
TSK, TSK, I'M JOKING.
I MEANT, WE COULD GO OUT FOR A DRINK. ♥

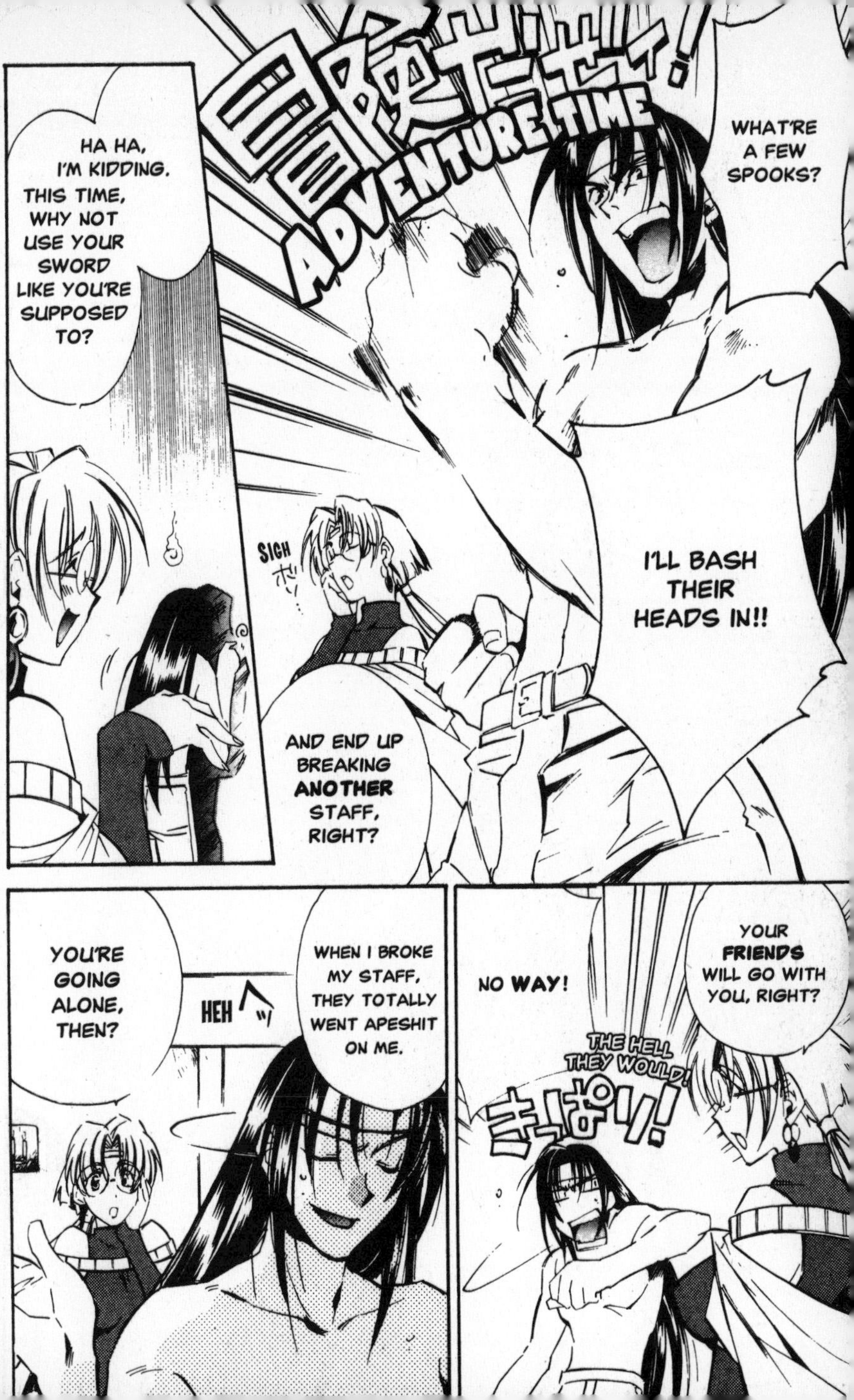

冒険だぜィ!
ADVENTURE TIME
WHAT'RE A FEW SPOOKS?
I'LL BASH THEIR HEADS IN!!
SIGH
AND END UP BREAKING ANOTHER STAFF, RIGHT?
HA HA, I'M KIDDING. THIS TIME, WHY NOT USE YOUR SWORD LIKE YOU'RE SUPPOSED TO?
YOUR FRIENDS WILL GO WITH YOU, RIGHT?
NO WAY!
THE HELL THEY WOULD!
きっぱり!
WHEN I BROKE MY STAFF, THEY TOTALLY WENT APESHIT ON ME.
HEH
YOU'RE GOING ALONE, THEN?

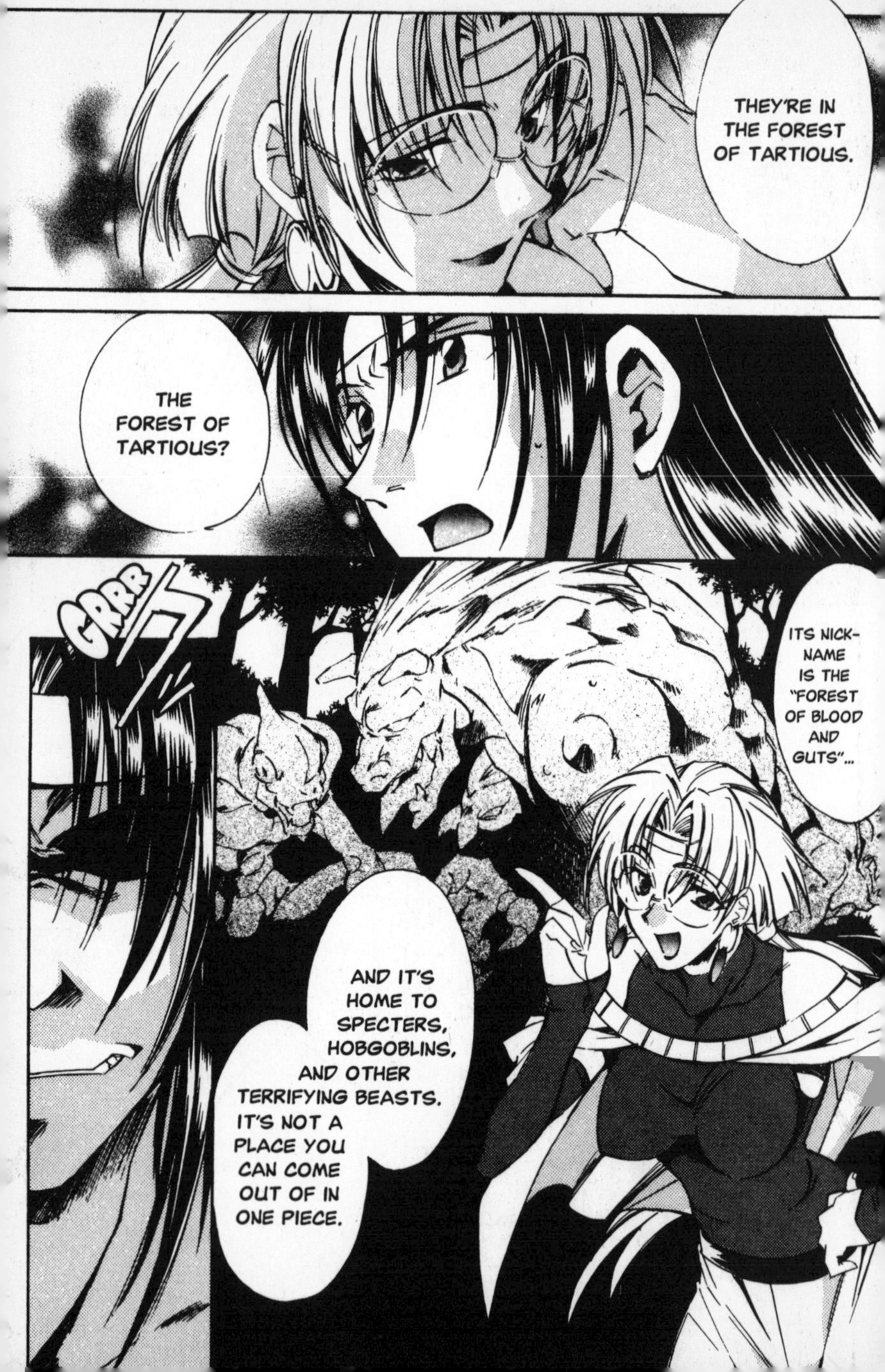
THEY'RE IN THE FOREST OF TARTIOUS.
THE FOREST OF TARTIOUS?
ITS NICK-NAME IS THE "FOREST OF BLOOD AND GUTS"...
GRRR
AND IT'S HOME TO SPECTERS, HOBGOBLINS, AND OTHER TERRIFYING BEASTS. IT'S NOT A PLACE YOU CAN COME OUT OF IN ONE PIECE.

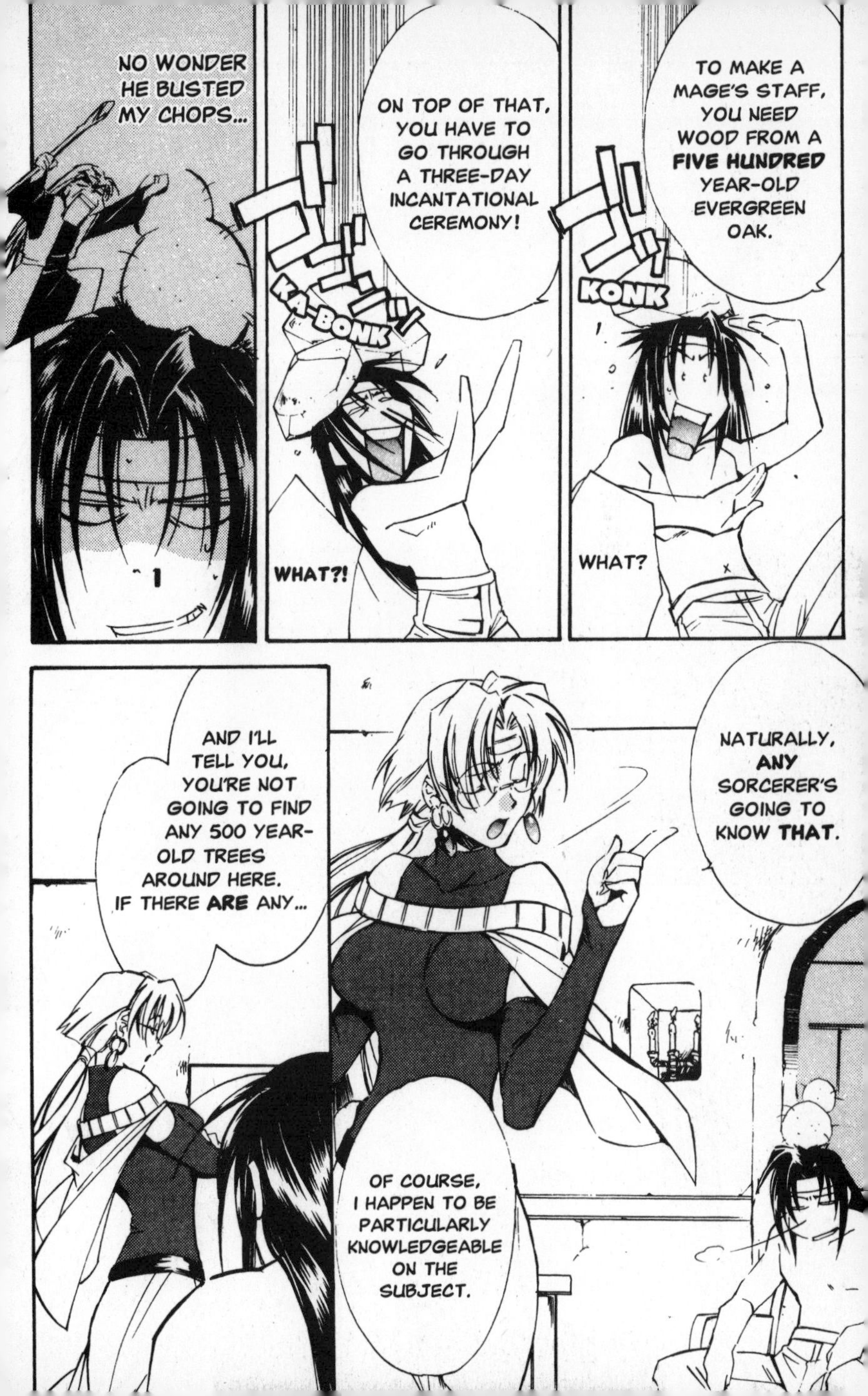
TO MAKE A MAGE'S STAFF, YOU NEED WOOD FROM A **FIVE HUNDRED** YEAR-OLD EVERGREEN OAK.
KONK
WHAT?
ON TOP OF THAT, YOU HAVE TO GO THROUGH A THREE-DAY INCANTATIONAL CEREMONY!
KA-BONK
WHAT?!
NO WONDER HE BUSTED MY CHOPS...
NATURALLY, **ANY** SORCERER'S GOING TO KNOW **THAT**.
AND I'LL TELL YOU, YOU'RE NOT GOING TO FIND ANY 500 YEAR-OLD TREES AROUND HERE. IF THERE **ARE** ANY...
OF COURSE, I HAPPEN TO BE PARTICULARLY KNOWLEDGEABLE ON THE SUBJECT.

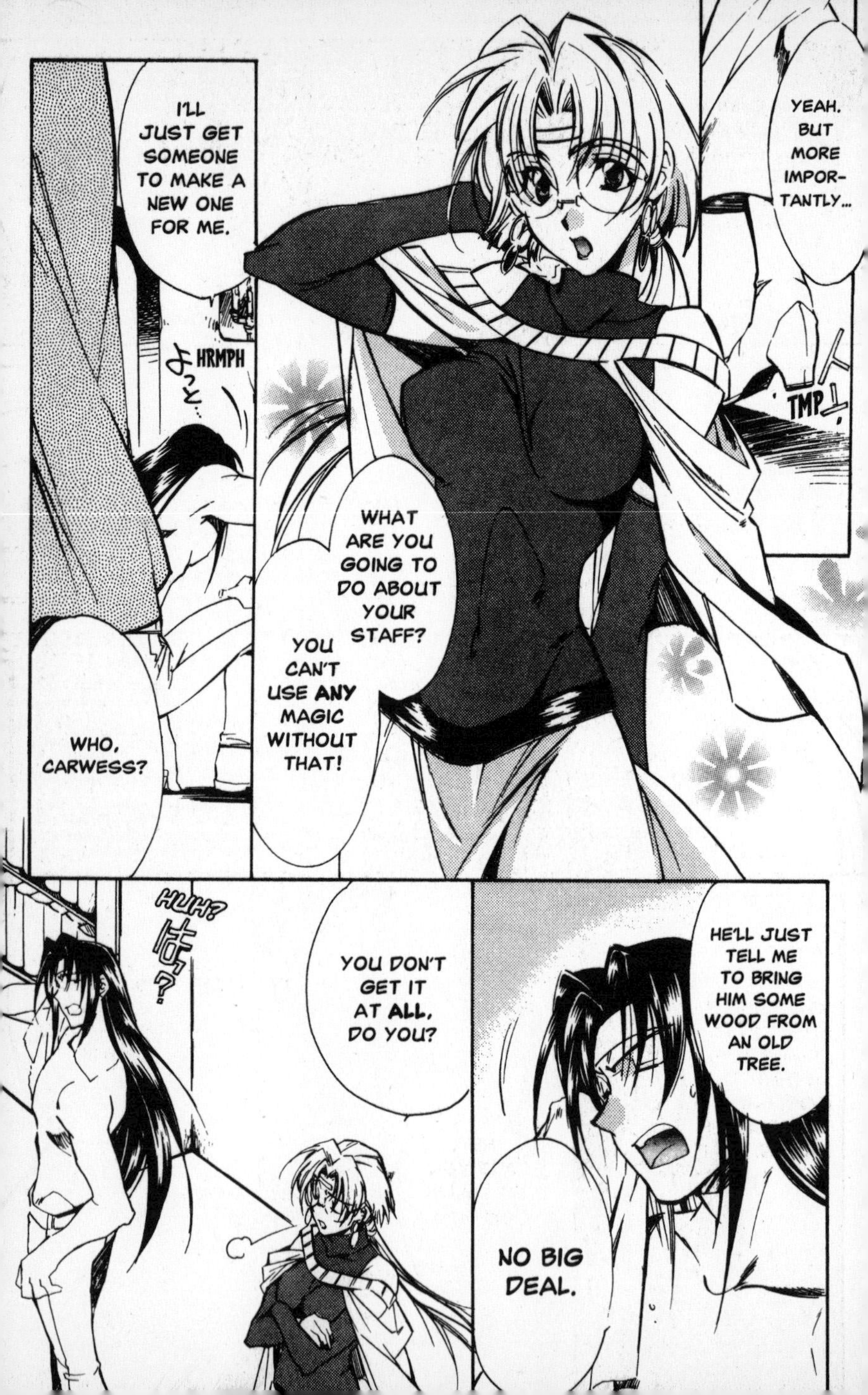
YEAH. BUT MORE IMPORTANTLY...
TMP
WHAT ARE YOU GOING TO DO ABOUT YOUR STAFF?
YOU CAN'T USE **ANY** MAGIC WITHOUT THAT!
I'LL JUST GET SOMEONE TO MAKE A NEW ONE FOR ME.
HRMPH
WHO, CARWESS?
HE'LL JUST TELL ME TO BRING HIM SOME WOOD FROM AN OLD TREE.
NO BIG DEAL.
YOU DON'T GET IT AT **ALL**, DO YOU?
HUH?

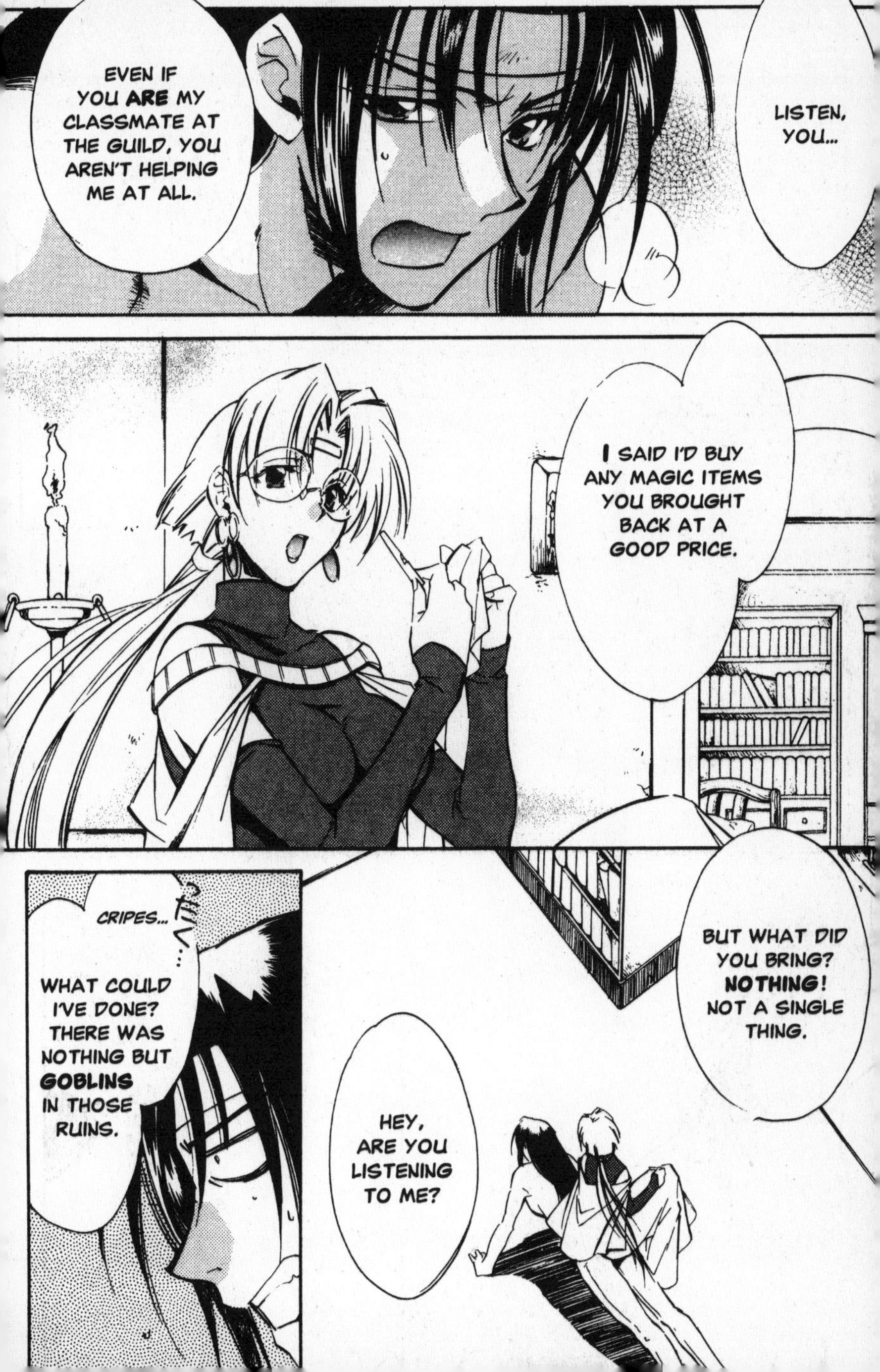
LISTEN, YOU...
EVEN IF YOU **ARE** MY CLASSMATE AT THE GUILD, YOU AREN'T HELPING ME AT ALL.
I SAID I'D BUY ANY MAGIC ITEMS YOU BROUGHT BACK AT A GOOD PRICE.
...
BUT WHAT DID YOU BRING? **NOTHING!** NOT A SINGLE THING.
HEY, ARE YOU LISTENING TO ME?
CRIPES...
WHAT COULD I'VE DONE? THERE WAS NOTHING BUT **GOBLINS** IN THOSE RUINS.

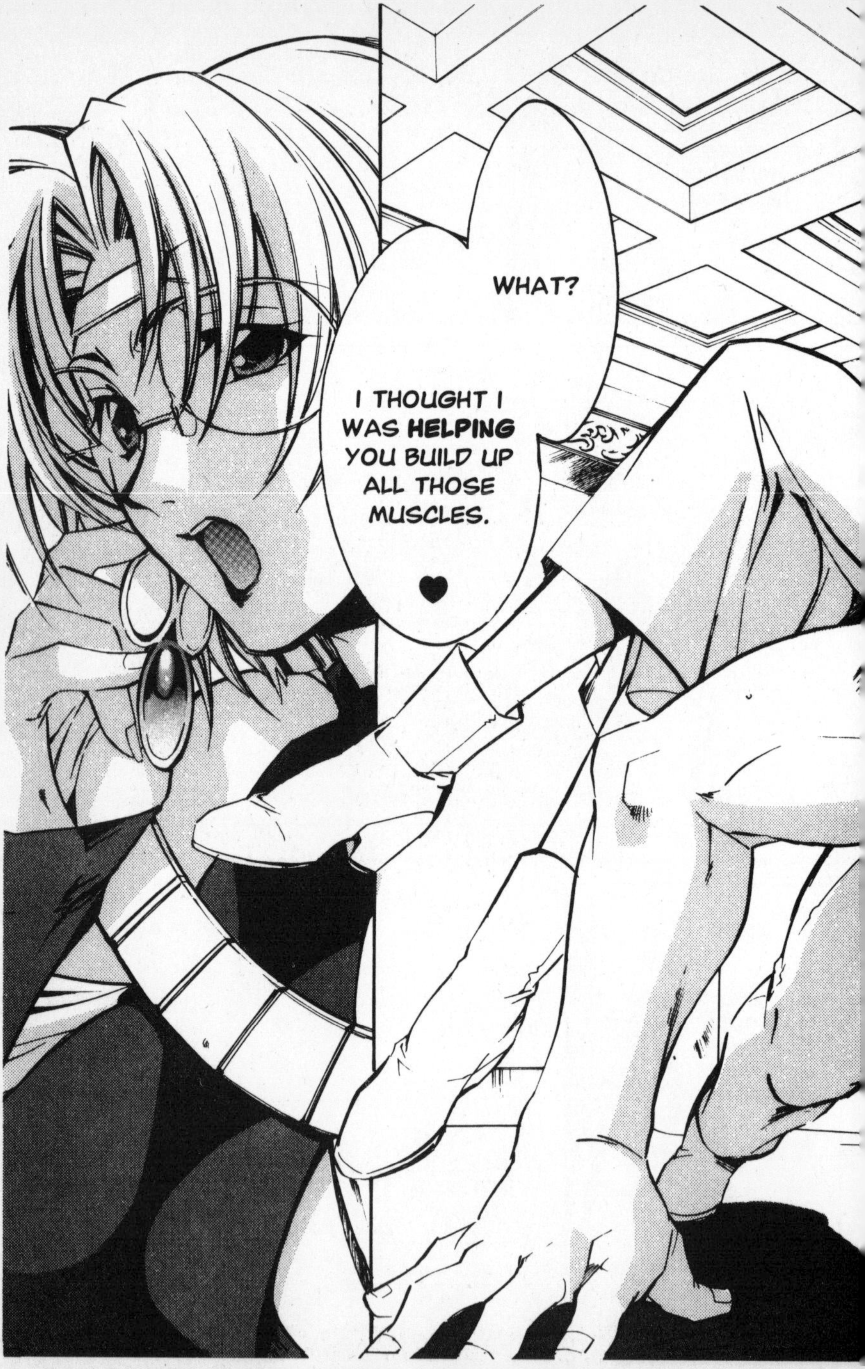
WHAT?
I THOUGHT I WAS **HELPING** YOU BUILD UP ALL THOSE MUSCLES. ♥

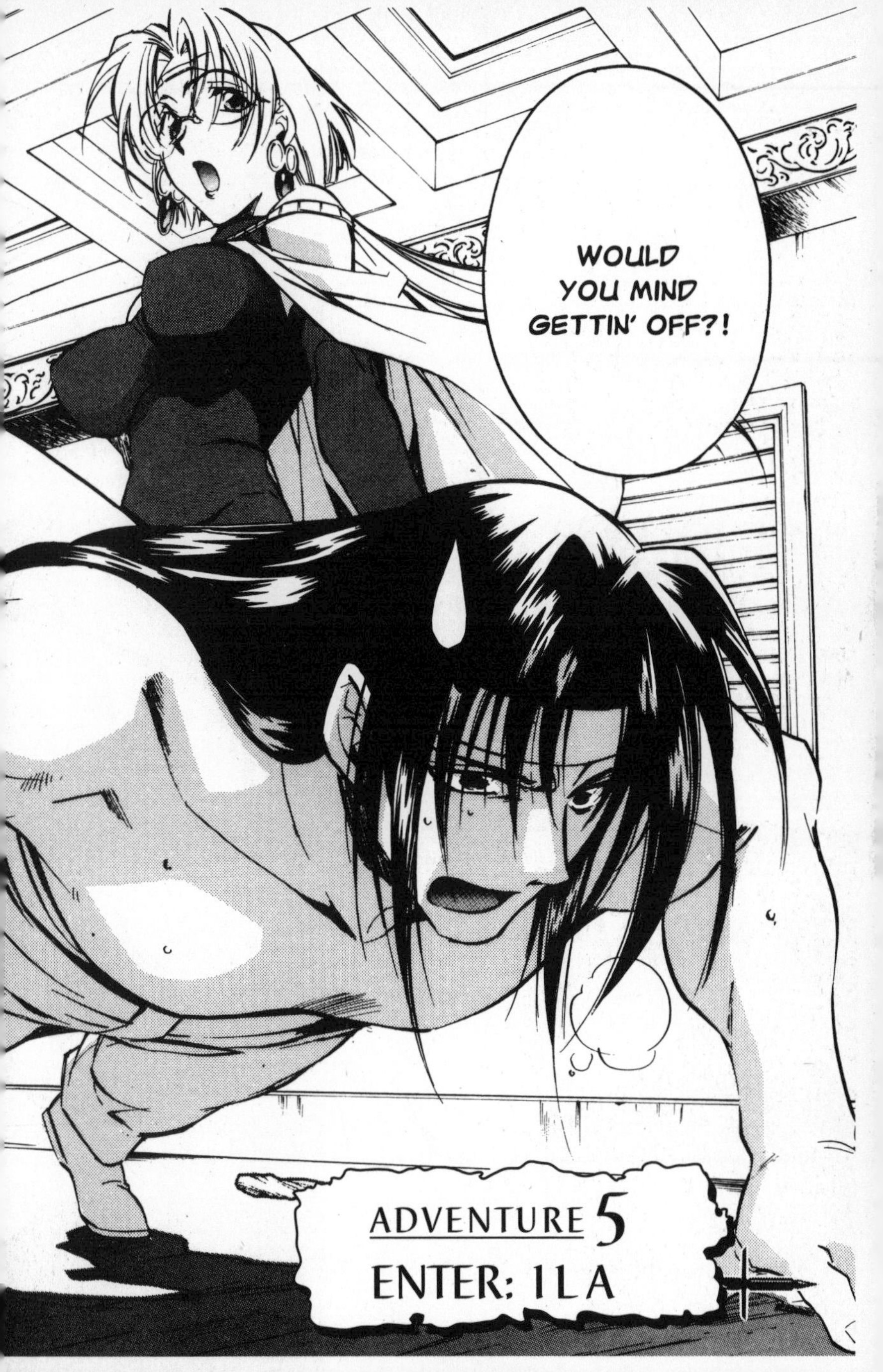
WOULD YOU MIND GETTIN' OFF?!
ADVENTURE 5
ENTER: ILA

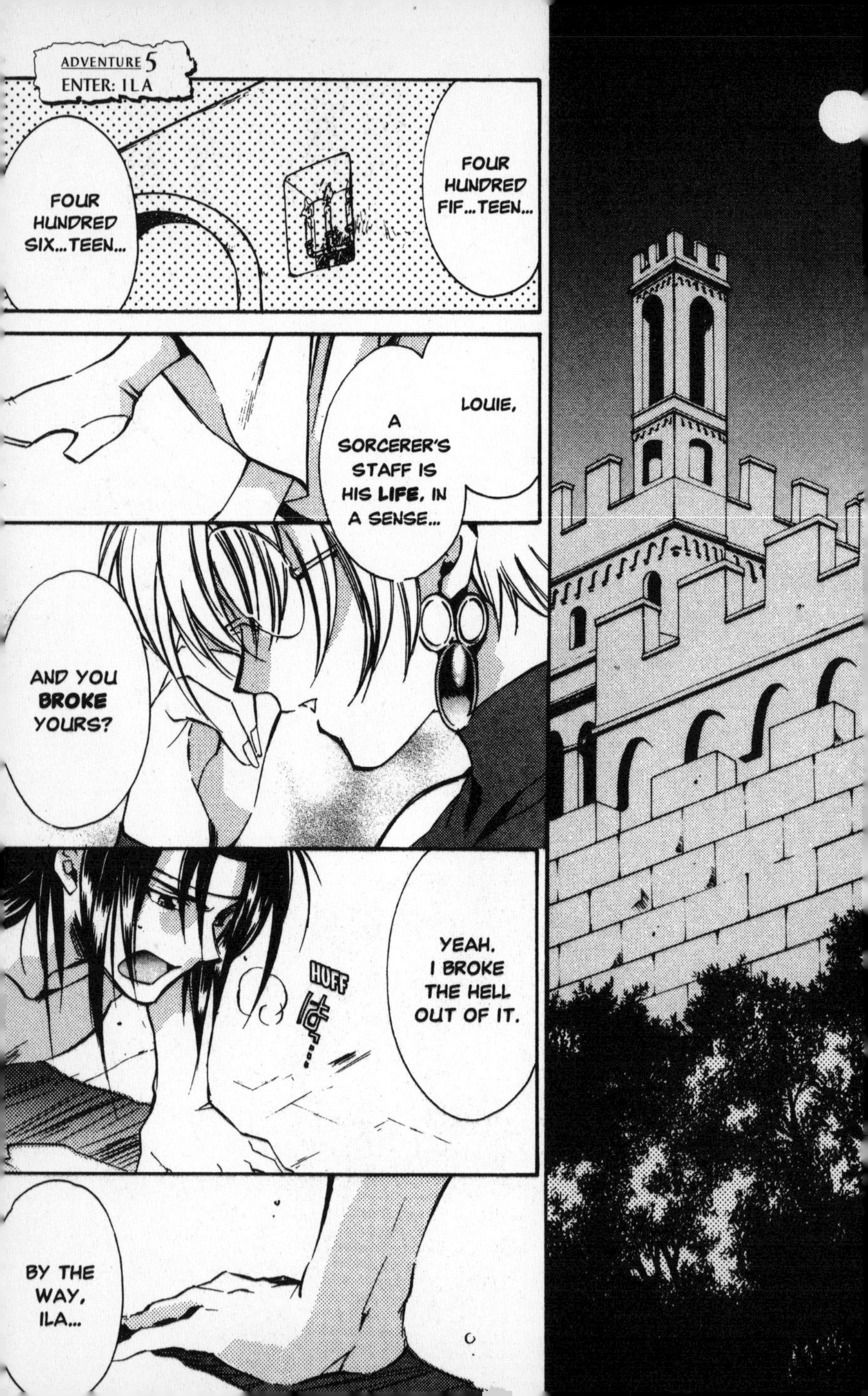
ADVENTURE 5
ENTER: ILA
FOUR HUNDRED FIF...TEEN...
FOUR HUNDRED SIX...TEEN...
LOUIE,
A SORCERER'S STAFF IS HIS LIFE, IN A SENSE...
AND YOU BROKE YOURS?
YEAH. I BROKE THE HELL OUT OF IT.
HUFF
BY THE WAY, ILA...

魔法戦士リウイ

LOUIE the RUNE SOLDIER

紅炎のバスタード

現実（げんじつ）……

REALITY…

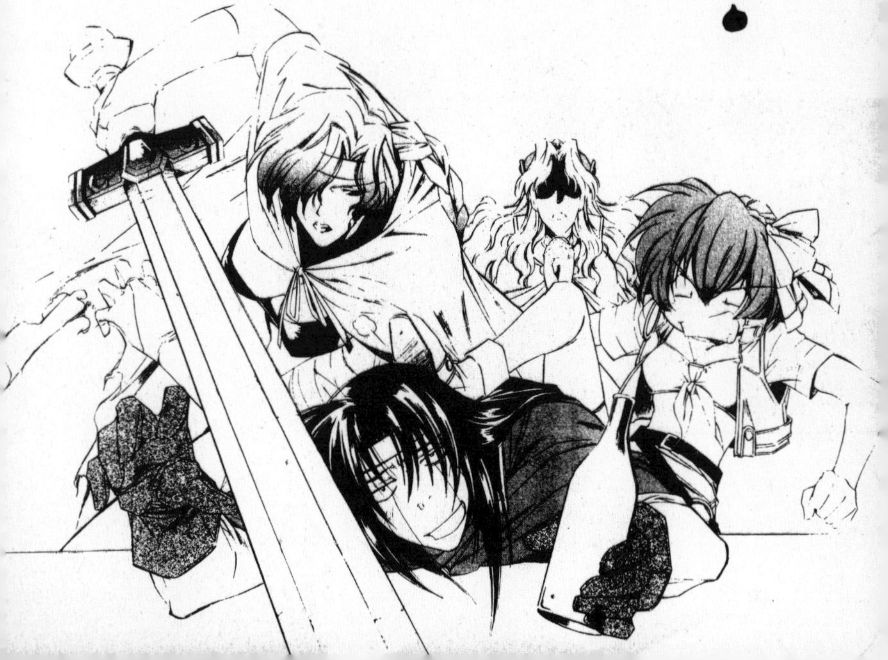

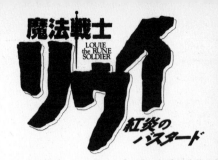

魔法戦士
LOUIE the RUNE SOLDIER
リウイ
紅炎のバスタード

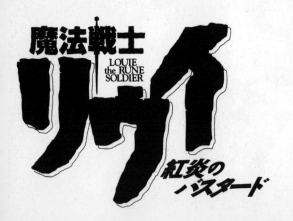

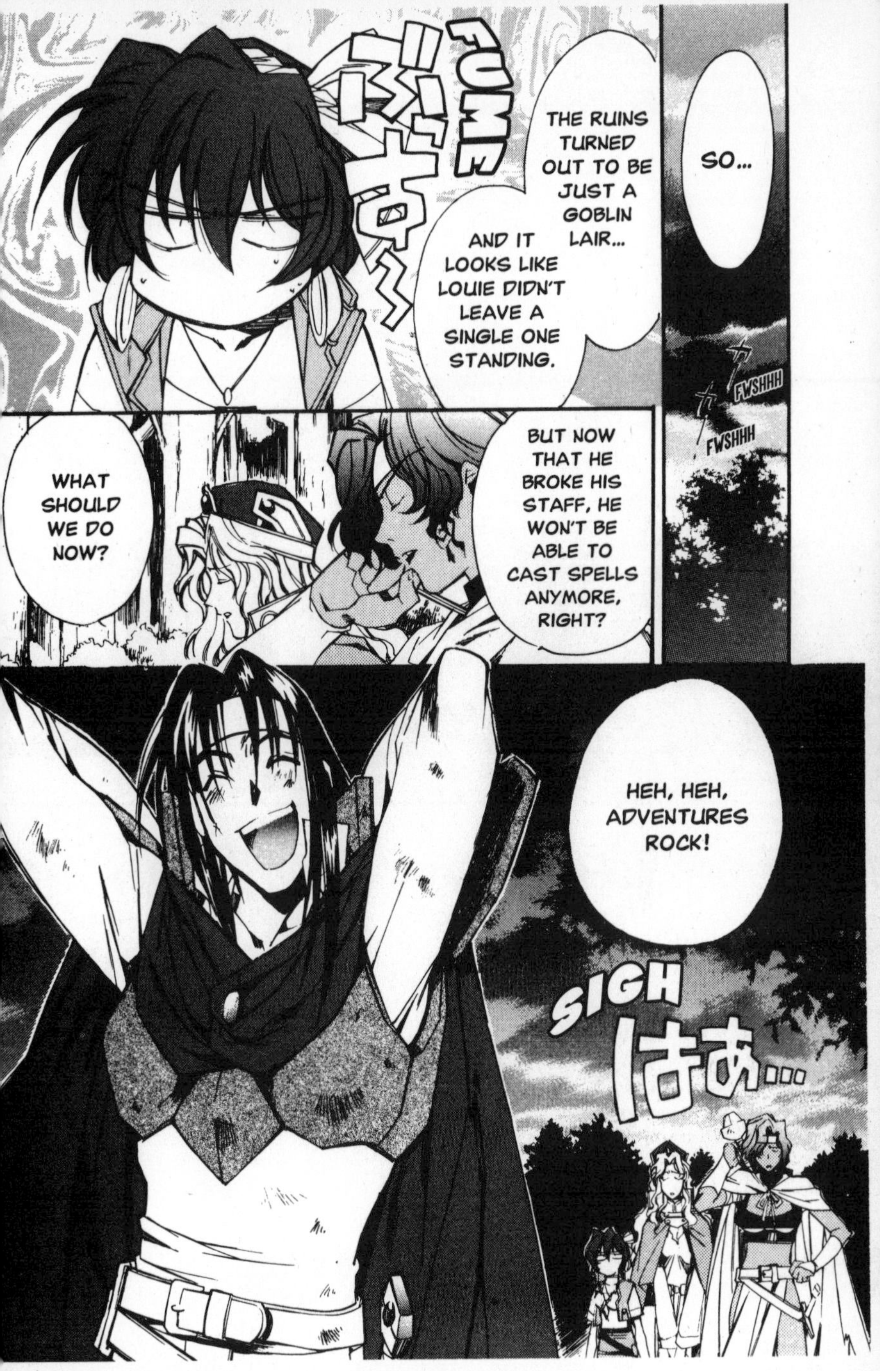
SO...
FWSHHH
FWSHHH
THE RUINS TURNED OUT TO BE JUST A GOBLIN LAIR...
AND IT LOOKS LIKE LOUIE DIDN'T LEAVE A SINGLE ONE STANDING.
FUME
BUT NOW THAT HE BROKE HIS STAFF, HE WON'T BE ABLE TO CAST SPELLS ANYMORE, RIGHT?
WHAT SHOULD WE DO NOW?
HEH, HEH, ADVENTURES ROCK!
SIGH
はあ...

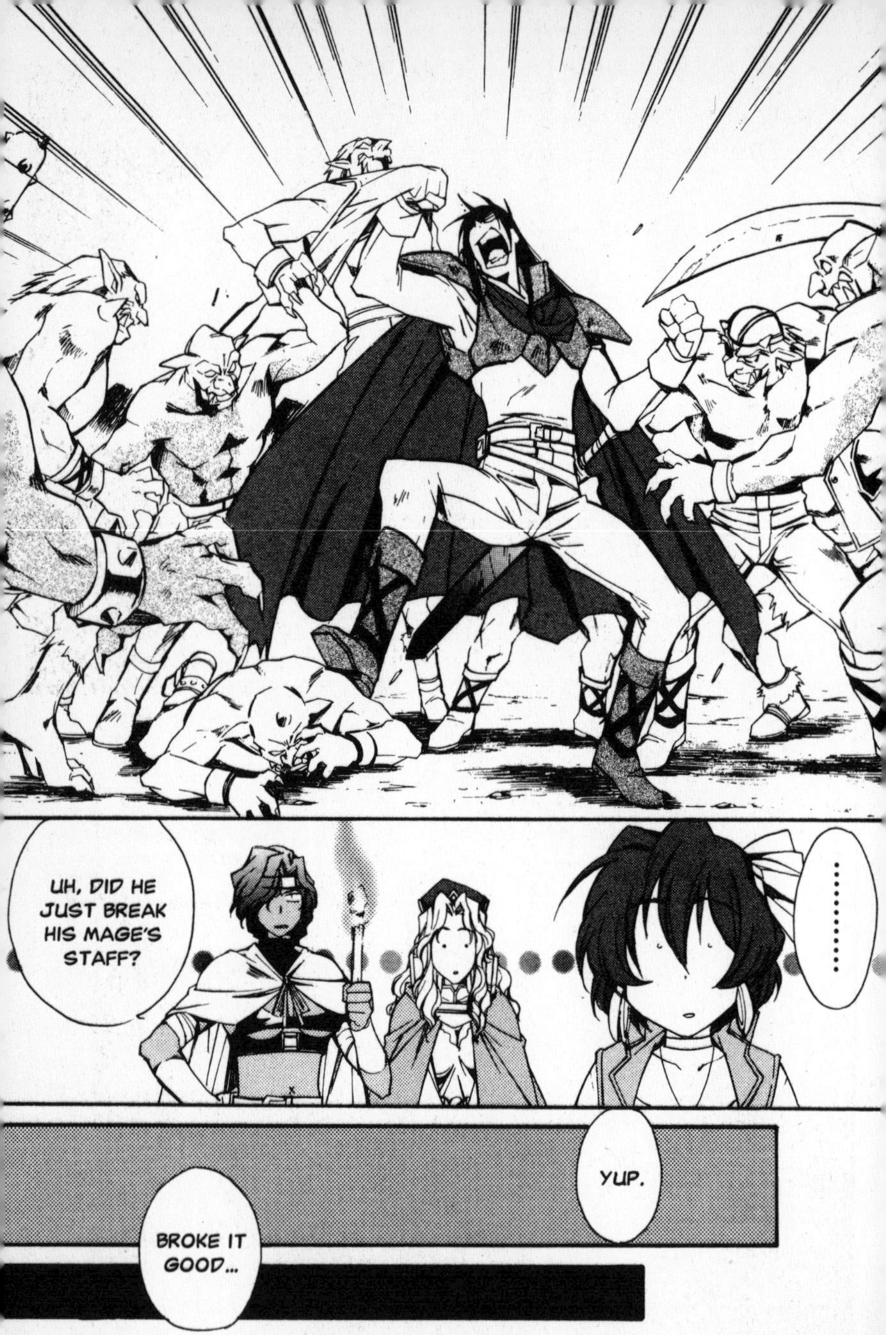
......
UH, DID HE JUST BREAK HIS MAGE'S STAFF?
YUP.
BROKE IT GOOD...

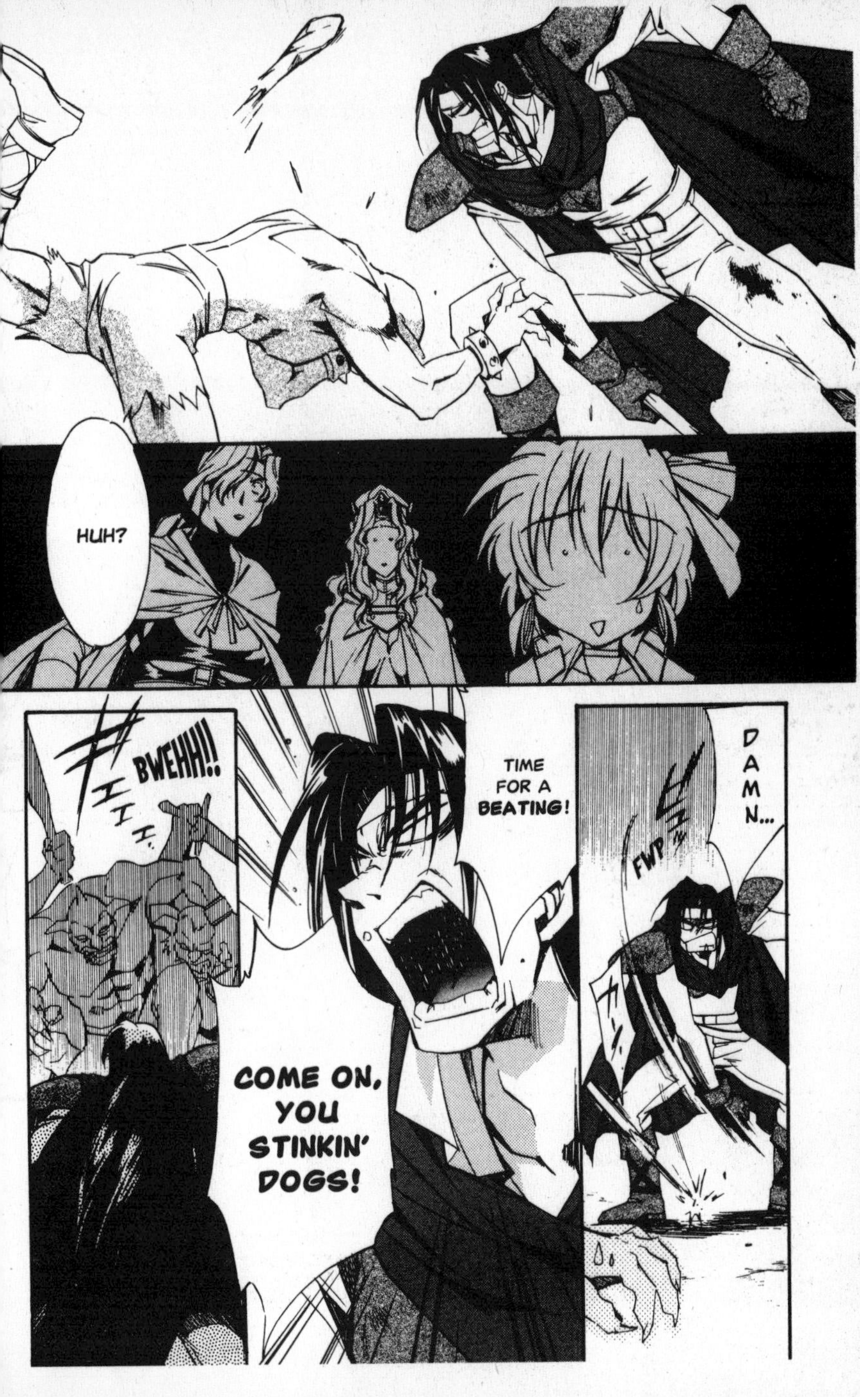
HUH?
DAMN...
FWP
TIME FOR A BEATING!
COME ON, YOU STINKIN' DOGS!
BWEHH!!

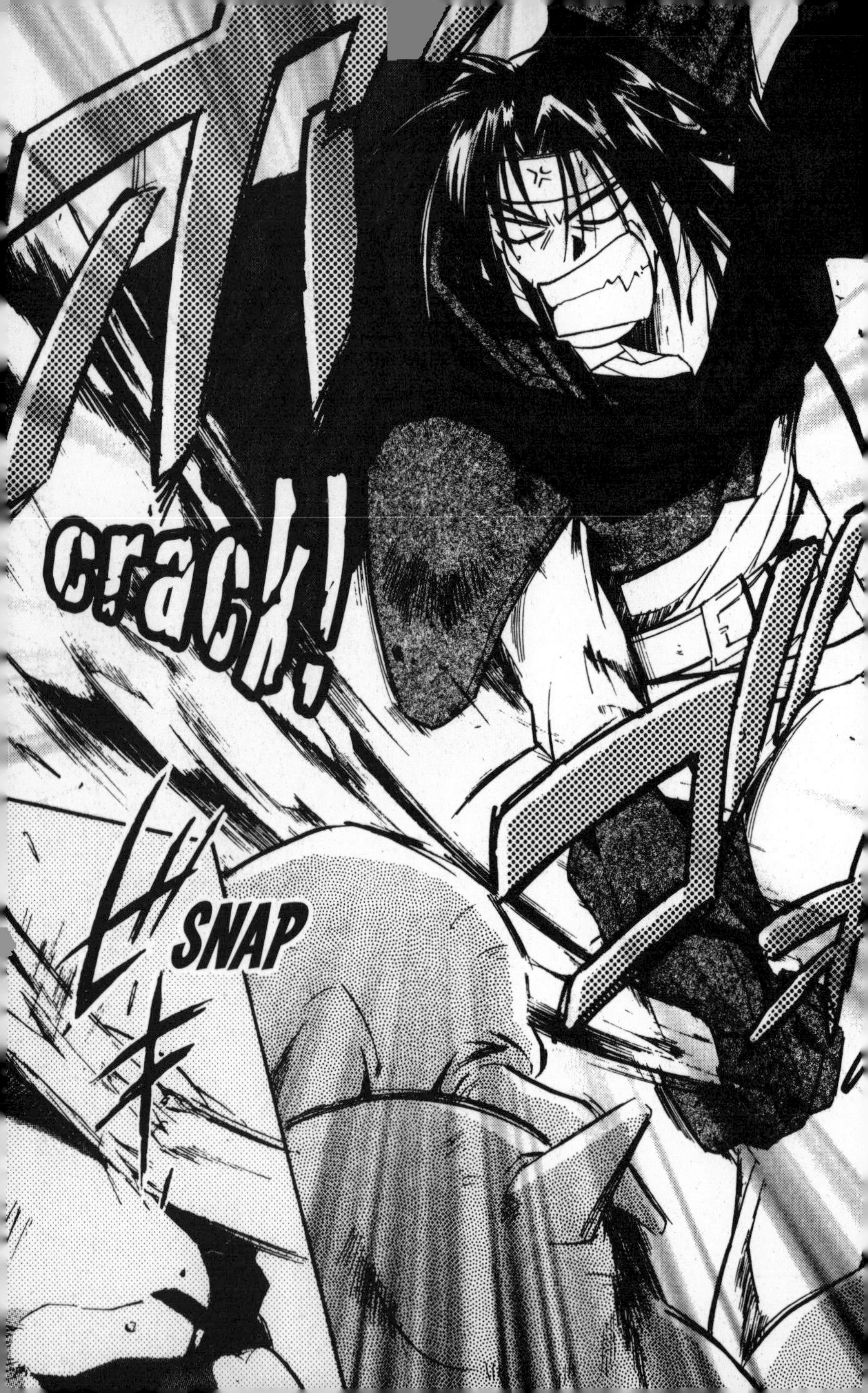
crack!
SNAP

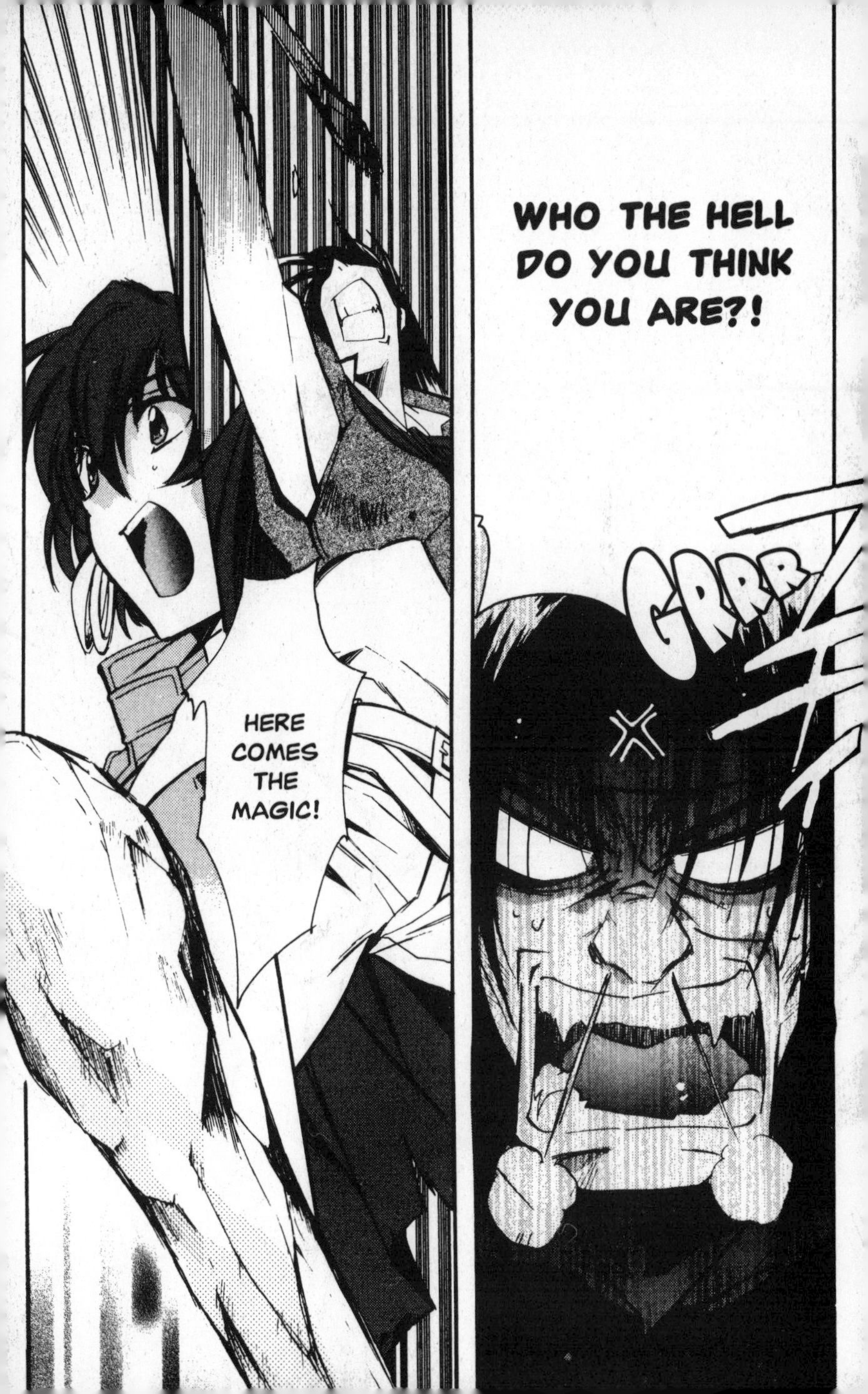
WHO THE HELL DO YOU THINK YOU ARE?!
GRRR
HERE COMES THE MAGIC!

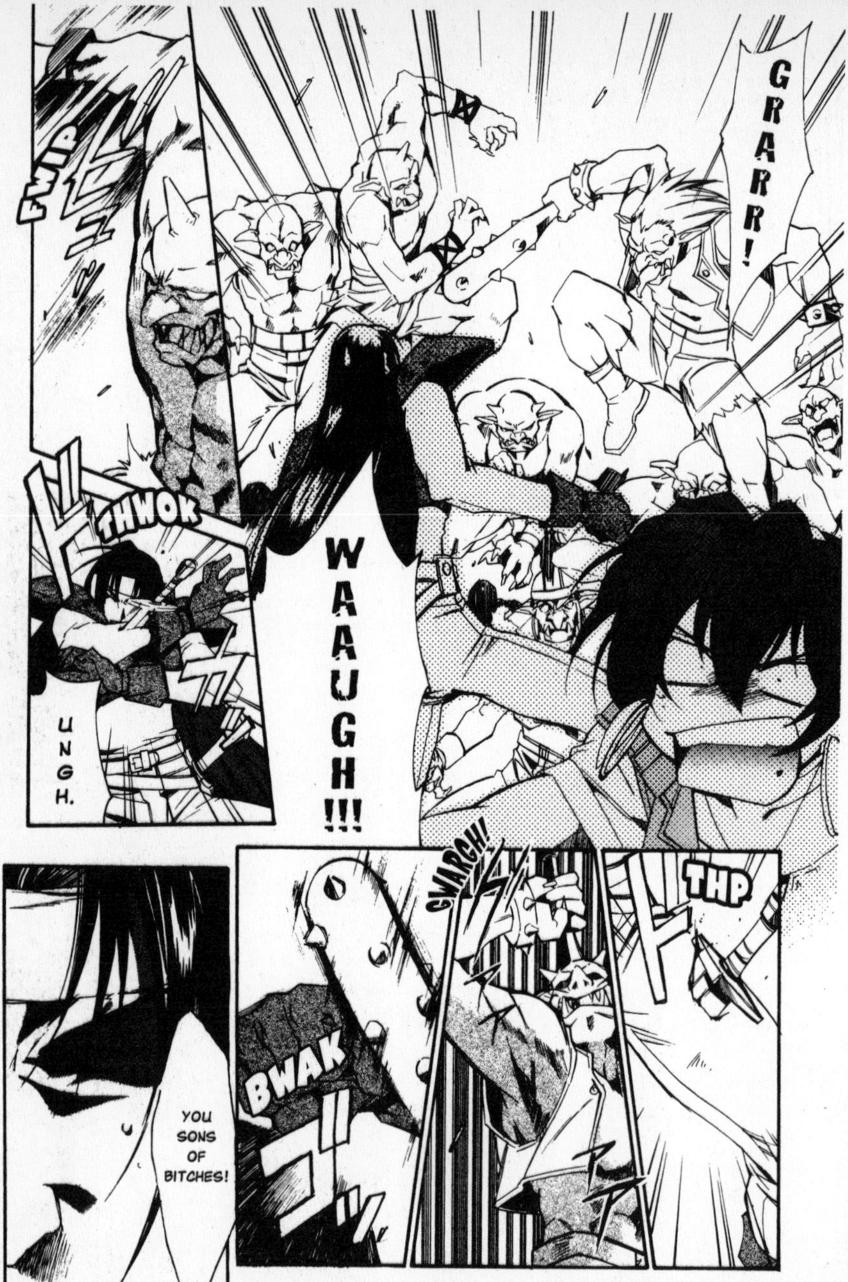
GRARR!
WAAUGH!!!
FWIP
THWOK
UNGH.
THP
GWARGH!
BWAK
YOU SONS OF BITCHES!

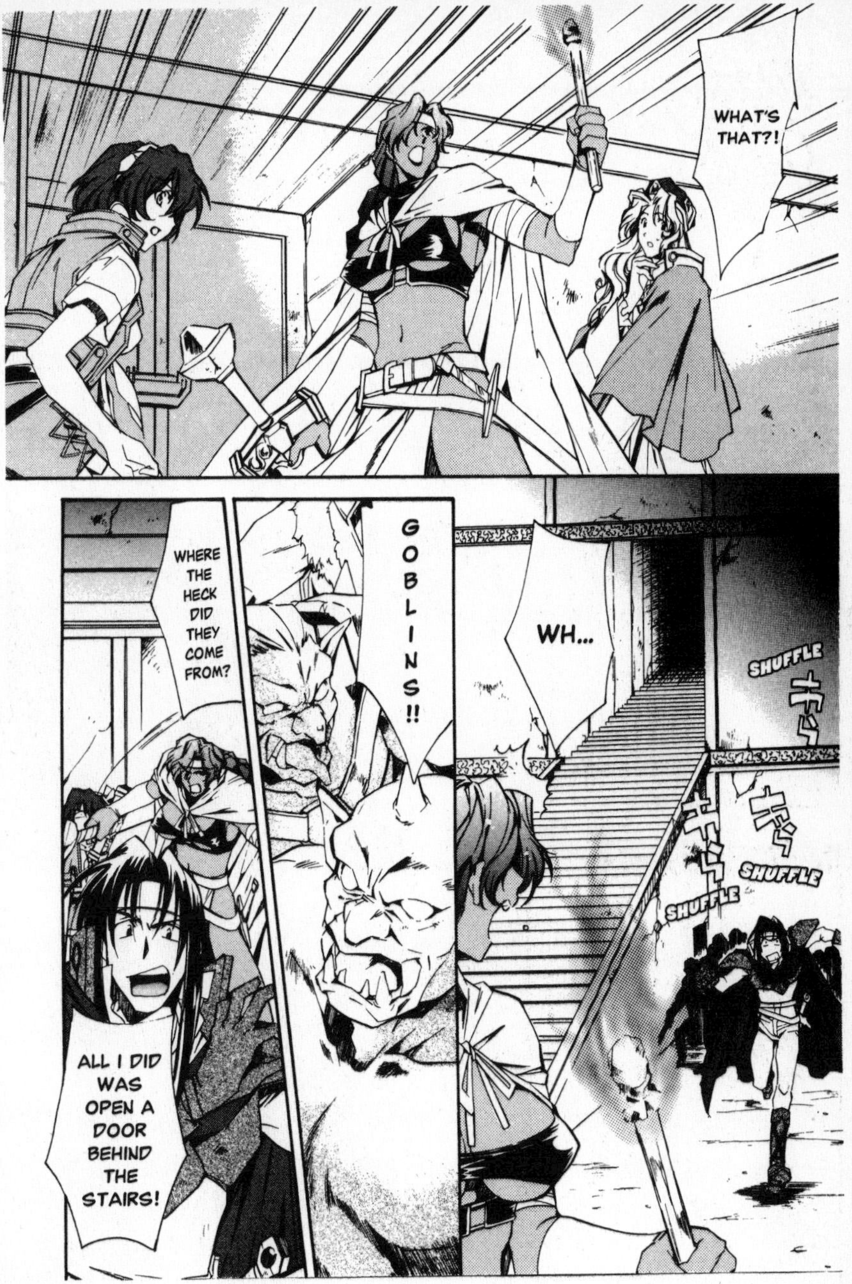
WHAT'S THAT?!
WH...
SHUFFLE
SHUFFLE
SHUFFLE
GOBLINS!!
WHERE THE HECK DID THEY COME FROM?
ALL I DID WAS OPEN A DOOR BEHIND THE STAIRS!

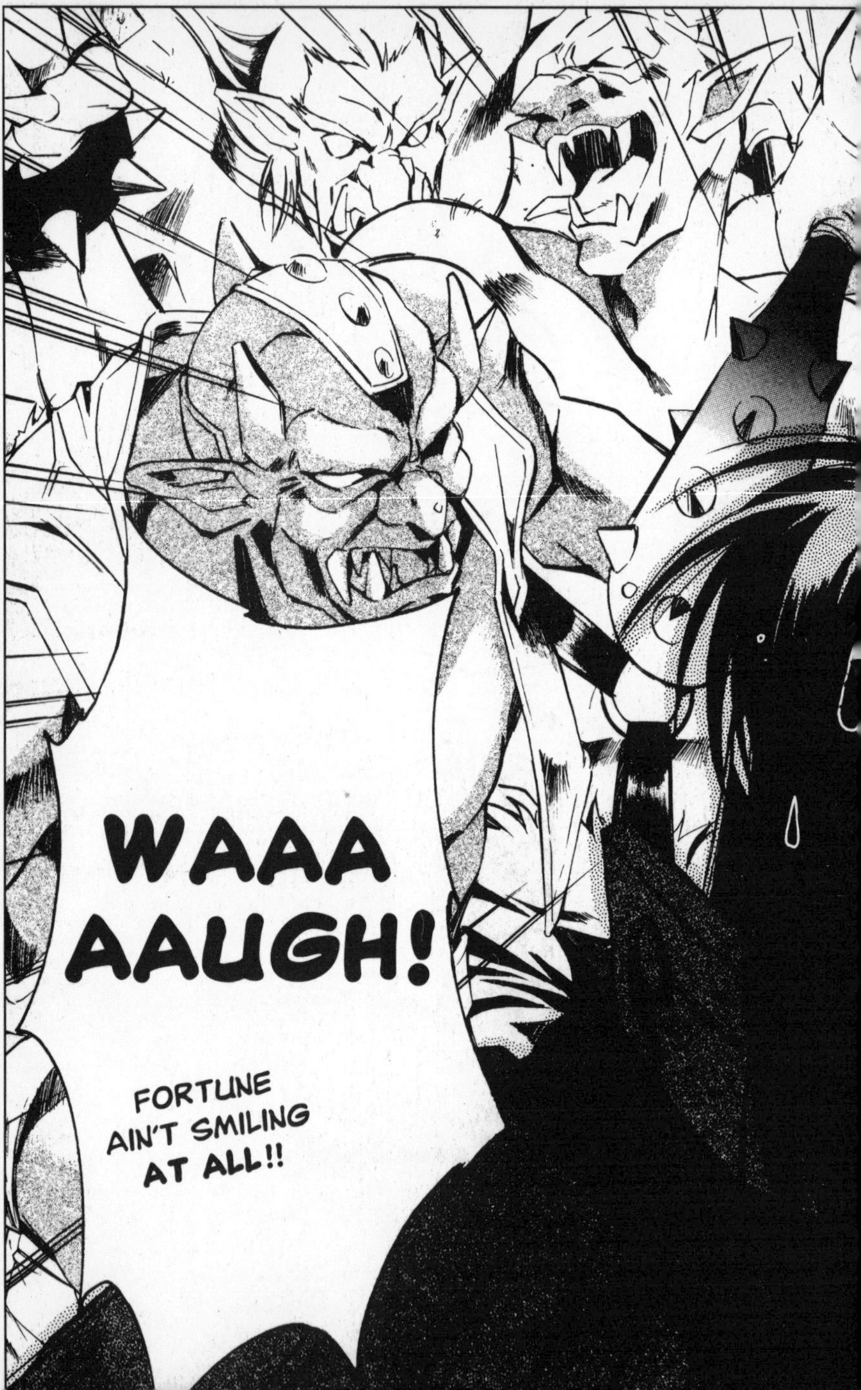
WAAA AAUGH!
FORTUNE AIN'T SMILING AT ALL!!

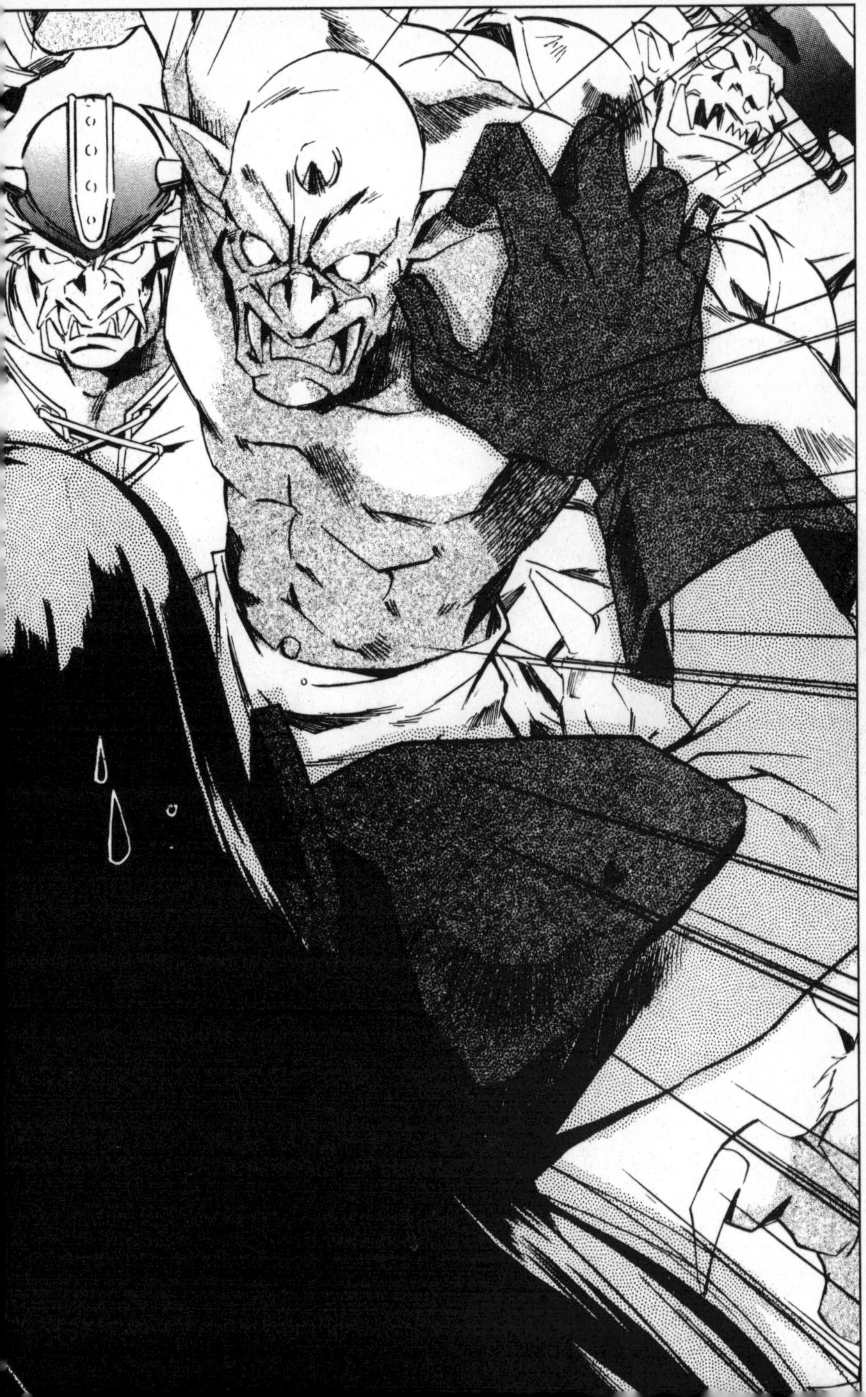

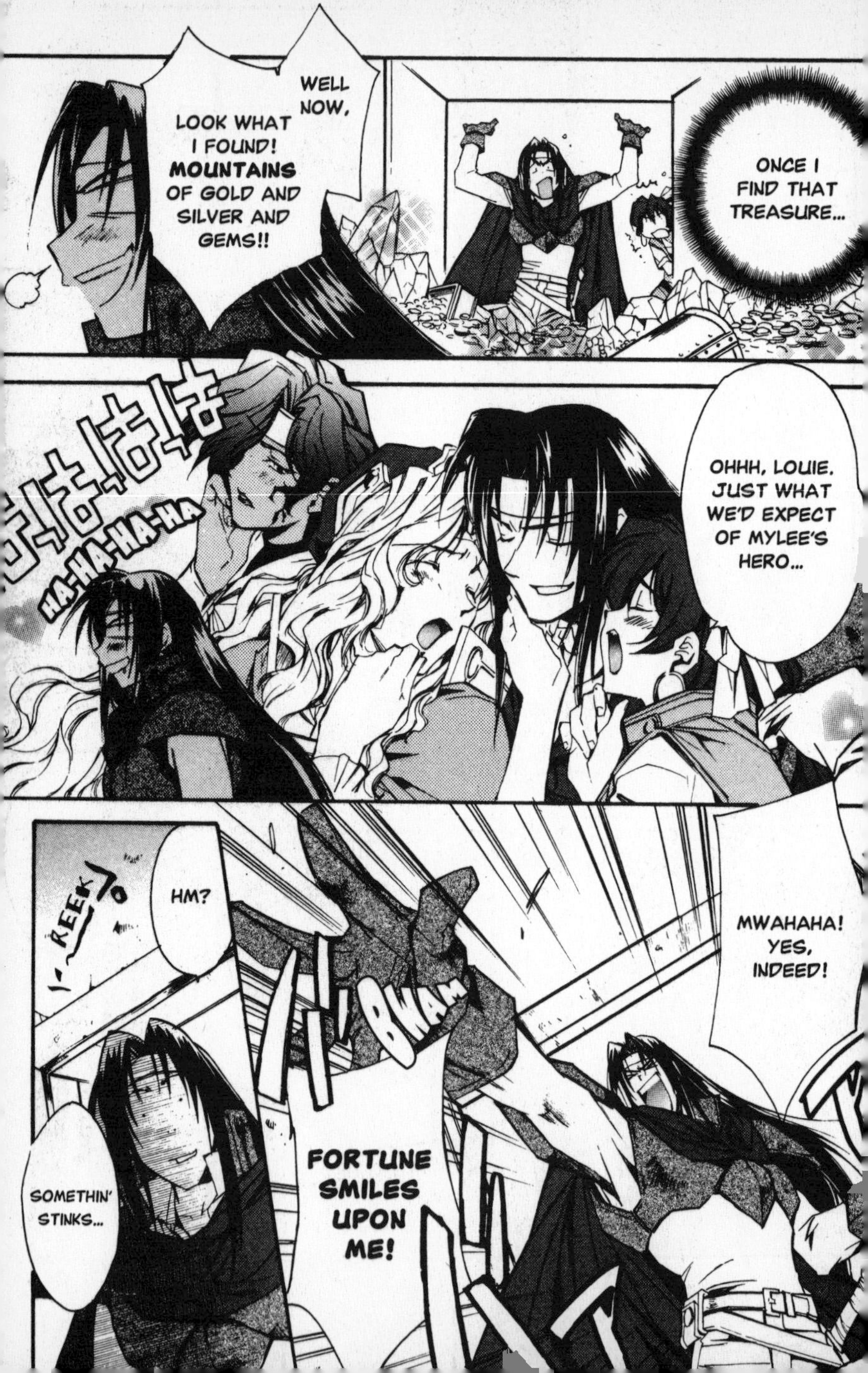
ONCE I FIND THAT TREASURE...
WELL NOW,
LOOK WHAT I FOUND! MOUNTAINS OF GOLD AND SILVER AND GEMS!!
OHHH, LOUIE. JUST WHAT WE'D EXPECT OF MYLEE'S HERO...
HA-HA-HA-HA
MWAHAHA! YES, INDEED!
FORTUNE SMILES UPON ME!
BWAM
HM?
KREEK
SOMETHIN' STINKS...

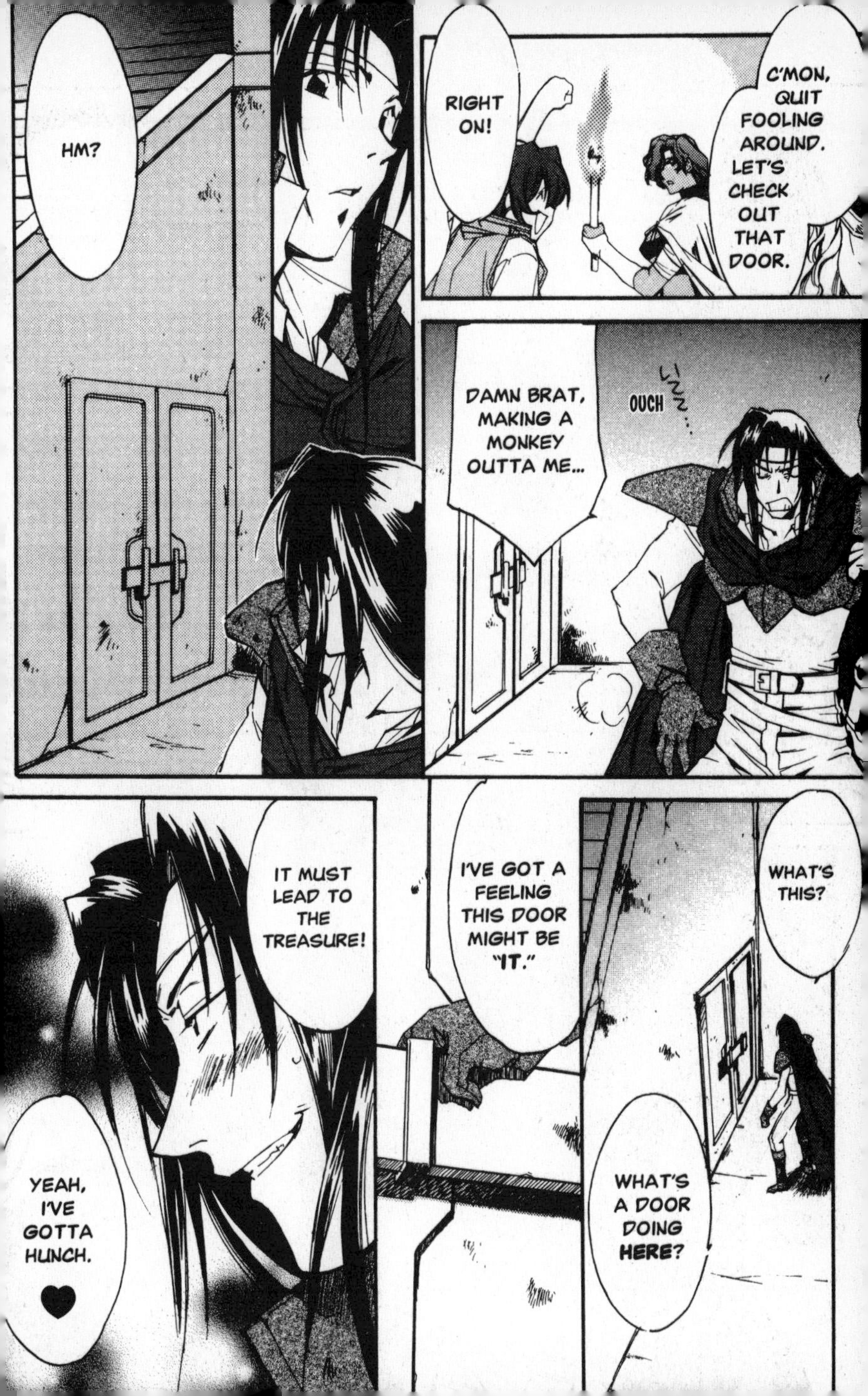
C'MON, QUIT FOOLING AROUND. LET'S CHECK OUT THAT DOOR.
RIGHT ON!
OUCH
DAMN BRAT, MAKING A MONKEY OUTTA ME...
HM?
WHAT'S THIS?
WHAT'S A DOOR DOING HERE?
I'VE GOT A FEELING THIS DOOR MIGHT BE "IT."
IT MUST LEAD TO THE TREASURE!
YEAH, I'VE GOTTA HUNCH. ♥

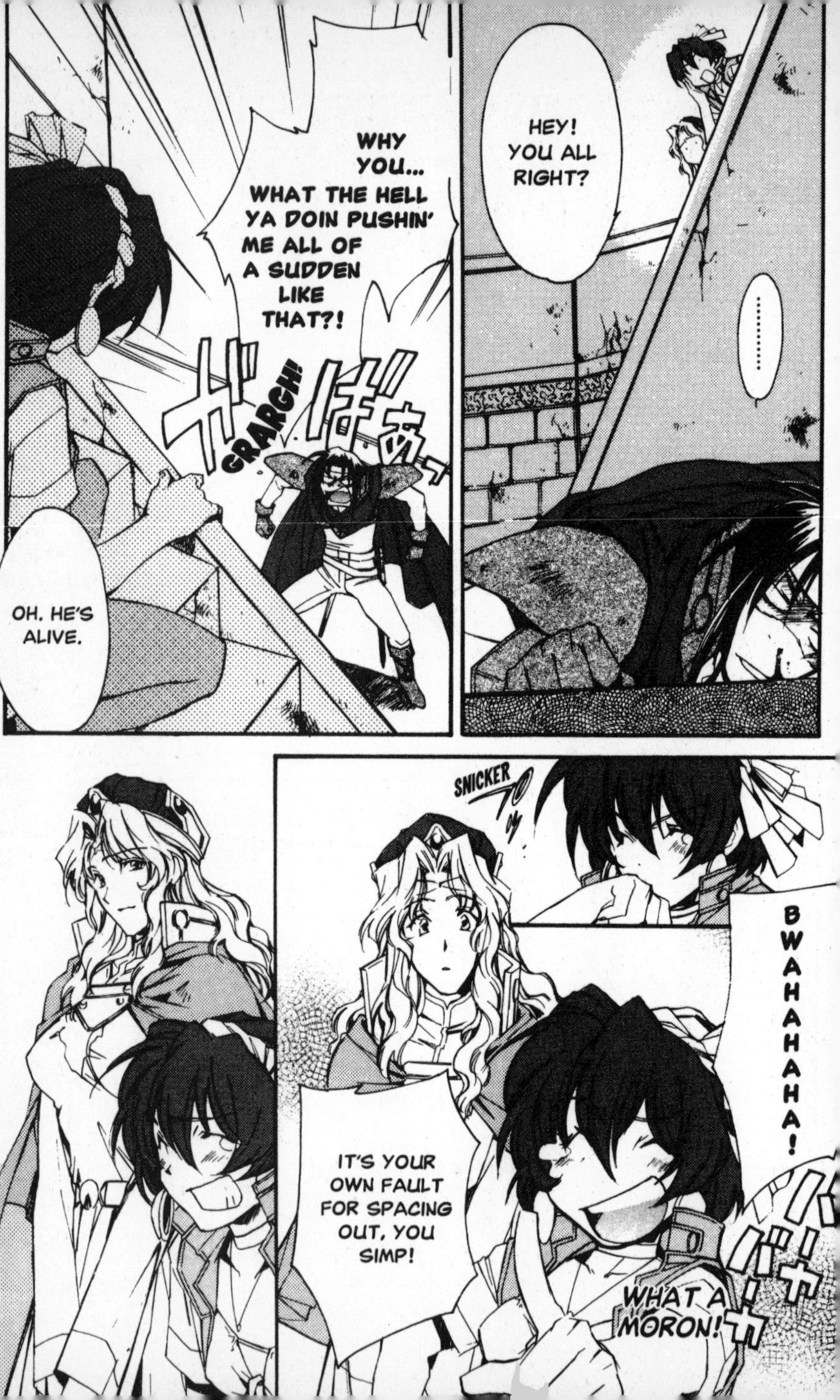
HEY! YOU ALL RIGHT?
......
WHY YOU... WHAT THE HELL YA DOIN PUSHIN' ME ALL OF A SUDDEN LIKE THAT?!
GRARGH!
OH. HE'S ALIVE.
SNICKER
BWAHAHAHA!
IT'S YOUR OWN FAULT FOR SPACING OUT, YOU SIMP!
WHAT A MORON!

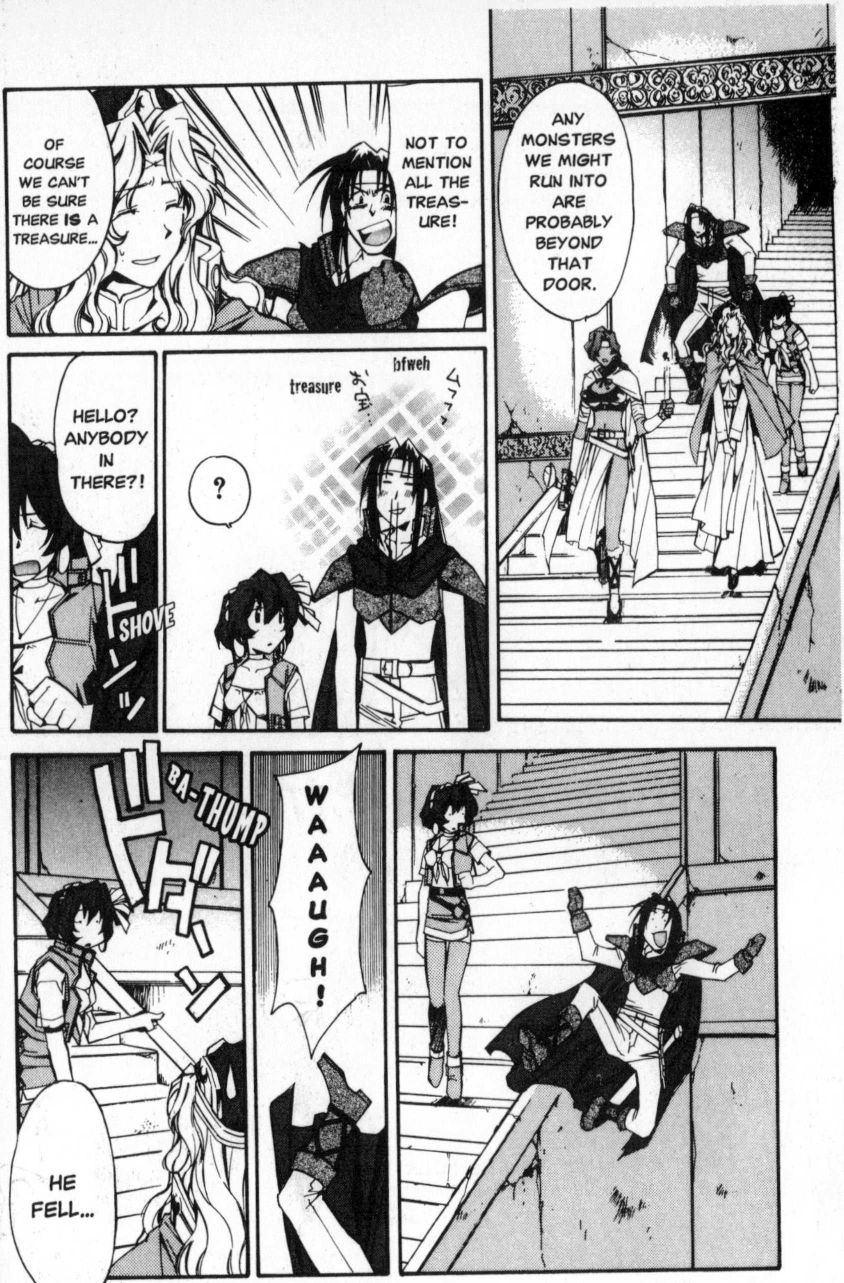
ANY MONSTERS WE MIGHT RUN INTO ARE PROBABLY BEYOND THAT DOOR.
NOT TO MENTION ALL THE TREAS-URE!
OF COURSE WE CAN'T BE SURE THERE **IS** A TREASURE...
bfweh
ムフフ
お宝…
treasure
?
HELLO? ANYBODY IN THERE?!
SHOVE
WAAAUGH!
BA-THUMP
HE FELL...

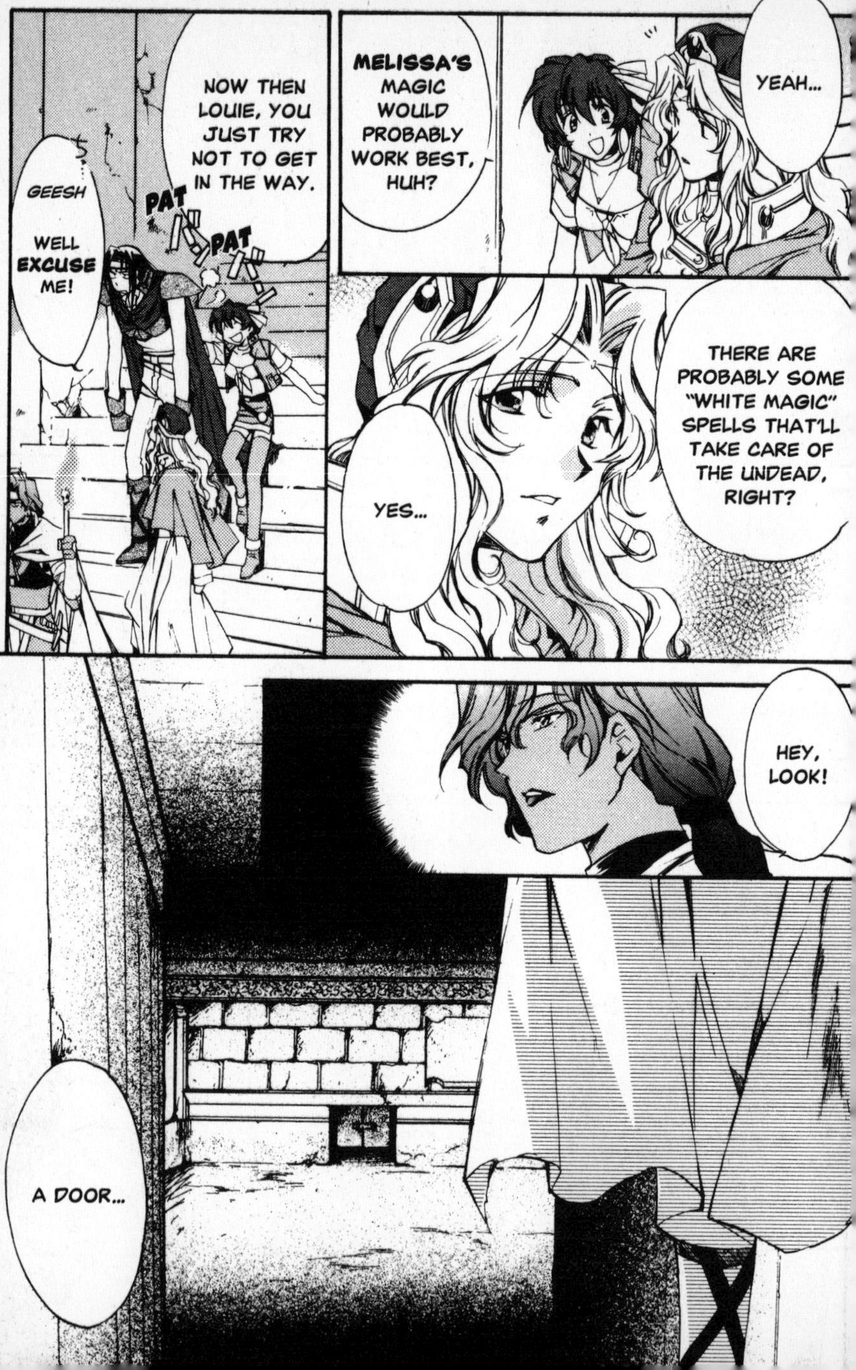
YEAH...
MELISSA'S MAGIC WOULD PROBABLY WORK BEST, HUH?
THERE ARE PROBABLY SOME "WHITE MAGIC" SPELLS THAT'LL TAKE CARE OF THE UNDEAD, RIGHT?
YES...
NOW THEN LOUIE, YOU JUST TRY NOT TO GET IN THE WAY.
PAT
PAT
GEESH
WELL EXCUSE ME!
HEY, LOOK!
A DOOR...

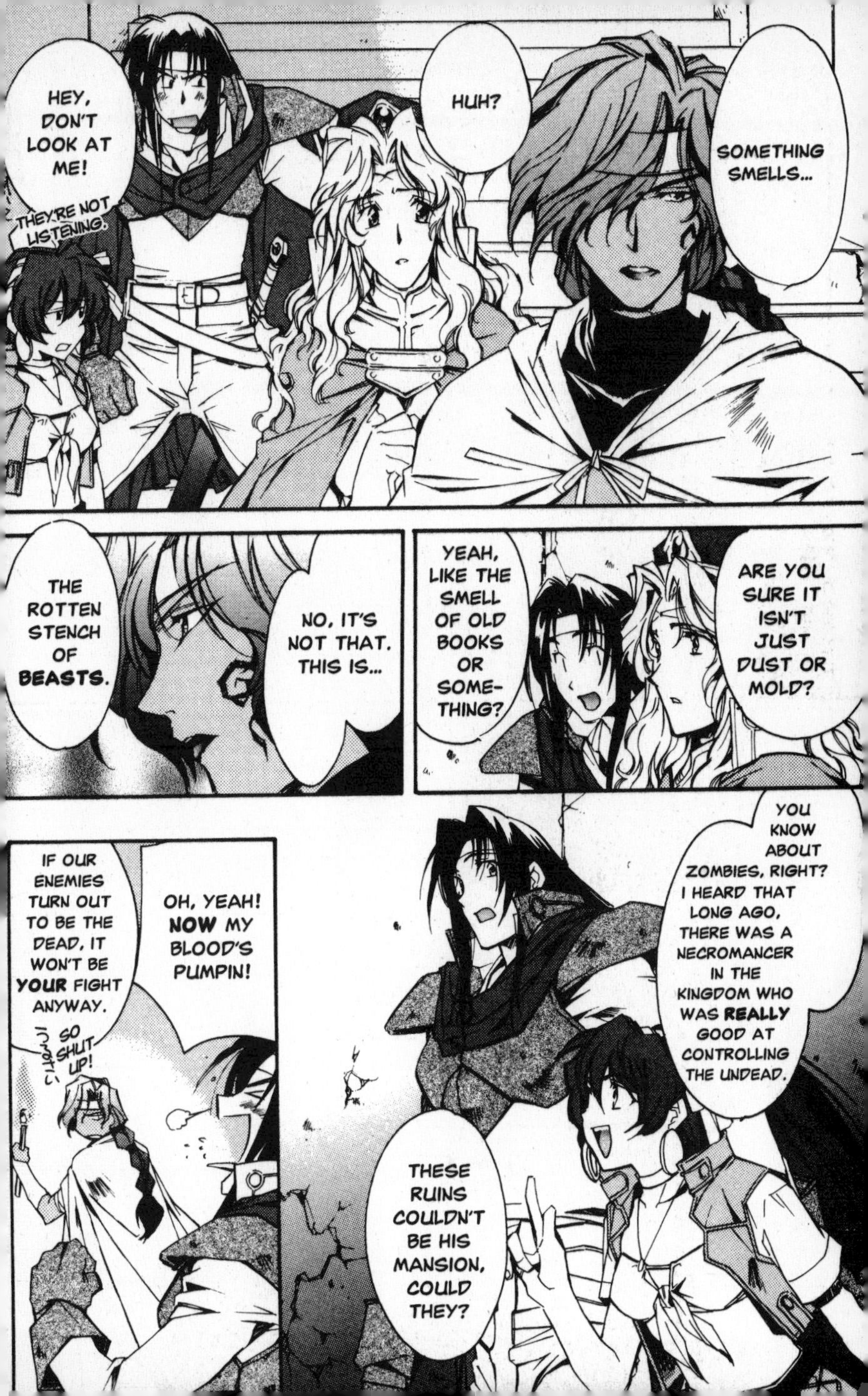
SOMETHING SMELLS...
HUH?
HEY, DON'T LOOK AT ME!
THEY'RE NOT LISTENING.
ARE YOU SURE IT ISN'T JUST DUST OR MOLD?
YEAH, LIKE THE SMELL OF OLD BOOKS OR SOME-THING?
NO, IT'S NOT THAT. THIS IS...
THE ROTTEN STENCH OF **BEASTS**.
YOU KNOW ABOUT ZOMBIES, RIGHT? I HEARD THAT LONG AGO, THERE WAS A NECROMANCER IN THE KINGDOM WHO WAS **REALLY** GOOD AT CONTROLLING THE UNDEAD.
THESE RUINS COULDN'T BE HIS MANSION, COULD THEY?
OH, YEAH! **NOW** MY BLOOD'S PUMPIN!
IF OUR ENEMIES TURN OUT TO BE THE DEAD, IT WON'T BE **YOUR** FIGHT ANYWAY.
SO SHUT UP!

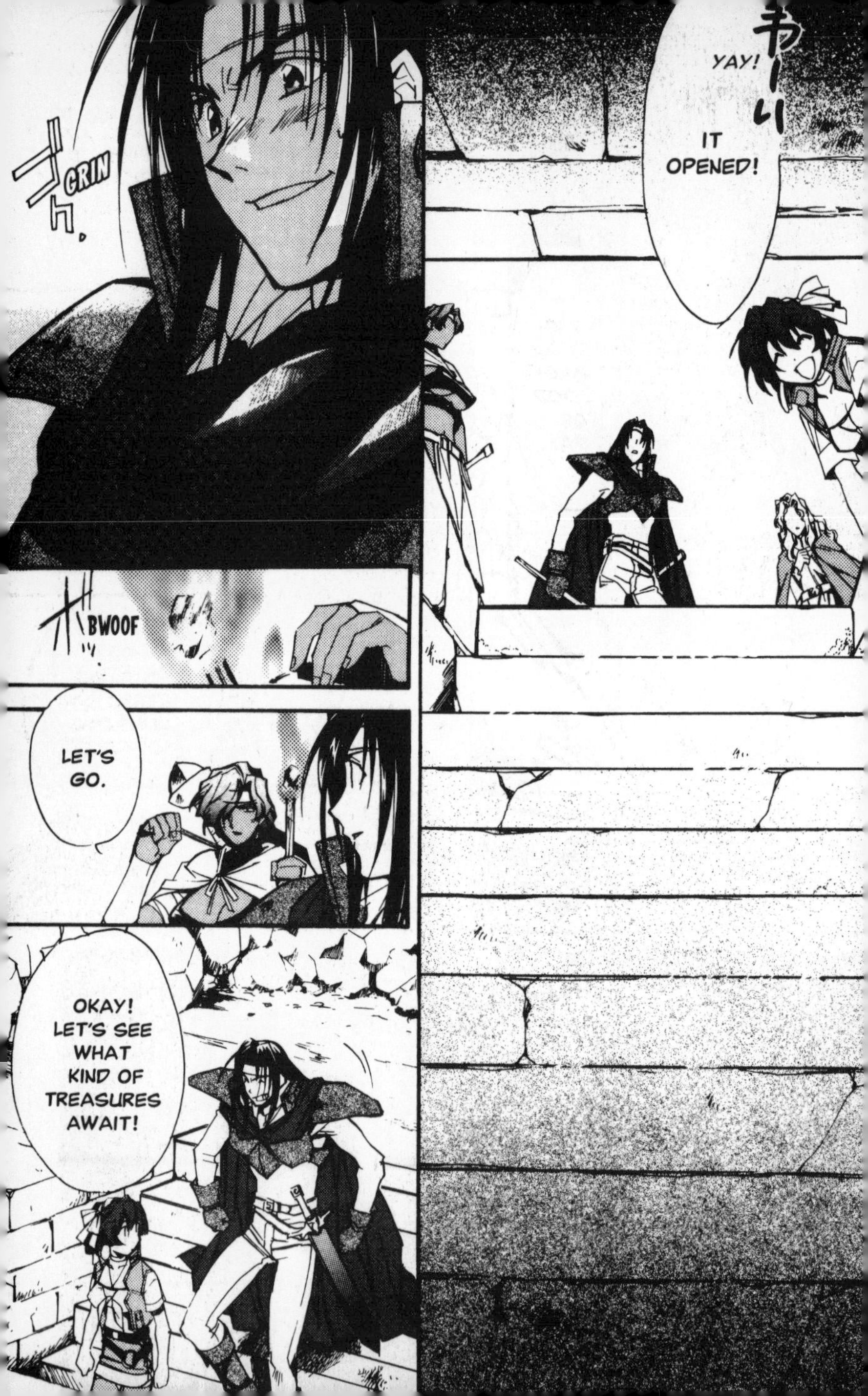
YAY!
IT OPENED!
GRIN
BWOOF
LET'S GO.
OKAY! LET'S SEE WHAT KIND OF TREASURES AWAIT!

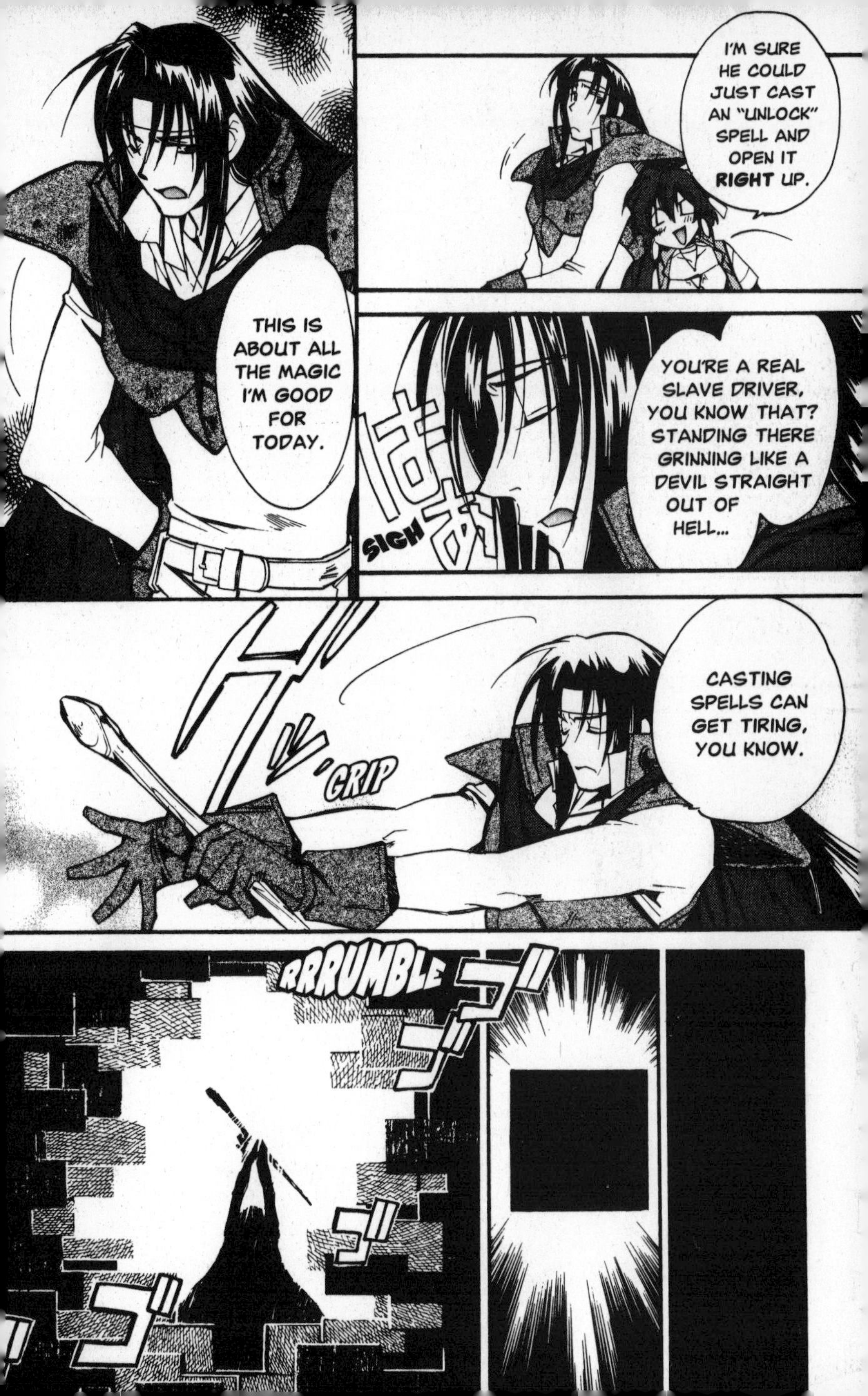
I'M SURE HE COULD JUST CAST AN "UNLOCK" SPELL AND OPEN IT **RIGHT** UP.
SIGH
YOU'RE A REAL SLAVE DRIVER, YOU KNOW THAT? STANDING THERE GRINNING LIKE A DEVIL STRAIGHT OUT OF HELL...
THIS IS ABOUT ALL THE MAGIC I'M GOOD FOR TODAY.
CASTING SPELLS CAN GET TIRING, YOU KNOW.
GRIP
RRRUMBLE

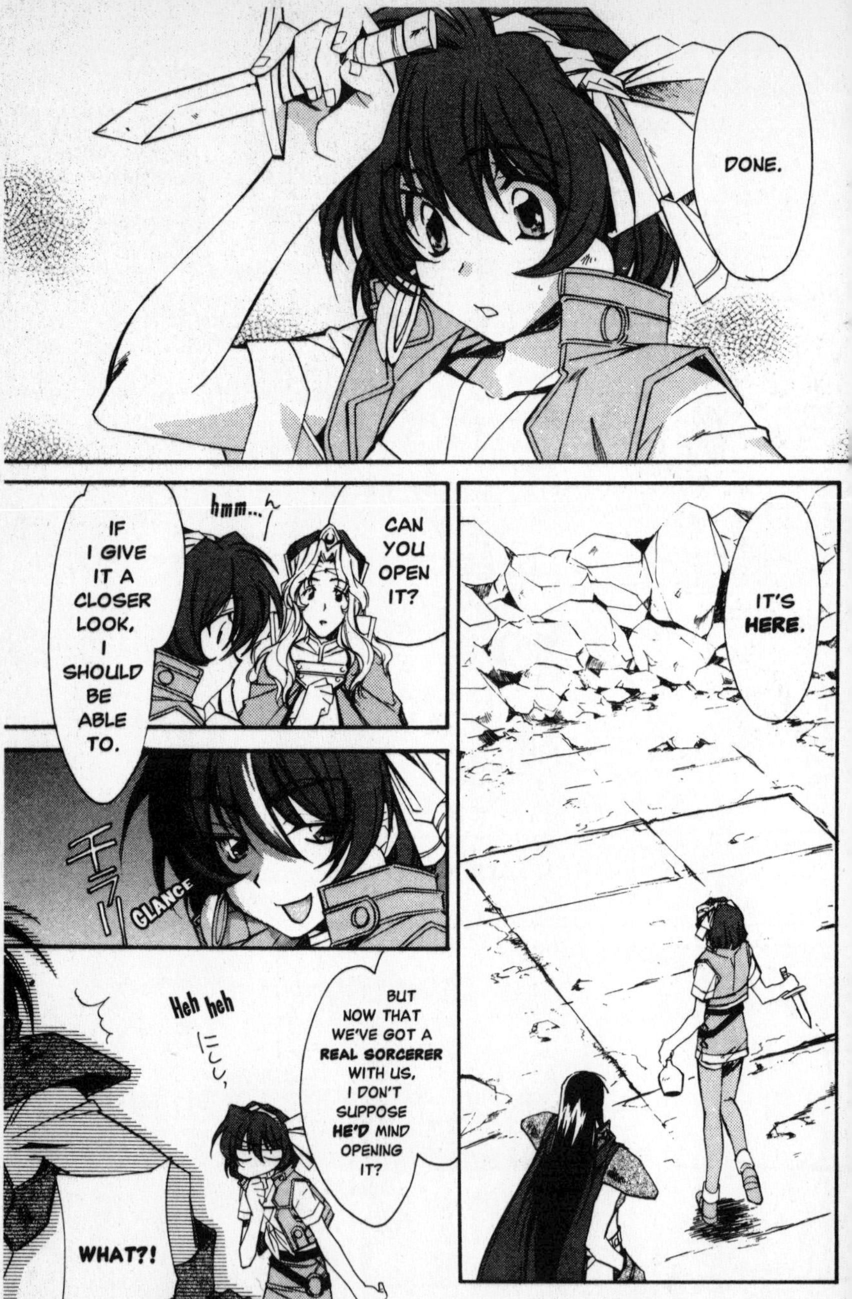
DONE.
IT'S HERE.
CAN YOU OPEN IT?
hmm...
IF I GIVE IT A CLOSER LOOK, I SHOULD BE ABLE TO.
GLANCE
BUT NOW THAT WE'VE GOT A REAL SORCERER WITH US, I DON'T SUPPOSE HE'D MIND OPENING IT?
Heh heh
WHAT?!

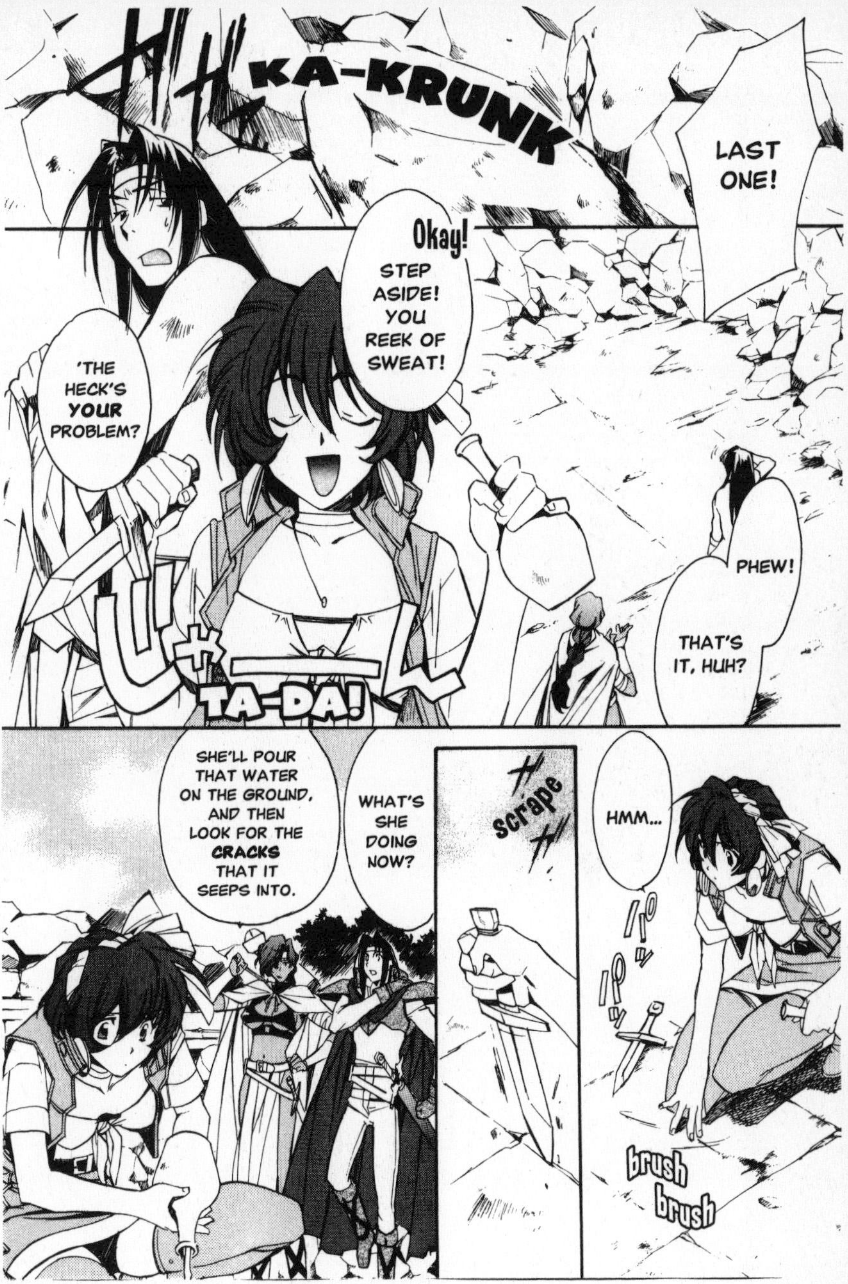
LAST ONE!
KA-KRUNK
PHEW!
THAT'S IT, HUH?
Okay!
STEP ASIDE! YOU REEK OF SWEAT!
'THE HECK'S YOUR PROBLEM?
TA-DA!
HMM...
brush brush
scrape
WHAT'S SHE DOING NOW?
SHE'LL POUR THAT WATER ON THE GROUND, AND THEN LOOK FOR THE CRACKS THAT IT SEEPS INTO.

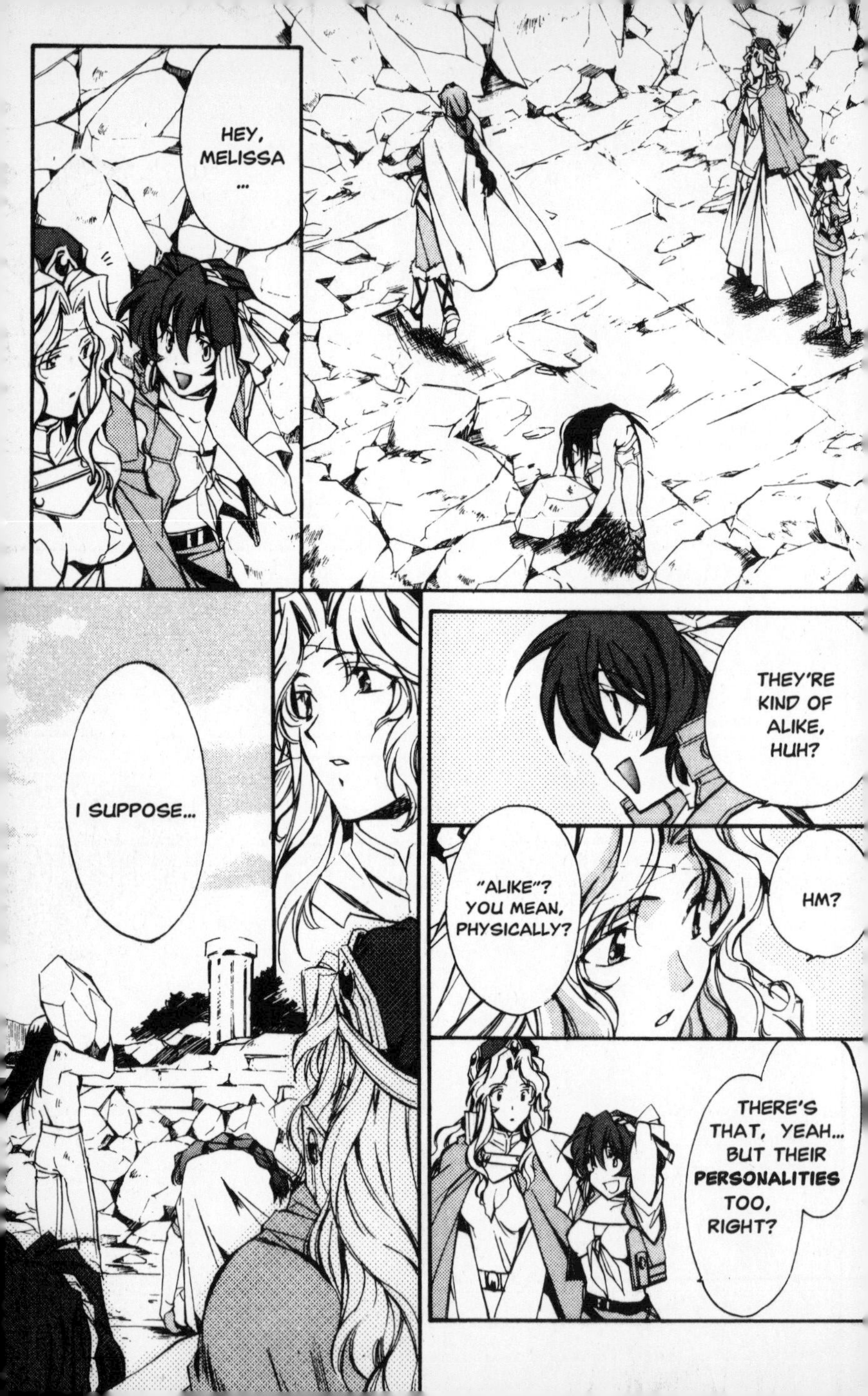
HEY, MELISSA ...
THEY'RE KIND OF ALIKE, HUH?
HM?
"ALIKE"? YOU MEAN, PHYSICALLY?
THERE'S THAT, YEAH... BUT THEIR PERSONALITIES TOO, RIGHT?
I SUPPOSE...

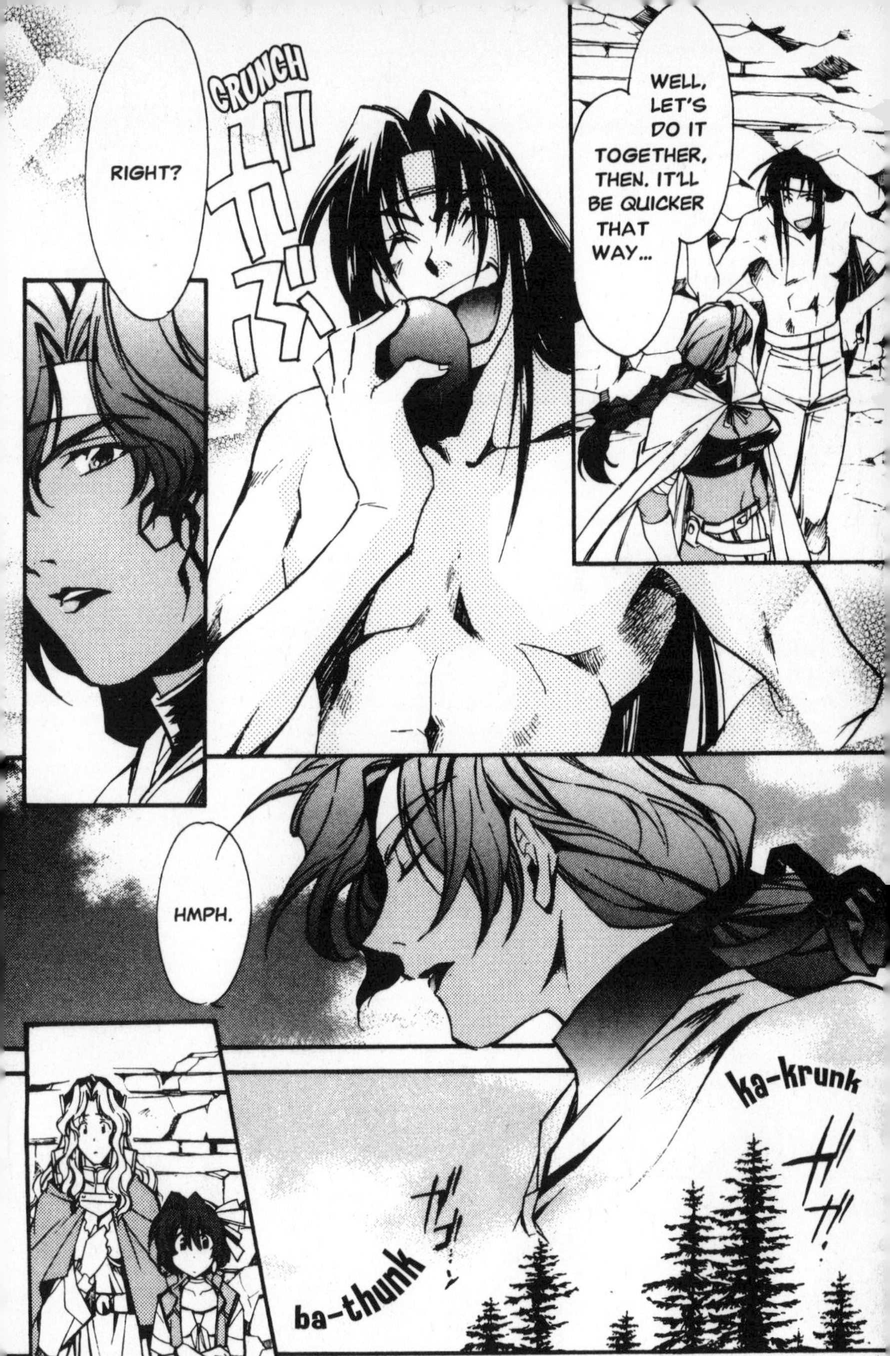
WELL, LET'S DO IT TOGETHER, THEN. IT'LL BE QUICKER THAT WAY...
CRUNCH
RIGHT?
HMPH.
ka-krunk
ba-thunk

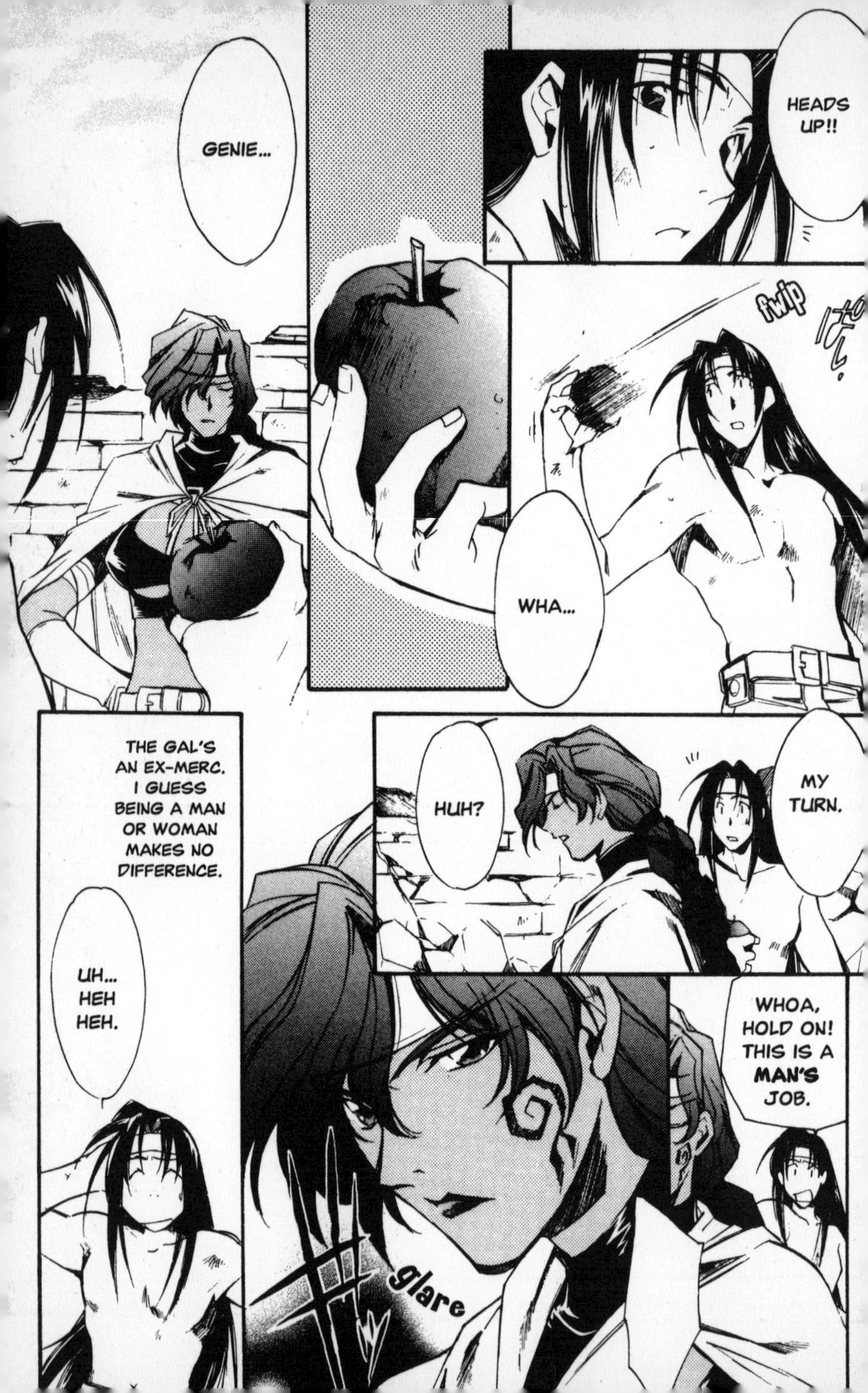
HEADS UP!!
fwip
ぱし
WHA...
GENIE...
MY TURN.
HUH?
WHOA, HOLD ON! THIS IS A **MAN'S** JOB.
glare
THE GAL'S AN EX-MERC. I GUESS BEING A MAN OR WOMAN MAKES NO DIFFERENCE.
UH... HEH HEH.

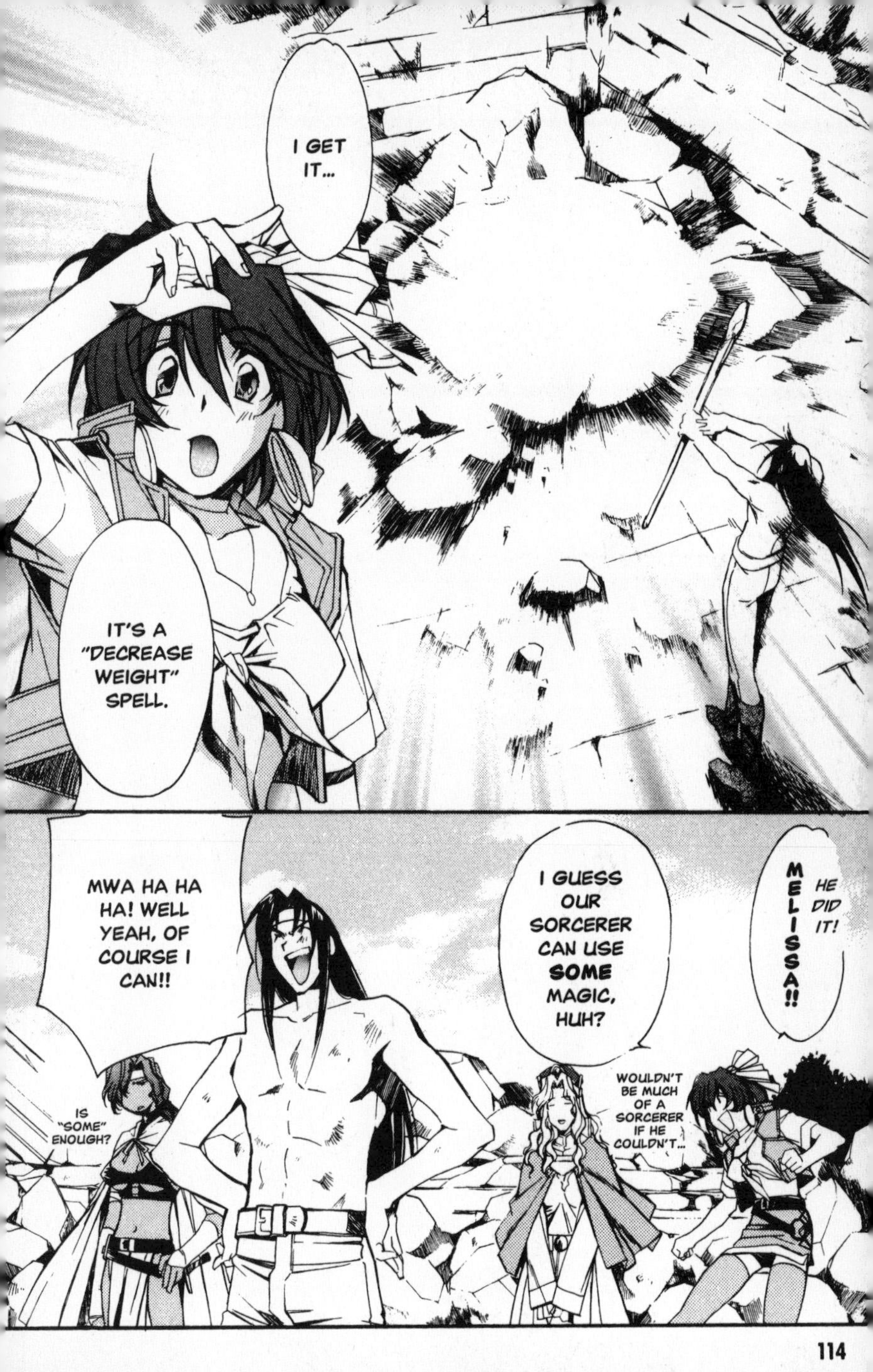
I GET IT...
IT'S A "DECREASE WEIGHT" SPELL.
MELISSA!!
HE DID IT!
I GUESS OUR SORCERER CAN USE **SOME** MAGIC, HUH?
WOULDN'T BE MUCH OF A SORCERER IF HE COULDN'T...
MWA HA HA HA! WELL YEAH, OF COURSE I CAN!!
IS "SOME" ENOUGH?

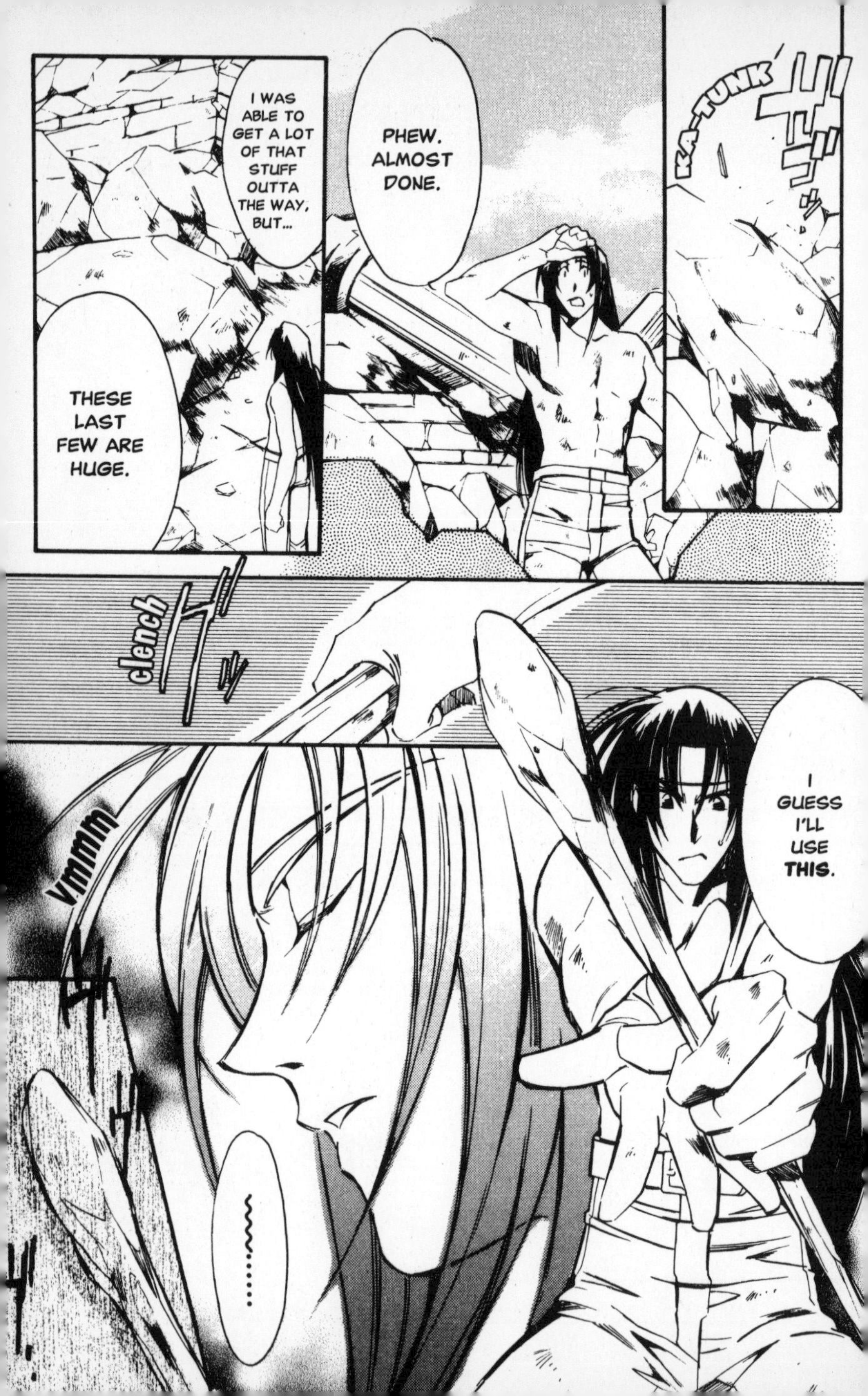
KA-TUNK
PHEW. ALMOST DONE.
I WAS ABLE TO GET A LOT OF THAT STUFF OUTTA THE WAY, BUT...
THESE LAST FEW ARE HUGE.
clench
I GUESS I'LL USE THIS.
Vmmm
......

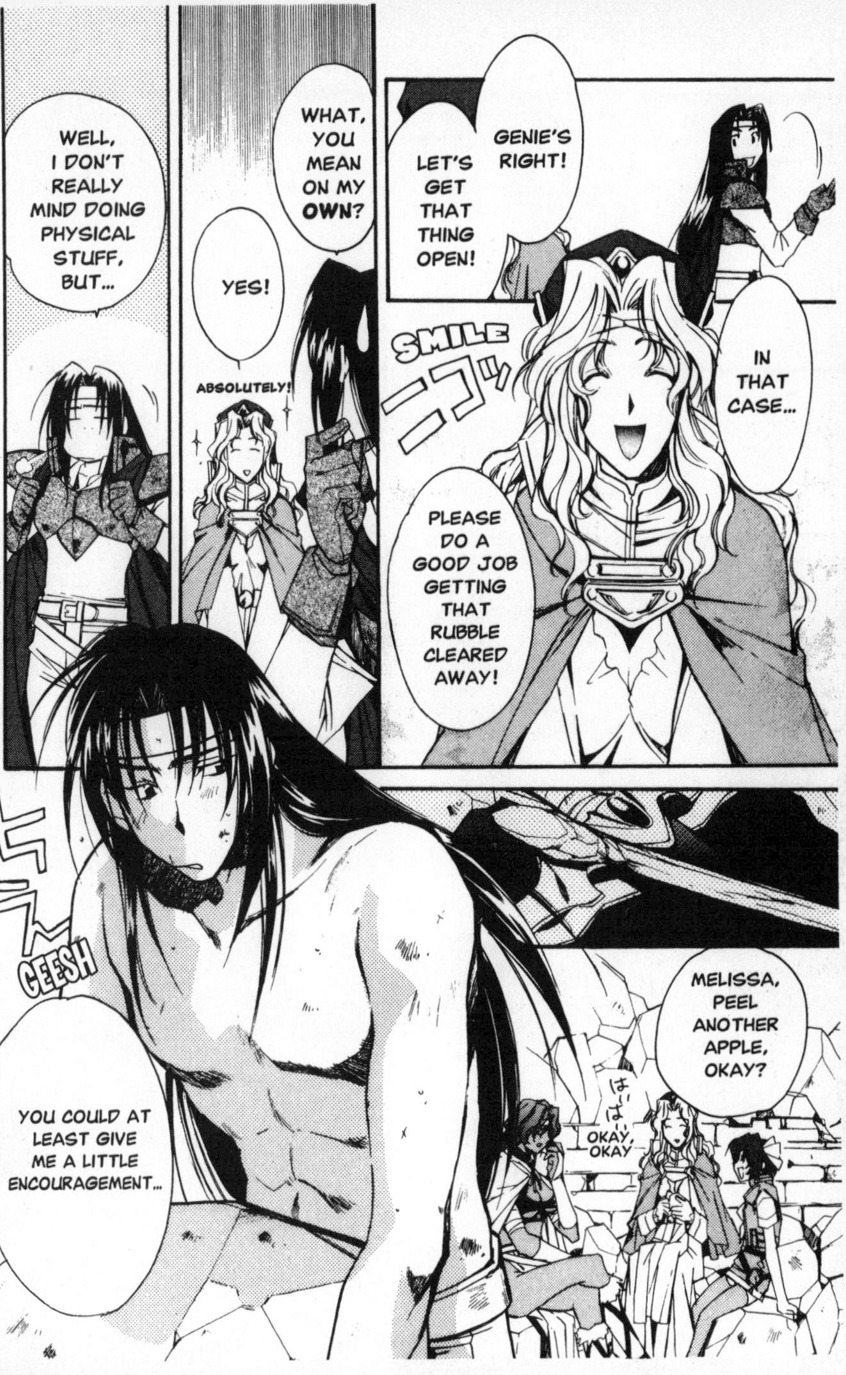
GENIE'S RIGHT!
LET'S GET THAT THING OPEN!
IN THAT CASE...
SMILE
ニコッ
PLEASE DO A GOOD JOB GETTING THAT RUBBLE CLEARED AWAY!
WHAT, YOU MEAN ON MY **OWN**?
YES!
ABSOLUTELY!
WELL, I DON'T REALLY MIND DOING PHYSICAL STUFF, BUT...
MELISSA, PEEL ANOTHER APPLE, OKAY?
はいはい
OKAY, OKAY
GEESH
YOU COULD AT LEAST GIVE ME A LITTLE ENCOURAGEMENT...

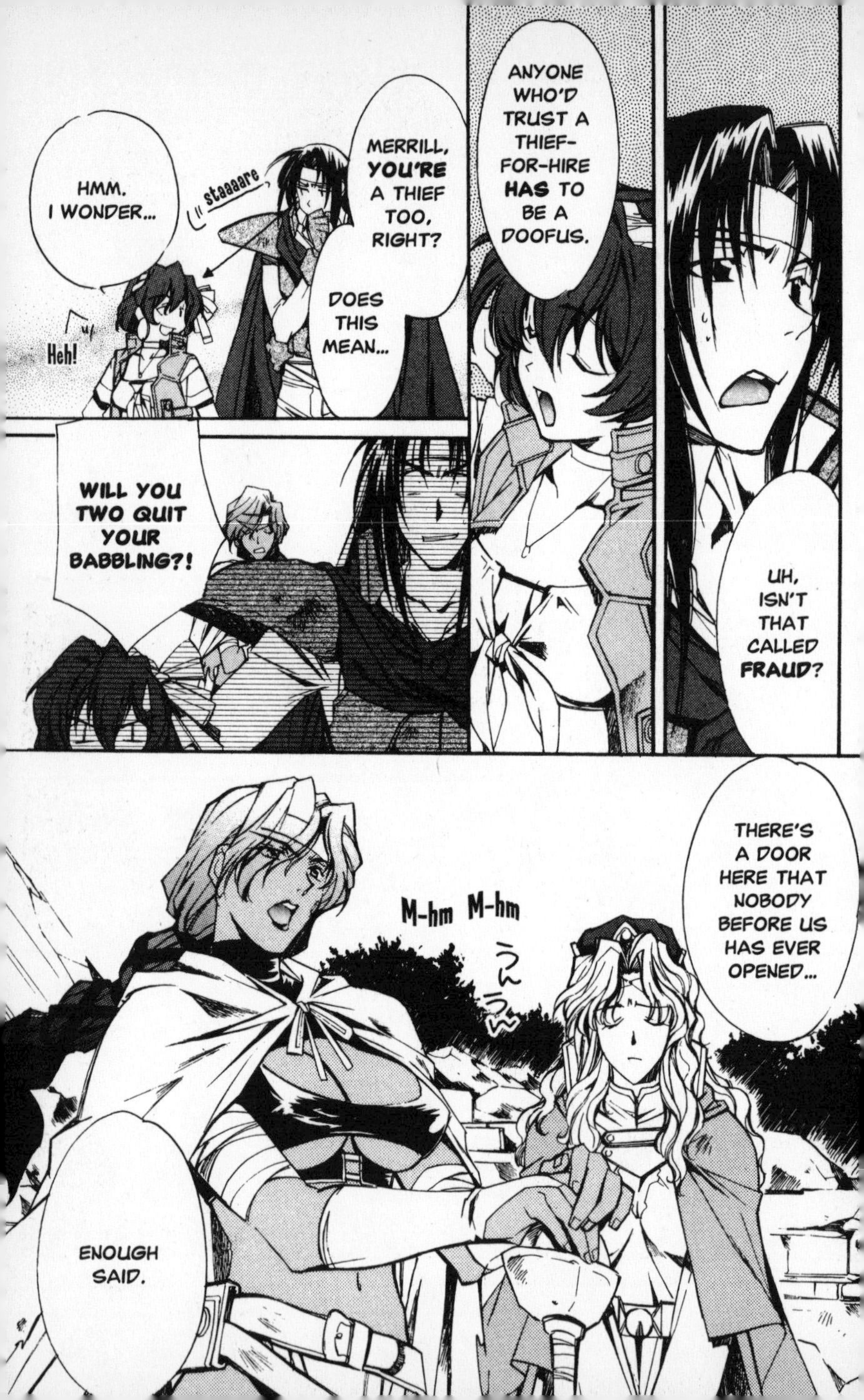
UH, ISN'T THAT CALLED FRAUD?
ANYONE WHO'D TRUST A THIEF-FOR-HIRE HAS TO BE A DOOFUS.
MERRILL, YOU'RE A THIEF TOO, RIGHT?
DOES THIS MEAN...
staaaare
HMM. I WONDER...
Heh!
WILL YOU TWO QUIT YOUR BABBLING?!
THERE'S A DOOR HERE THAT NOBODY BEFORE US HAS EVER OPENED...
M-hm M-hm
うんうん
ENOUGH SAID.

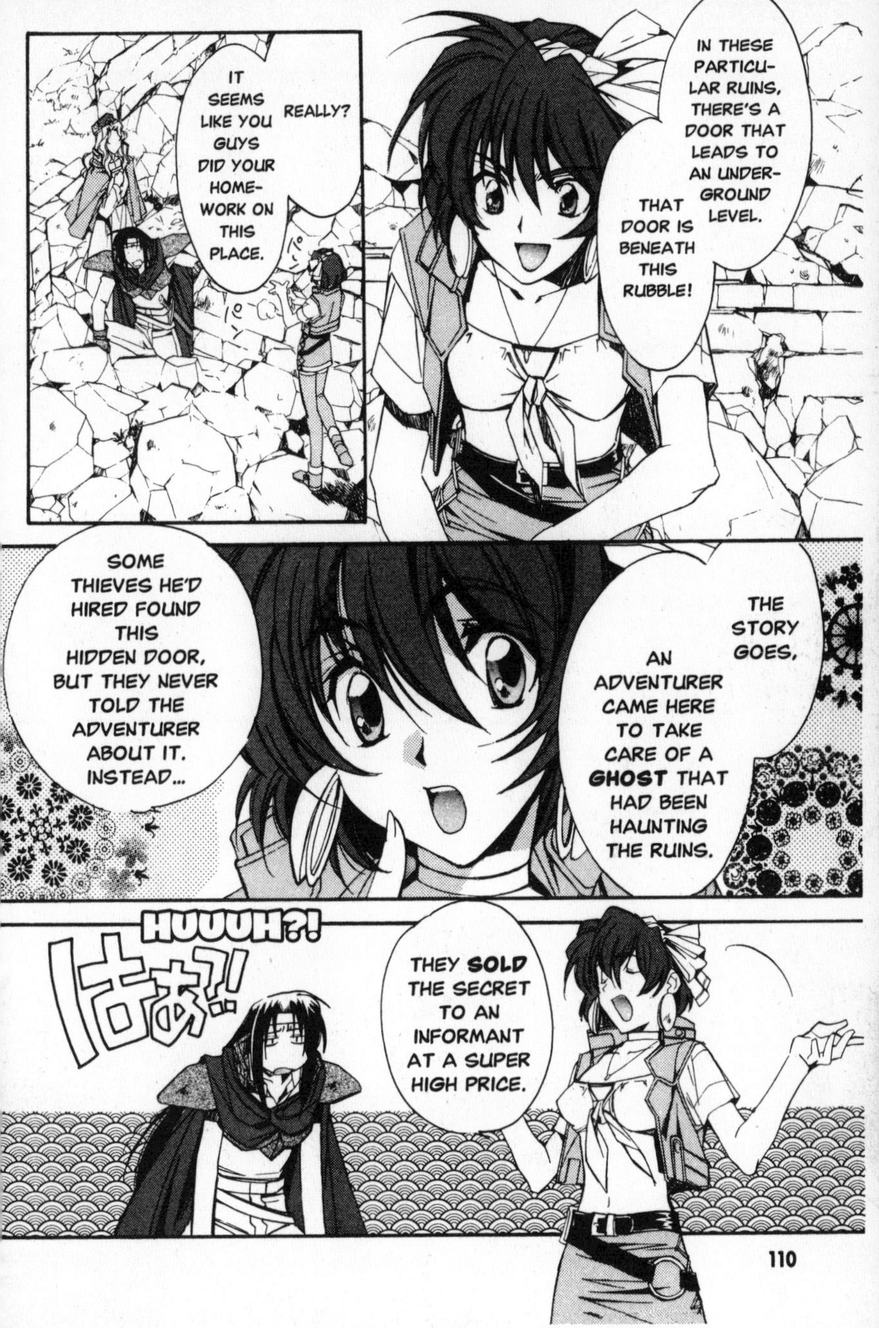
IN THESE PARTICULAR RUINS, THERE'S A DOOR THAT LEADS TO AN UNDERGROUND LEVEL.
THAT DOOR IS BENEATH THIS RUBBLE!
REALLY?
IT SEEMS LIKE YOU GUYS DID YOUR HOMEWORK ON THIS PLACE.
THE STORY GOES,
AN ADVENTURER CAME HERE TO TAKE CARE OF A **GHOST** THAT HAD BEEN HAUNTING THE RUINS.
SOME THIEVES HE'D HIRED FOUND THIS HIDDEN DOOR, BUT THEY NEVER TOLD THE ADVENTURER ABOUT IT. INSTEAD...
THEY **SOLD** THE SECRET TO AN INFORMANT AT A SUPER HIGH PRICE.
HUUUH?!
はぁ?!

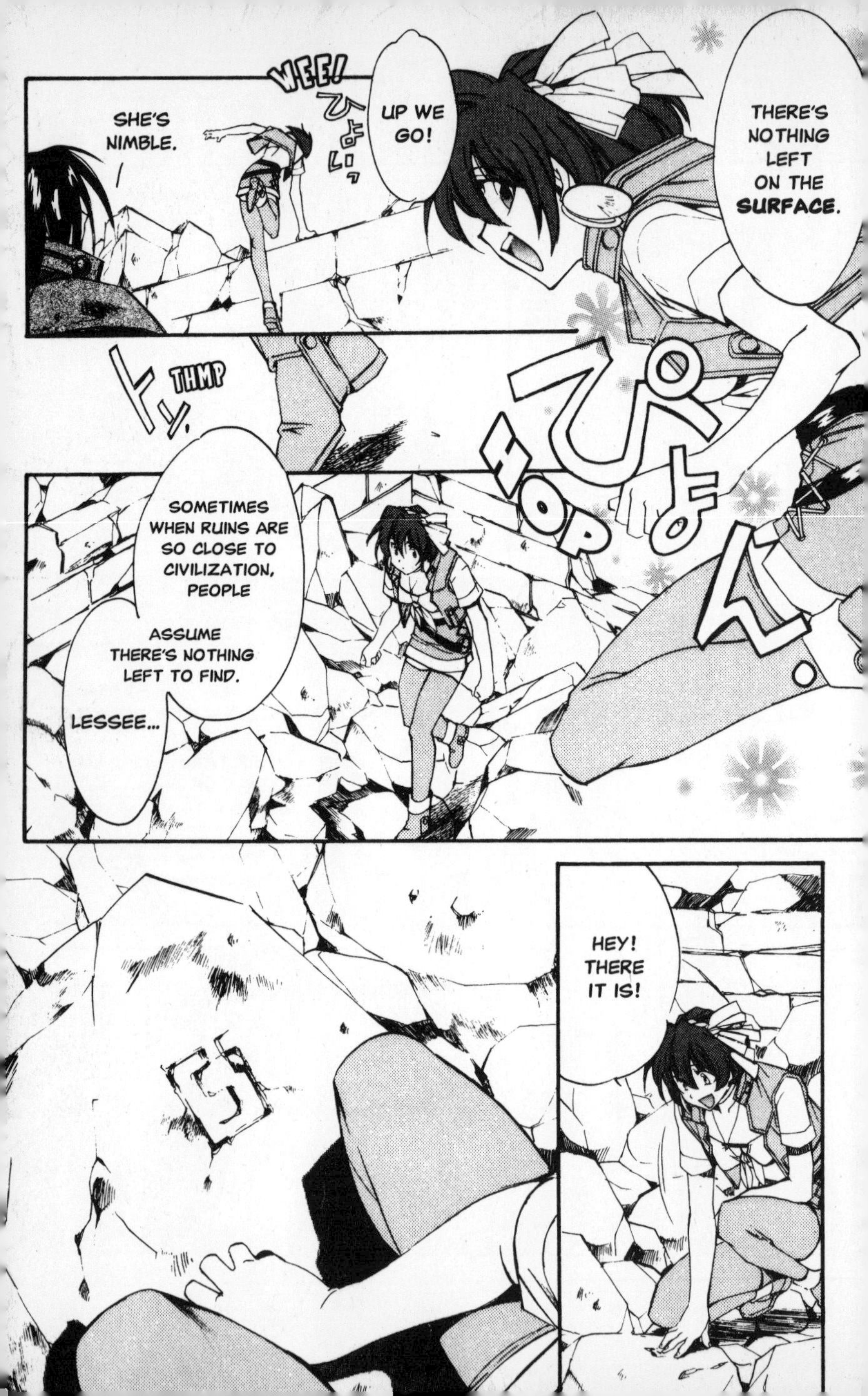
THERE'S NOTHING LEFT ON THE SURFACE.
ぴょん
HOP
UP WE GO!
WEE!
ひょいっ
SHE'S NIMBLE.
トッ
THMP
SOMETIMES WHEN RUINS ARE SO CLOSE TO CIVILIZATION, PEOPLE
ASSUME THERE'S NOTHING LEFT TO FIND.
LESSEE...
HEY! THERE IT IS!

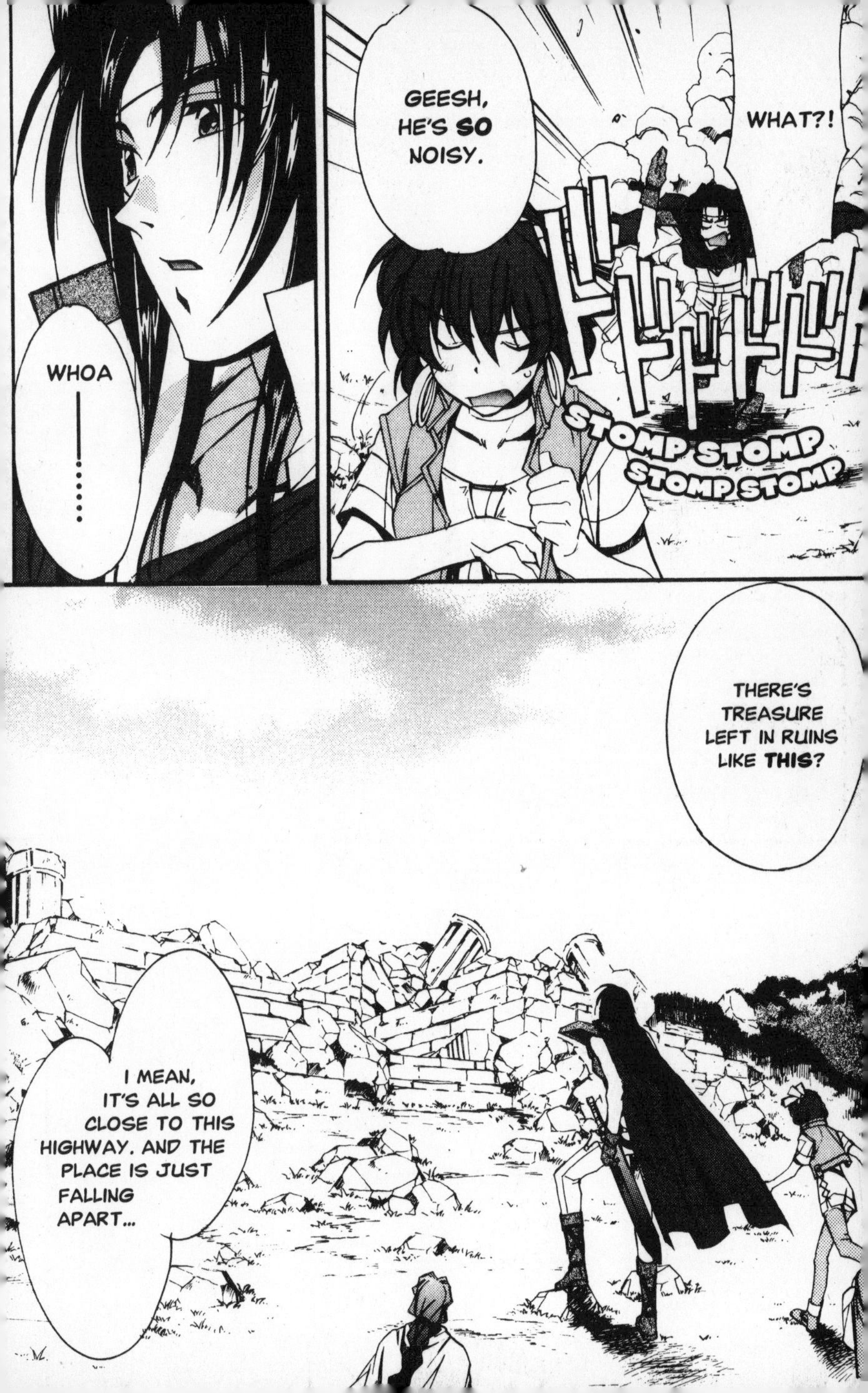
WHAT?!
GEESH, HE'S SO NOISY.
STOMP STOMP STOMP STOMP
WHOA ―――……
THERE'S TREASURE LEFT IN RUINS LIKE THIS?
I MEAN, IT'S ALL SO CLOSE TO THIS HIGHWAY. AND THE PLACE IS JUST FALLING APART...

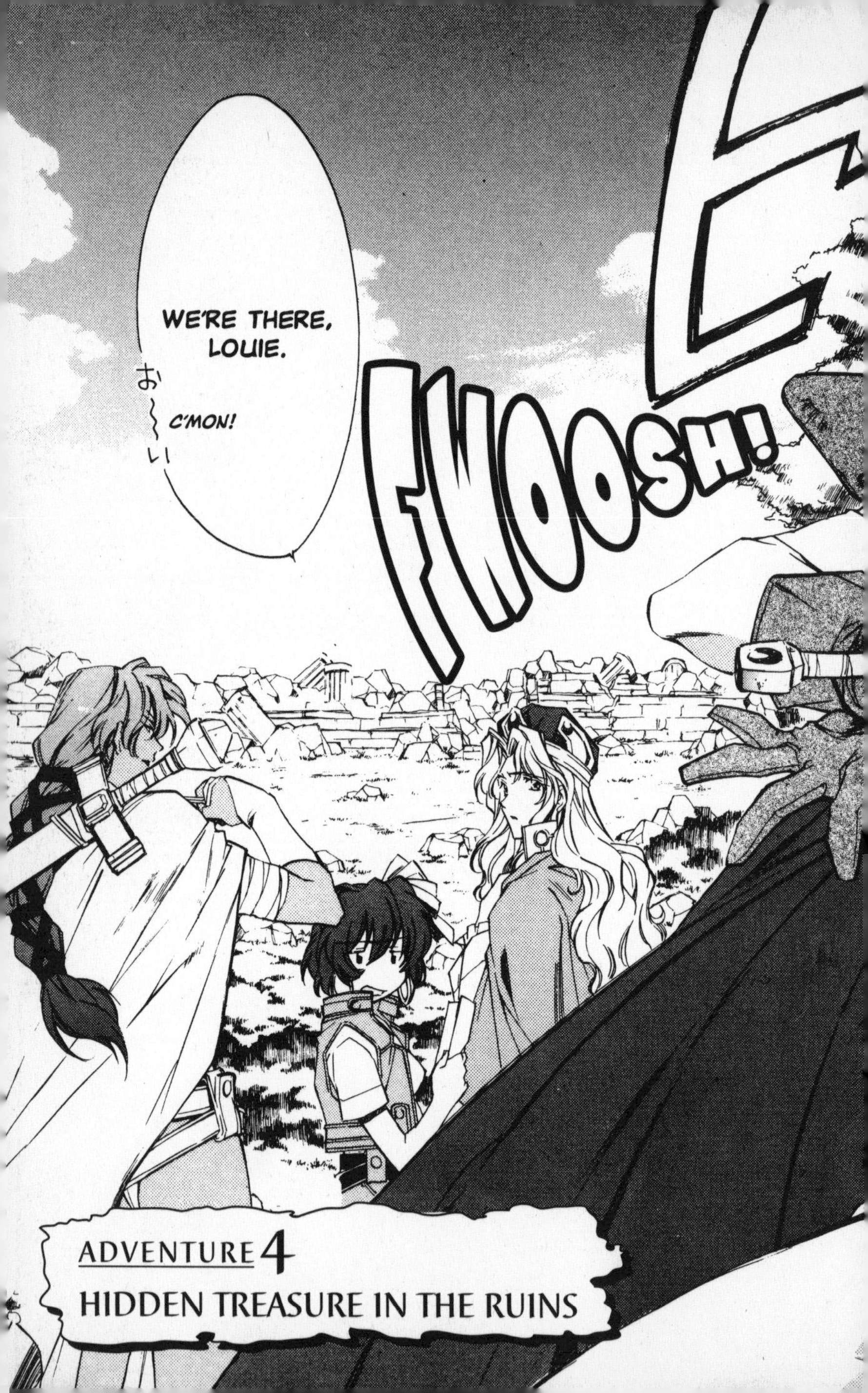
FWOOSH!
WE'RE THERE, LOUIE.
お～い
C'MON!
ADVENTURE 4
HIDDEN TREASURE IN THE RUINS

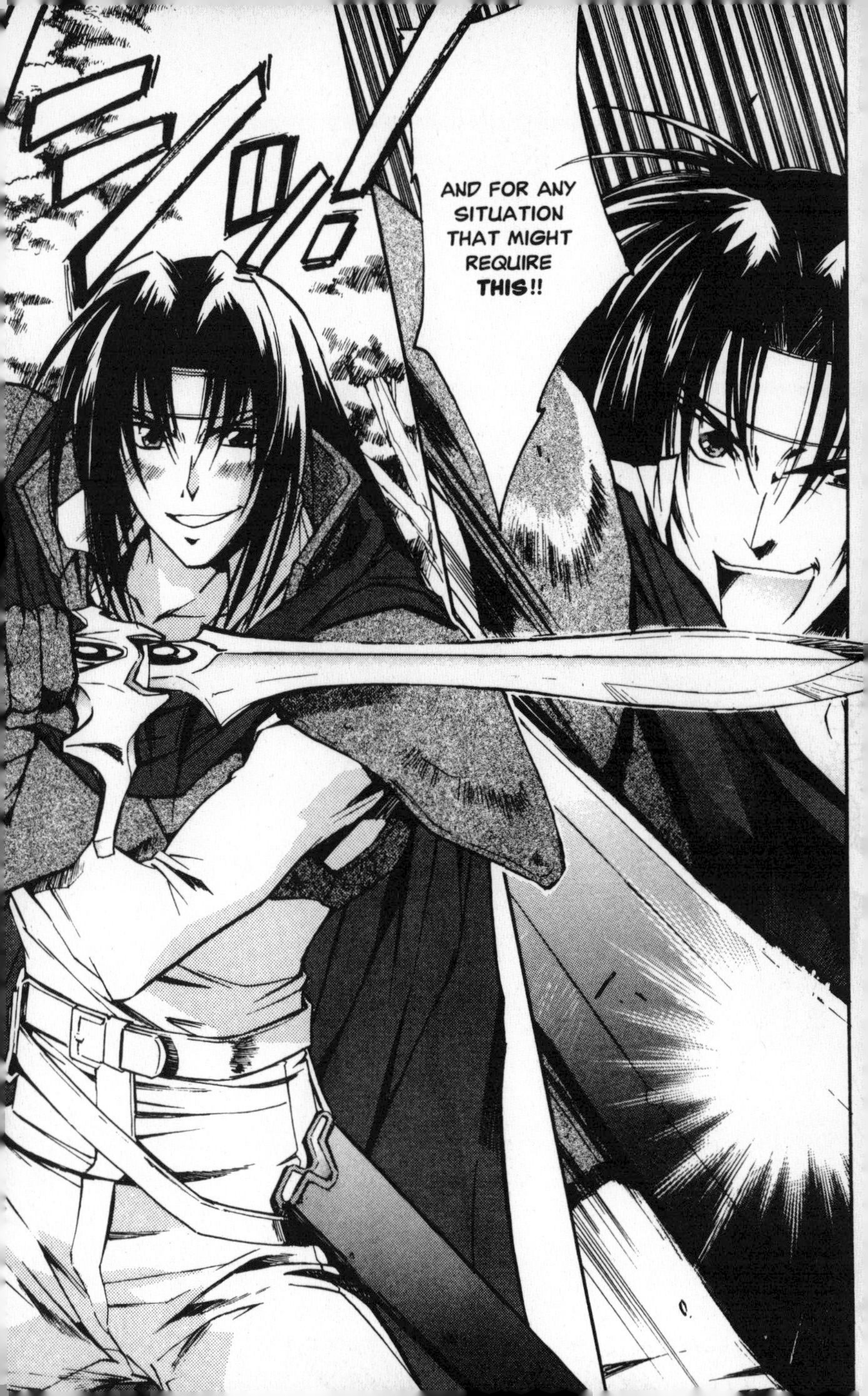
AND FOR ANY SITUATION THAT MIGHT REQUIRE **THIS**!!

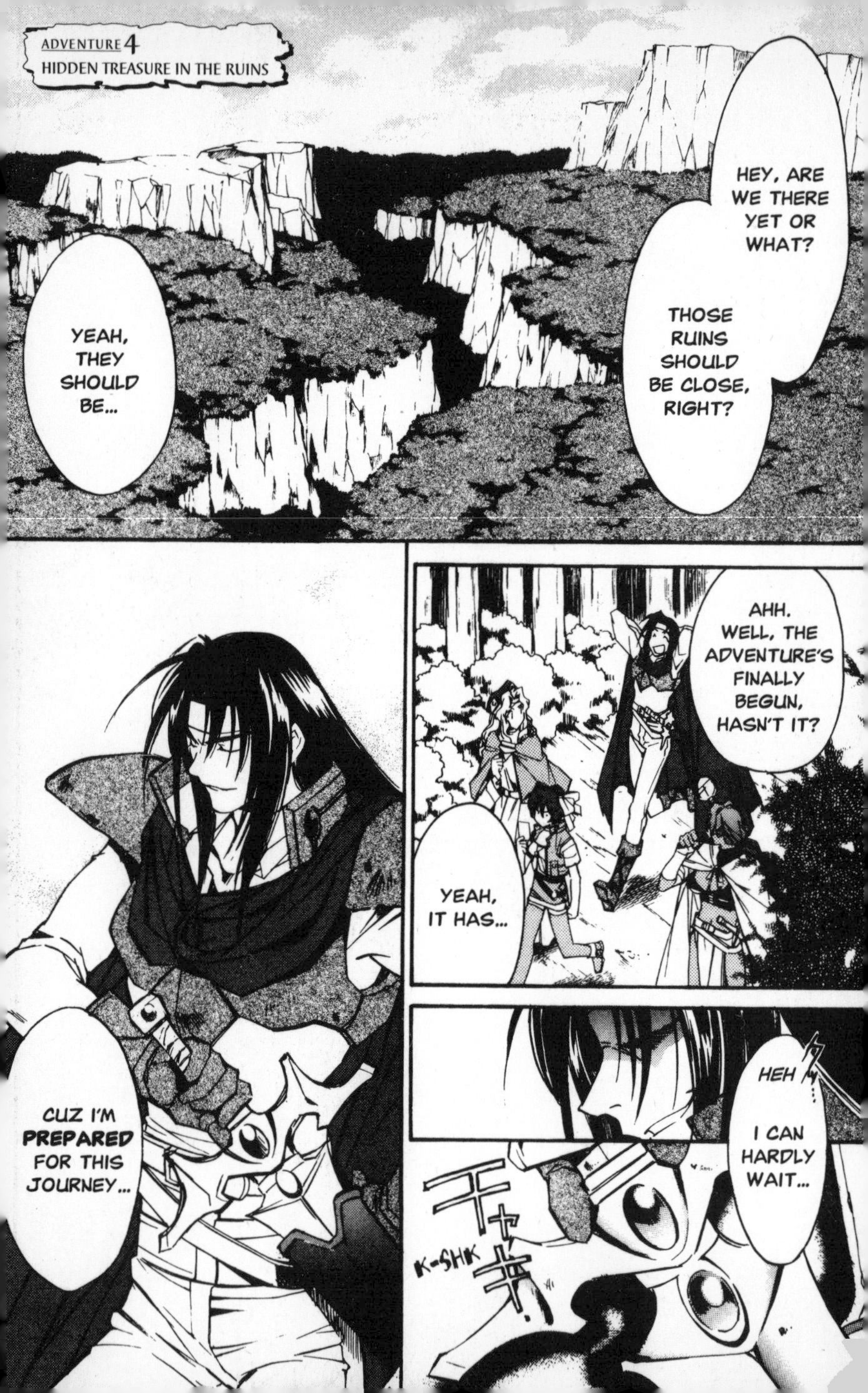
ADVENTURE 4
HIDDEN TREASURE IN THE RUINS
HEY, ARE WE THERE YET OR WHAT?
THOSE RUINS SHOULD BE CLOSE, RIGHT?
YEAH, THEY SHOULD BE...
AHH. WELL, THE ADVENTURE'S FINALLY BEGUN, HASN'T IT?
YEAH, IT HAS...
HEH
I CAN HARDLY WAIT...
K-SHK
CUZ I'M **PREPARED** FOR THIS JOURNEY...

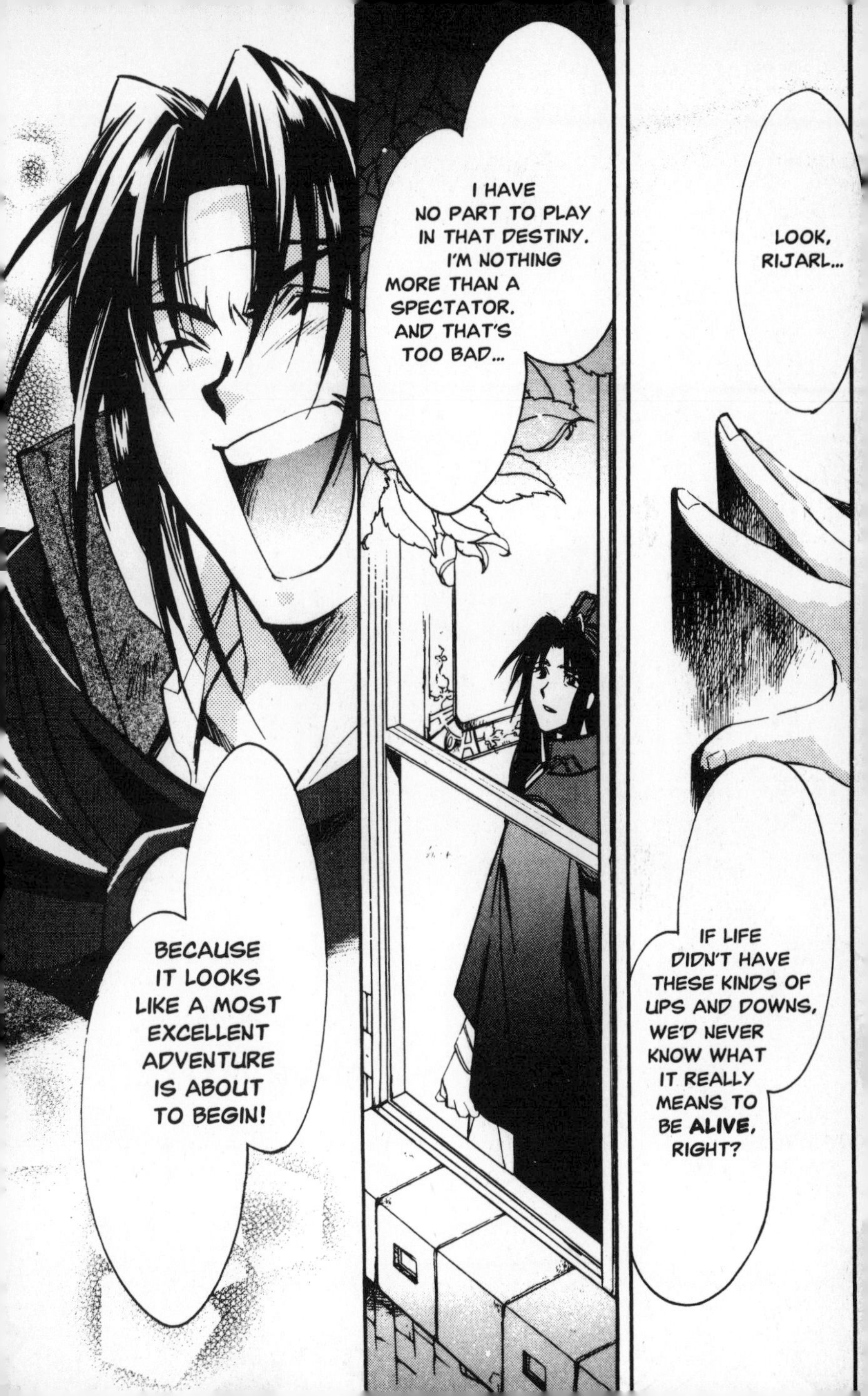
LOOK, RIJARL...
IF LIFE DIDN'T HAVE THESE KINDS OF UPS AND DOWNS, WE'D NEVER KNOW WHAT IT REALLY MEANS TO BE **ALIVE**, RIGHT?
I HAVE NO PART TO PLAY IN THAT DESTINY. I'M NOTHING MORE THAN A SPECTATOR. AND THAT'S TOO BAD...
BECAUSE IT LOOKS LIKE A MOST EXCELLENT ADVENTURE IS ABOUT TO BEGIN!

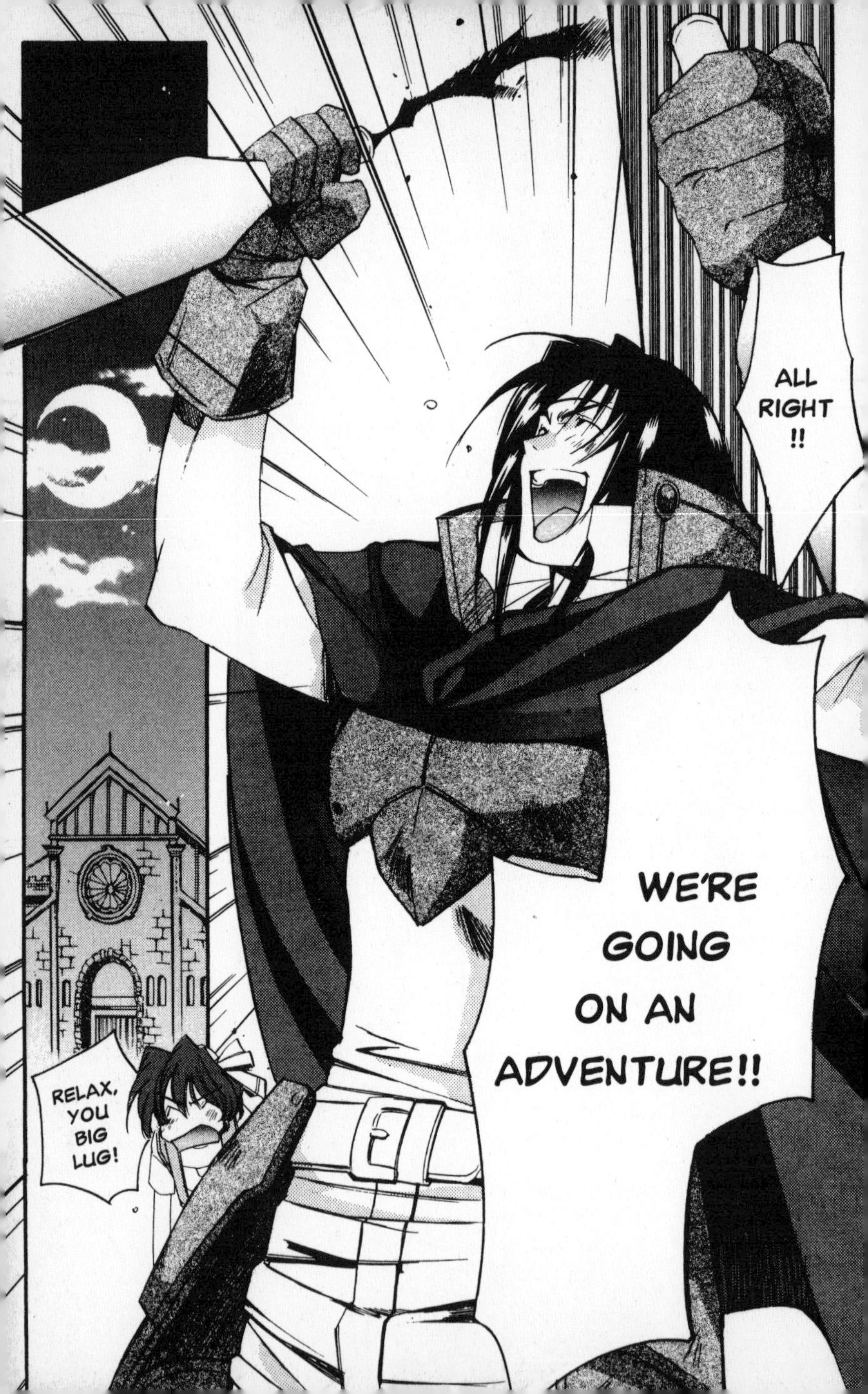
ALL RIGHT !!
WE'RE GOING ON AN ADVENTURE!!
RELAX, YOU BIG LUG!

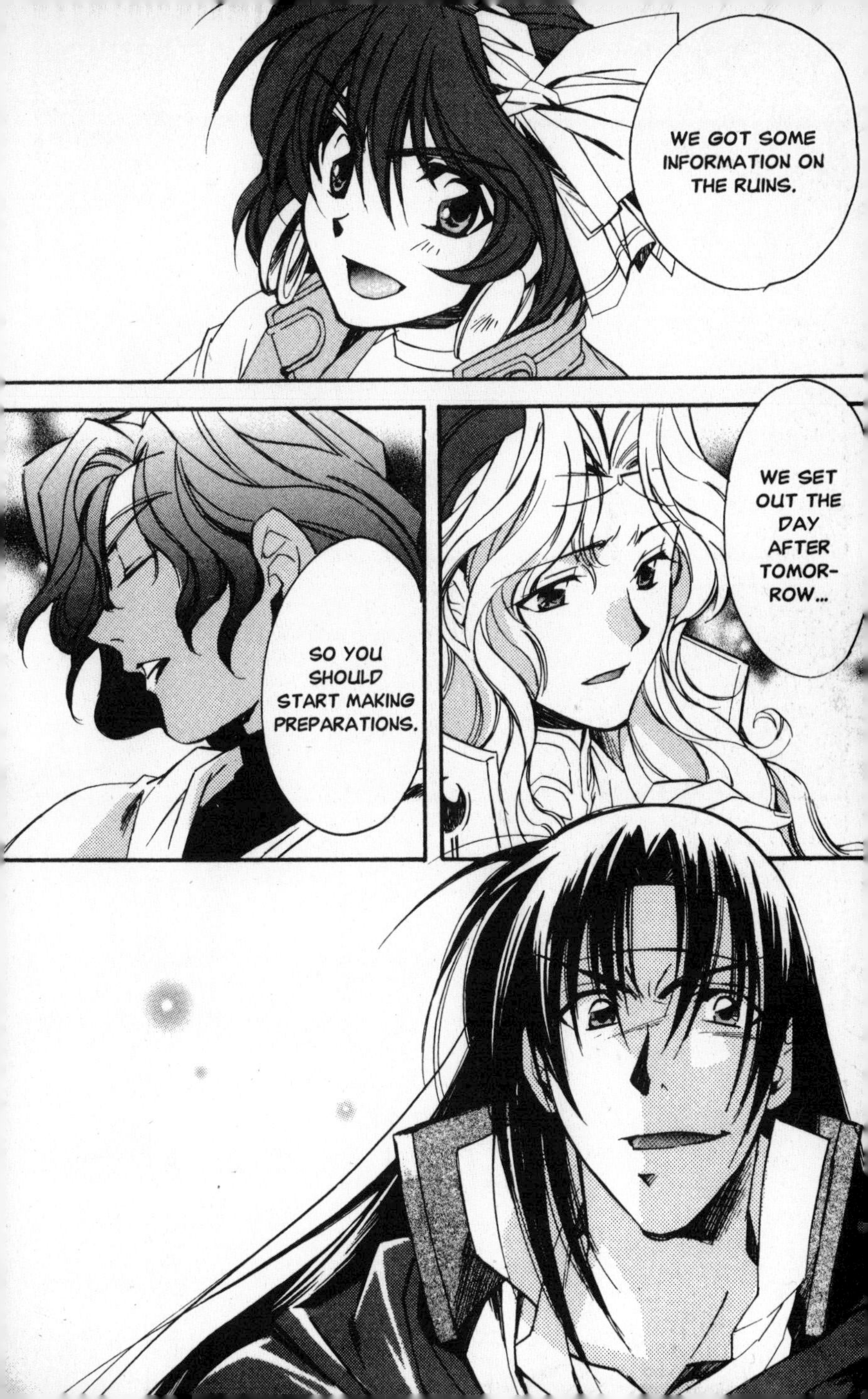
WE GOT SOME INFORMATION ON THE RUINS.
WE SET OUT THE DAY AFTER TOMOR-ROW...
SO YOU SHOULD START MAKING PREPARATIONS.

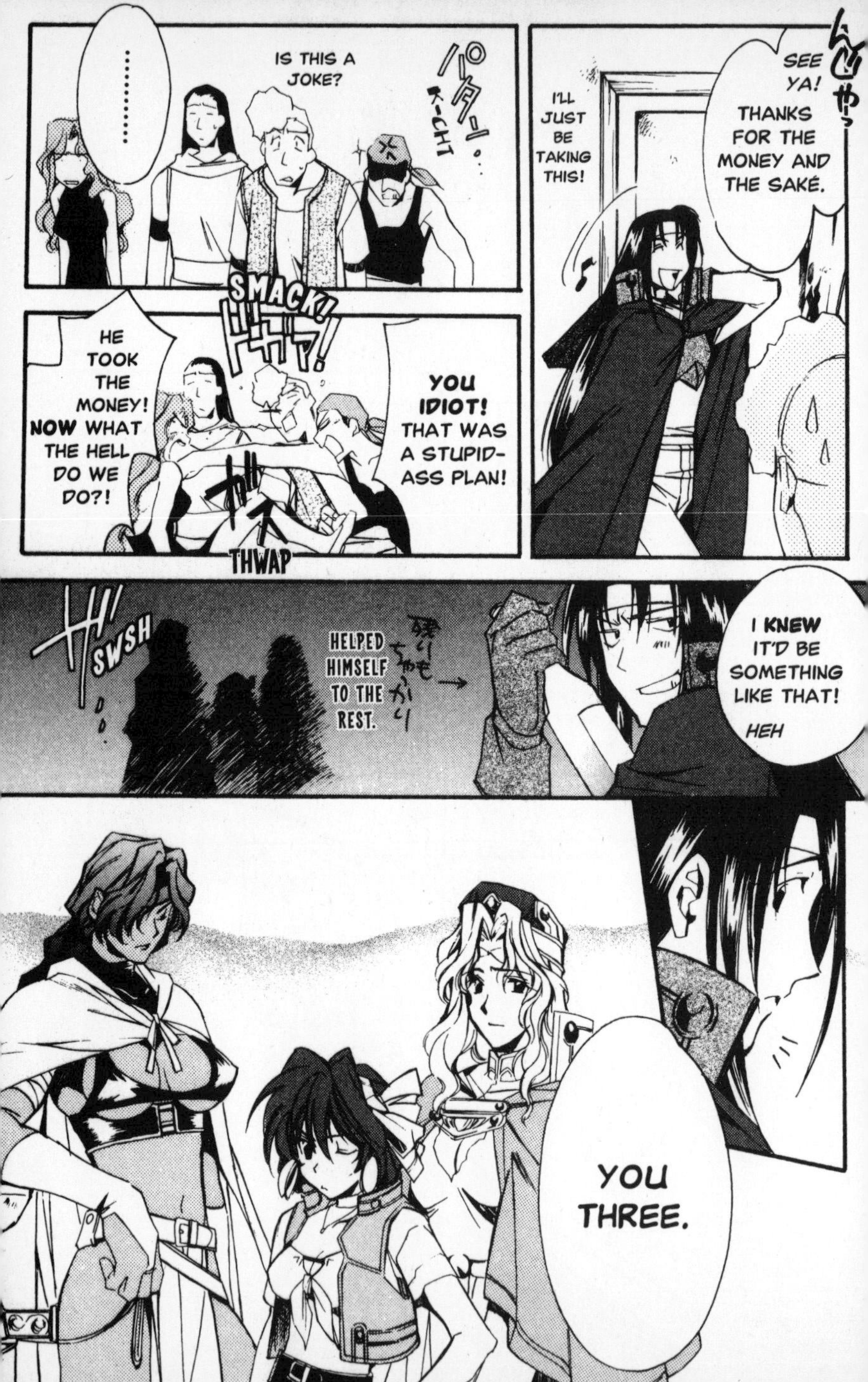
SEE YA!
THANKS FOR THE MONEY AND THE SAKÉ.
I'LL JUST BE TAKING THIS!
IS THIS A JOKE?
K-CHI
......
SMACK!
YOU IDIOT! THAT WAS A STUPID-ASS PLAN!
HE TOOK THE MONEY! NOW WHAT THE HELL DO WE DO?!
THWAP
I KNEW IT'D BE SOMETHING LIKE THAT!
HEH
HELPED HIMSELF TO THE REST.
SWSH
YOU THREE.

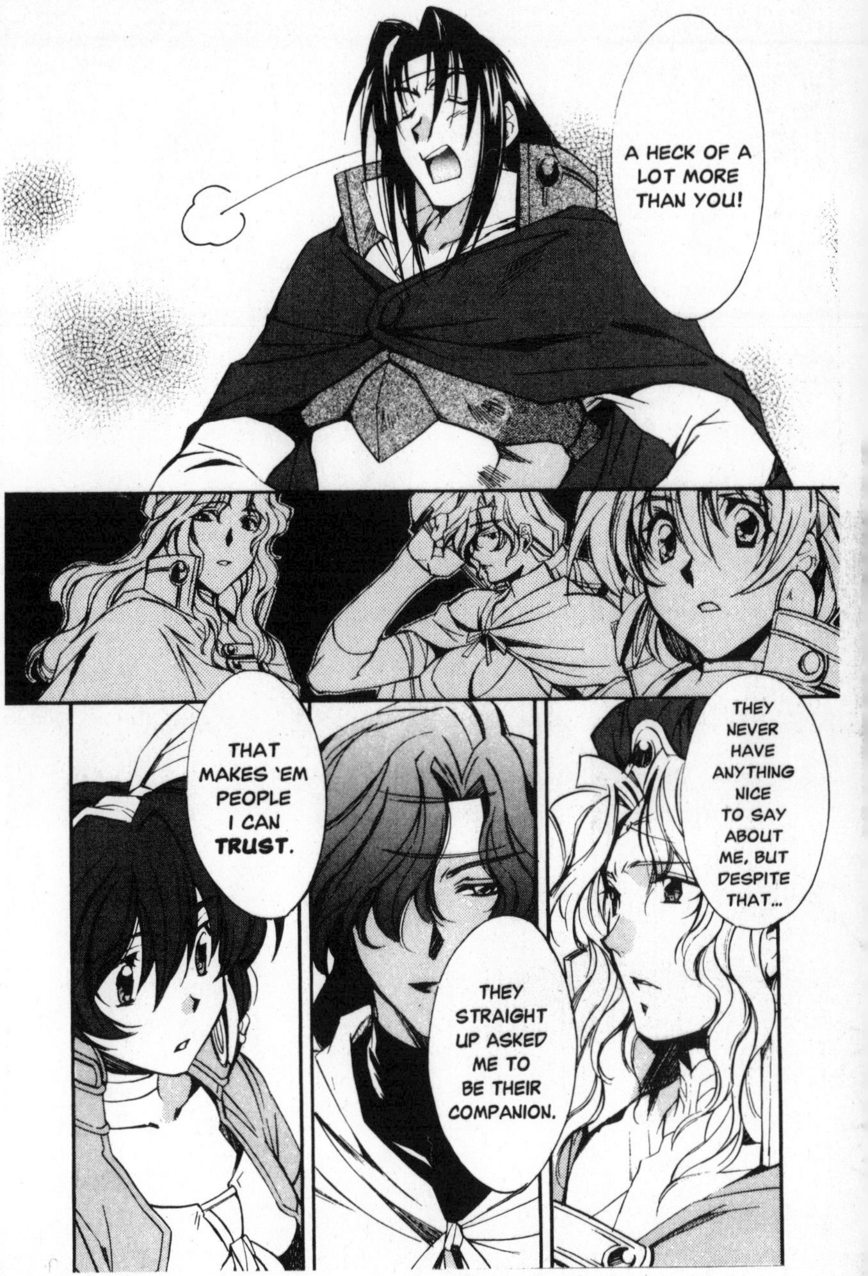
A HECK OF A LOT MORE THAN YOU!
THEY NEVER HAVE ANYTHING NICE TO SAY ABOUT ME, BUT DESPITE THAT...
THEY STRAIGHT UP ASKED ME TO BE THEIR COMPANION.
THAT MAKES 'EM PEOPLE I CAN **TRUST**.

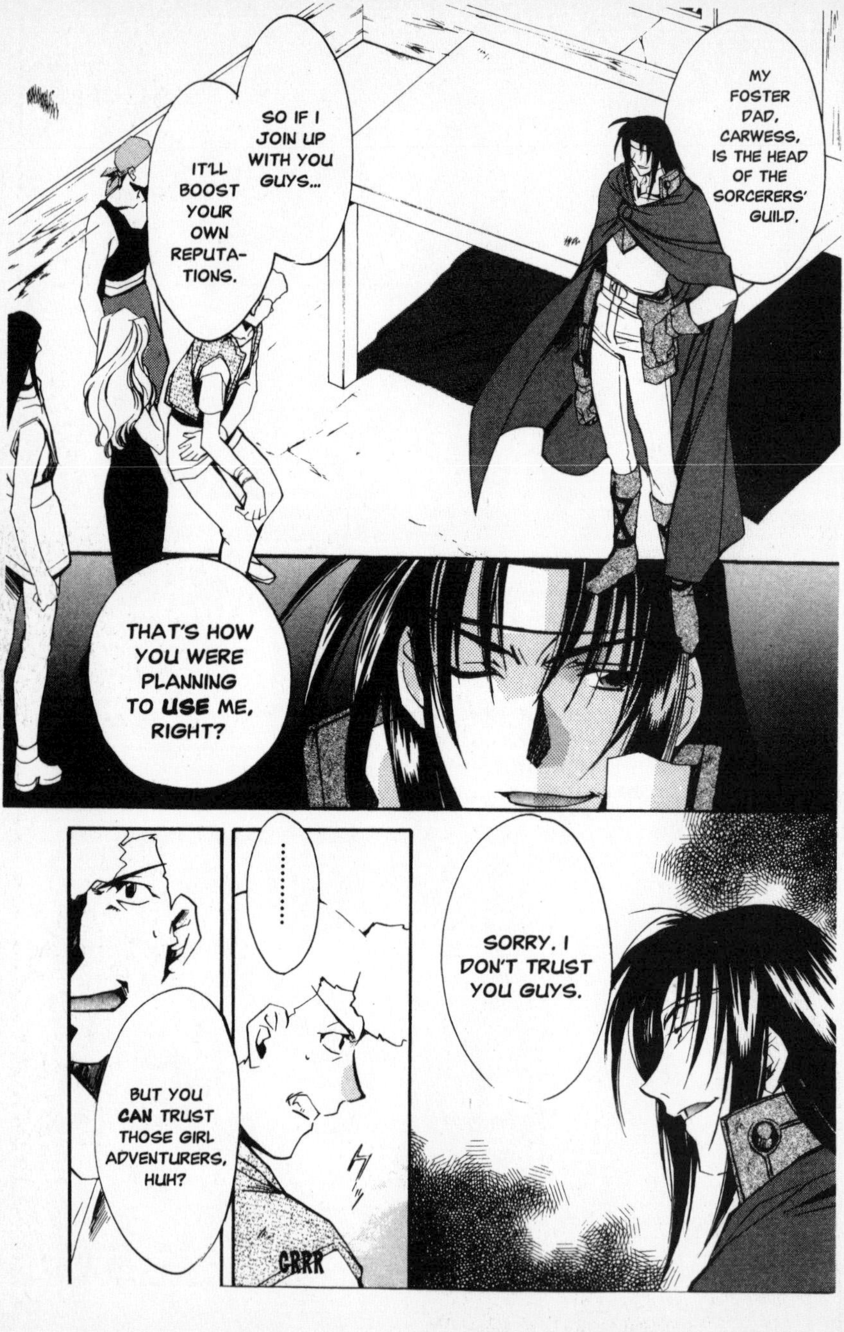
MY FOSTER DAD, CARWESS, IS THE HEAD OF THE SORCERERS' GUILD.
SO IF I JOIN UP WITH YOU GUYS...
IT'LL BOOST YOUR OWN REPUTATIONS.
THAT'S HOW YOU WERE PLANNING TO USE ME, RIGHT?
SORRY. I DON'T TRUST YOU GUYS.
......
BUT YOU CAN TRUST THOSE GIRL ADVENTURERS, HUH?
GRRR

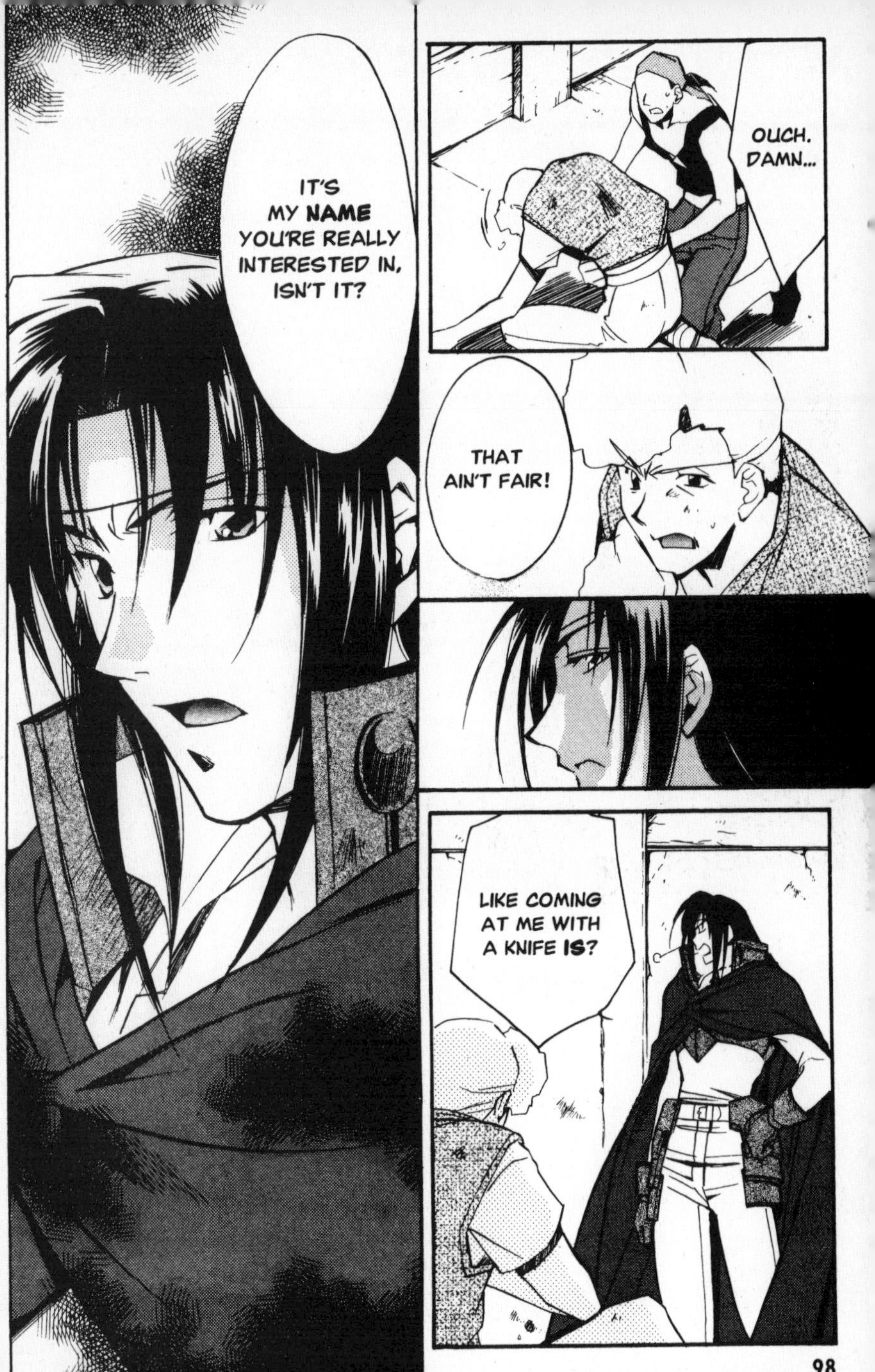
OUCH. DAMN...
THAT AIN'T FAIR!
LIKE COMING AT ME WITH A KNIFE **IS**?
IT'S MY **NAME** YOU'RE REALLY INTERESTED IN, ISN'T IT?

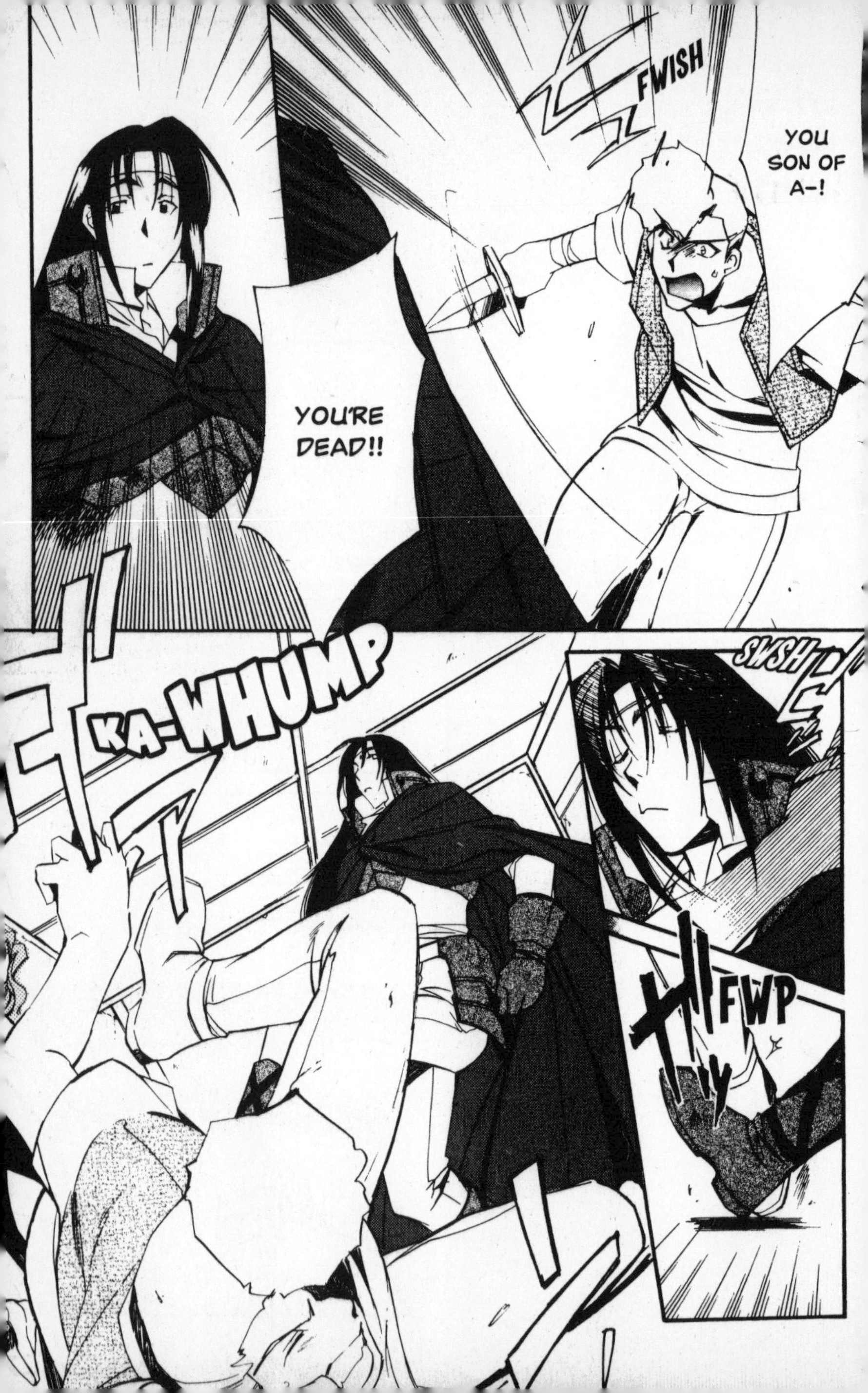
FWISH
YOU SON OF A-!
YOU'RE DEAD!!
SWSH
FWP
KA-WHUMP

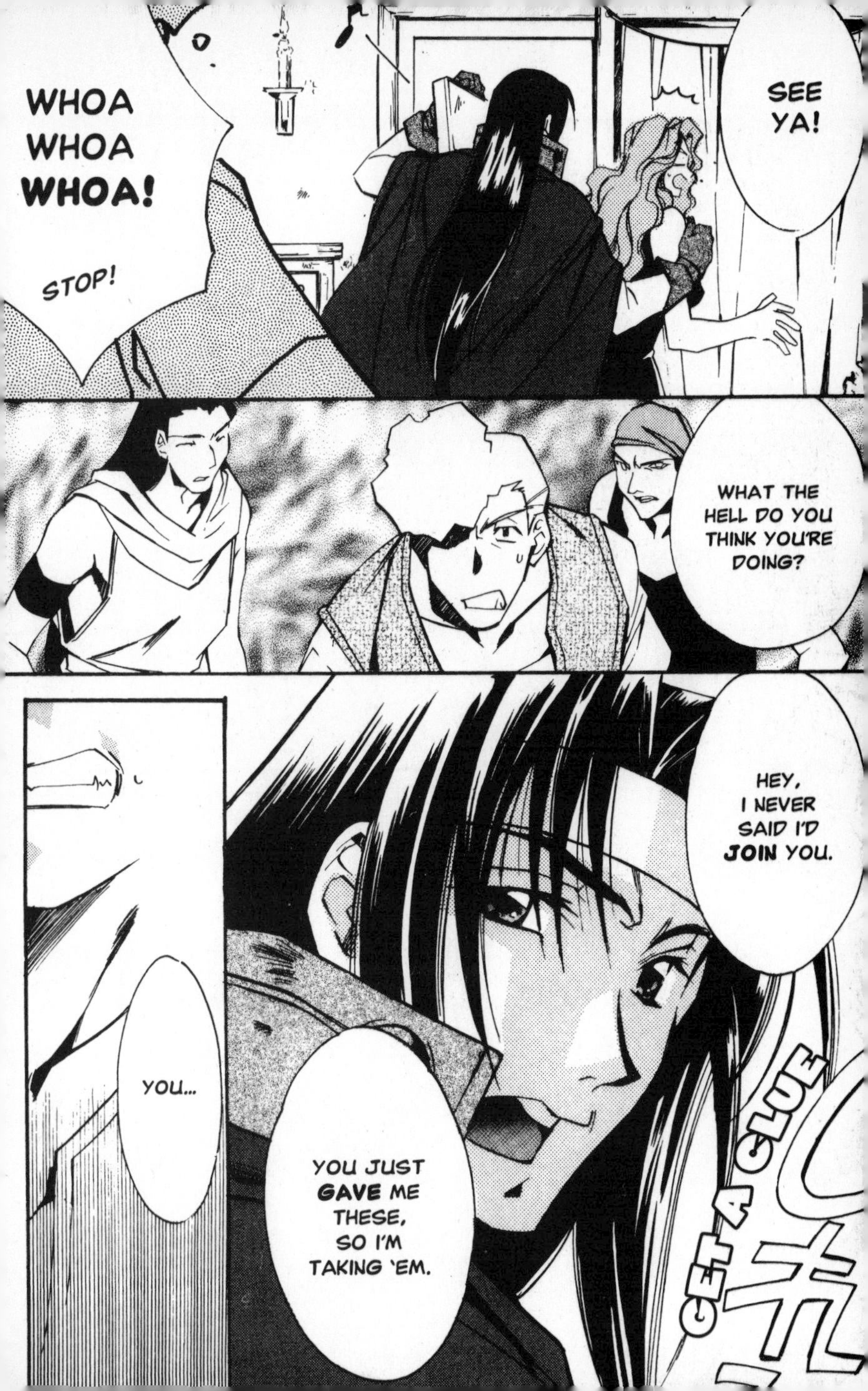
SEE YA!
WHOA WHOA WHOA!
STOP!
WHAT THE HELL DO YOU THINK YOU'RE DOING?
HEY, I NEVER SAID I'D JOIN YOU.
YOU JUST GAVE ME THESE, SO I'M TAKING 'EM.
GET A CLUE
YOU...

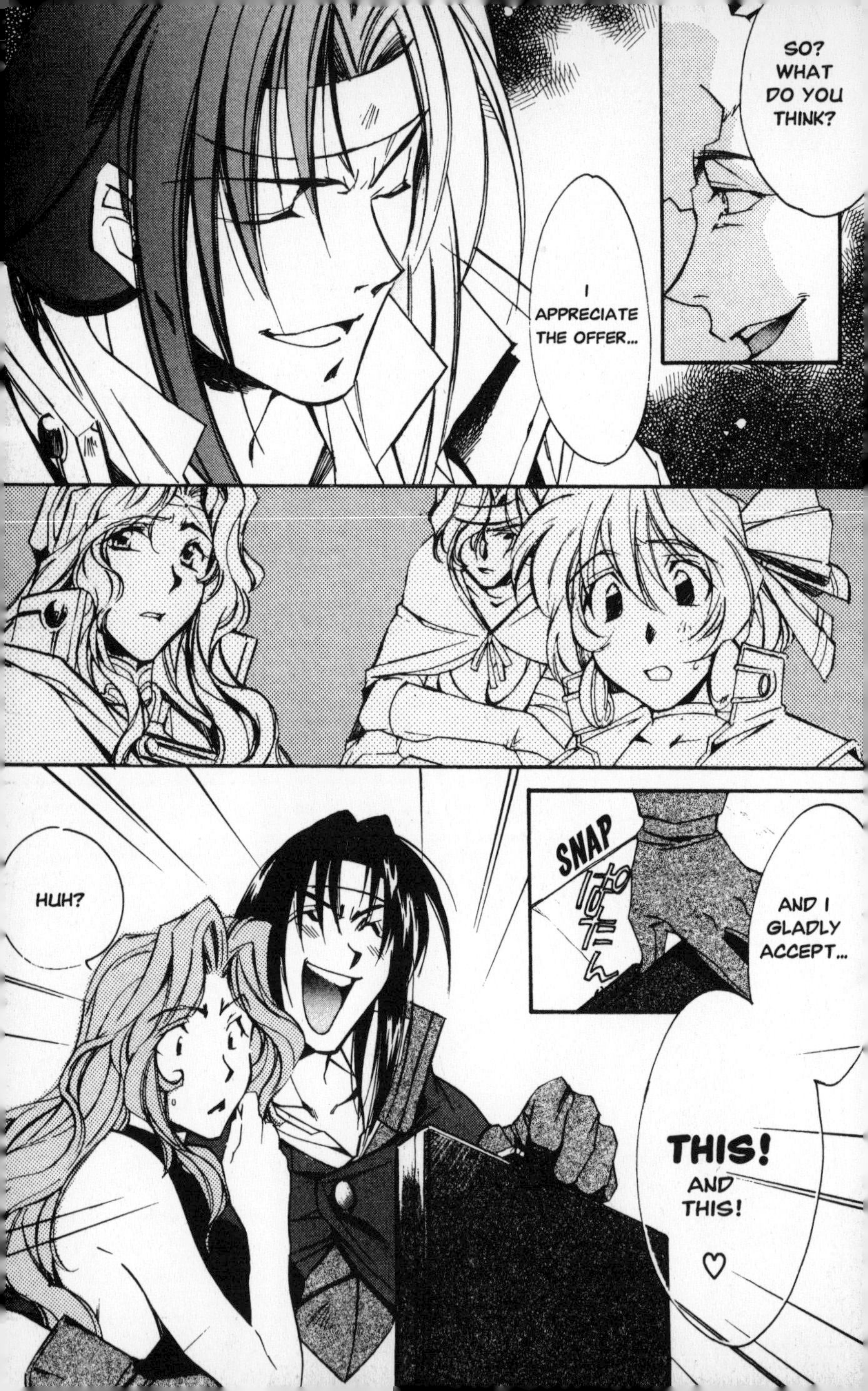
SO? WHAT DO YOU THINK?
I APPRECIATE THE OFFER...
SNAP
ぱたん
AND I GLADLY ACCEPT...
THIS! AND THIS! ♡
HUH?

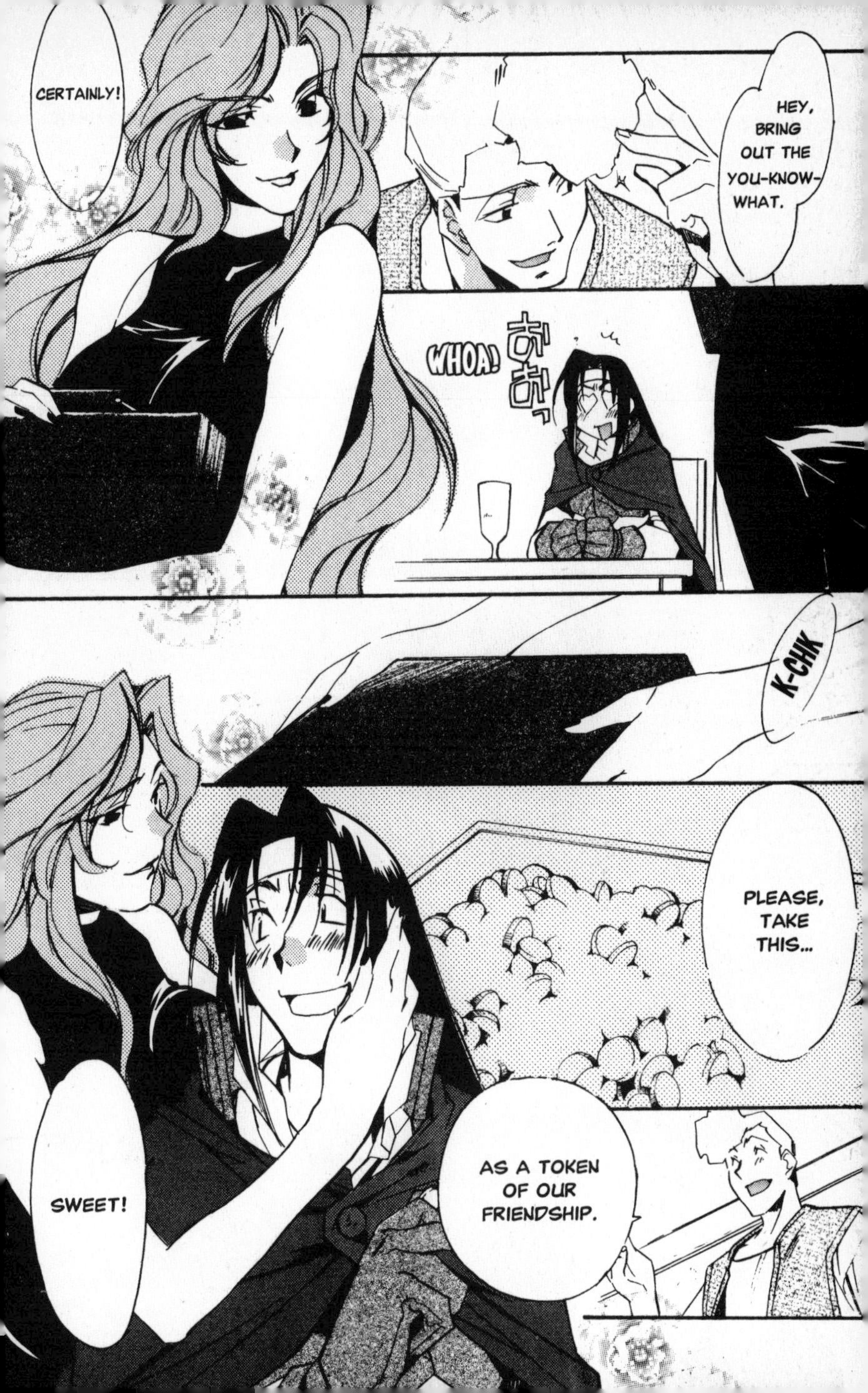
HEY, BRING OUT THE YOU-KNOW-WHAT.
CERTAINLY!
WHOA!
おおっ
K-CHK
PLEASE, TAKE THIS...
AS A TOKEN OF OUR FRIENDSHIP.
SWEET!

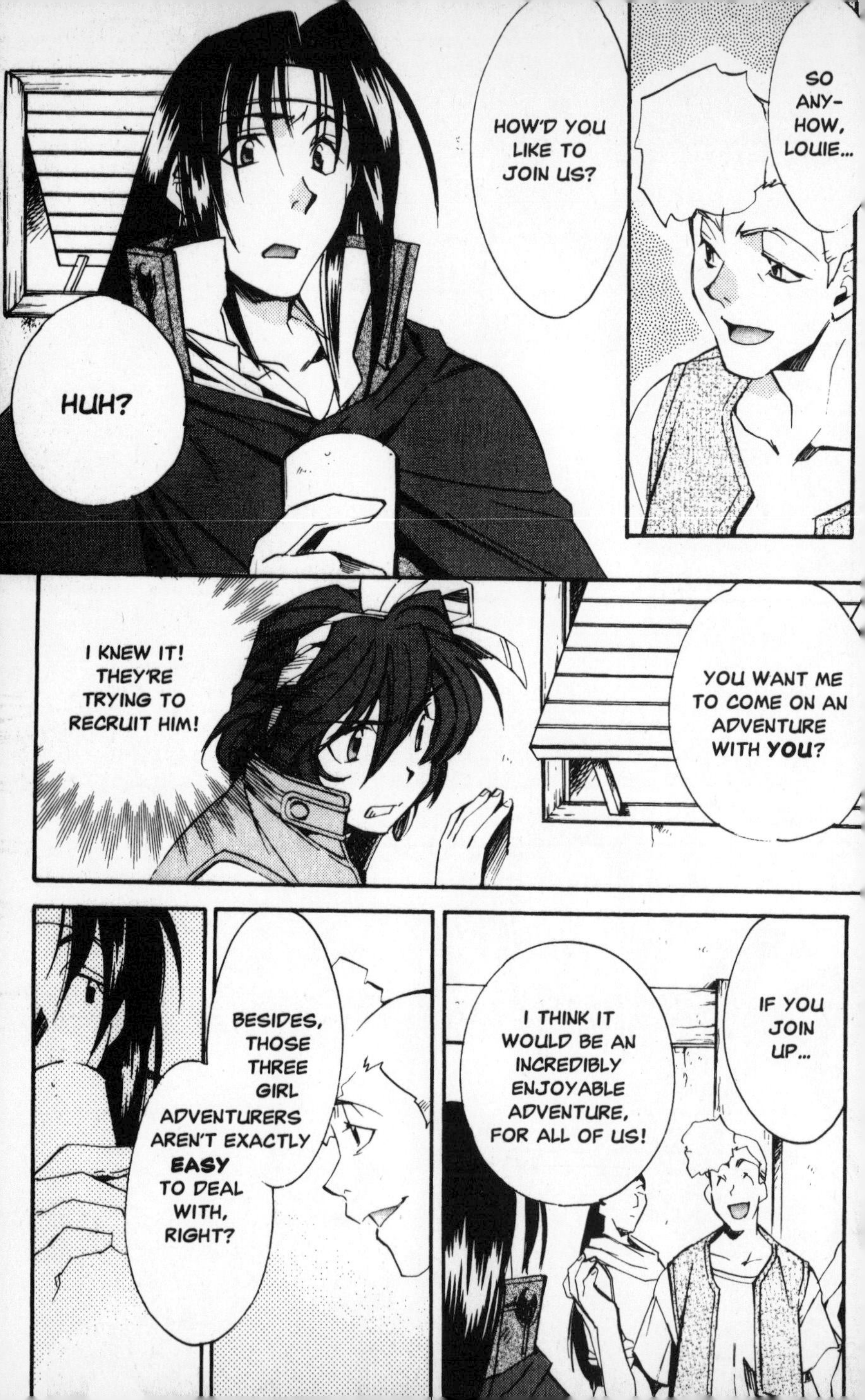
SO ANY-HOW, LOUIE...
HOW'D YOU LIKE TO JOIN US?
HUH?
YOU WANT ME TO COME ON AN ADVENTURE WITH **YOU**?
I KNEW IT! THEY'RE TRYING TO RECRUIT HIM!
IF YOU JOIN UP...
I THINK IT WOULD BE AN INCREDIBLY ENJOYABLE ADVENTURE, FOR ALL OF US!
BESIDES, THOSE THREE GIRL ADVENTURERS AREN'T EXACTLY **EASY** TO DEAL WITH, RIGHT?

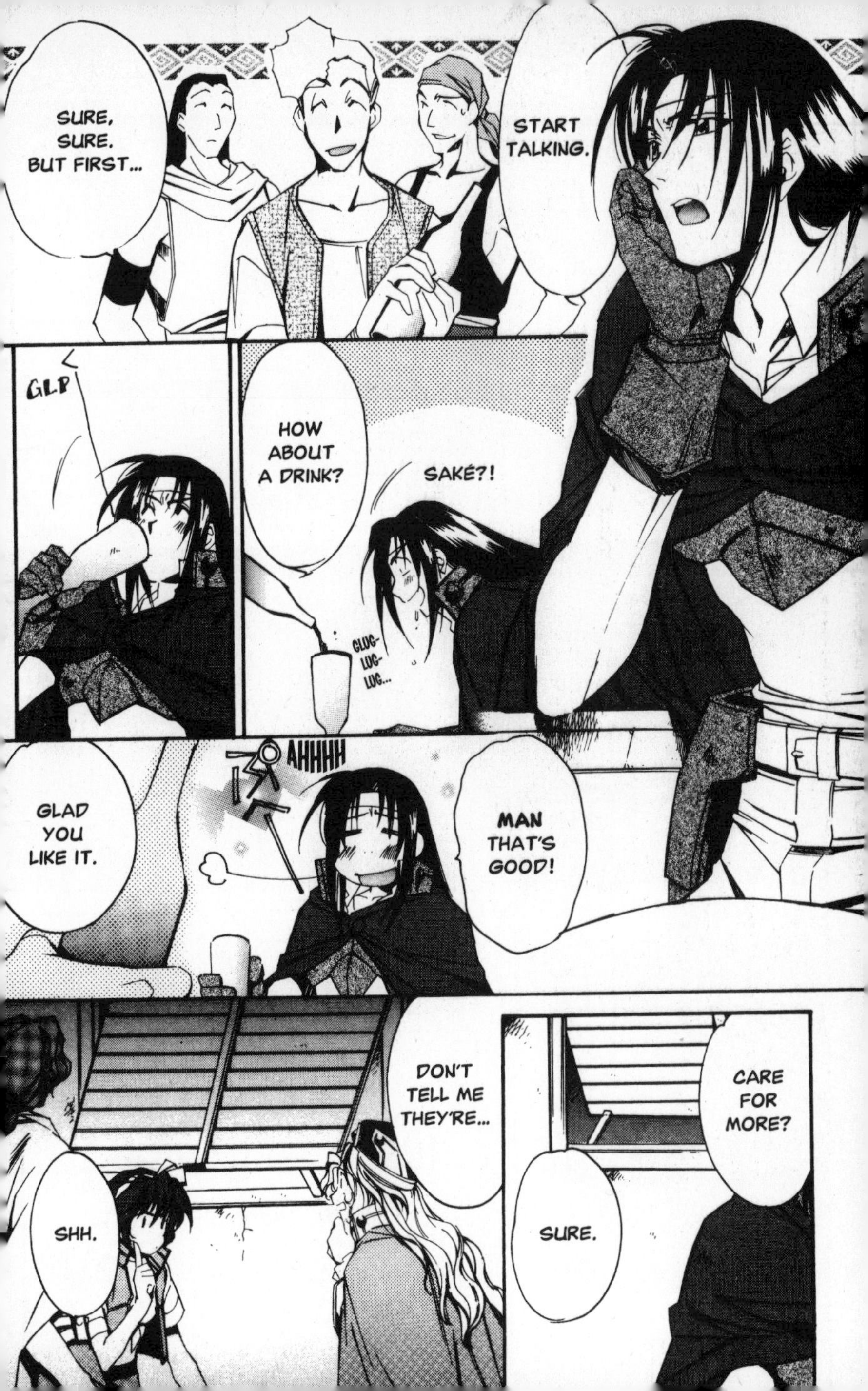
START TALKING.
SURE, SURE. BUT FIRST...
HOW ABOUT A DRINK?
SAKÉ?!
GLUG-LUG-LUG...
GLP
AHHHH
MAN THAT'S GOOD!
GLAD YOU LIKE IT.
CARE FOR MORE?
SURE.
DON'T TELL ME THEY'RE...
SHH.

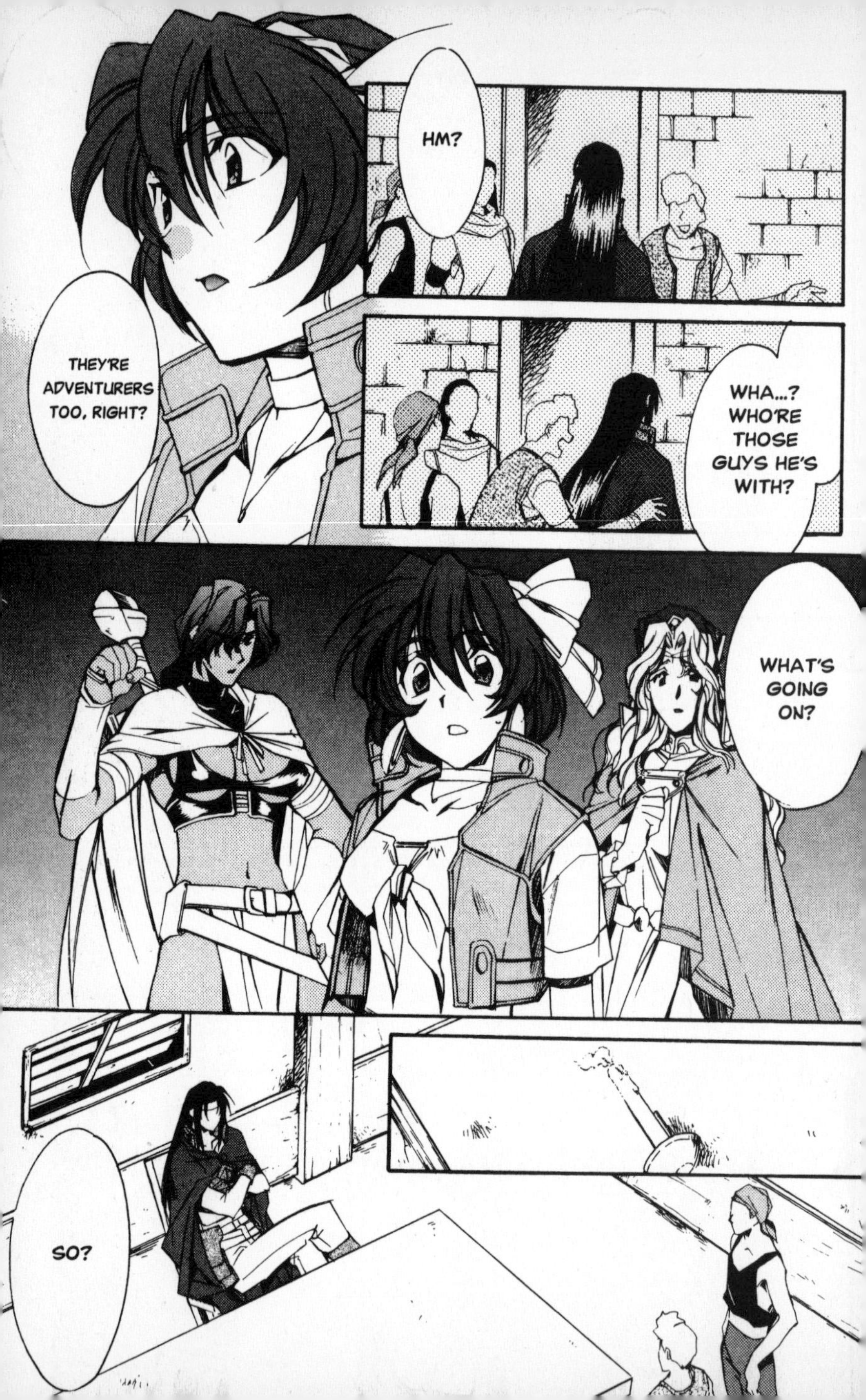
HM?
WHA...? WHO'RE THOSE GUYS HE'S WITH?
THEY'RE ADVENTURERS TOO, RIGHT?
WHAT'S GOING ON?
SO?

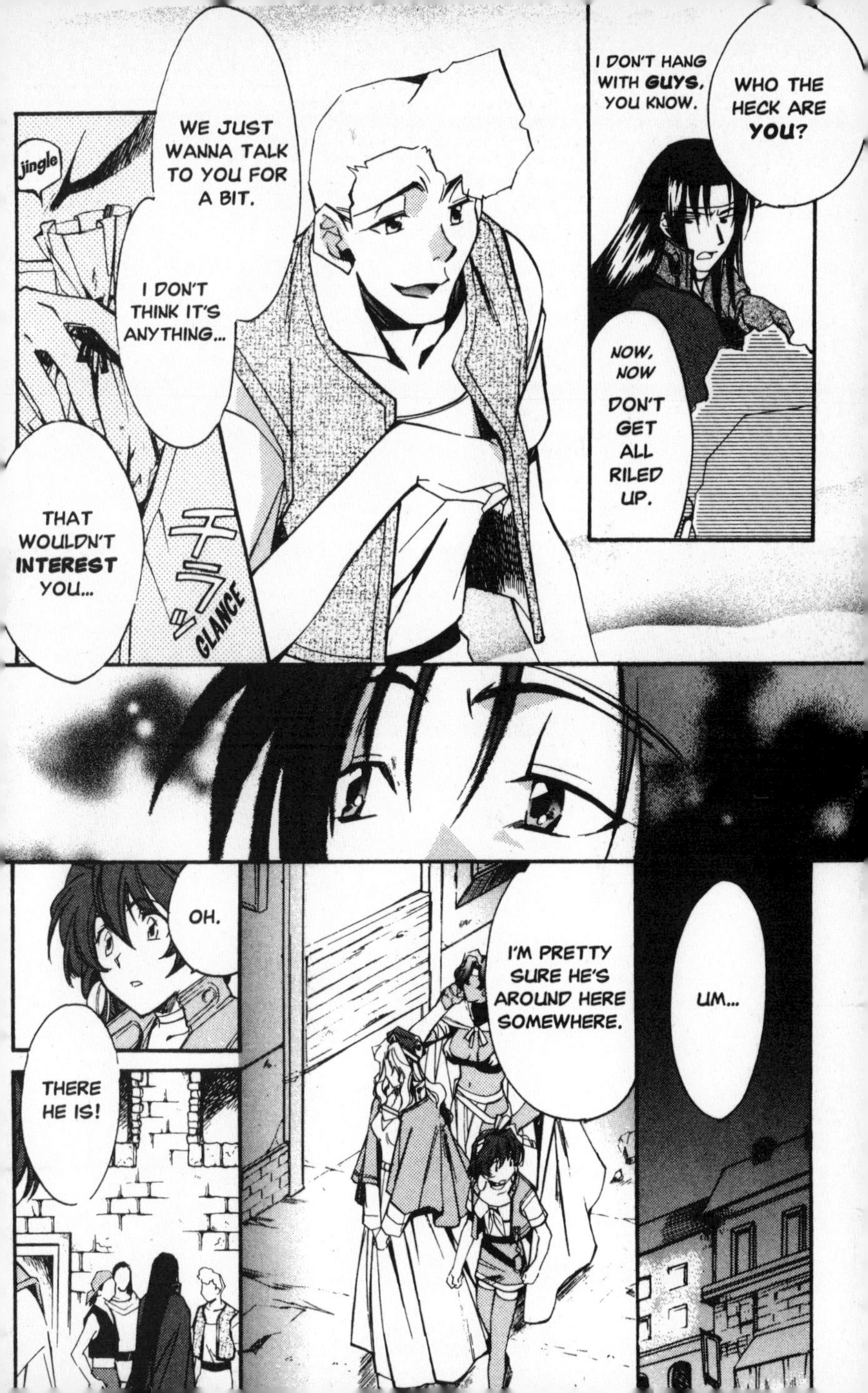
WHO THE HECK ARE YOU?
I DON'T HANG WITH GUYS, YOU KNOW.
NOW, NOW DON'T GET ALL RILED UP.
WE JUST WANNA TALK TO YOU FOR A BIT.
jingle
I DON'T THINK IT'S ANYTHING...
チラッ GLANCE
THAT WOULDN'T INTEREST YOU...
UM...
I'M PRETTY SURE HE'S AROUND HERE SOMEWHERE.
OH.
THERE HE IS!

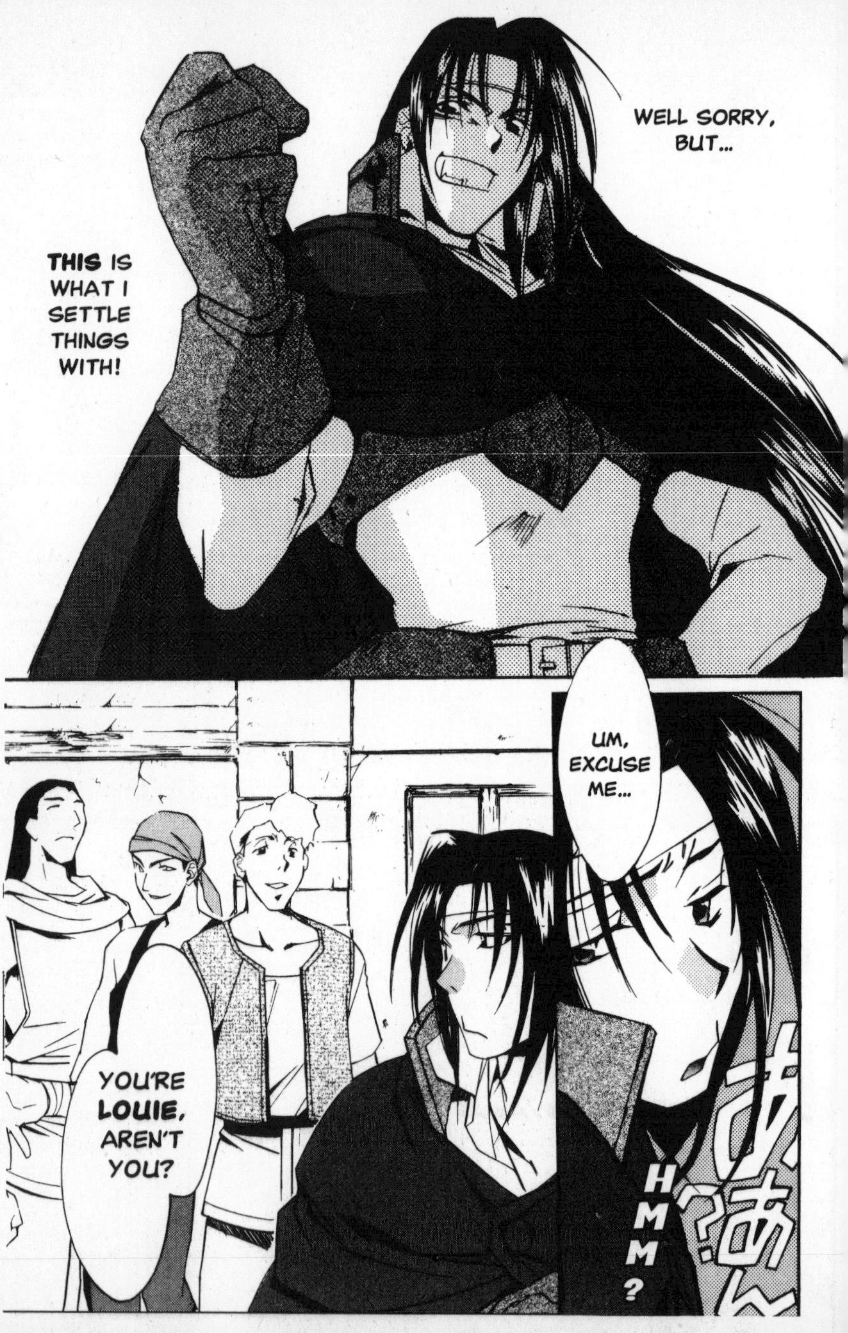
WELL SORRY, BUT...
THIS IS WHAT I SETTLE THINGS WITH!
UM, EXCUSE ME...
HMM?
YOU'RE **LOUIE**, AREN'T YOU?

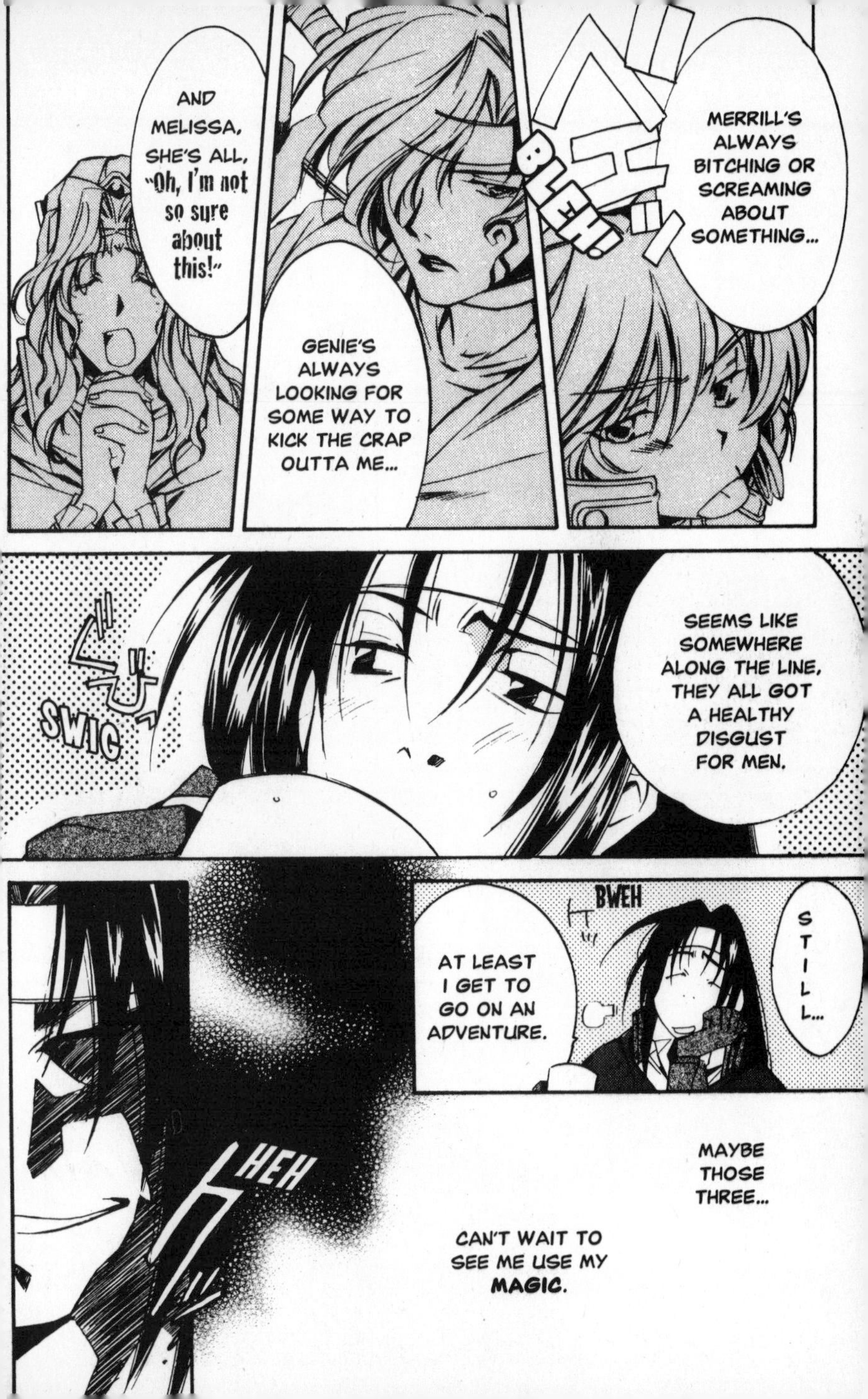
MERRILL'S ALWAYS BITCHING OR SCREAMING ABOUT SOMETHING...
BLEH!
GENIE'S ALWAYS LOOKING FOR SOME WAY TO KICK THE CRAP OUTTA ME...
AND MELISSA, SHE'S ALL, "Oh, I'm not so sure about this!"
SEEMS LIKE SOMEWHERE ALONG THE LINE, THEY ALL GOT A HEALTHY DISGUST FOR MEN.
SWIG
STILL...
BWEH
AT LEAST I GET TO GO ON AN ADVENTURE.
MAYBE THOSE THREE...
CAN'T WAIT TO SEE ME USE MY **MAGIC**.
HEH

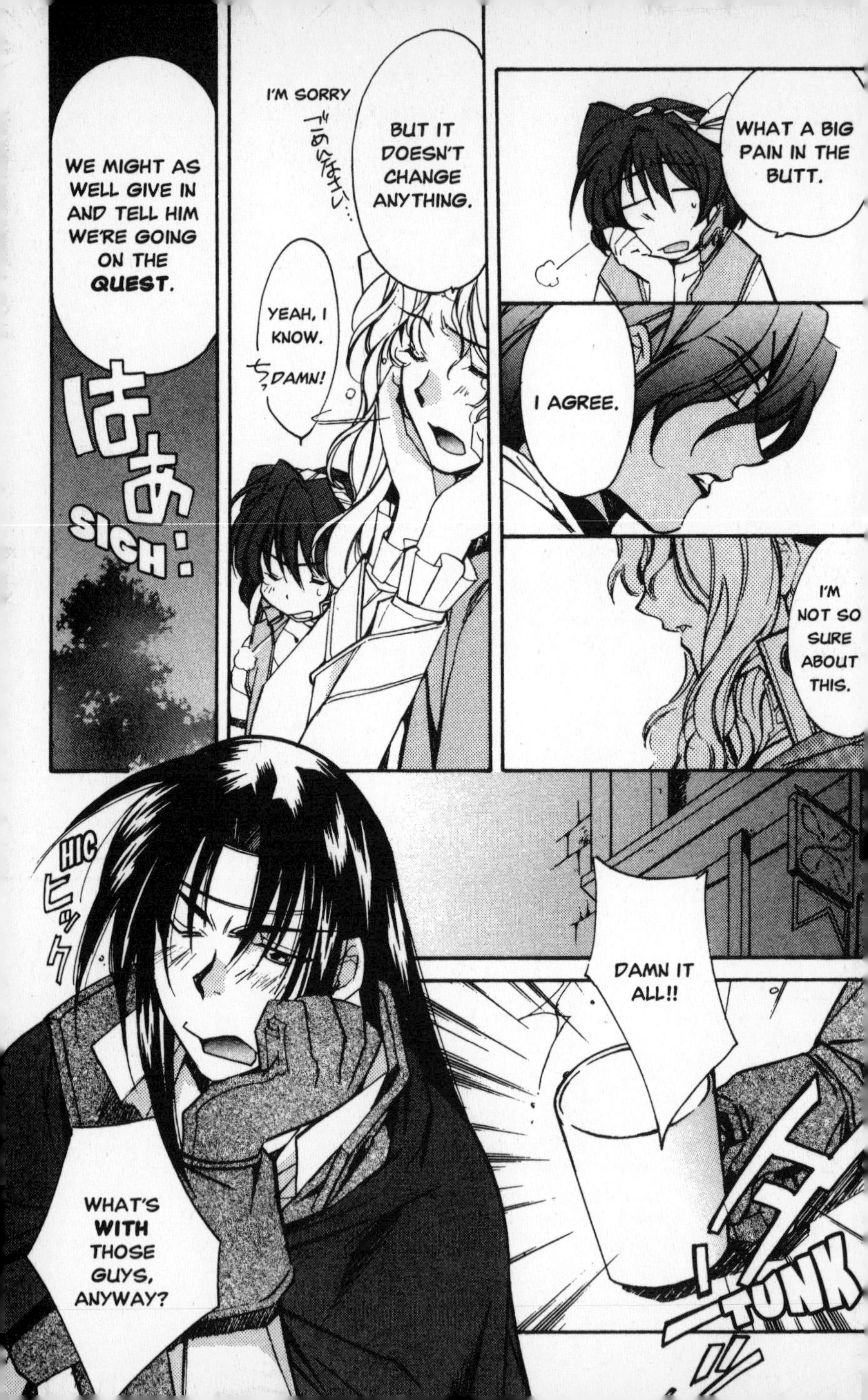
WHAT A BIG PAIN IN THE BUTT.
I AGREE.
I'M NOT SO SURE ABOUT THIS.
BUT IT DOESN'T CHANGE ANYTHING.
I'M SORRY
YEAH, I KNOW.
DAMN!
WE MIGHT AS WELL GIVE IN AND TELL HIM WE'RE GOING ON THE **QUEST**.
はあ
SIGH
DAMN IT ALL!!
TUNK
HIC
ヒック
WHAT'S **WITH** THOSE GUYS, ANYWAY?

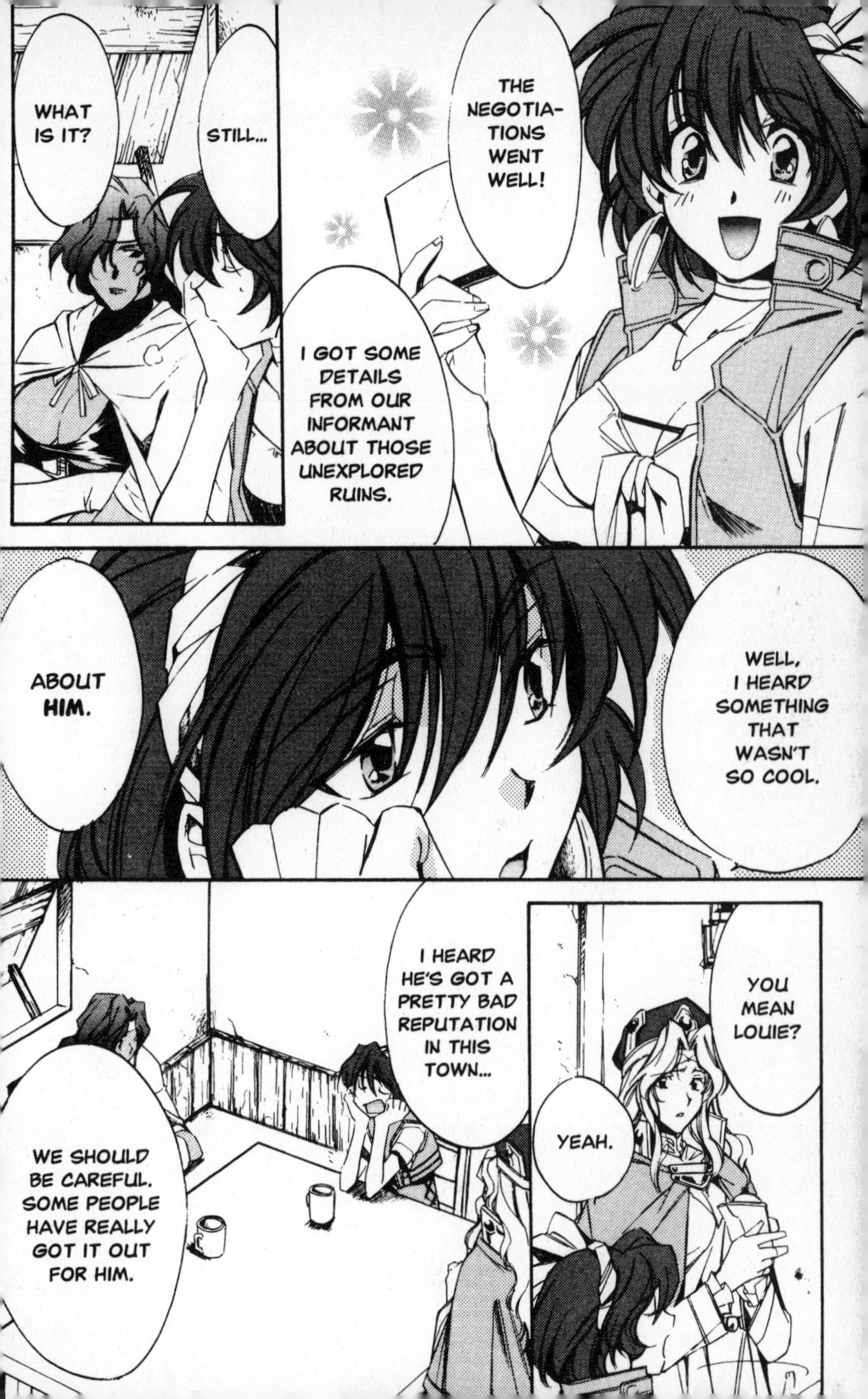
THE NEGOTIATIONS WENT WELL!
I GOT SOME DETAILS FROM OUR INFORMANT ABOUT THOSE UNEXPLORED RUINS.
STILL...
WHAT IS IT?
WELL, I HEARD SOMETHING THAT WASN'T SO COOL.
ABOUT **HIM**.
YOU MEAN LOUIE?
YEAH.
I HEARD HE'S GOT A PRETTY BAD REPUTATION IN THIS TOWN...
WE SHOULD BE CAREFUL. SOME PEOPLE HAVE REALLY GOT IT OUT FOR HIM.

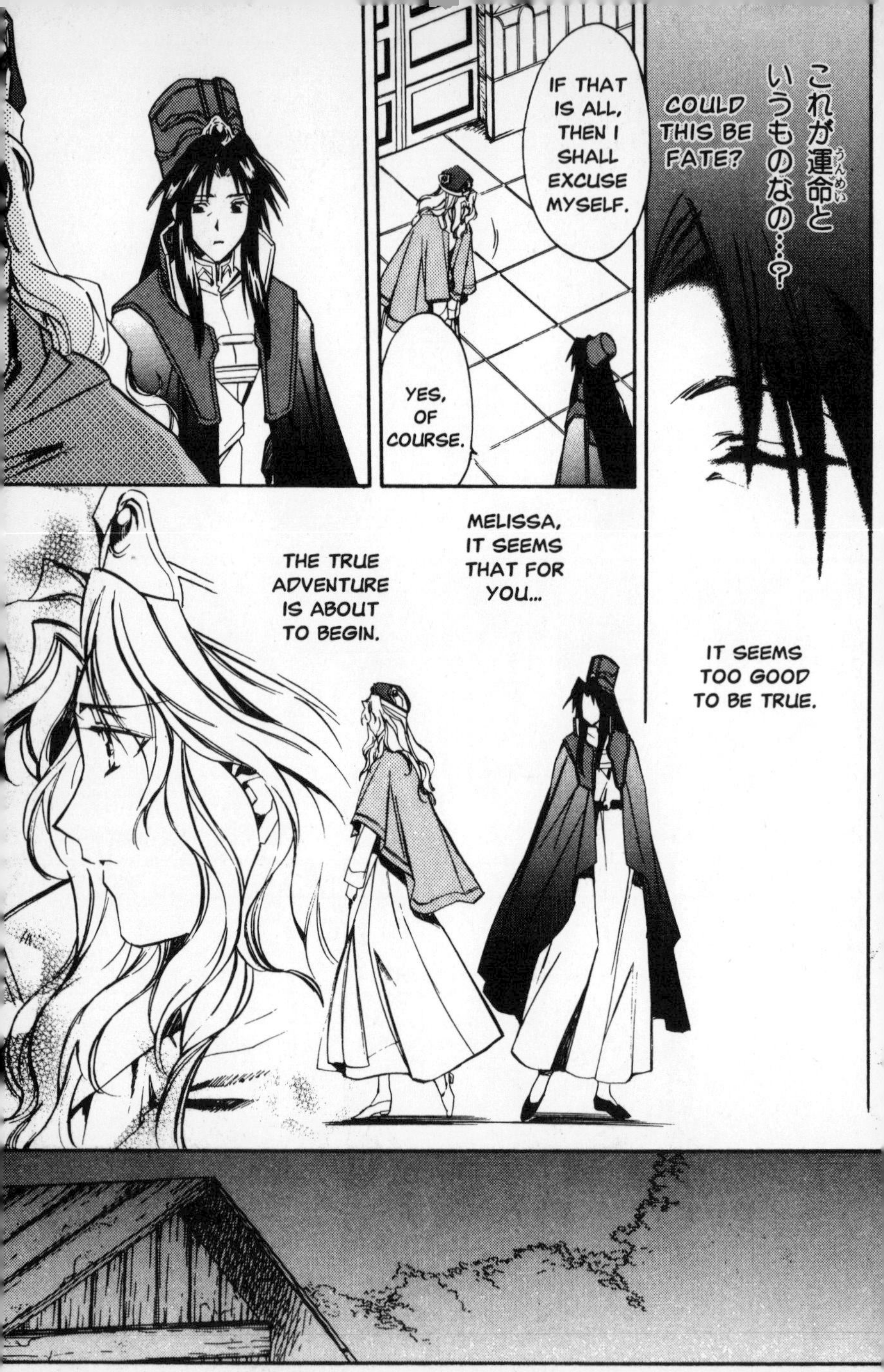
これが運命というものなの…？
COULD THIS BE FATE?
IT SEEMS TOO GOOD TO BE TRUE.
IF THAT IS ALL, THEN I SHALL EXCUSE MYSELF.
YES, OF COURSE.
MELISSA, IT SEEMS THAT FOR YOU...
THE TRUE ADVENTURE IS ABOUT TO BEGIN.

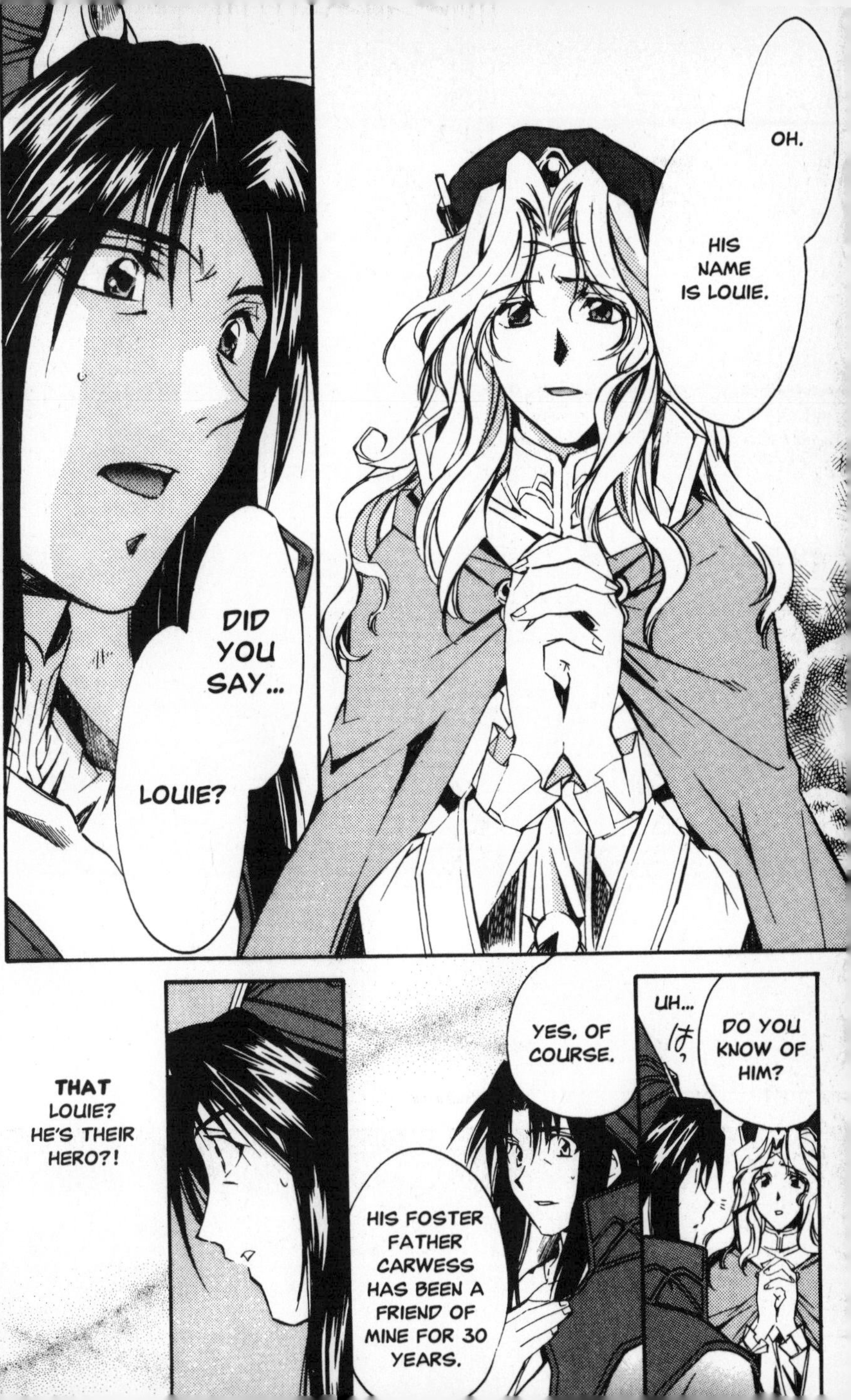
OH.
HIS NAME IS LOUIE.
DID YOU SAY...
LOUIE?
UH...
は、
DO YOU KNOW OF HIM?
YES, OF COURSE.
HIS FOSTER FATHER CARWESS HAS BEEN A FRIEND OF MINE FOR 30 YEARS.
THAT LOUIE? HE'S THEIR HERO?!

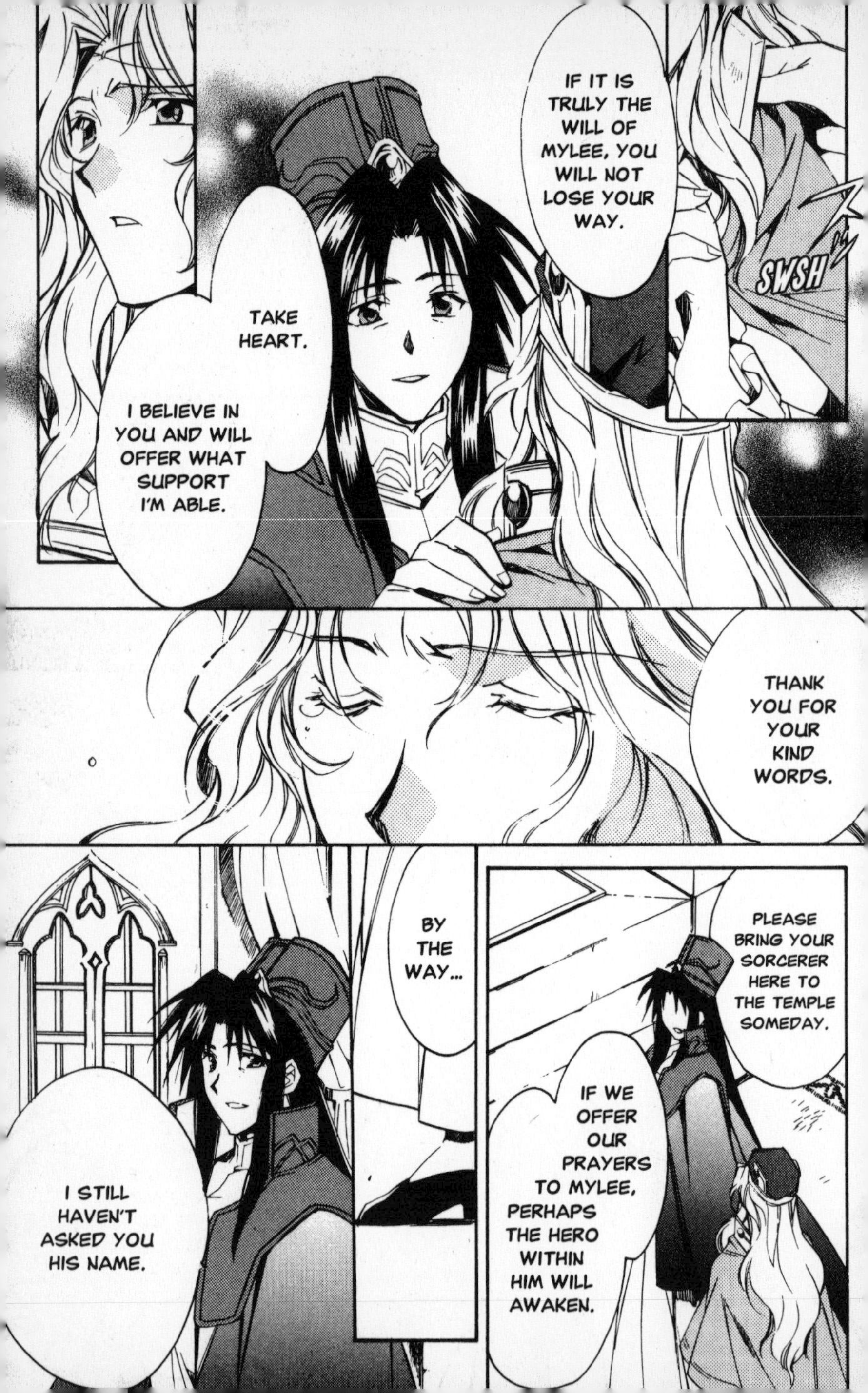
SWSH
IF IT IS TRULY THE WILL OF MYLEE, YOU WILL NOT LOSE YOUR WAY.
TAKE HEART.
I BELIEVE IN YOU AND WILL OFFER WHAT SUPPORT I'M ABLE.
THANK YOU FOR YOUR KIND WORDS.
PLEASE BRING YOUR SORCERER HERE TO THE TEMPLE SOMEDAY.
IF WE OFFER OUR PRAYERS TO MYLEE, PERHAPS THE HERO WITHIN HIM WILL AWAKEN.
BY THE WAY...
I STILL HAVEN'T ASKED YOU HIS NAME.

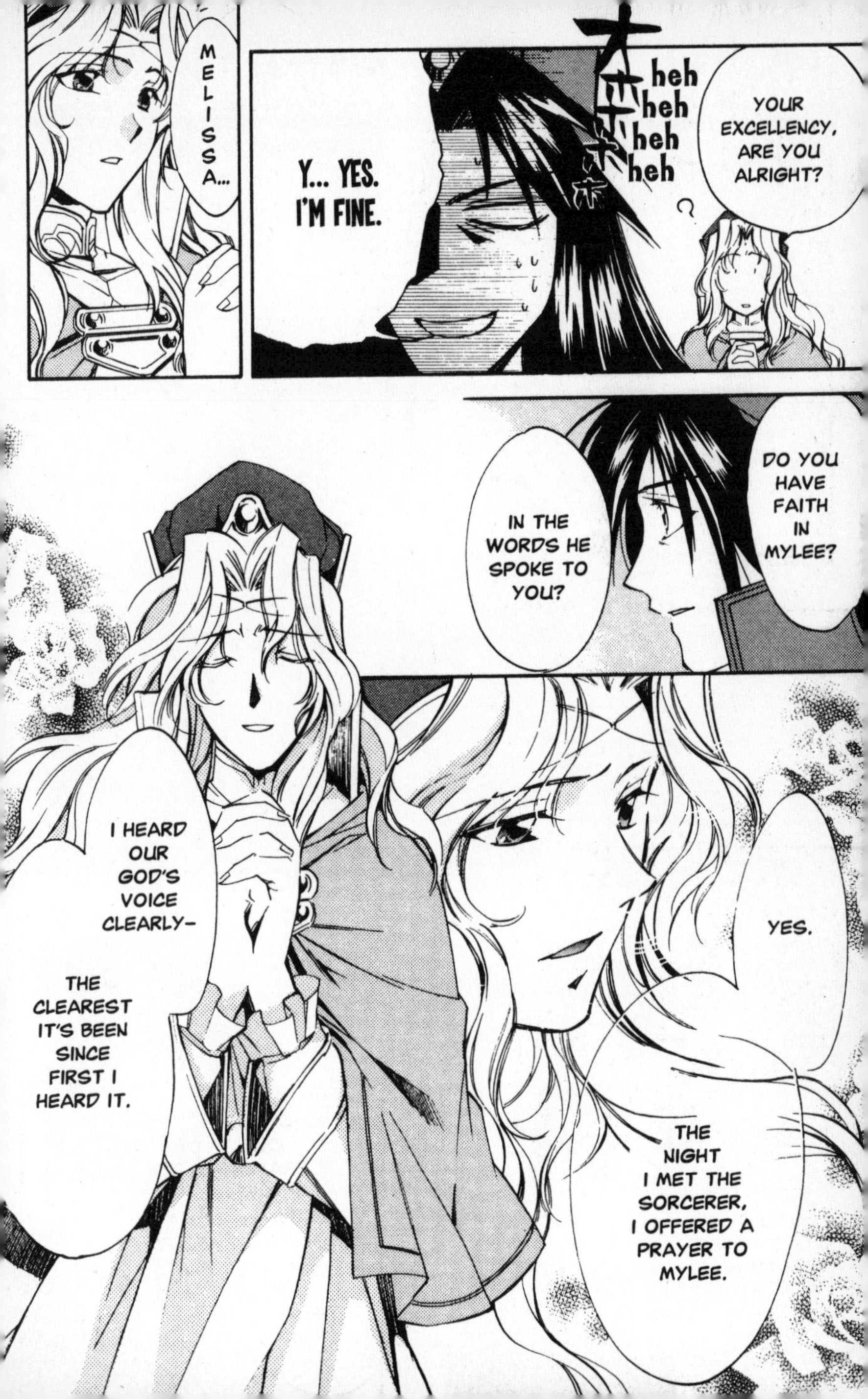
YOUR EXCELLENCY, ARE YOU ALRIGHT?
heh heh heh heh
Y... YES. I'M FINE.
MELISSA...
DO YOU HAVE FAITH IN MYLEE?
IN THE WORDS HE SPOKE TO YOU?
YES.
THE NIGHT I MET THE SORCERER, I OFFERED A PRAYER TO MYLEE.
I HEARD OUR GOD'S VOICE CLEARLY-
THE CLEAREST IT'S BEEN SINCE FIRST I HEARD IT.

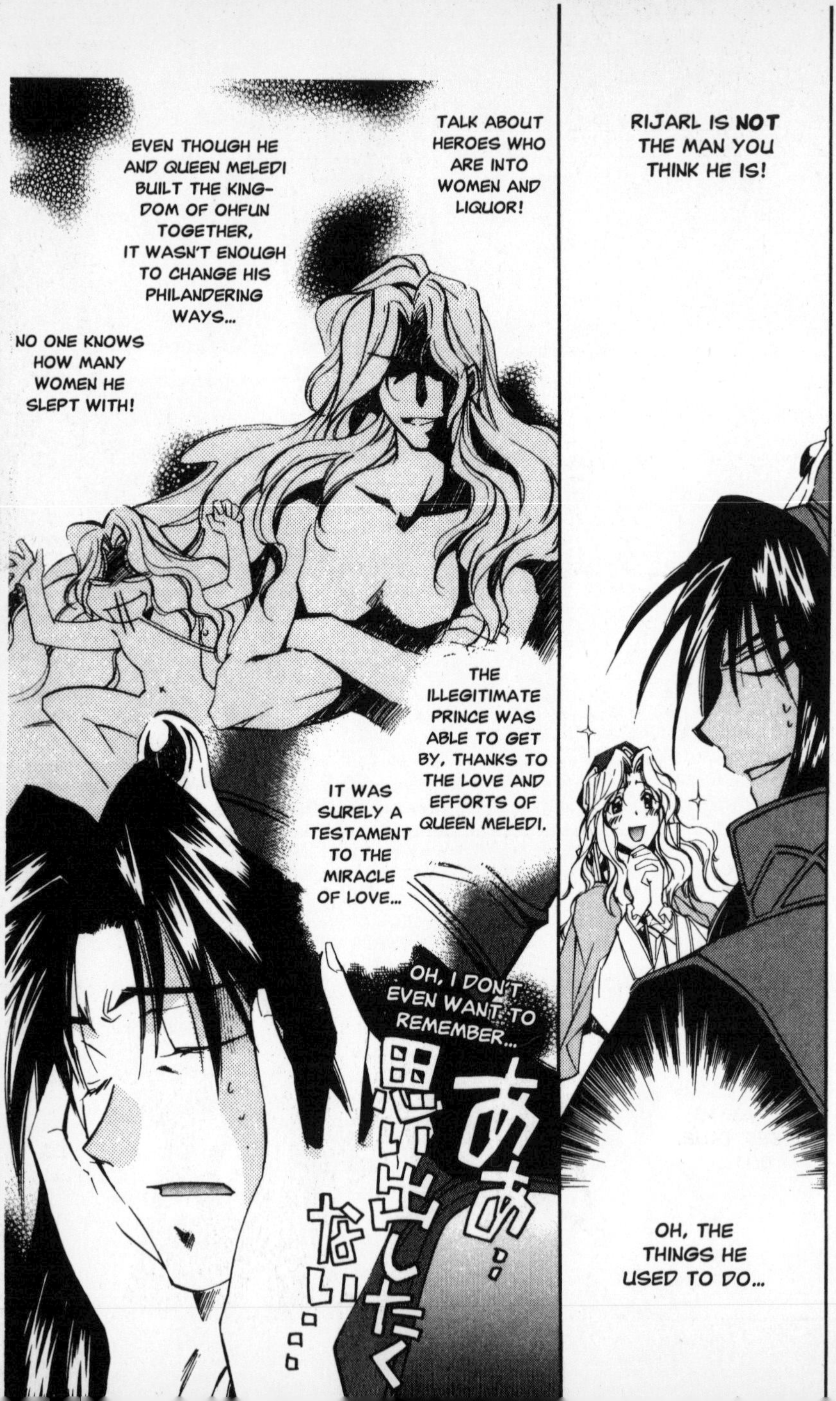
RIJARL IS **NOT** THE MAN YOU THINK HE IS!
OH, THE THINGS HE USED TO DO...
TALK ABOUT HEROES WHO ARE INTO WOMEN AND LIQUOR!
EVEN THOUGH HE AND QUEEN MELEDI BUILT THE KING-DOM OF OHFUN TOGETHER, IT WASN'T ENOUGH TO CHANGE HIS PHILANDERING WAYS...
NO ONE KNOWS HOW MANY WOMEN HE SLEPT WITH!
THE ILLEGITIMATE PRINCE WAS ABLE TO GET BY, THANKS TO THE LOVE AND EFFORTS OF QUEEN MELEDI.
IT WAS SURELY A TESTAMENT TO THE MIRACLE OF LOVE...
OH, I DON'T EVEN WANT TO REMEMBER...
ああ思い出したくない…

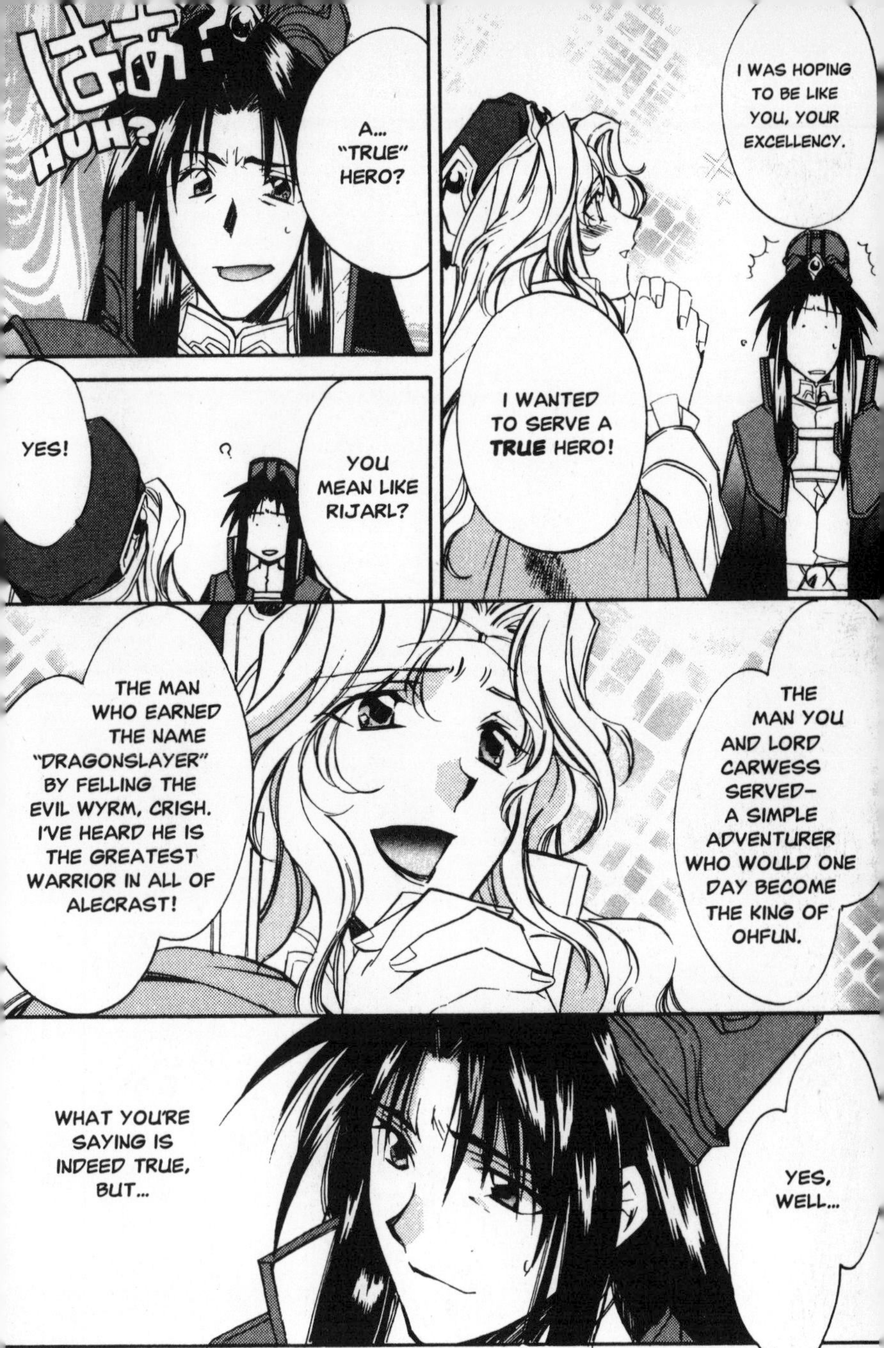
I WAS HOPING TO BE LIKE YOU, YOUR EXCELLENCY.
I WANTED TO SERVE A **TRUE** HERO!
はあ?
HUH?
A... "TRUE" HERO?
YOU MEAN LIKE RIJARL?
YES!
THE MAN YOU AND LORD CARWESS SERVED— A SIMPLE ADVENTURER WHO WOULD ONE DAY BECOME THE KING OF OHFUN.
THE MAN WHO EARNED THE NAME "DRAGONSLAYER" BY FELLING THE EVIL WYRM, CRISH. I'VE HEARD HE IS THE GREATEST WARRIOR IN ALL OF ALECRAST!
YES, WELL...
WHAT YOU'RE SAYING IS INDEED TRUE, BUT...

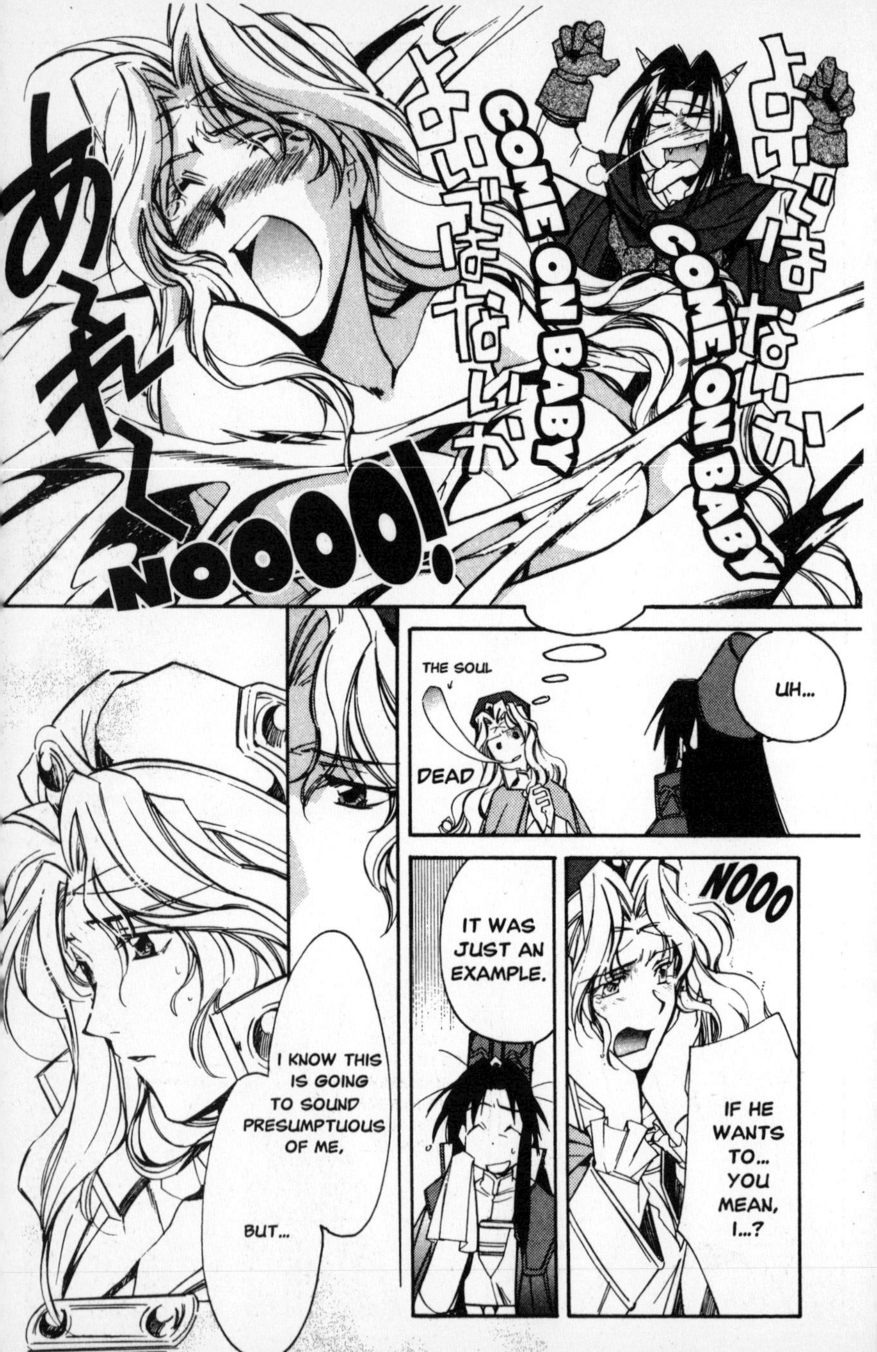
よいではないか
COME ON BABY
COME ON BABY
よいではないか
あれ〜
NOOOO!
UH...
THE SOUL
DEAD
NOOO
IF HE WANTS TO... YOU MEAN, I...?
IT WAS JUST AN EXAMPLE.
I KNOW THIS IS GOING TO SOUND PRESUMPTUOUS OF ME,
BUT...

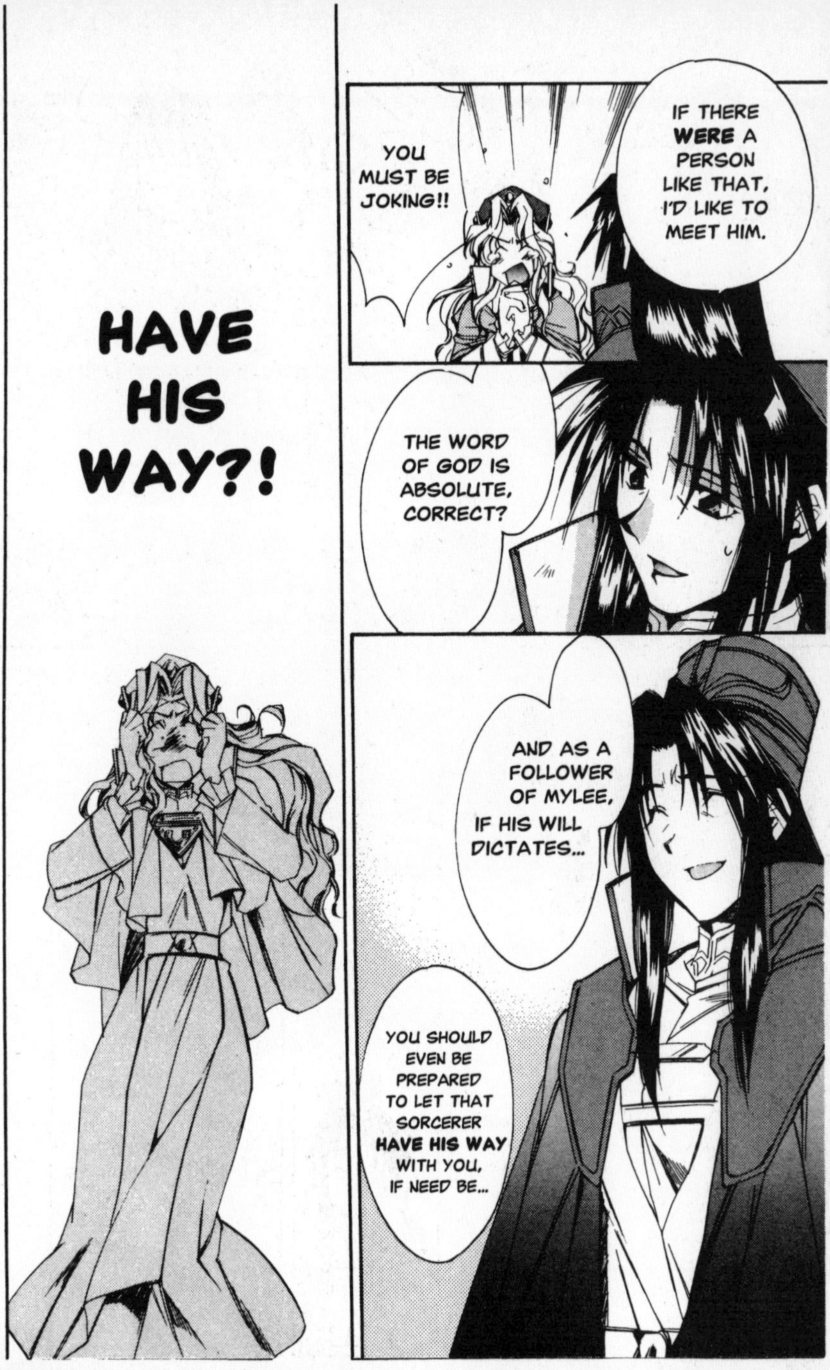
IF THERE WERE A PERSON LIKE THAT, I'D LIKE TO MEET HIM.
YOU MUST BE JOKING!!
THE WORD OF GOD IS ABSOLUTE, CORRECT?
AND AS A FOLLOWER OF MYLEE, IF HIS WILL DICTATES...
YOU SHOULD EVEN BE PREPARED TO LET THAT SORCERER HAVE HIS WAY WITH YOU, IF NEED BE...
HAVE HIS WAY?!

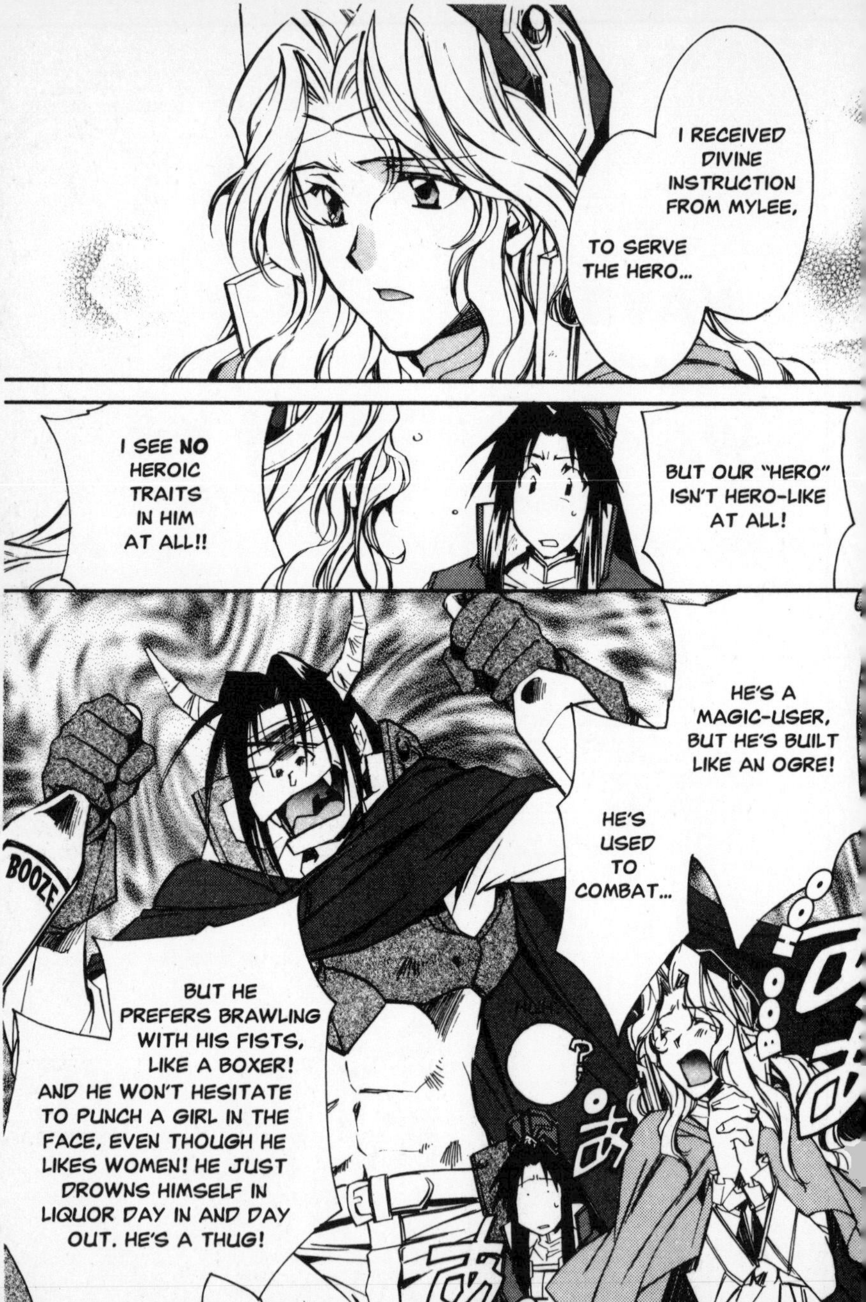
I RECEIVED DIVINE INSTRUCTION FROM MYLEE,
TO SERVE THE HERO...
BUT OUR "HERO" ISN'T HERO-LIKE AT ALL!
I SEE **NO** HEROIC TRAITS IN HIM AT ALL!!
HE'S A MAGIC-USER, BUT HE'S BUILT LIKE AN OGRE!
HE'S USED TO COMBAT...
BUT HE PREFERS BRAWLING WITH HIS FISTS, LIKE A BOXER! AND HE WON'T HESITATE TO PUNCH A GIRL IN THE FACE, EVEN THOUGH HE LIKES WOMEN! HE JUST DROWNS HIMSELF IN LIQUOR DAY IN AND DAY OUT. HE'S A THUG!
BOOZE

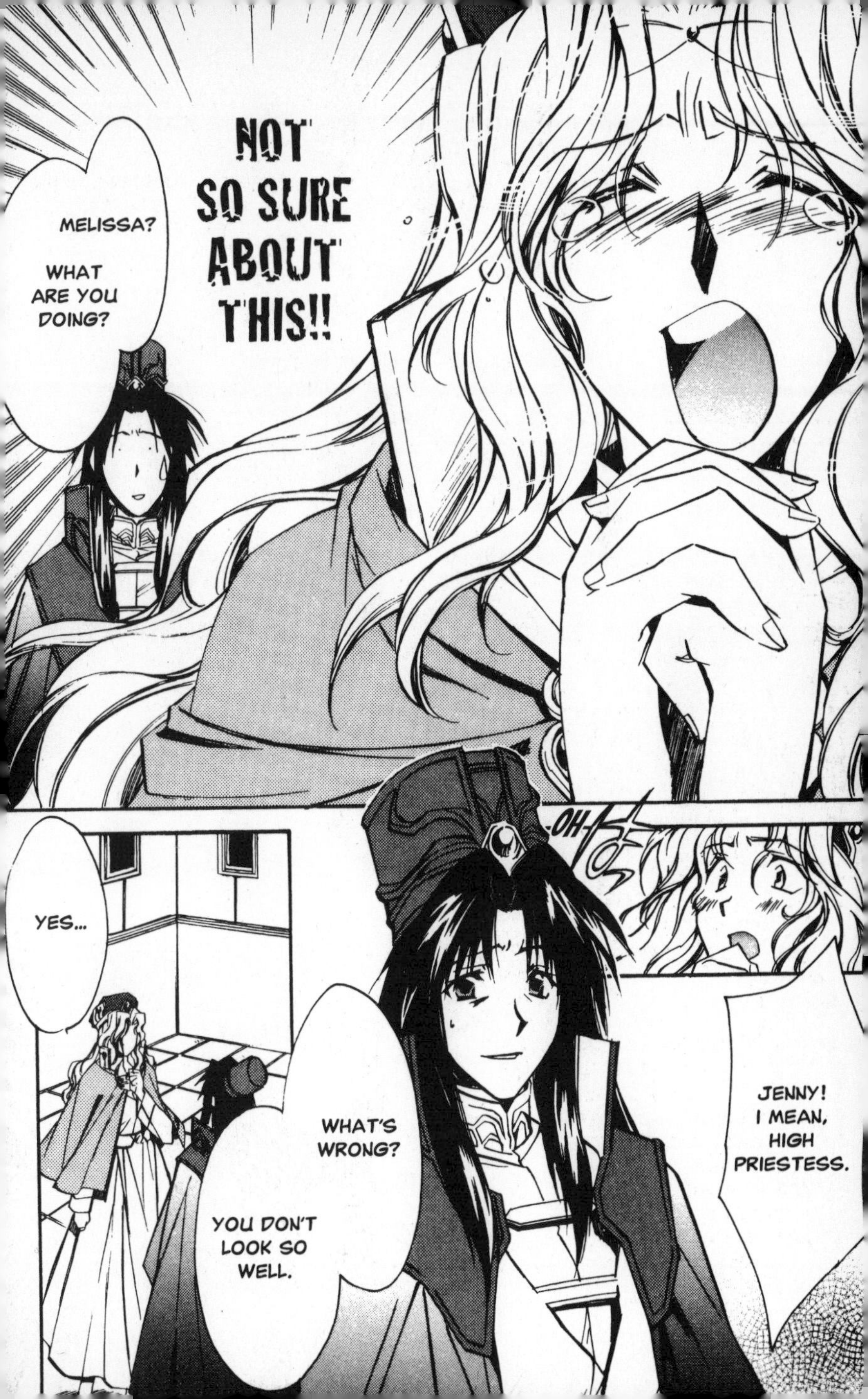
NOT SO SURE ABOUT THIS!!
MELISSA? WHAT ARE YOU DOING?
-OH-
JENNY! I MEAN, HIGH PRIESTESS.
WHAT'S WRONG?
YOU DON'T LOOK SO WELL.
YES...

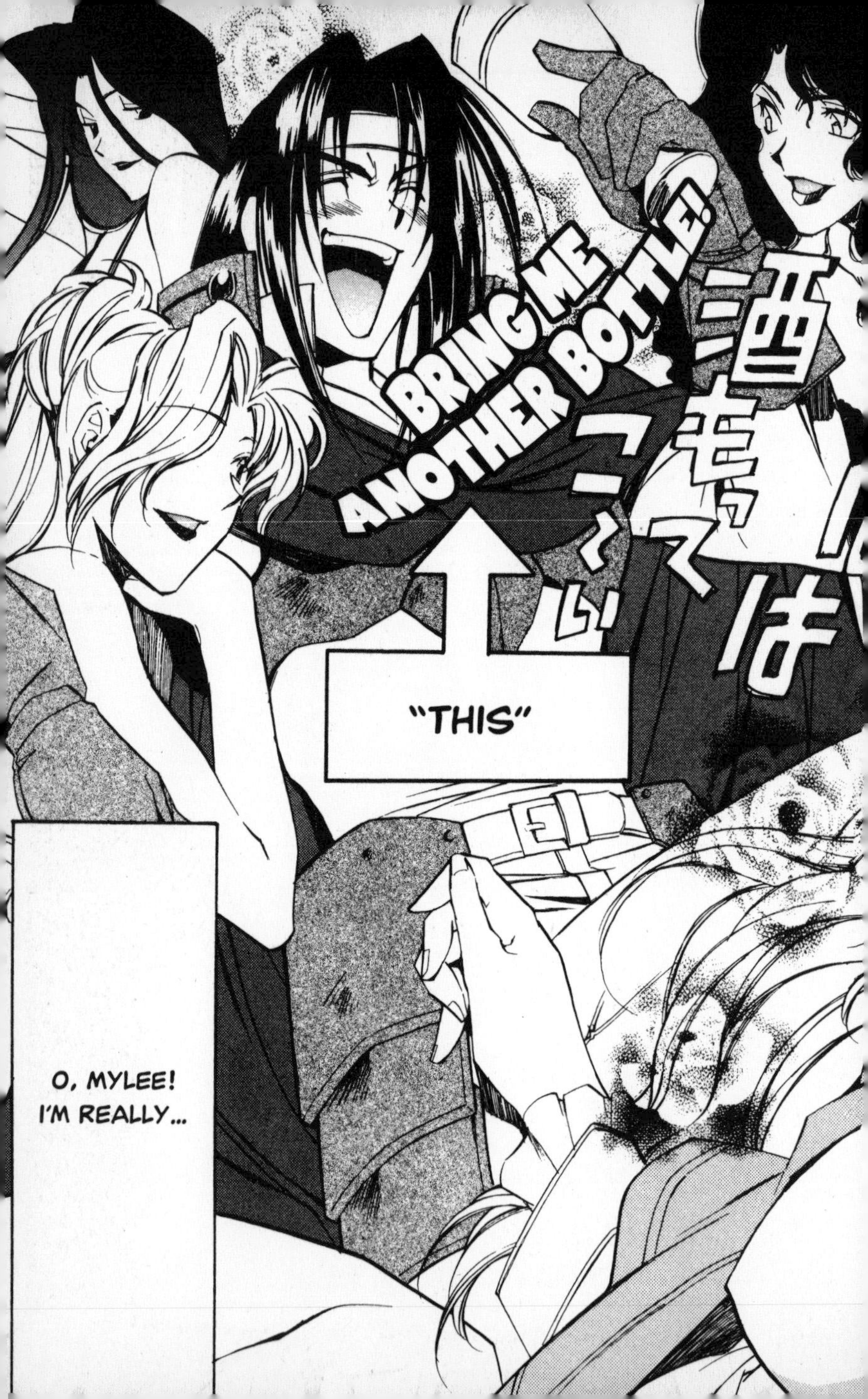

BRING ME ANOTHER BOTTLE!
酒もってこ〜い
"THIS"
O, MYLEE! I'M REALLY...

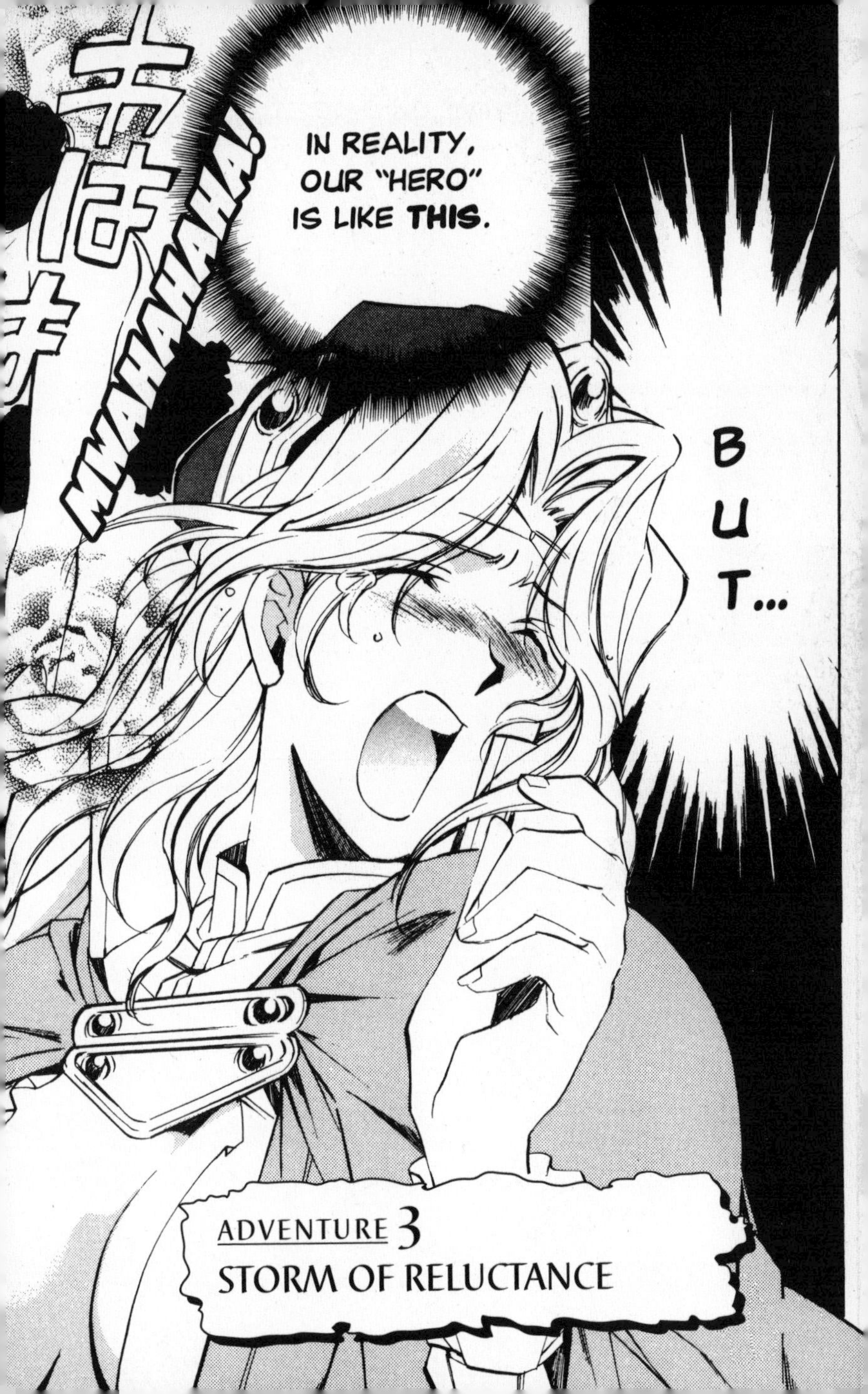
BUT...
IN REALITY, OUR "HERO" IS LIKE THIS.
MWAHAHAHA!
ADVENTURE 3
STORM OF RELUCTANCE

ADVENTURE 3
STORM OF RELUCTANCE

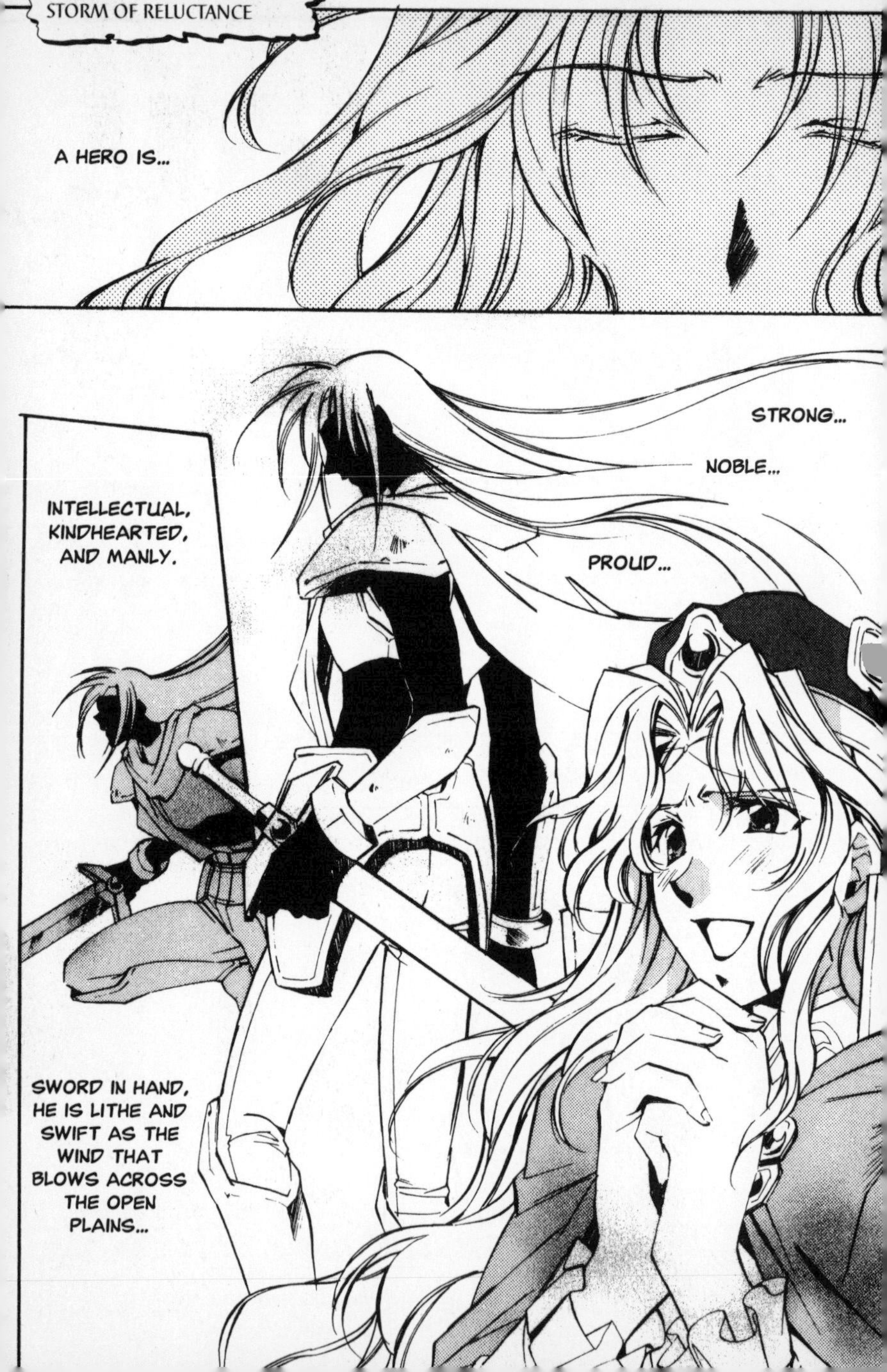
A HERO IS...
STRONG...
NOBLE...
PROUD...
INTELLECTUAL, KINDHEARTED, AND MANLY.
SWORD IN HAND, HE IS LITHE AND SWIFT AS THE WIND THAT BLOWS ACROSS THE OPEN PLAINS...

魔法戦士リウイ

LOUIE the RUNE SOLDIER

紅炎のバスタード

夢・・・!?

DREAM...?!

HA HA HA HA HA
はっはっはははっ

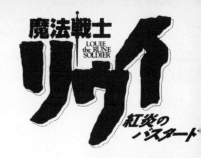

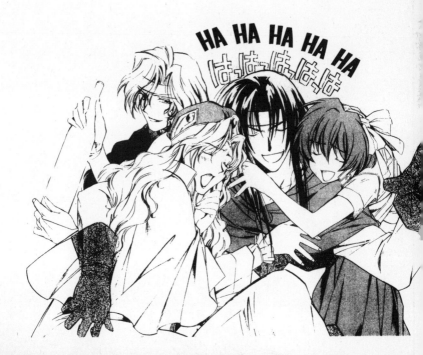

魔法戦士
LOUIE
the RUNE
SOLDIER
リウイ
紅炎の
バスタード

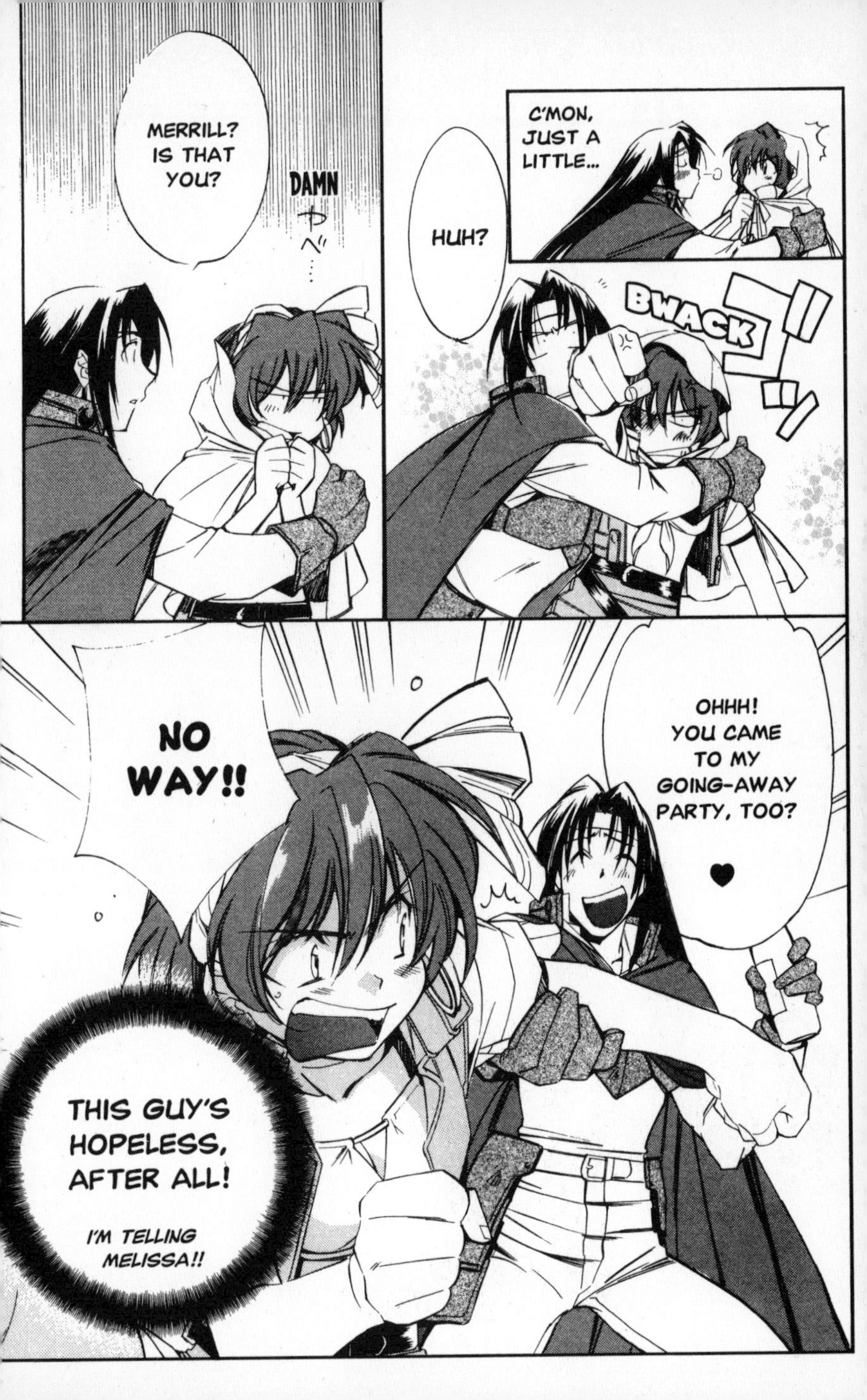
C'MON, JUST A LITTLE...
HUH?
BWACK
MERRILL? IS THAT YOU?
DAMN
ヤベ…
OHHH! YOU CAME TO MY GOING-AWAY PARTY, TOO?
NO WAY!!
THIS GUY'S HOPELESS, AFTER ALL!
I'M TELLING MELISSA!!

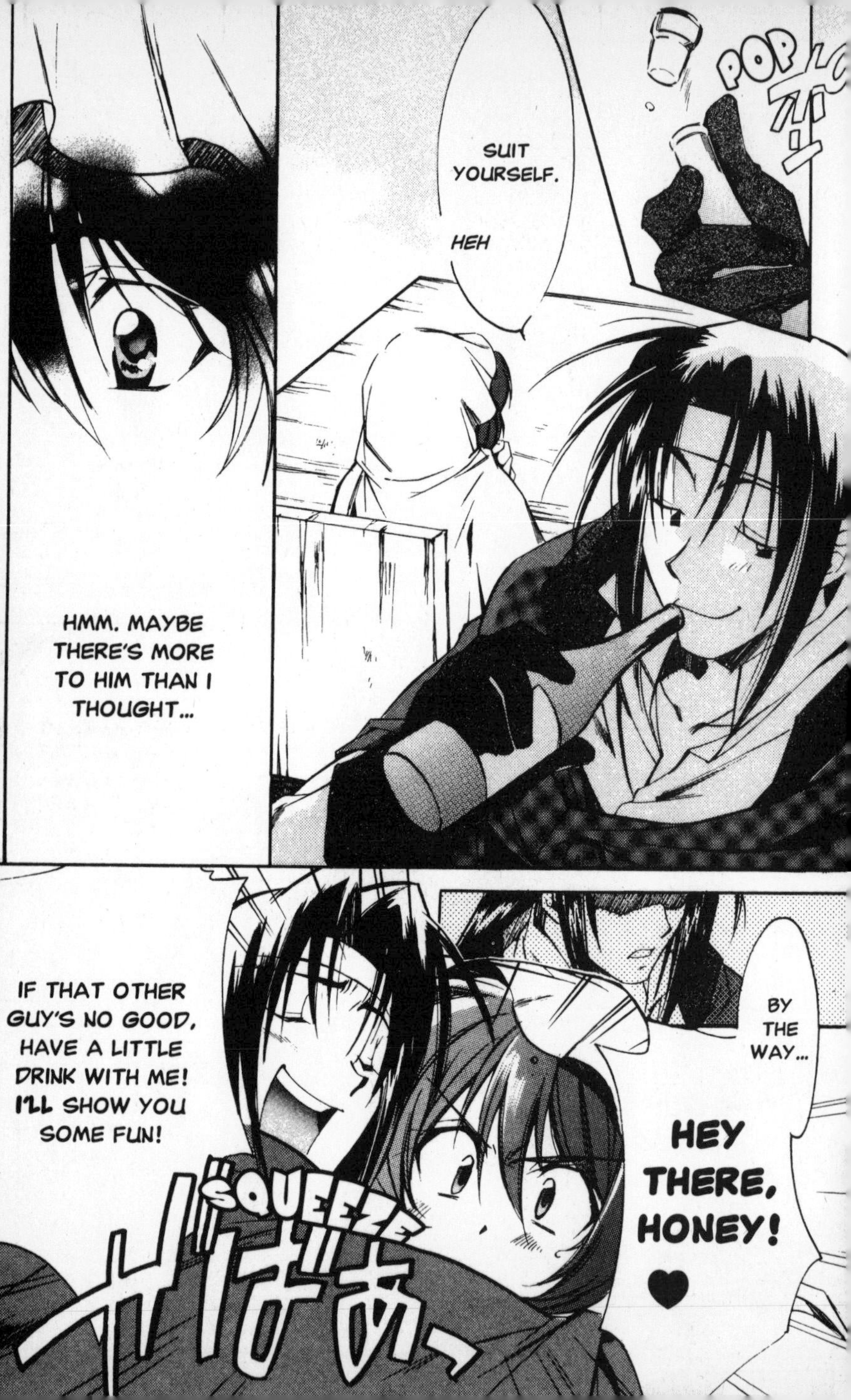
POP
SUIT YOURSELF.
HEH
HMM. MAYBE THERE'S MORE TO HIM THAN I THOUGHT...
BY THE WAY...
HEY THERE, HONEY! ♥
IF THAT OTHER GUY'S NO GOOD, HAVE A LITTLE DRINK WITH ME! I'LL SHOW YOU SOME FUN!
SQUEEZE

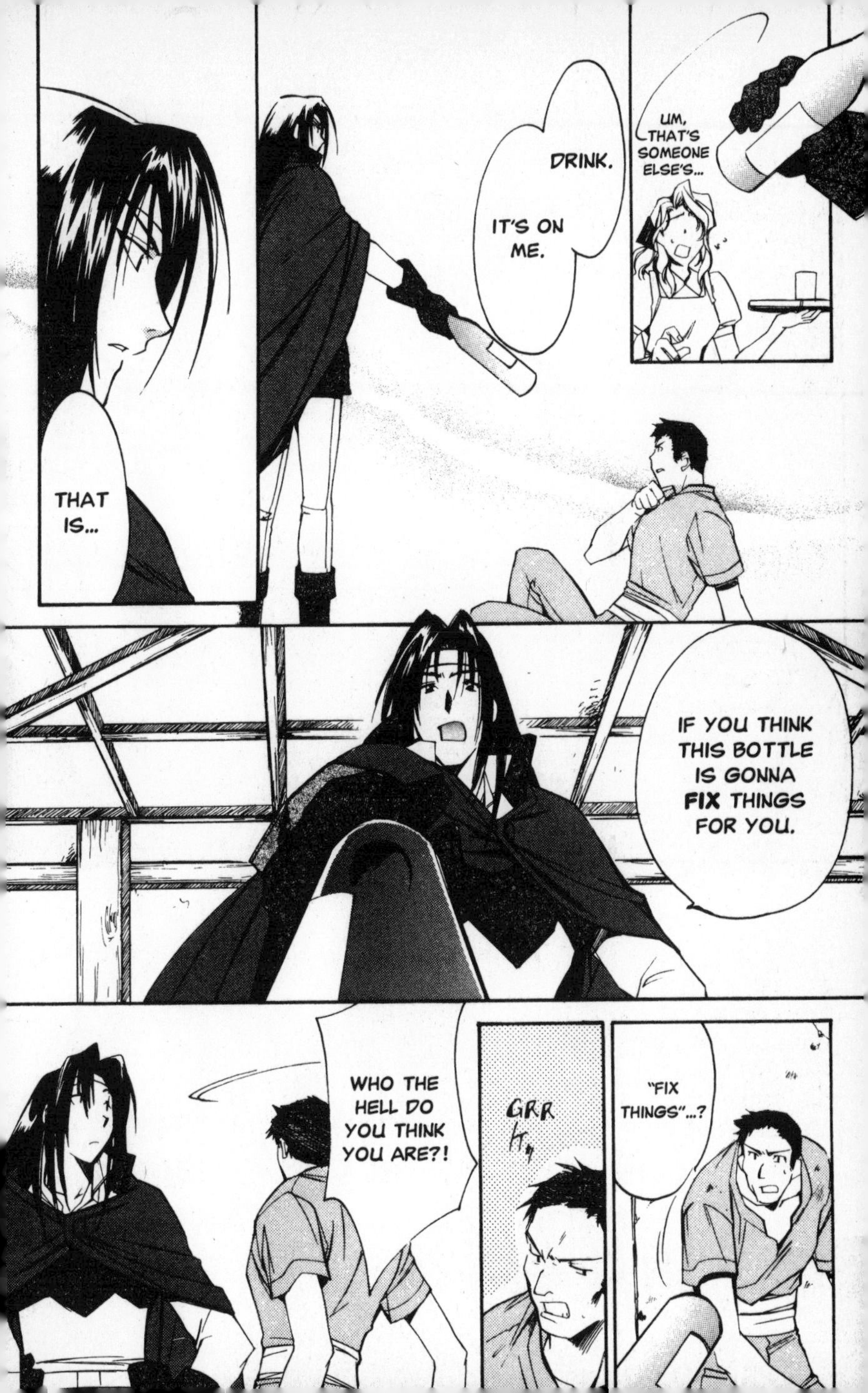
UM, THAT'S SOMEONE ELSE'S...
DRINK.
IT'S ON ME.
THAT IS...
IF YOU THINK THIS BOTTLE IS GONNA FIX THINGS FOR YOU.
"FIX THINGS"...?
GRR
WHO THE HELL DO YOU THINK YOU ARE?!

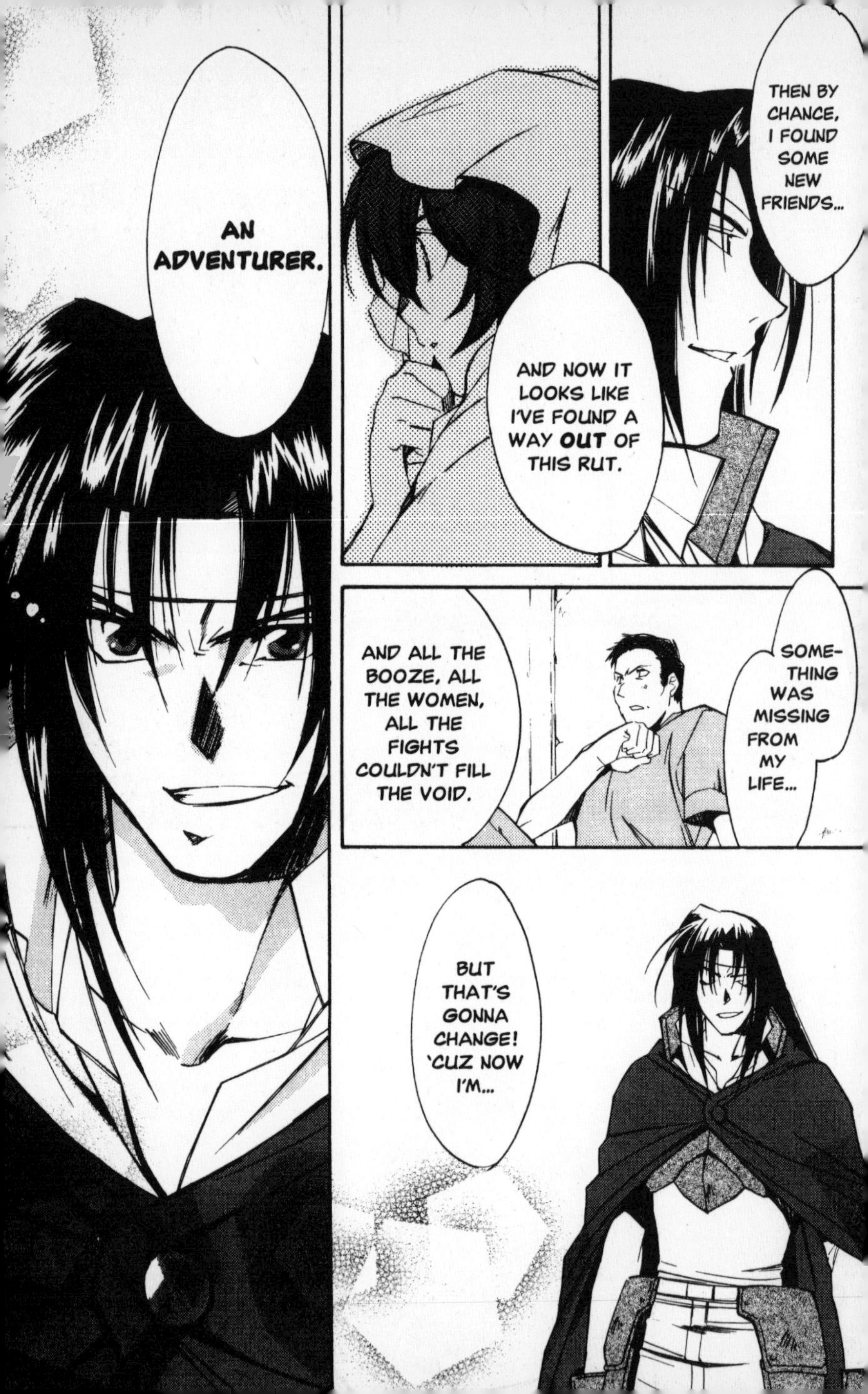
THEN BY CHANCE, I FOUND SOME NEW FRIENDS...
AND NOW IT LOOKS LIKE I'VE FOUND A WAY OUT OF THIS RUT.
SOME-THING WAS MISSING FROM MY LIFE...
AND ALL THE BOOZE, ALL THE WOMEN, ALL THE FIGHTS COULDN'T FILL THE VOID.
BUT THAT'S GONNA CHANGE! 'CUZ NOW I'M...
AN ADVENTURER.

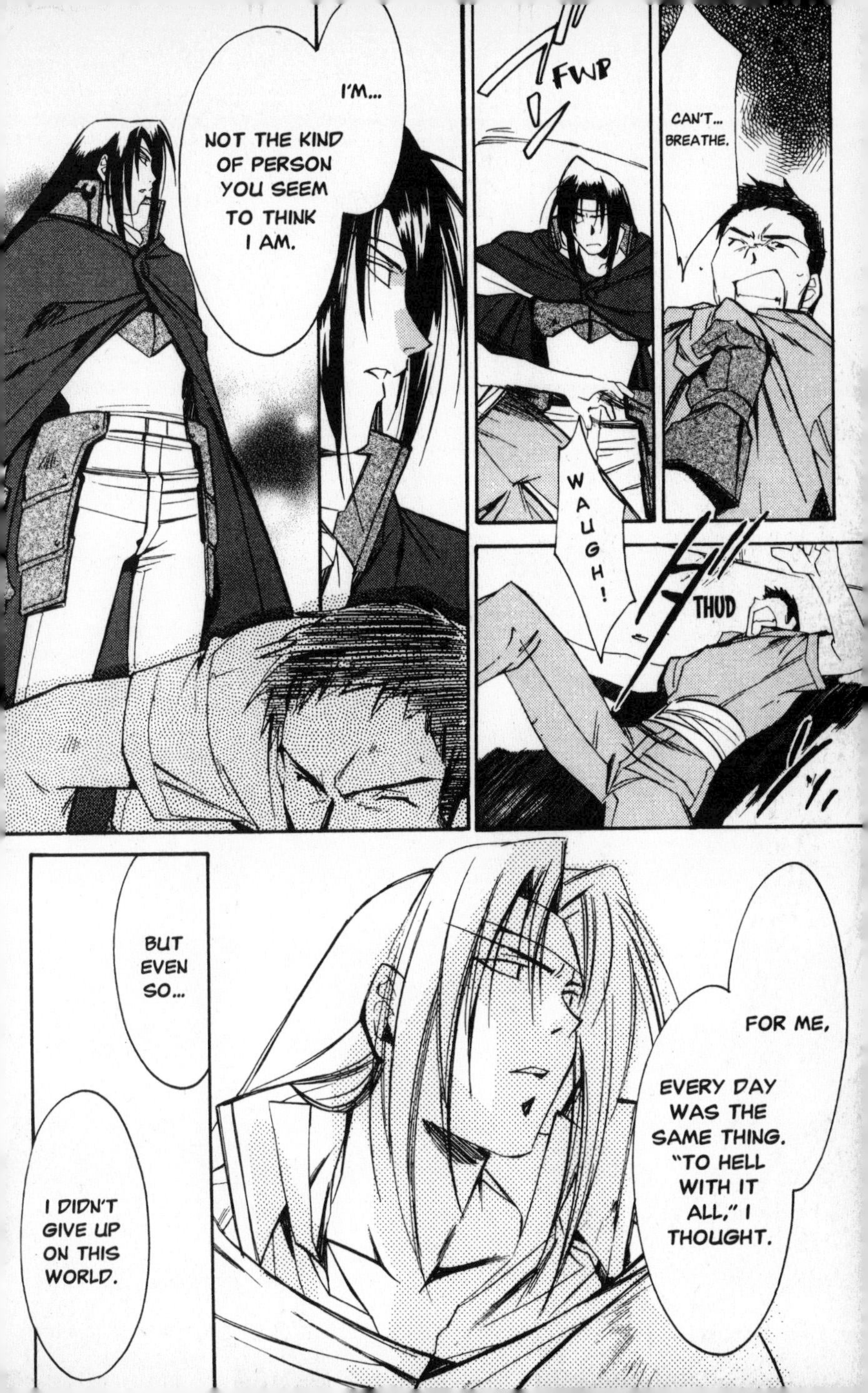
FWP
CAN'T... BREATHE.
WAUGH!
THUD
I'M...
NOT THE KIND OF PERSON YOU SEEM TO THINK I AM.
FOR ME,
EVERY DAY WAS THE SAME THING. "TO HELL WITH IT ALL," I THOUGHT.
BUT EVEN SO...
I DIDN'T GIVE UP ON THIS WORLD.

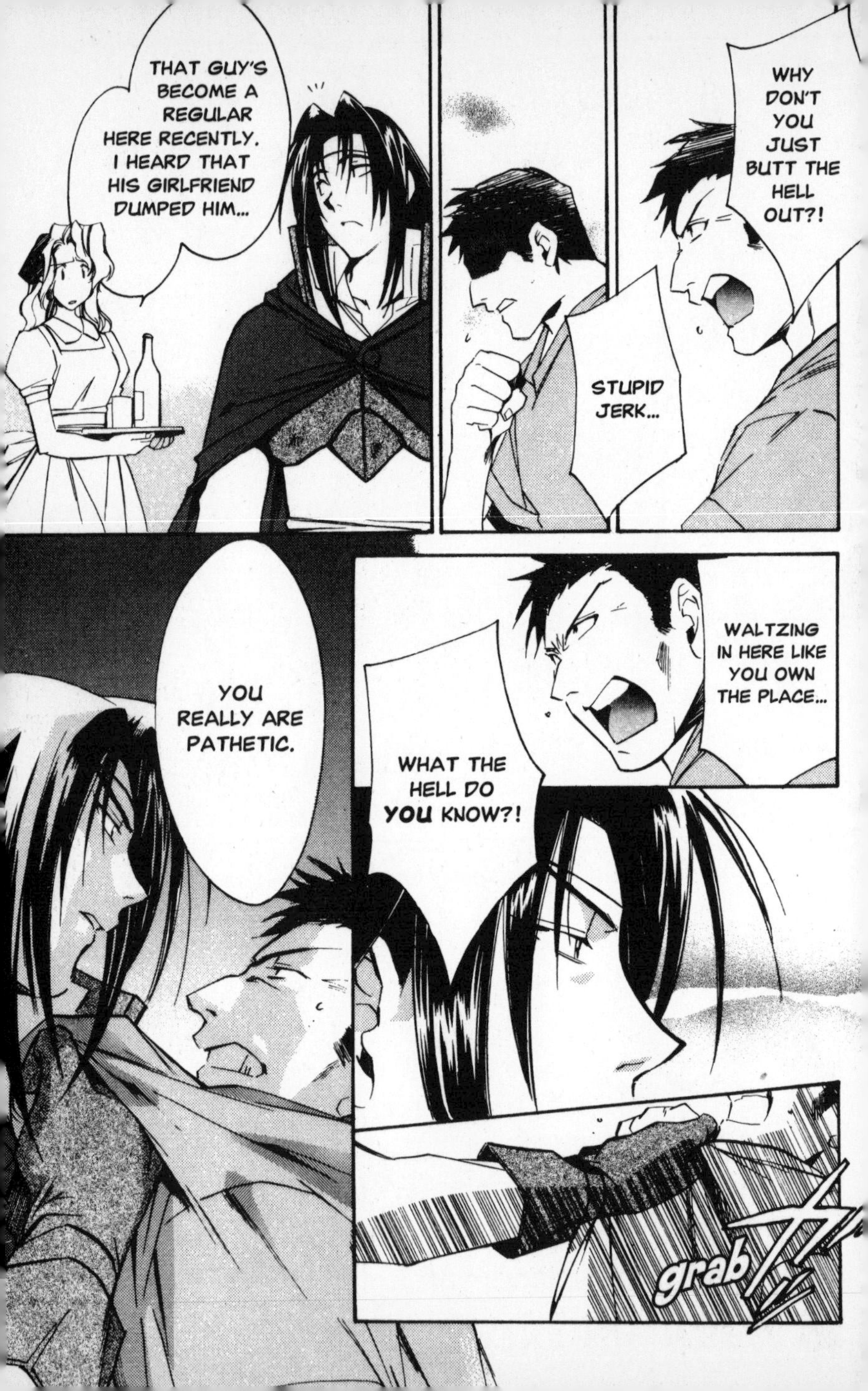
WHY DON'T YOU JUST BUTT THE HELL OUT?!
STUPID JERK...
THAT GUY'S BECOME A REGULAR HERE RECENTLY. I HEARD THAT HIS GIRLFRIEND DUMPED HIM...
WALTZING IN HERE LIKE YOU OWN THE PLACE...
WHAT THE HELL DO **YOU** KNOW?!
grab
YOU REALLY ARE PATHETIC.

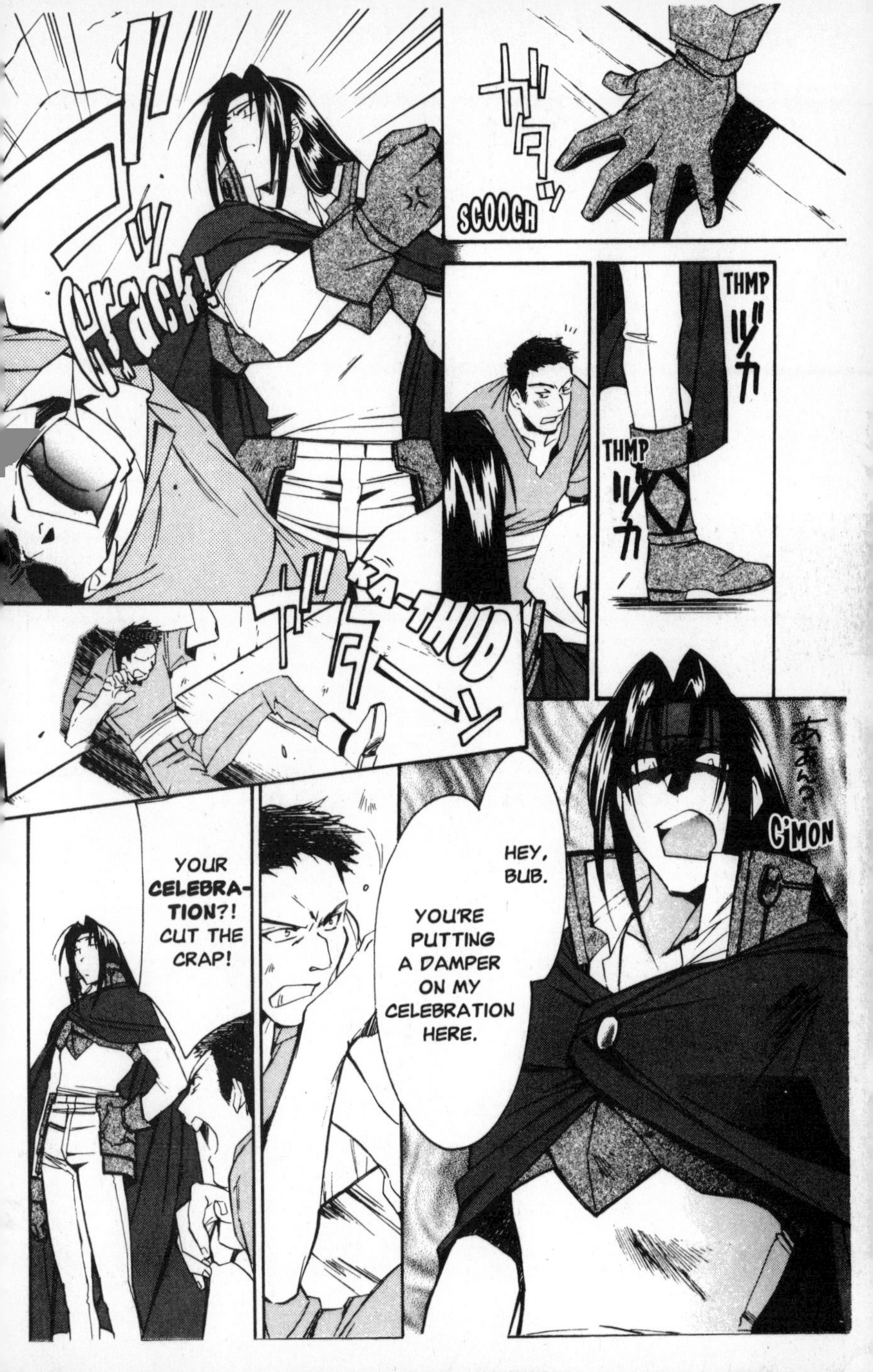
ガタッ
SCOOCH
ゴッ
Crack!
THMP
ヅカ
THMP
ヅカ
ガターン
KA-THUD
あぁん?
C'MON
HEY, BUB.
YOU'RE PUTTING A DAMPER ON MY CELEBRATION HERE.
YOUR **CELEBRATION**?! CUT THE CRAP!

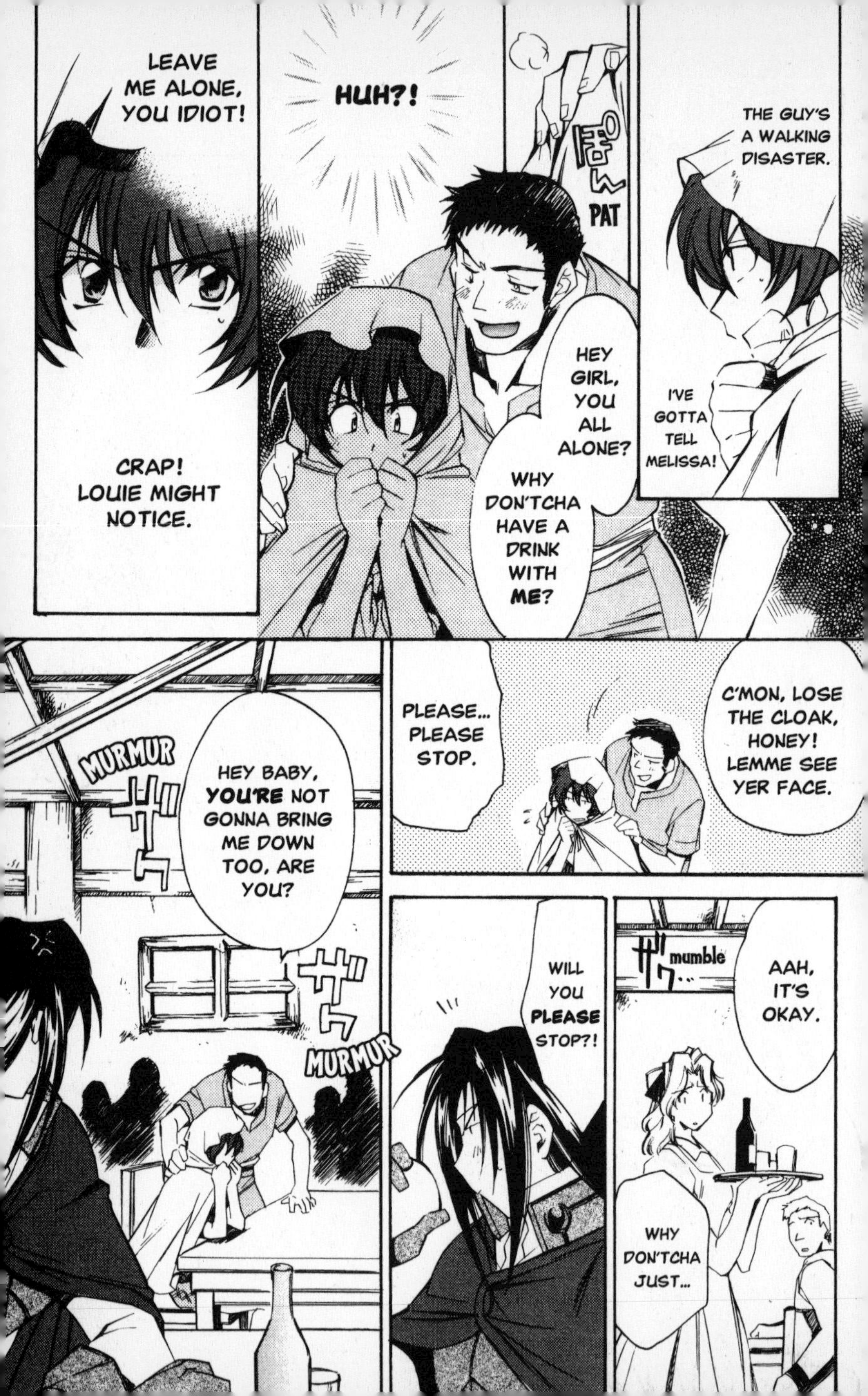
THE GUY'S A WALKING DISASTER.
I'VE GOTTA TELL MELISSA!
HUH?!
ぽん
PAT
HEY GIRL, YOU ALL ALONE?
WHY DON'TCHA HAVE A DRINK WITH ME?
LEAVE ME ALONE, YOU IDIOT!
CRAP! LOUIE MIGHT NOTICE.
C'MON, LOSE THE CLOAK, HONEY! LEMME SEE YER FACE.
PLEASE... PLEASE STOP.
AAH, IT'S OKAY.
ザワ mumble
WHY DON'TCHA JUST...
WILL YOU PLEASE STOP?!
HEY BABY, YOU'RE NOT GONNA BRING ME DOWN TOO, ARE YOU?
MURMUR
ザワ
ザワ
MURMUR

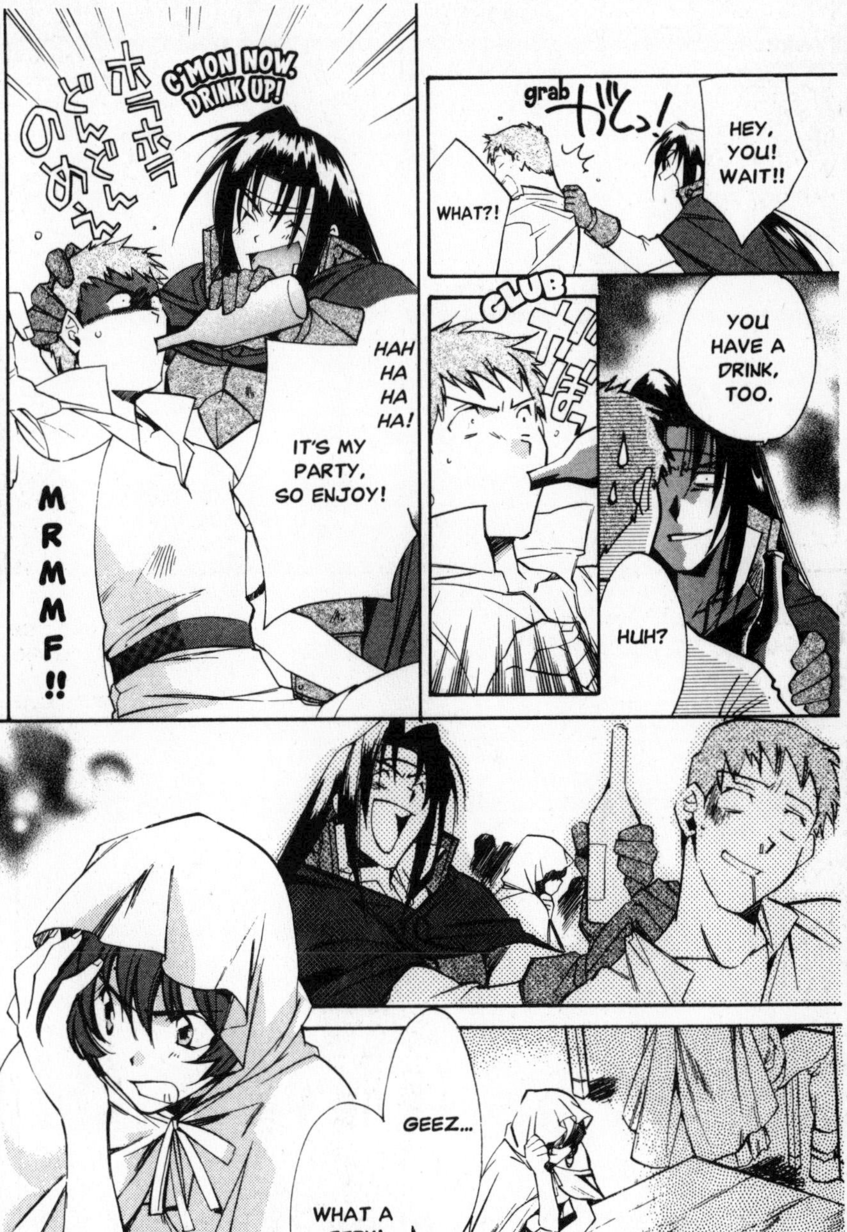
grab
HEY, YOU! WAIT!!
WHAT?!
GLUB
YOU HAVE A DRINK, TOO.
HUH?
C'MON NOW. DRINK UP!
ホラホラどんどんのめぇ
HAH HA HA HA!
IT'S MY PARTY, SO ENJOY!
MRMMMF!!
GEEZ...
WHAT A JERK!

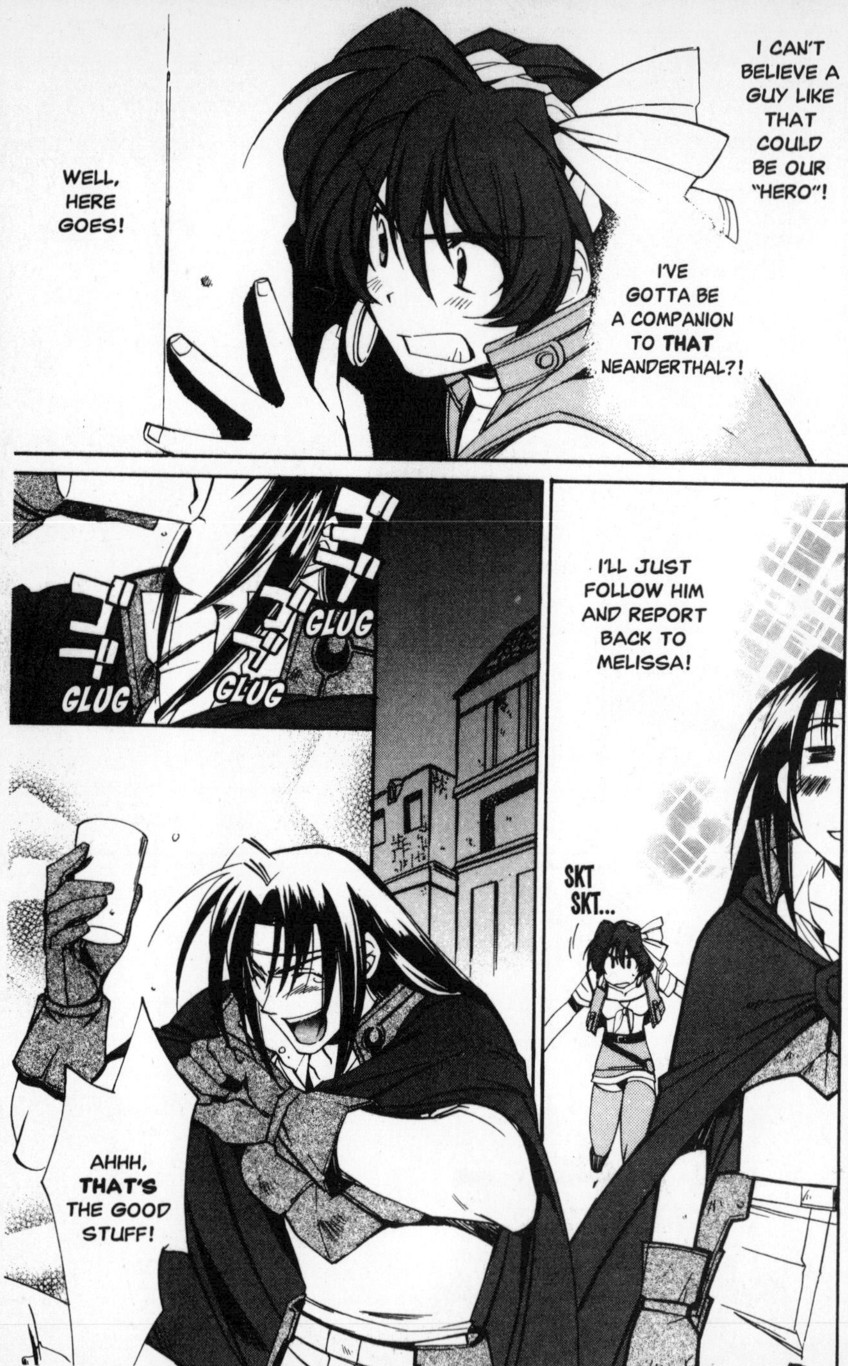

I CAN'T BELIEVE A GUY LIKE THAT COULD BE OUR "HERO"!
I'VE GOTTA BE A COMPANION TO **THAT** NEANDERTHAL?!
WELL, HERE GOES!
I'LL JUST FOLLOW HIM AND REPORT BACK TO MELISSA!
SKT SKT...
GLUG
GLUG
GLUG
AHHH, **THAT'S** THE GOOD STUFF!

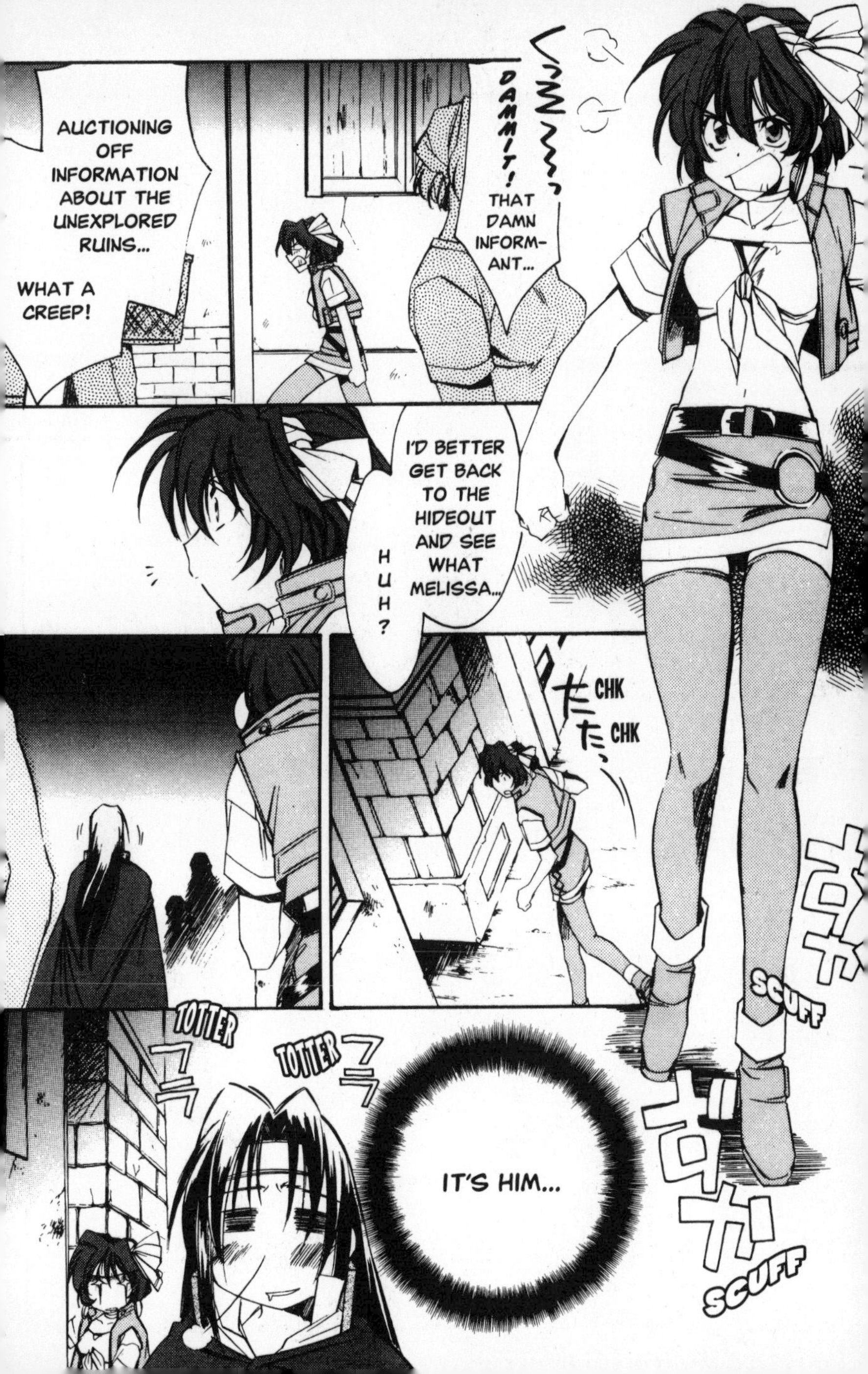
DAMMIT!
THAT DAMN INFORM-ANT...
AUCTIONING OFF INFORMATION ABOUT THE UNEXPLORED RUINS...
WHAT A CREEP!
SCUFF
SCUFF
I'D BETTER GET BACK TO THE HIDEOUT AND SEE WHAT MELISSA...
HUH?
CHK
CHK
IT'S HIM...
TOTTER
TOTTER

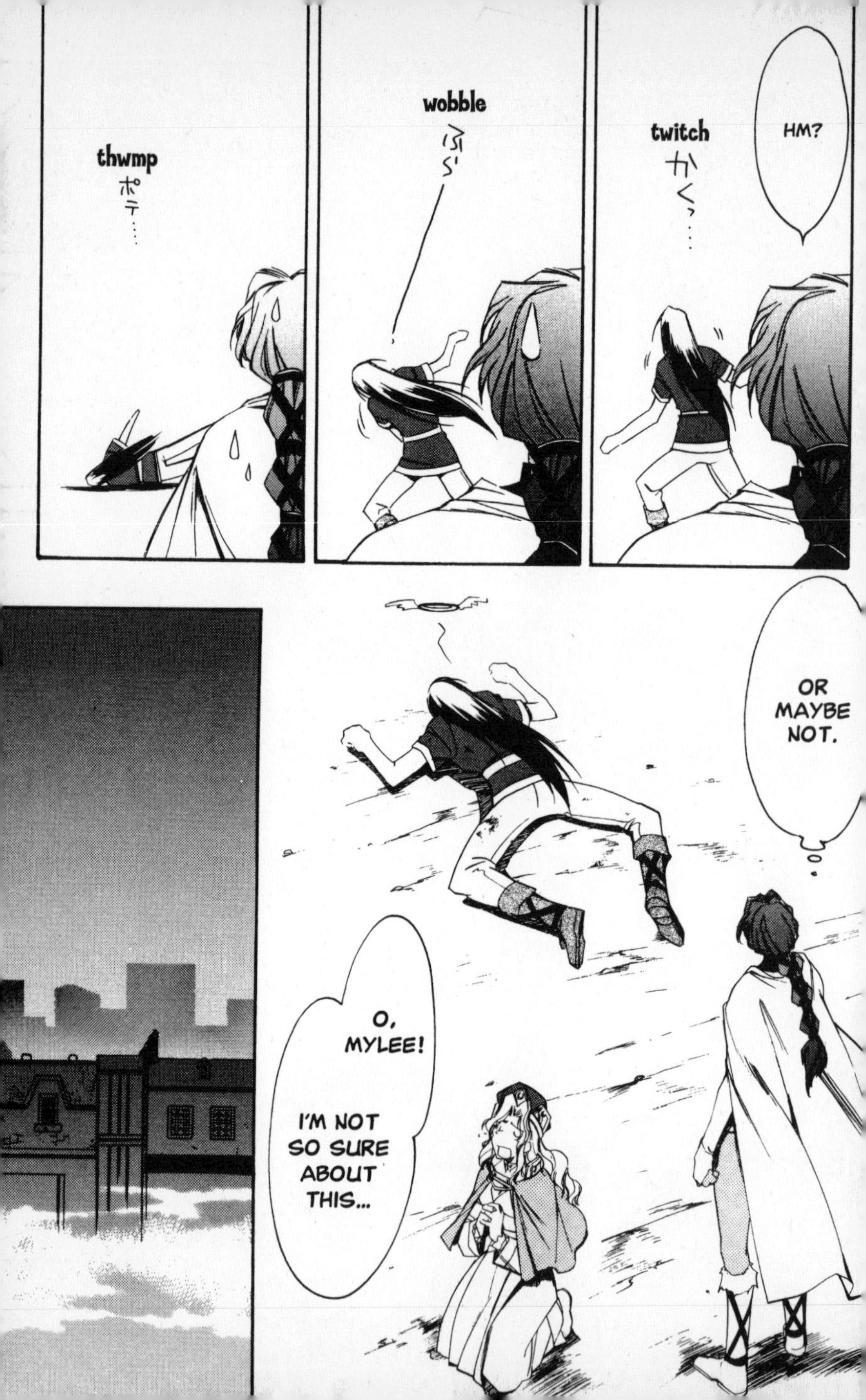
HM?
twitch
かくっ…
wobble
ふら
thwmp
ポテ…
OR MAYBE NOT.
O, MYLEE!
I'M NOT SO SURE ABOUT THIS...

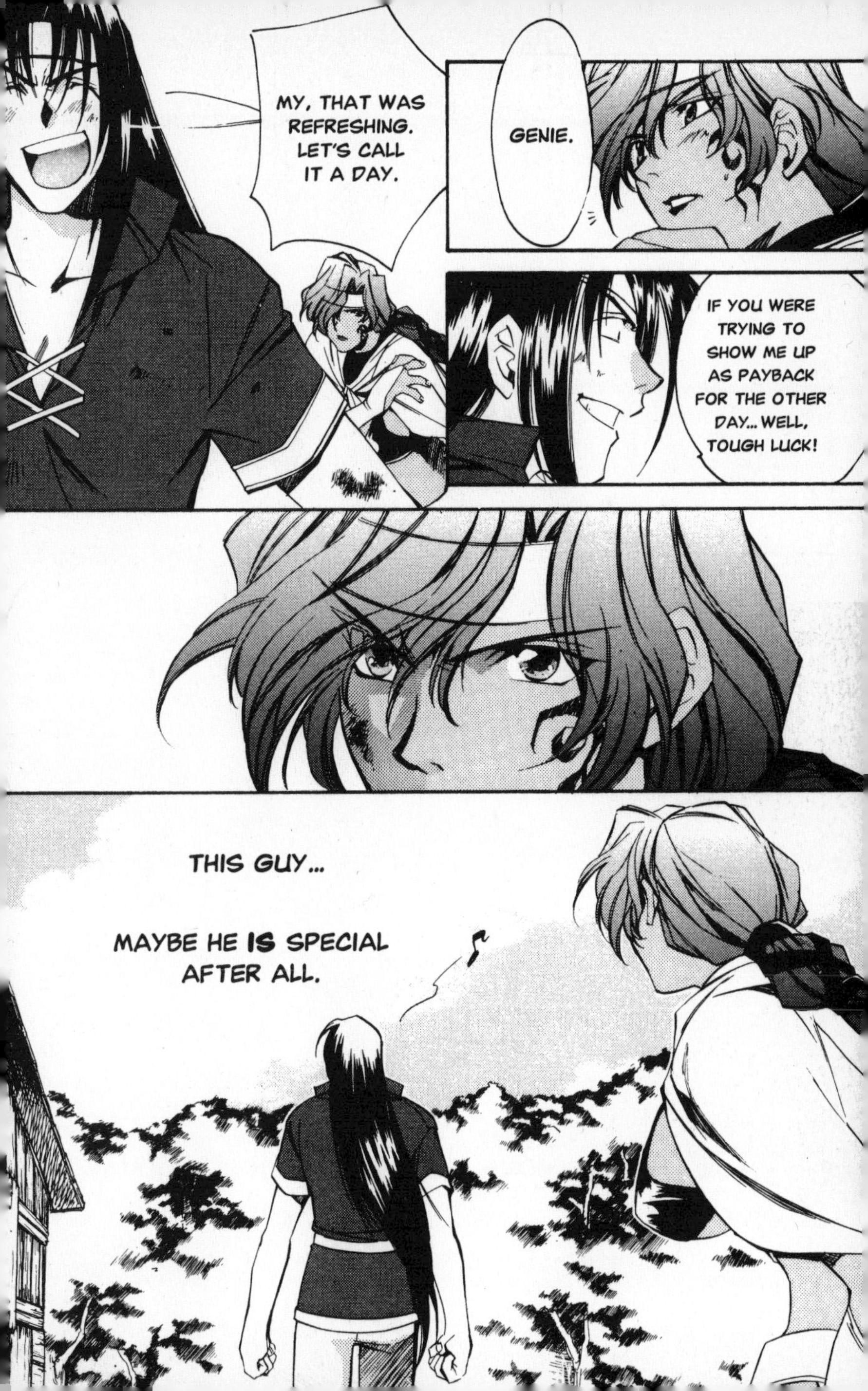
GENIE.
IF YOU WERE TRYING TO SHOW ME UP AS PAYBACK FOR THE OTHER DAY... WELL, TOUGH LUCK!
MY, THAT WAS REFRESHING. LET'S CALL IT A DAY.
THIS GUY...
MAYBE HE **IS** SPECIAL AFTER ALL.

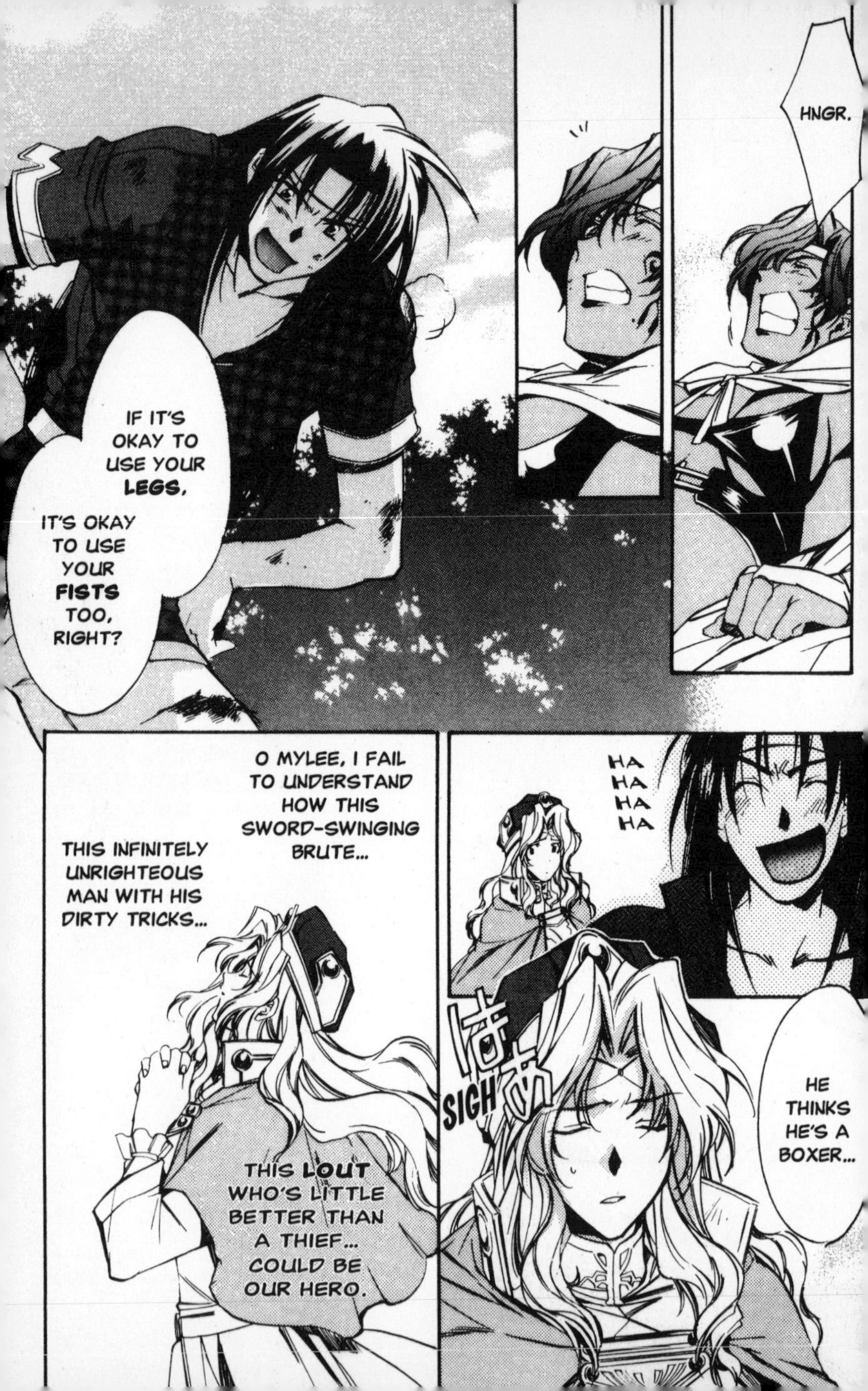
HNGR.
IF IT'S OKAY TO USE YOUR **LEGS**, IT'S OKAY TO USE YOUR **FISTS** TOO, RIGHT?
HA HA HA HA
SIGH はあ
HE THINKS HE'S A BOXER...
O MYLEE, I FAIL TO UNDERSTAND HOW THIS SWORD-SWINGING BRUTE...
THIS INFINITELY UNRIGHTEOUS MAN WITH HIS DIRTY TRICKS...
THIS **LOUT** WHO'S LITTLE BETTER THAN A THIEF... COULD BE OUR HERO.

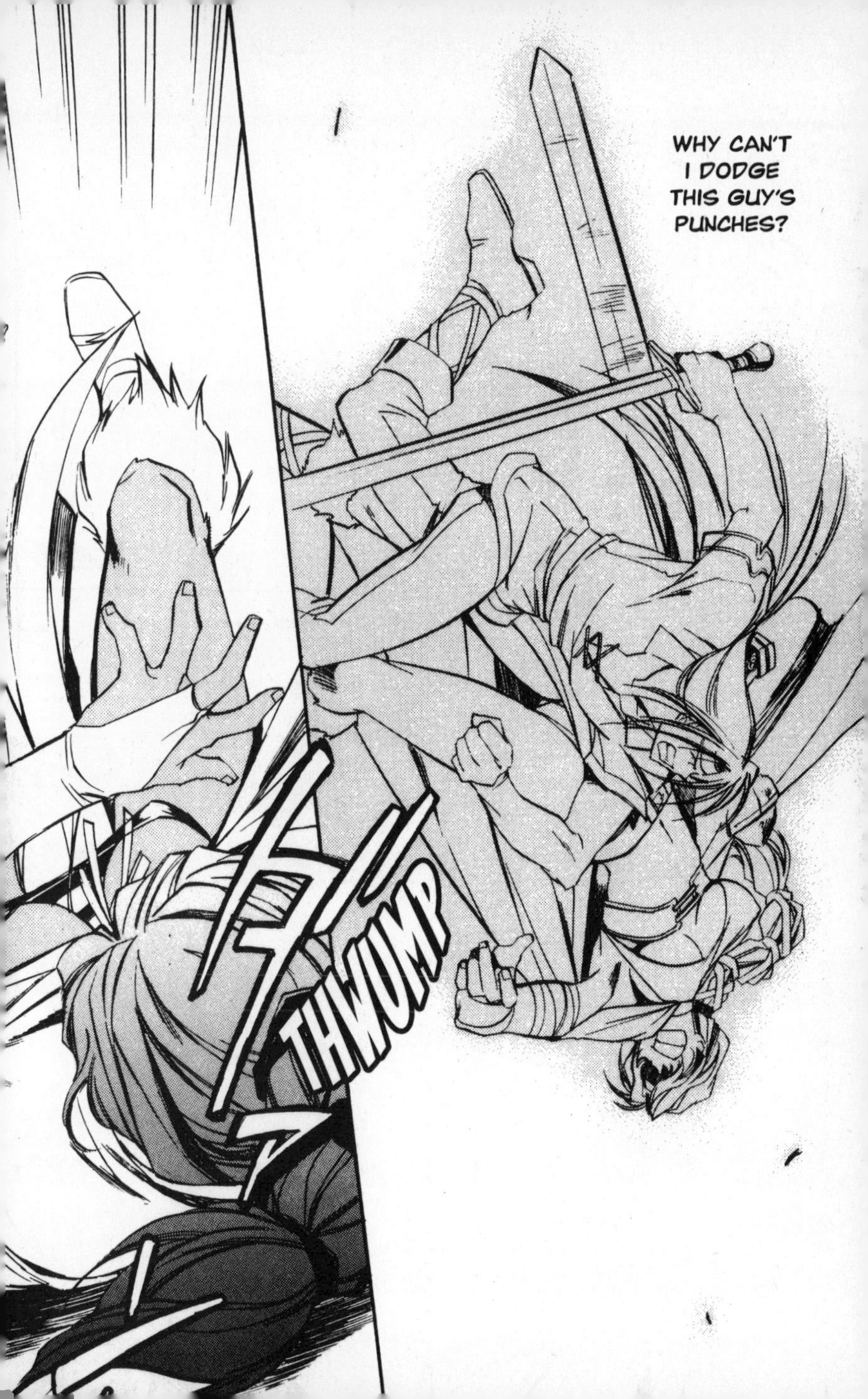
WHY CAN'T I DODGE THIS GUY'S PUNCHES?
THWUMP

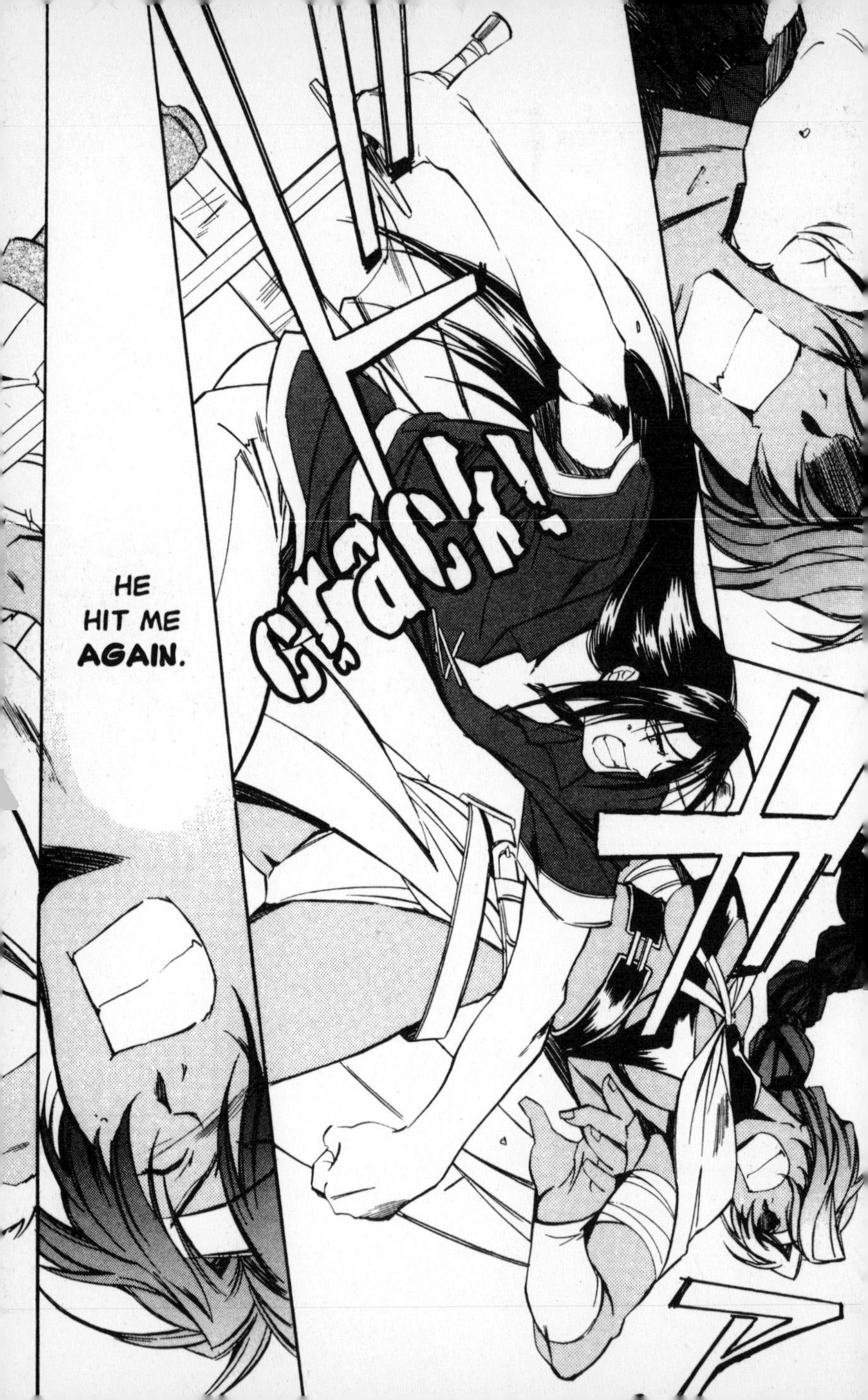
HE HIT ME AGAIN.
Crack!

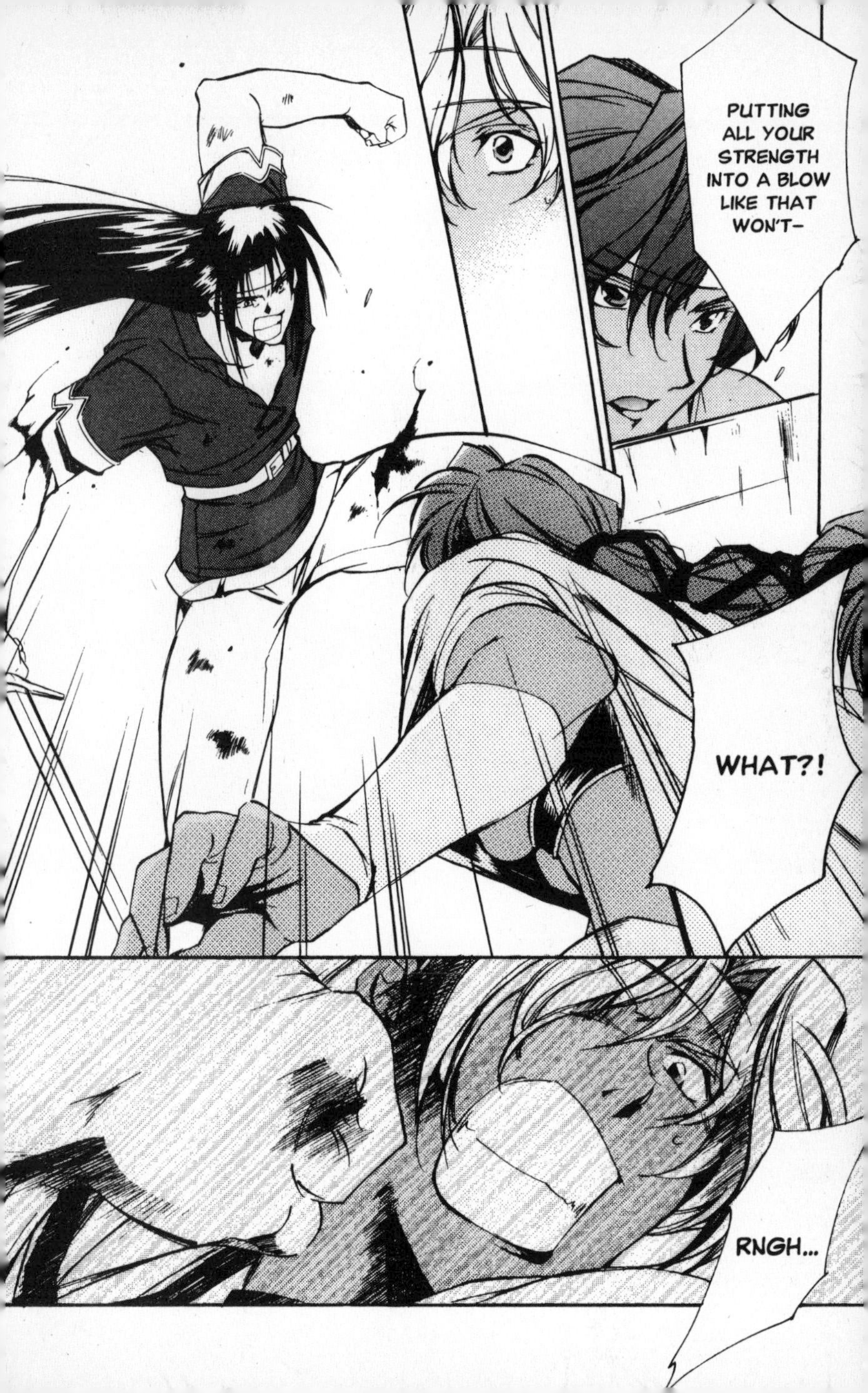
PUTTING ALL YOUR STRENGTH INTO A BLOW LIKE THAT WON'T-
WHAT?!
RNGH...

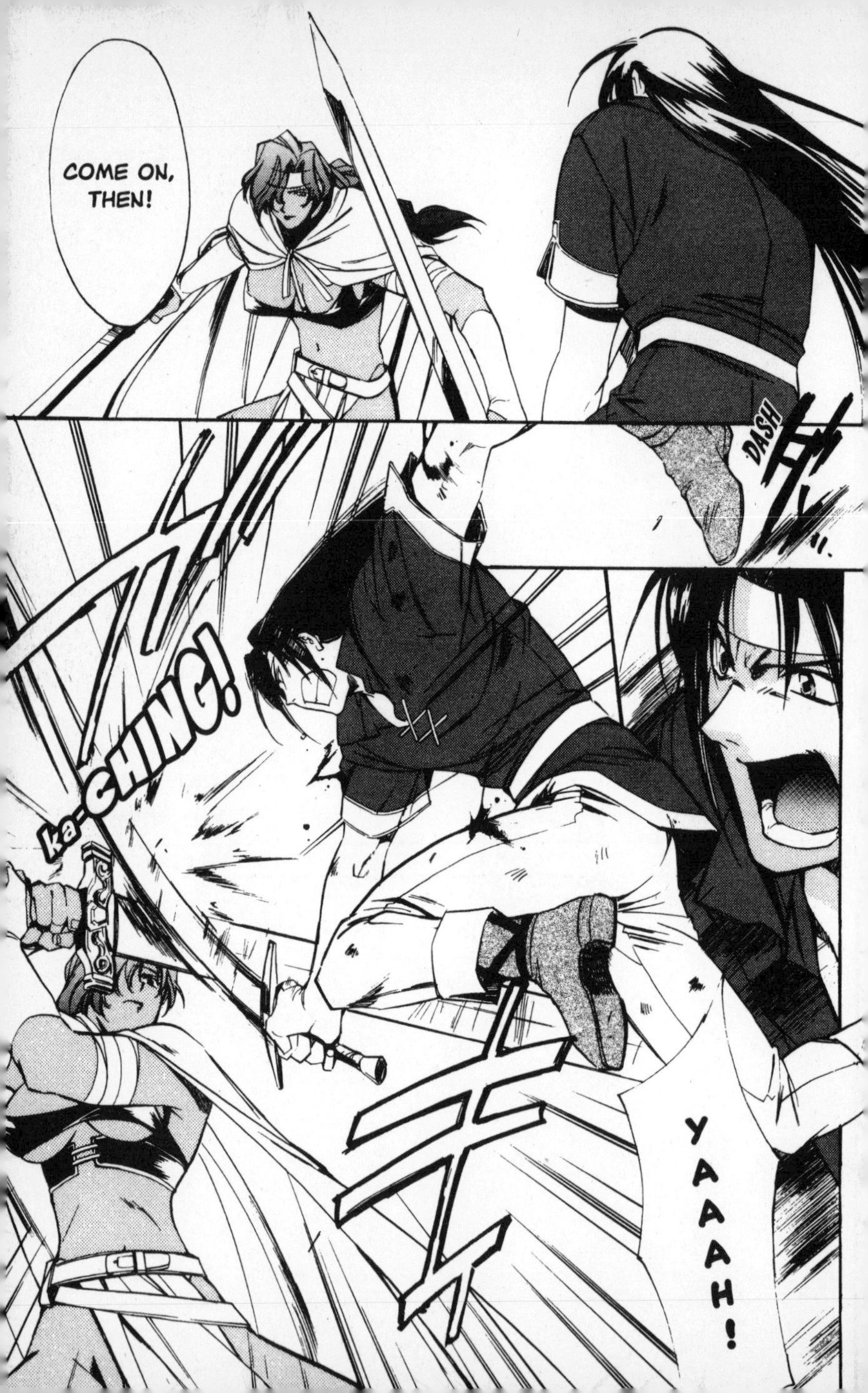
COME ON, THEN!
DASH
ka-CHING!
YAAAAH!

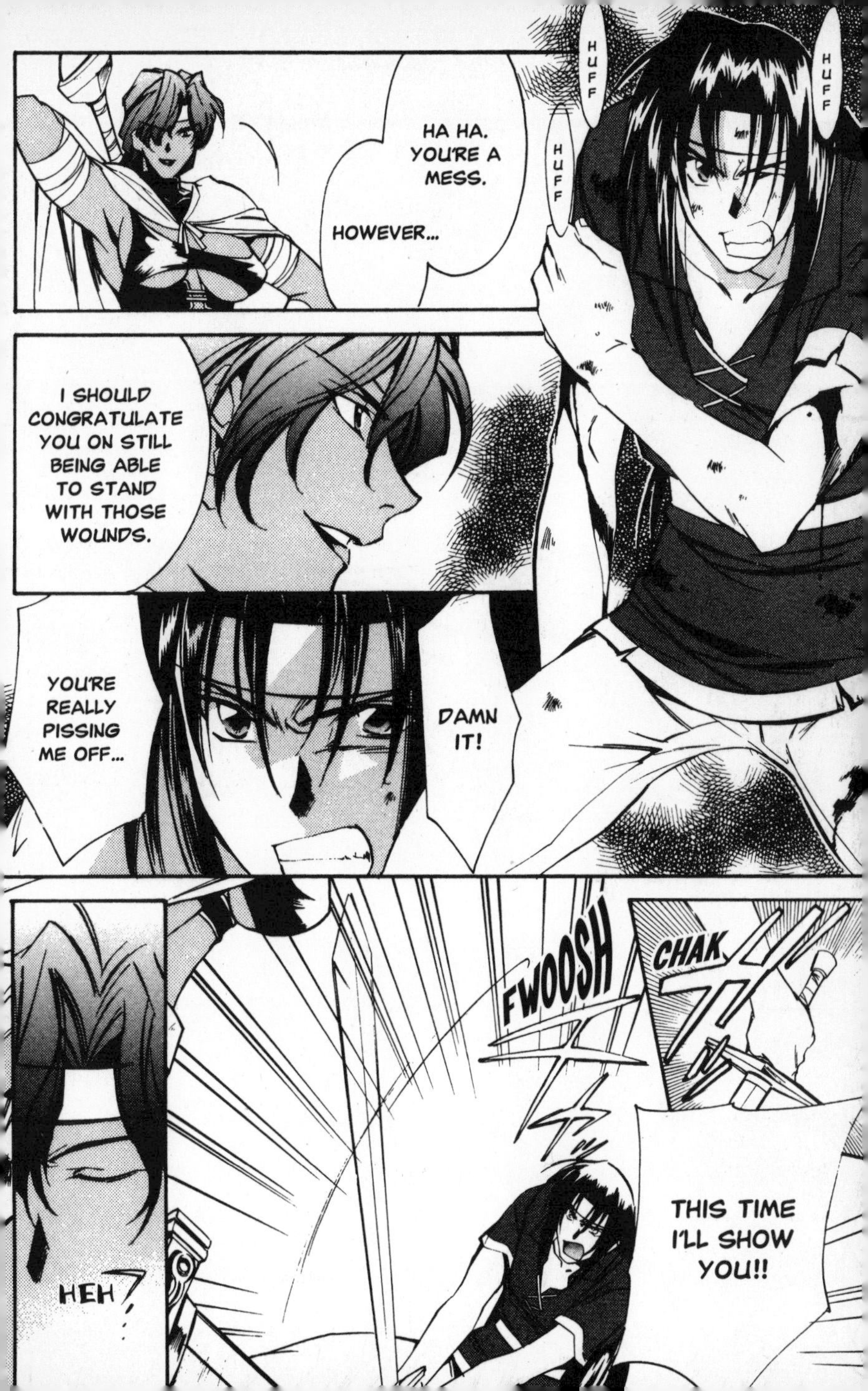
HUFF
HUFF
HUFF
HA HA. YOU'RE A MESS.
HOWEVER...
I SHOULD CONGRATULATE YOU ON STILL BEING ABLE TO STAND WITH THOSE WOUNDS.
DAMN IT!
YOU'RE REALLY PISSING ME OFF...
CHAK
FWOOSH
THIS TIME I'LL SHOW YOU!!
HEH

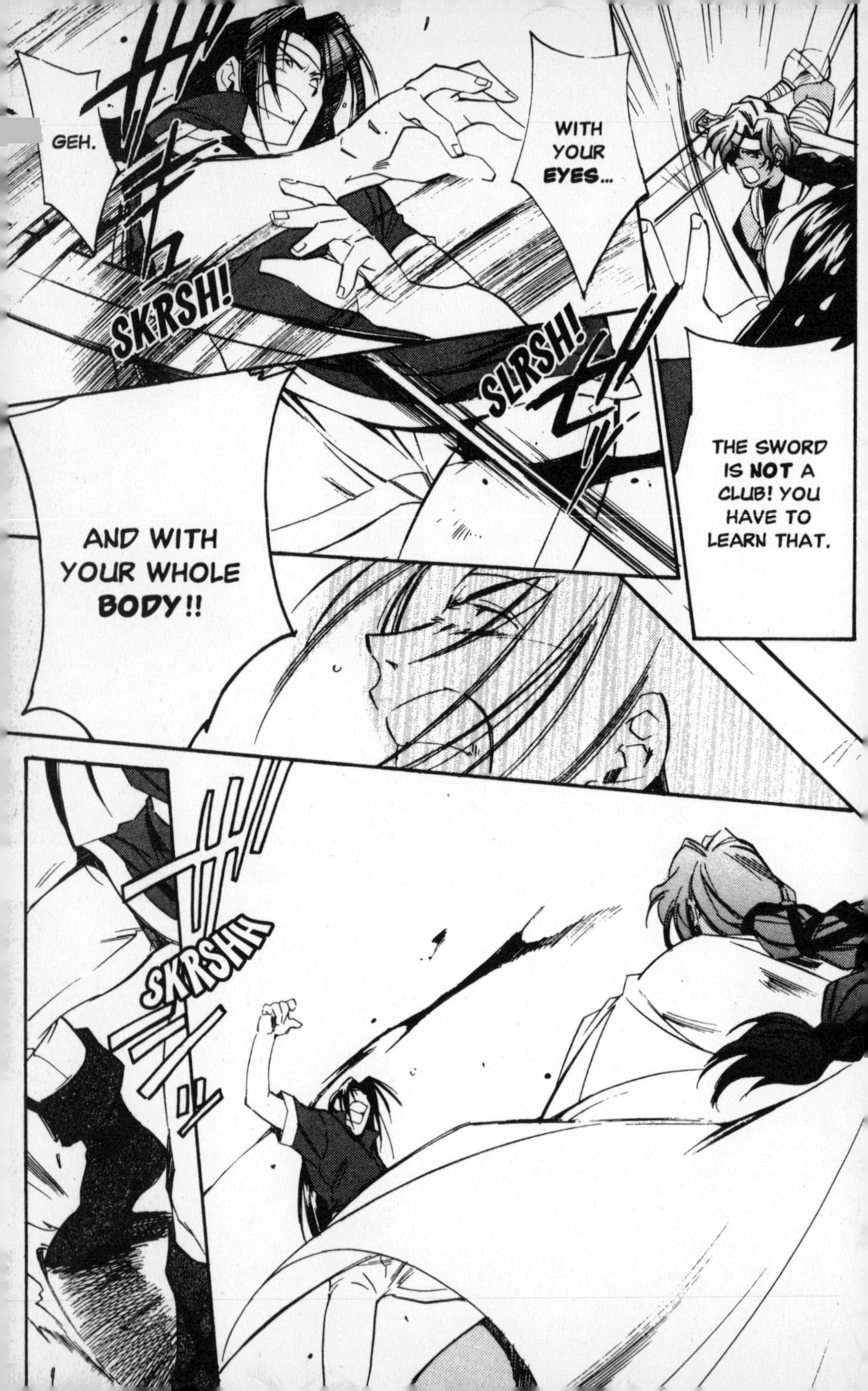
WITH YOUR EYES...
GEH.
SKRSH!
SLRSH!
THE SWORD IS NOT A CLUB! YOU HAVE TO LEARN THAT.
AND WITH YOUR WHOLE BODY!!
SKRSHH

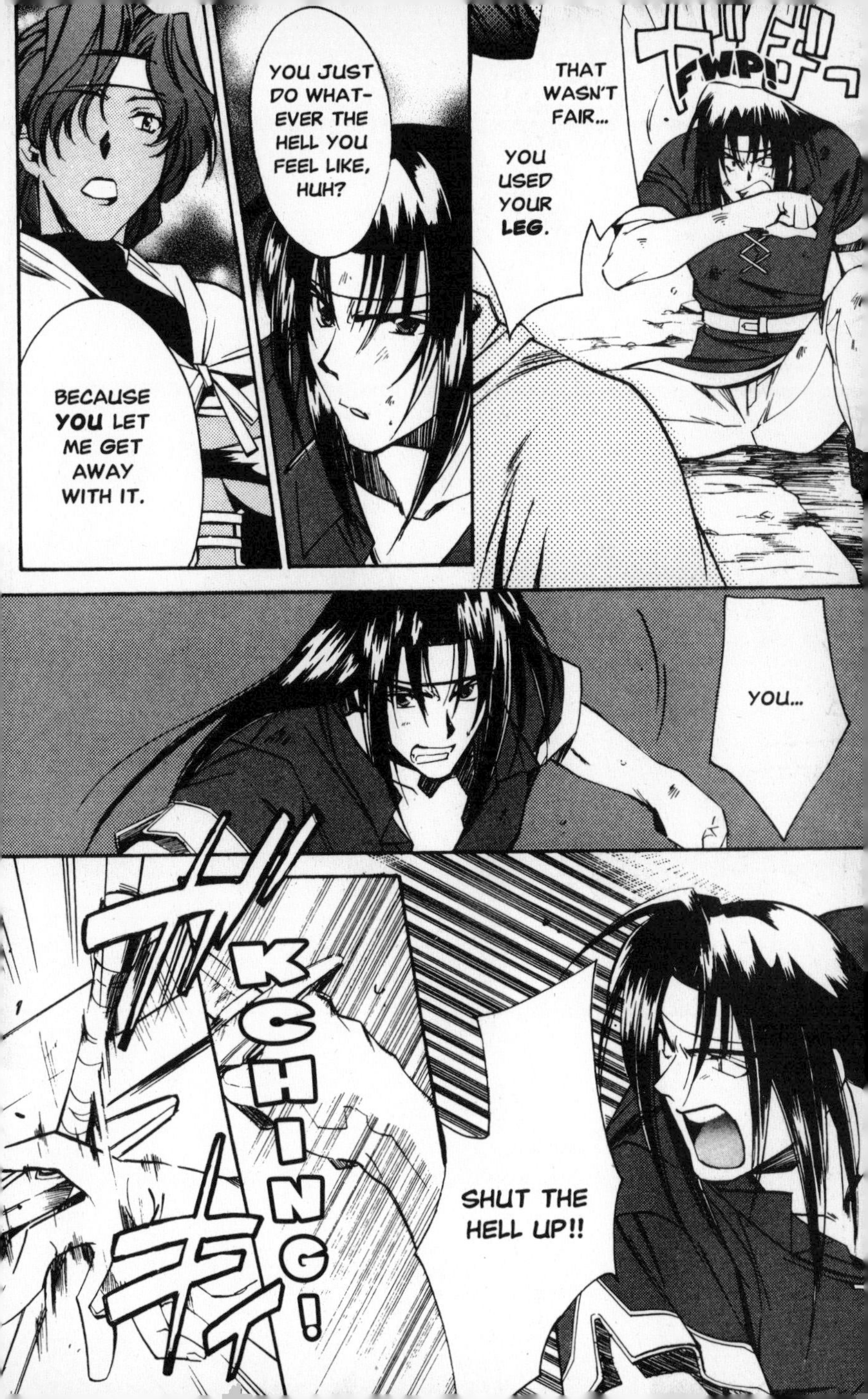
FWP!
THAT WASN'T FAIR...
YOU USED YOUR LEG.
YOU JUST DO WHAT-EVER THE HELL YOU FEEL LIKE, HUH?
BECAUSE YOU LET ME GET AWAY WITH IT.
YOU...
KCHING!
SHUT THE HELL UP!!

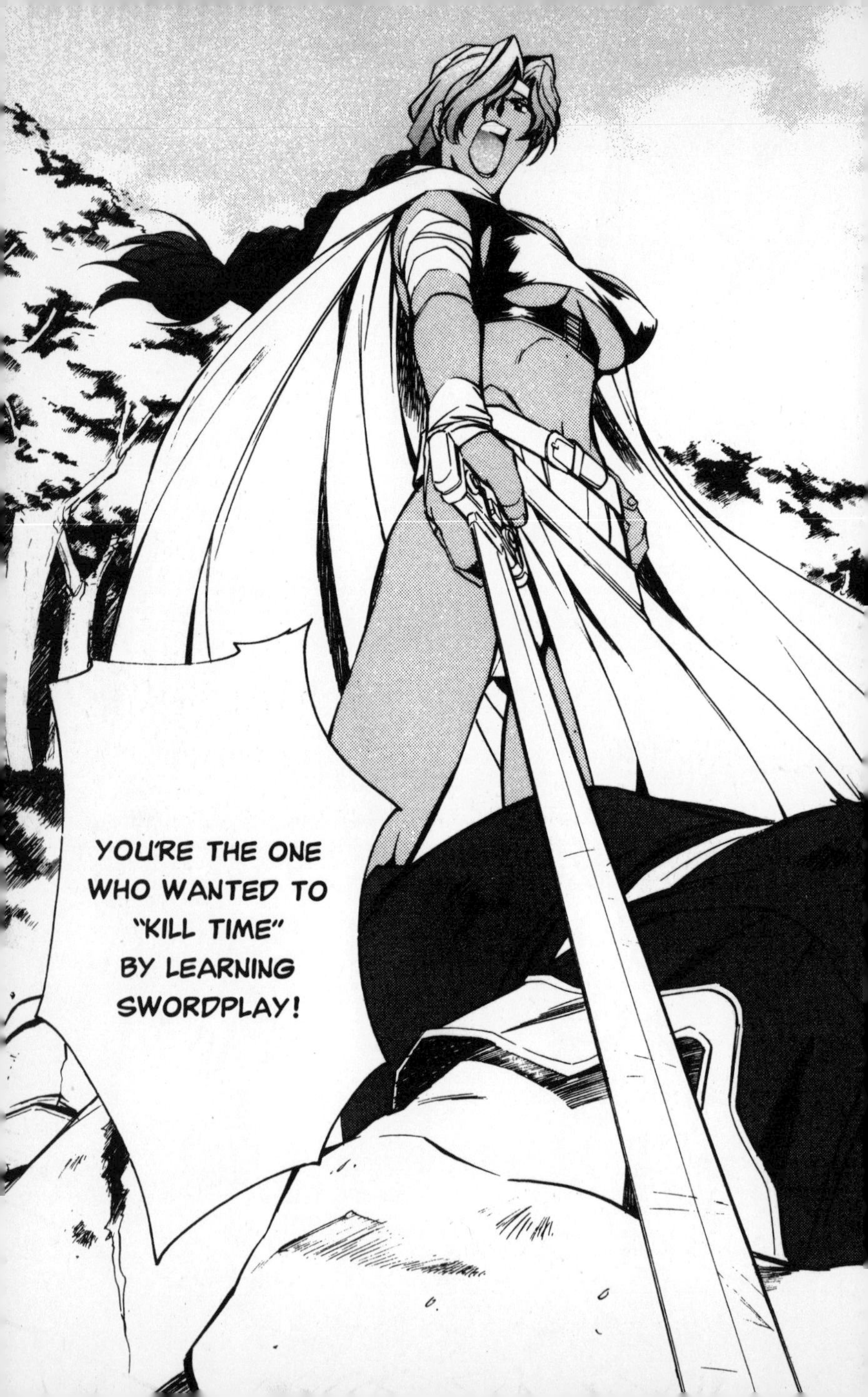
YOU'RE THE ONE WHO WANTED TO "KILL TIME" BY LEARNING SWORDPLAY!

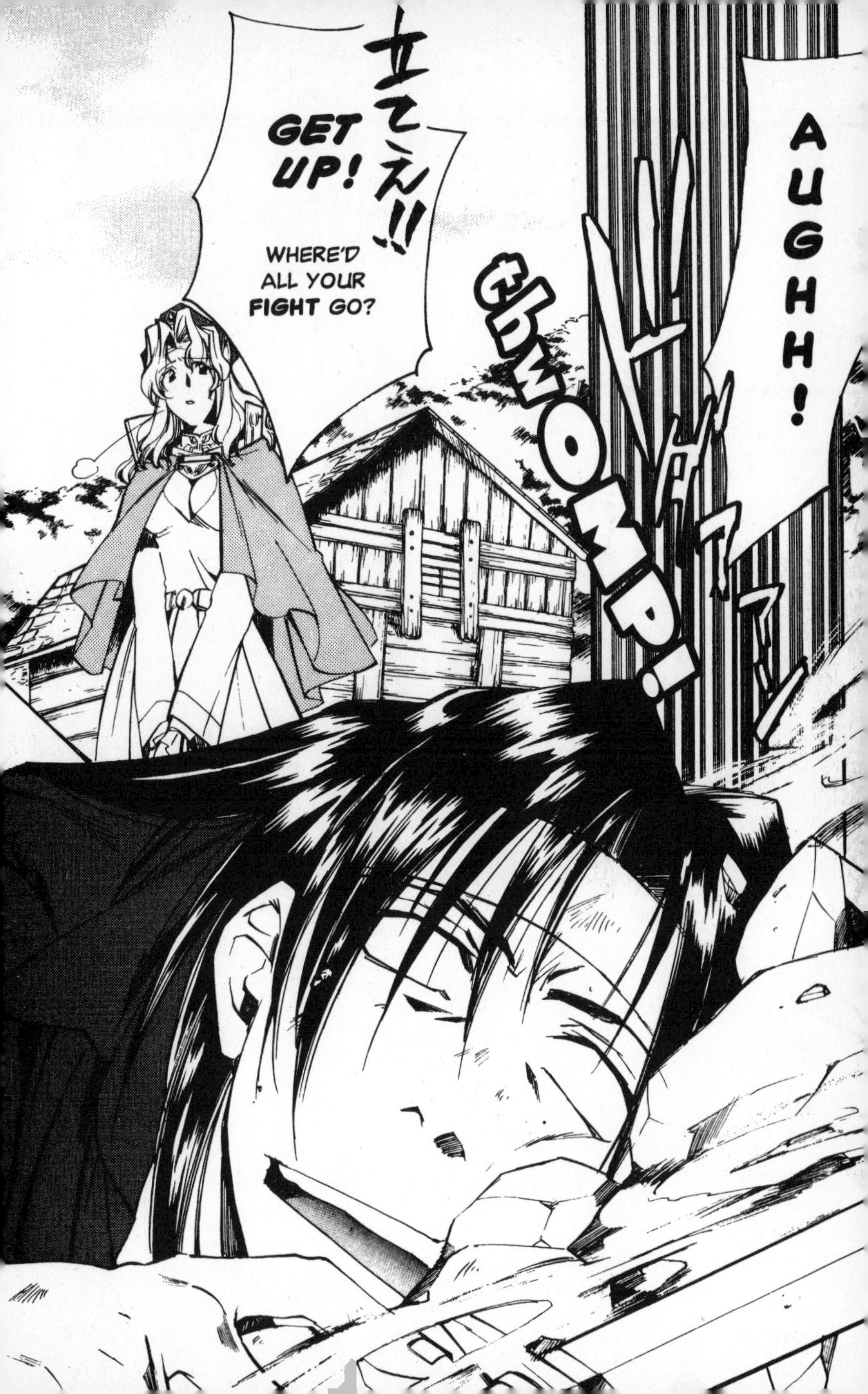
AUGHH!
WHOMP!
立てぇ!!
GET UP!
WHERE'D ALL YOUR FIGHT GO?

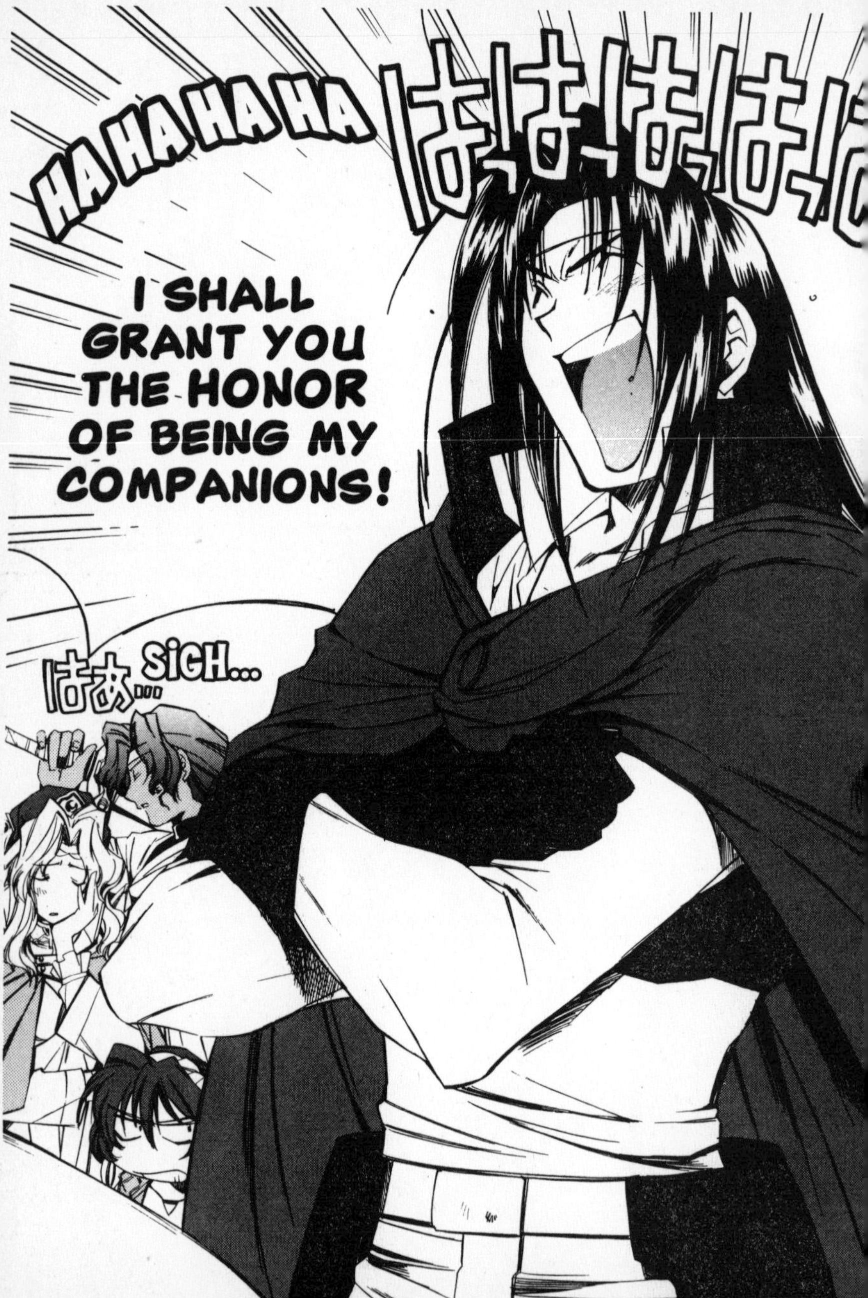
HA HA HA HA HA
はっはっはっはっは
I SHALL GRANT YOU THE HONOR OF BEING MY COMPANIONS!
はあ… SIGH...

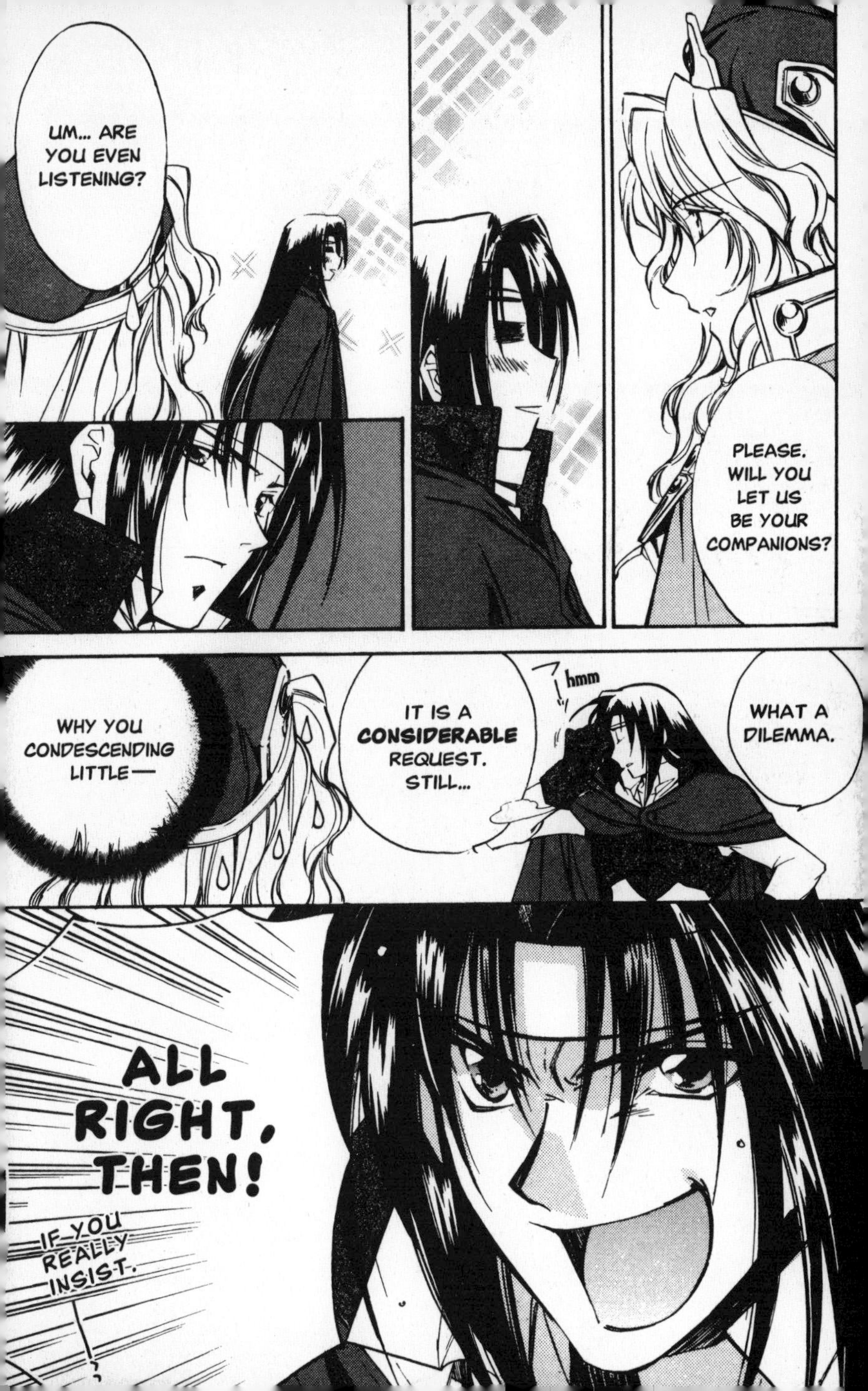
PLEASE. WILL YOU LET US BE YOUR COMPANIONS?
UM... ARE YOU EVEN LISTENING?
WHAT A DILEMMA.
hmm
IT IS A **CONSIDERABLE** REQUEST. STILL...
WHY YOU CONDESCENDING LITTLE—
ALL RIGHT, THEN!
IF YOU REALLY INSIST.

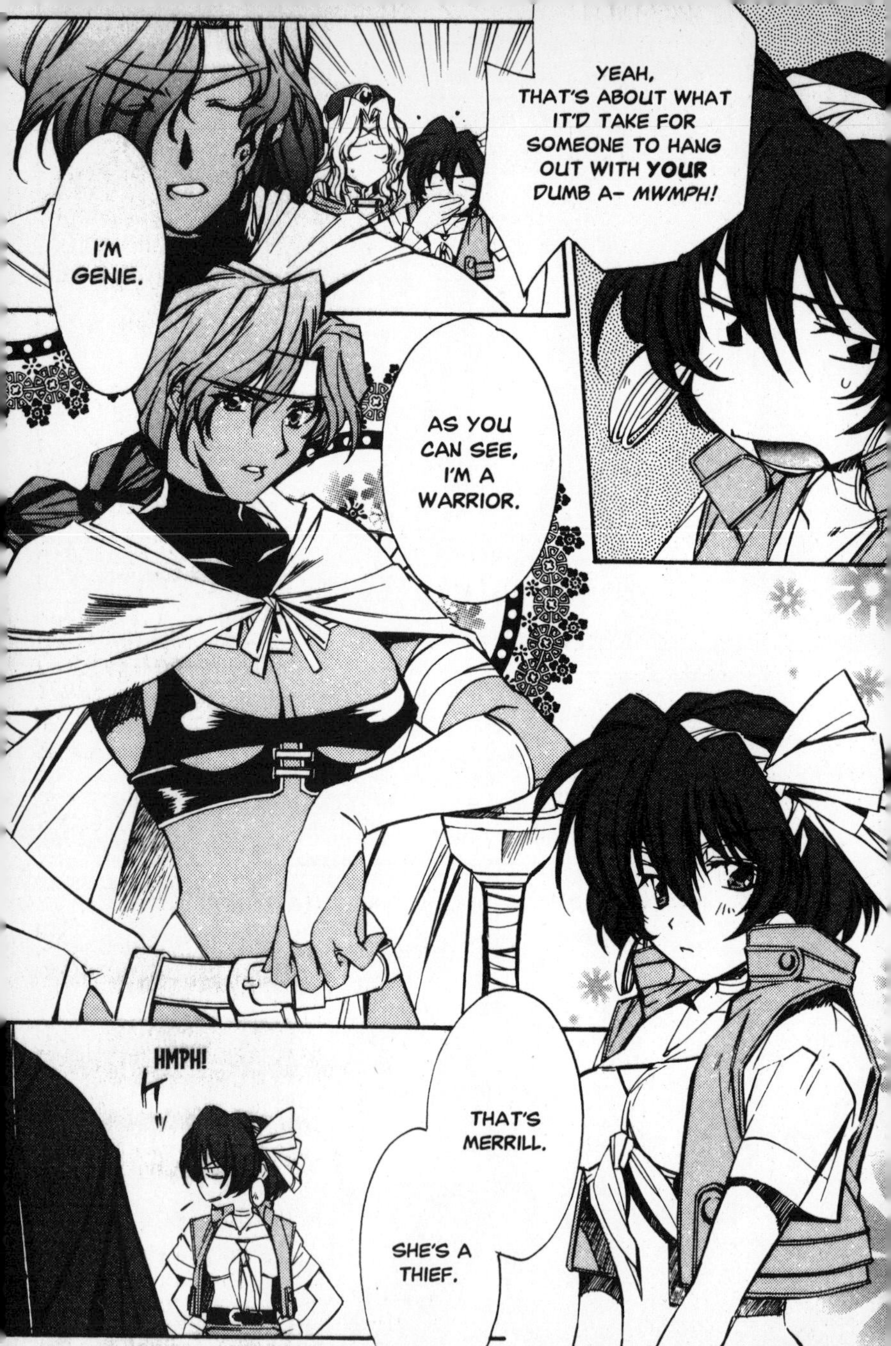

YEAH, THAT'S ABOUT WHAT IT'D TAKE FOR SOMEONE TO HANG OUT WITH **YOUR** DUMB A- *MWMPH!*
I'M GENIE.
AS YOU CAN SEE, I'M A WARRIOR.
THAT'S MERRILL.
SHE'S A THIEF.
HMPH!

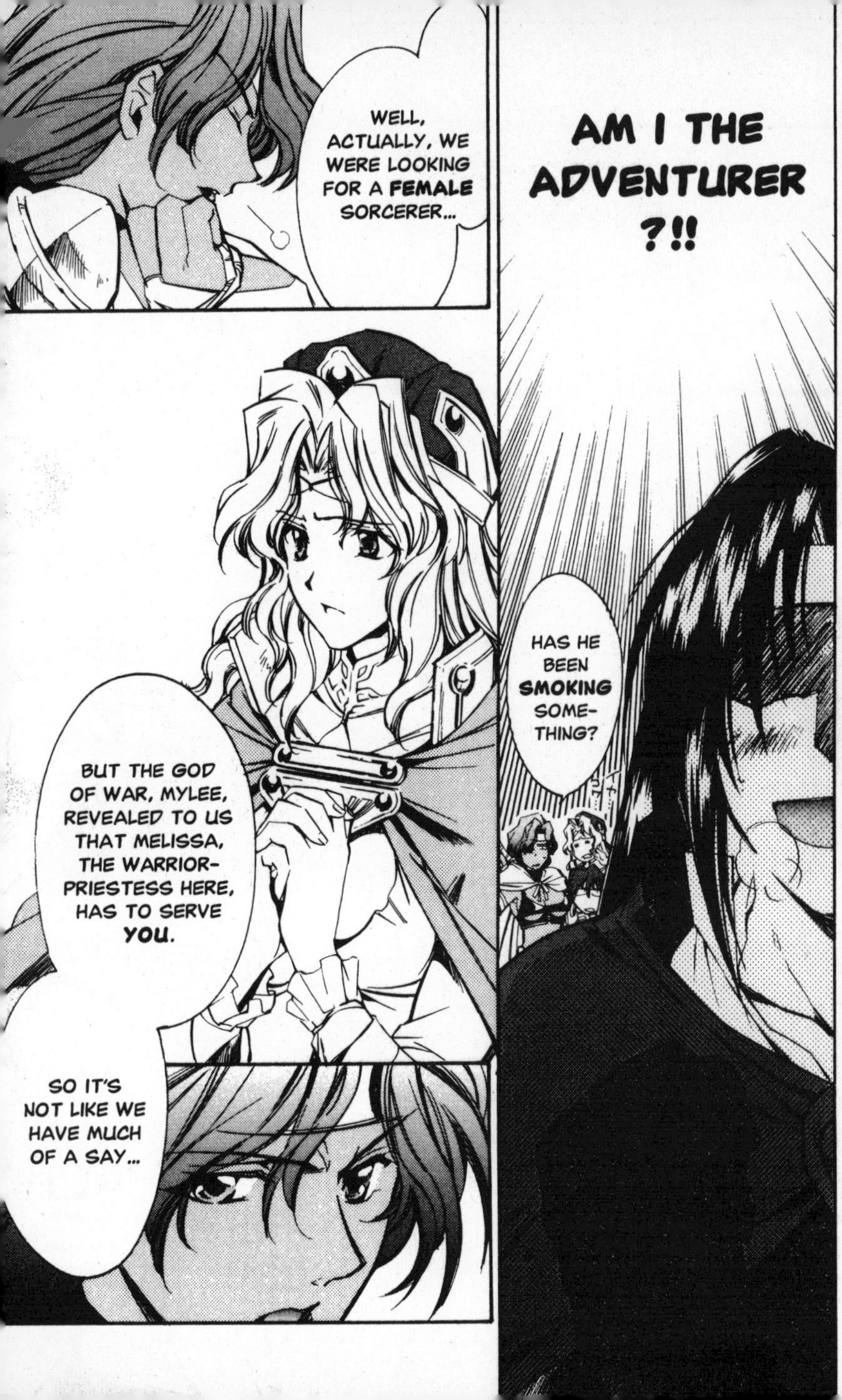
AM I THE ADVENTURER ?!!
HAS HE BEEN SMOKING SOME-THING?
WELL, ACTUALLY, WE WERE LOOKING FOR A **FEMALE** SORCERER...
BUT THE GOD OF WAR, MYLEE, REVEALED TO US THAT MELISSA, THE WARRIOR-PRIESTESS HERE, HAS TO SERVE **YOU**.
SO IT'S NOT LIKE WE HAVE MUCH OF A SAY...

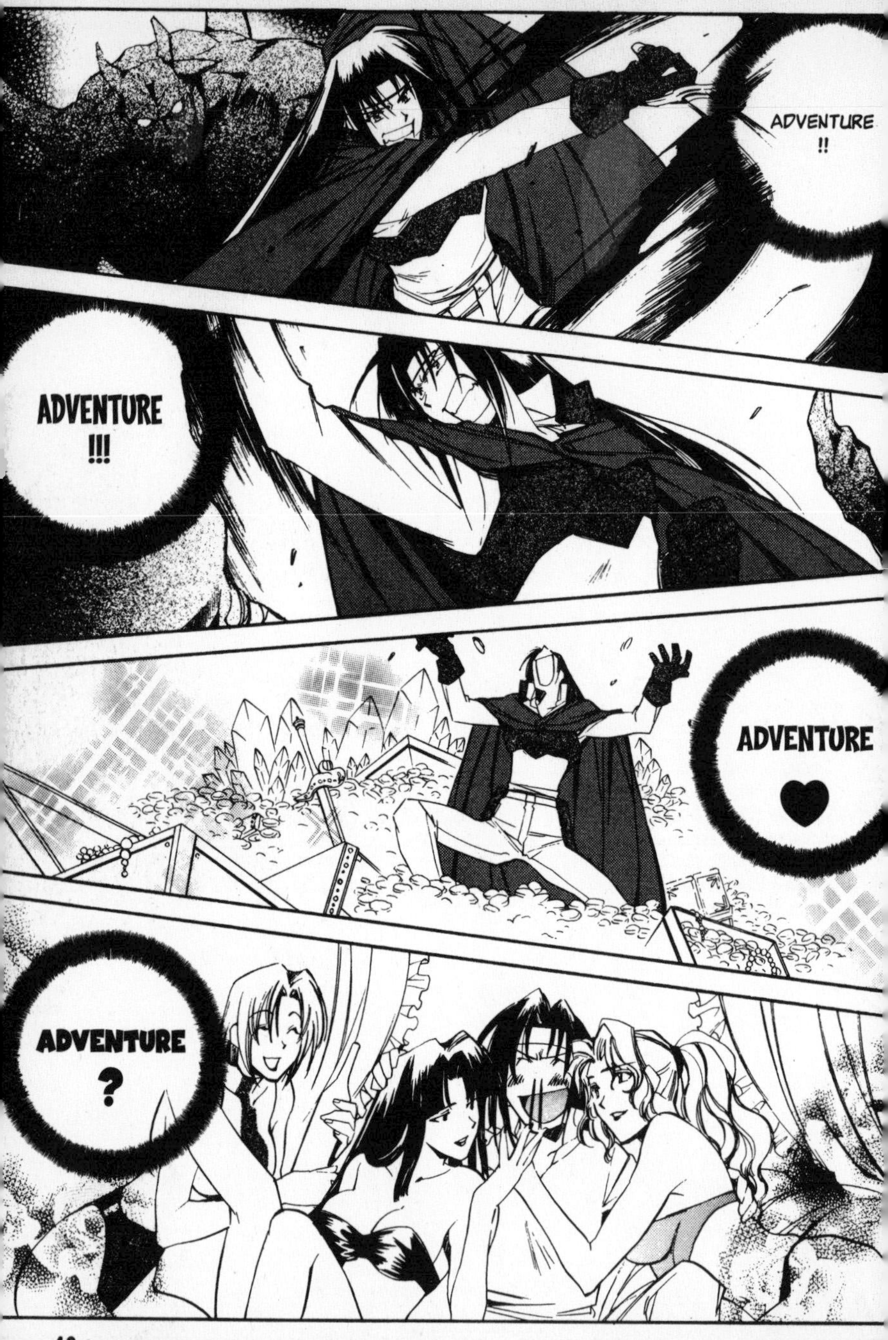
ADVENTURE !!
ADVENTURE !!!
ADVENTURE ♥
ADVENTURE ?

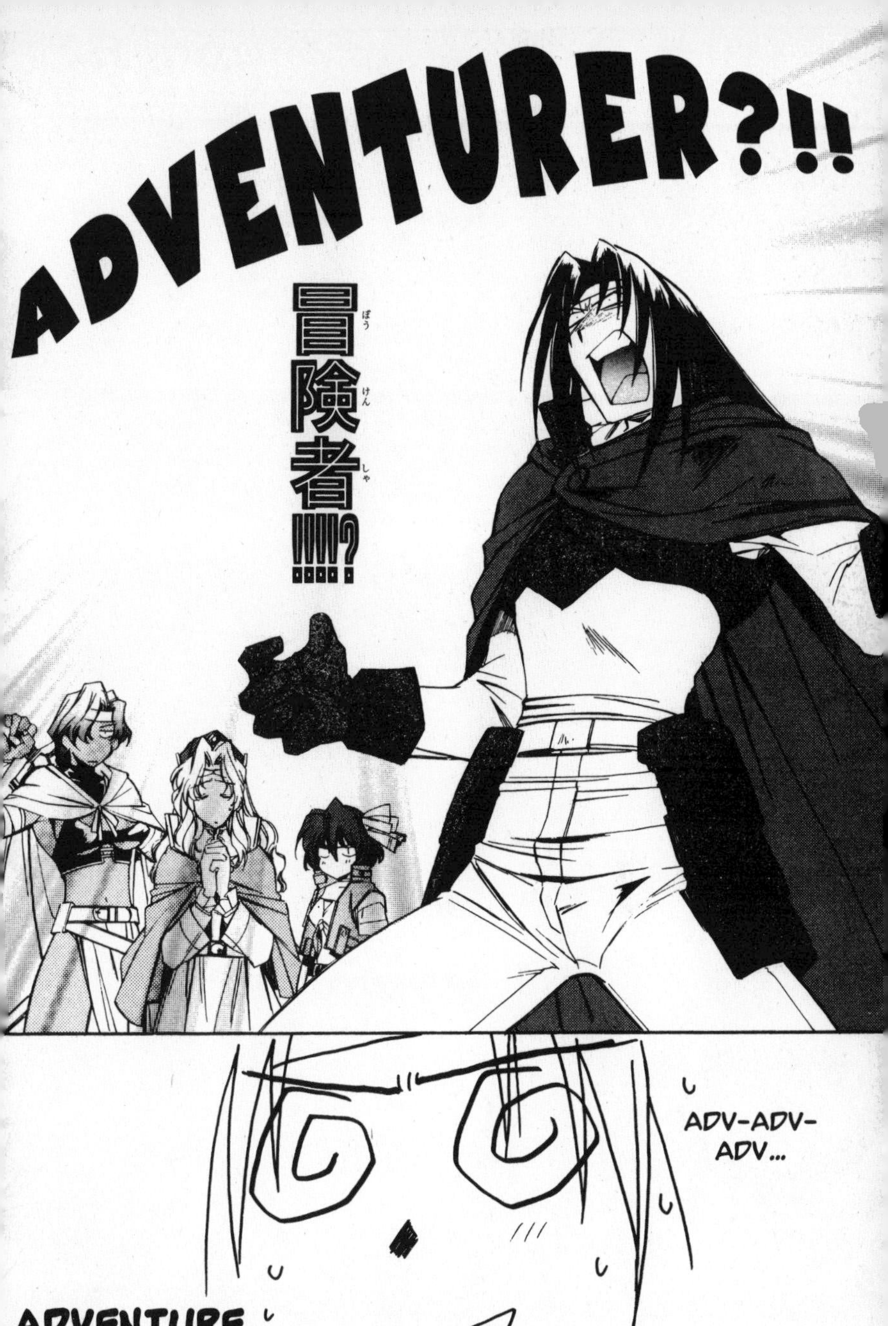
ADVENTURER?!!
冒険者!!!!?
ADV-ADV-ADV...
ADVENTURE...

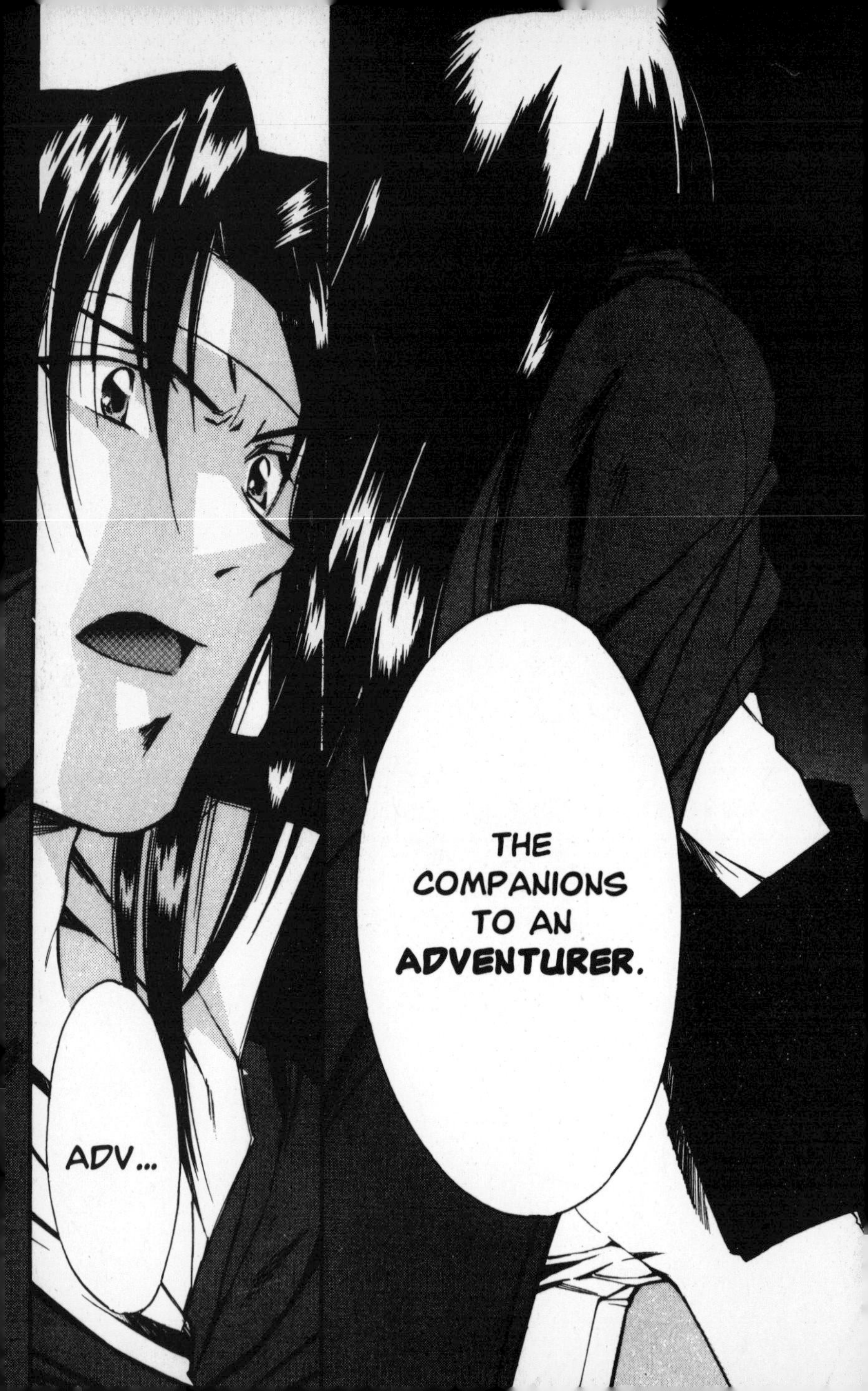
THE COMPANIONS TO AN ADVENTURER.
ADV...

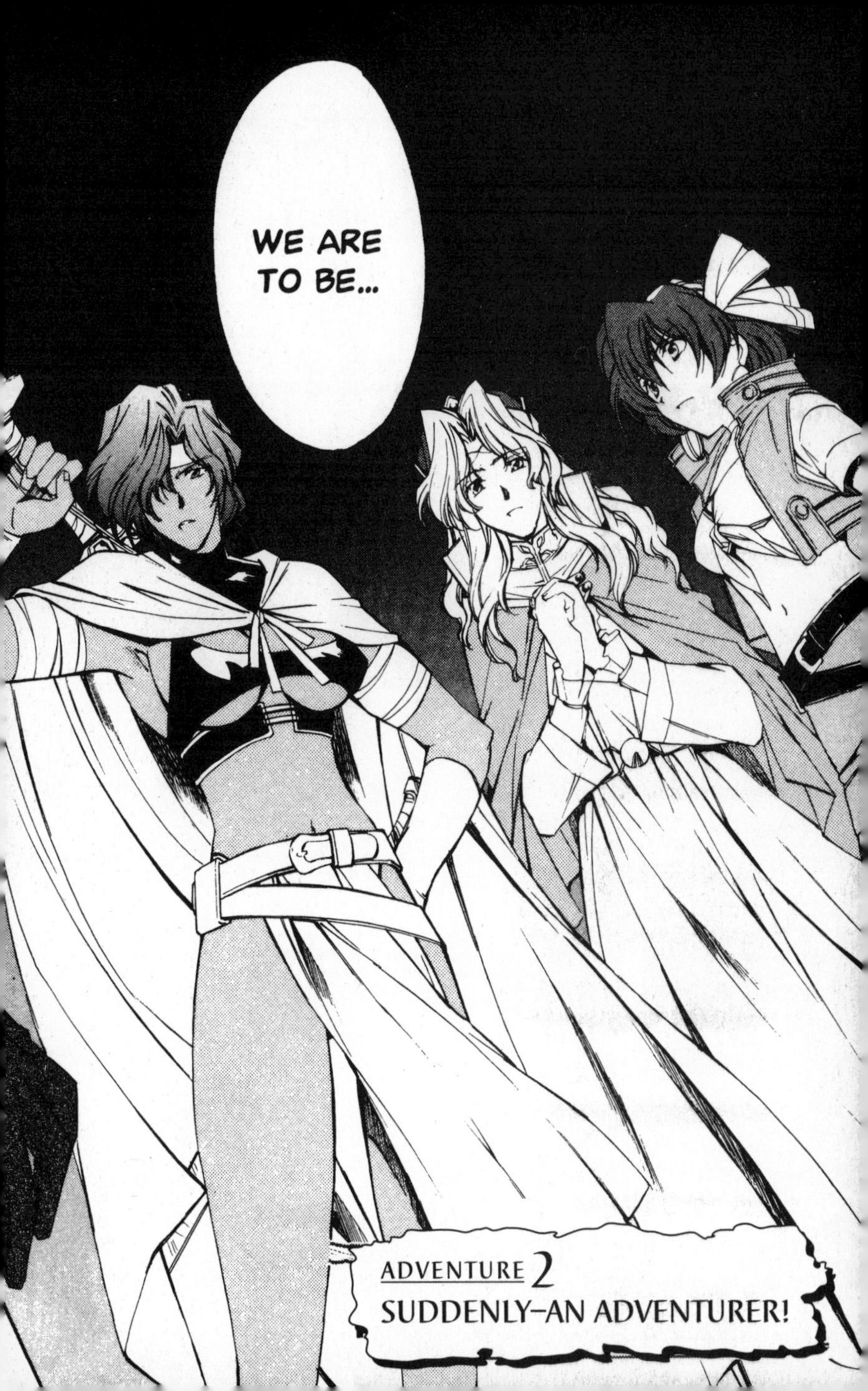
WE ARE TO BE...
ADVENTURE 2
SUDDENLY—AN ADVENTURER!

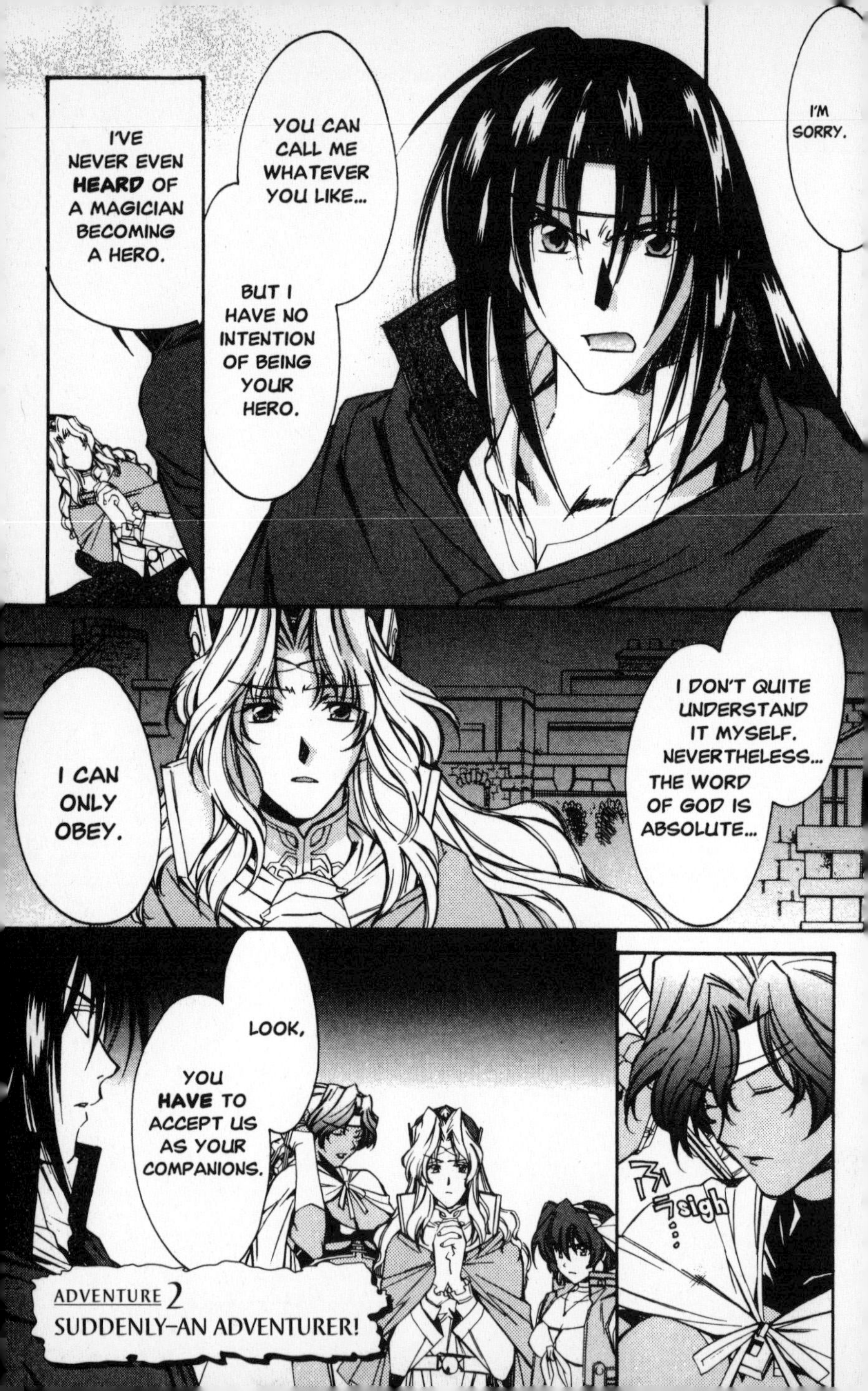

I'M SORRY.
YOU CAN CALL ME WHATEVER YOU LIKE...
BUT I HAVE NO INTENTION OF BEING YOUR HERO.
I'VE NEVER EVEN HEARD OF A MAGICIAN BECOMING A HERO.
I DON'T QUITE UNDERSTAND IT MYSELF. NEVERTHELESS... THE WORD OF GOD IS ABSOLUTE...
I CAN ONLY OBEY.
sigh...
LOOK,
YOU HAVE TO ACCEPT US AS YOUR COMPANIONS.
ADVENTURE 2
SUDDENLY—AN ADVENTURER!

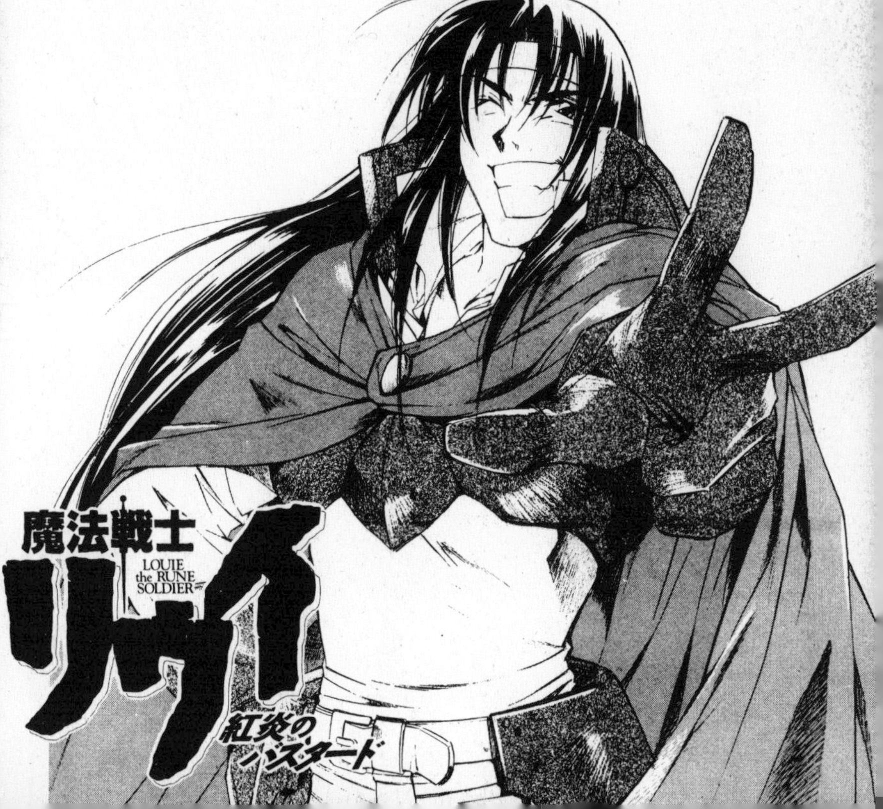
魔法戦士
リウイ
LOUIE the RUNE SOLDIER
紅炎のバスタード

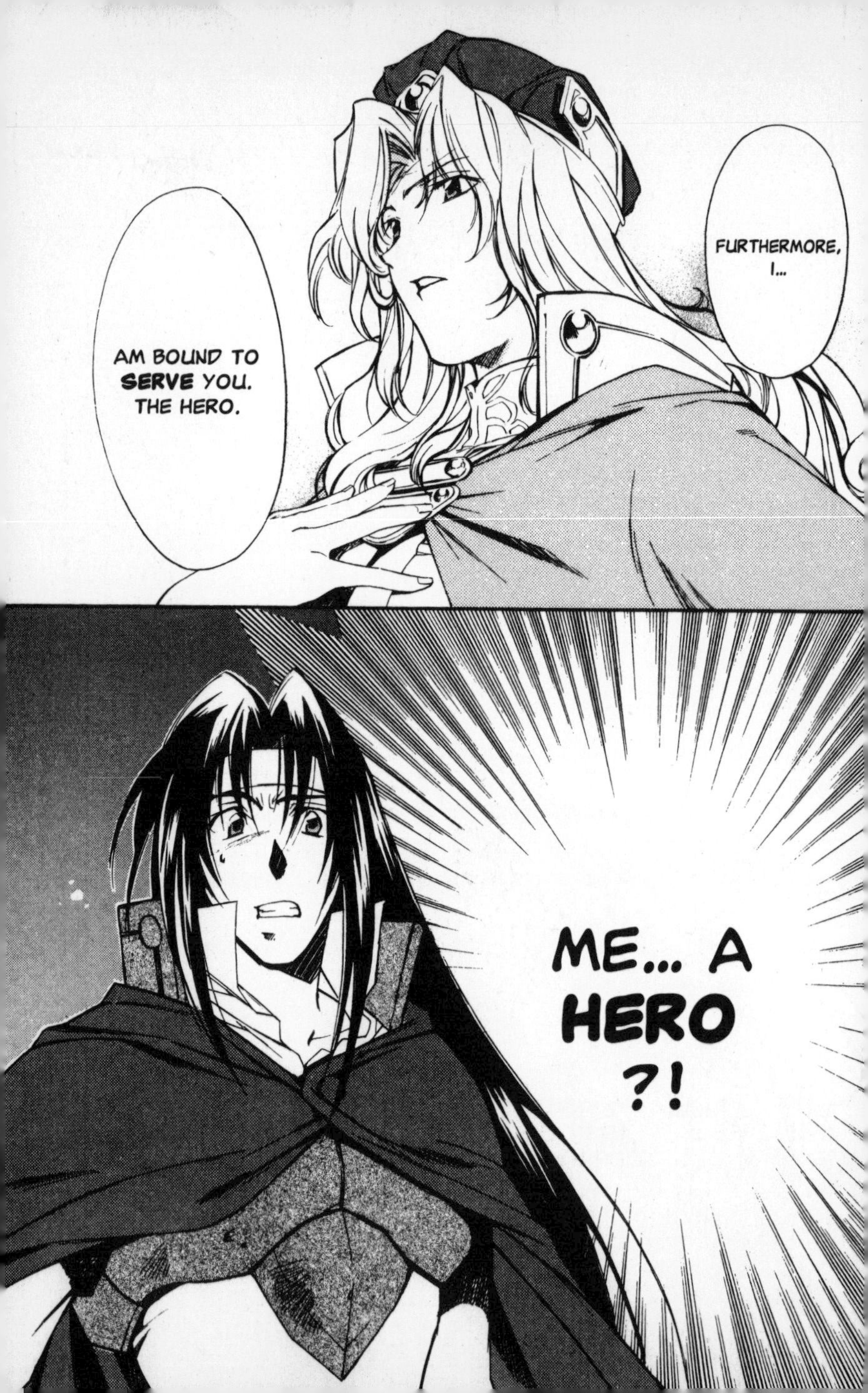
FURTHERMORE, I...
AM BOUND TO SERVE YOU. THE HERO.
ME... A HERO ?!

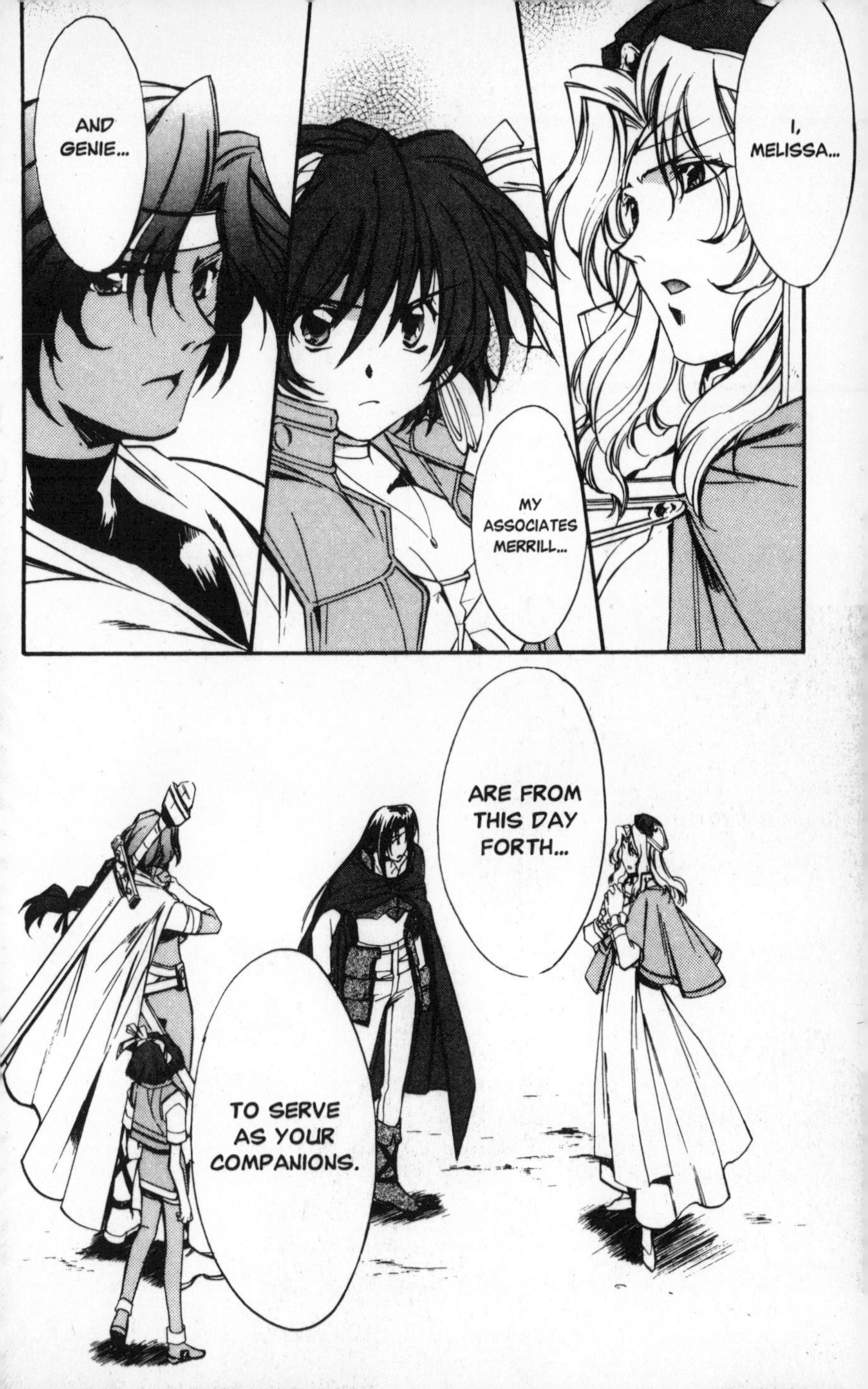
I, MELISSA...
MY ASSOCIATES MERRILL...
AND GENIE...
ARE FROM THIS DAY FORTH...
TO SERVE AS YOUR COMPANIONS.

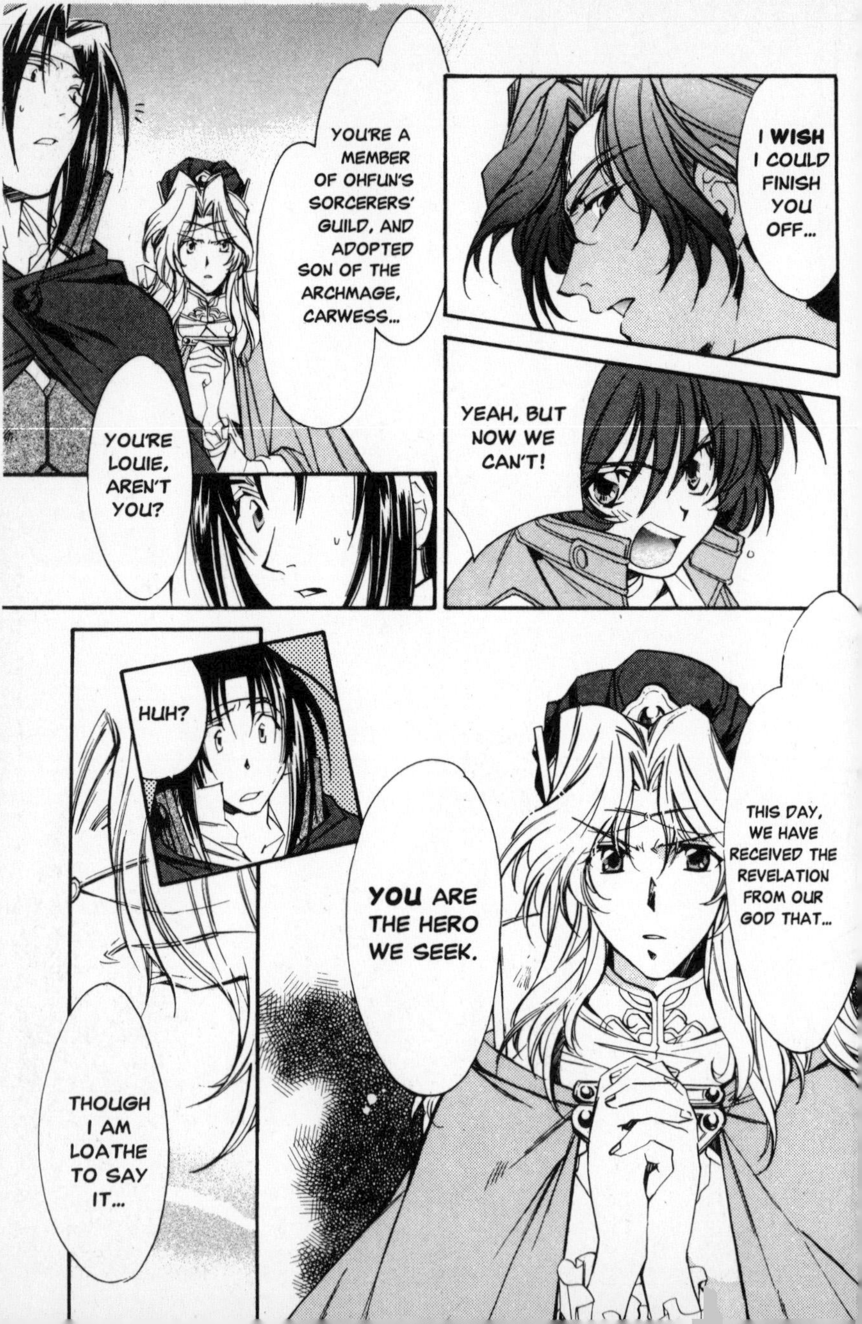
I **WISH** I COULD FINISH YOU OFF...
YEAH, BUT NOW WE CAN'T!
YOU'RE A MEMBER OF OHFUN'S SORCERERS' GUILD, AND ADOPTED SON OF THE ARCHMAGE, CARWESS...
YOU'RE LOUIE, AREN'T YOU?
THIS DAY, WE HAVE RECEIVED THE REVELATION FROM OUR GOD THAT...
YOU ARE THE HERO WE SEEK.
HUH?
THOUGH I AM LOATHE TO SAY IT...

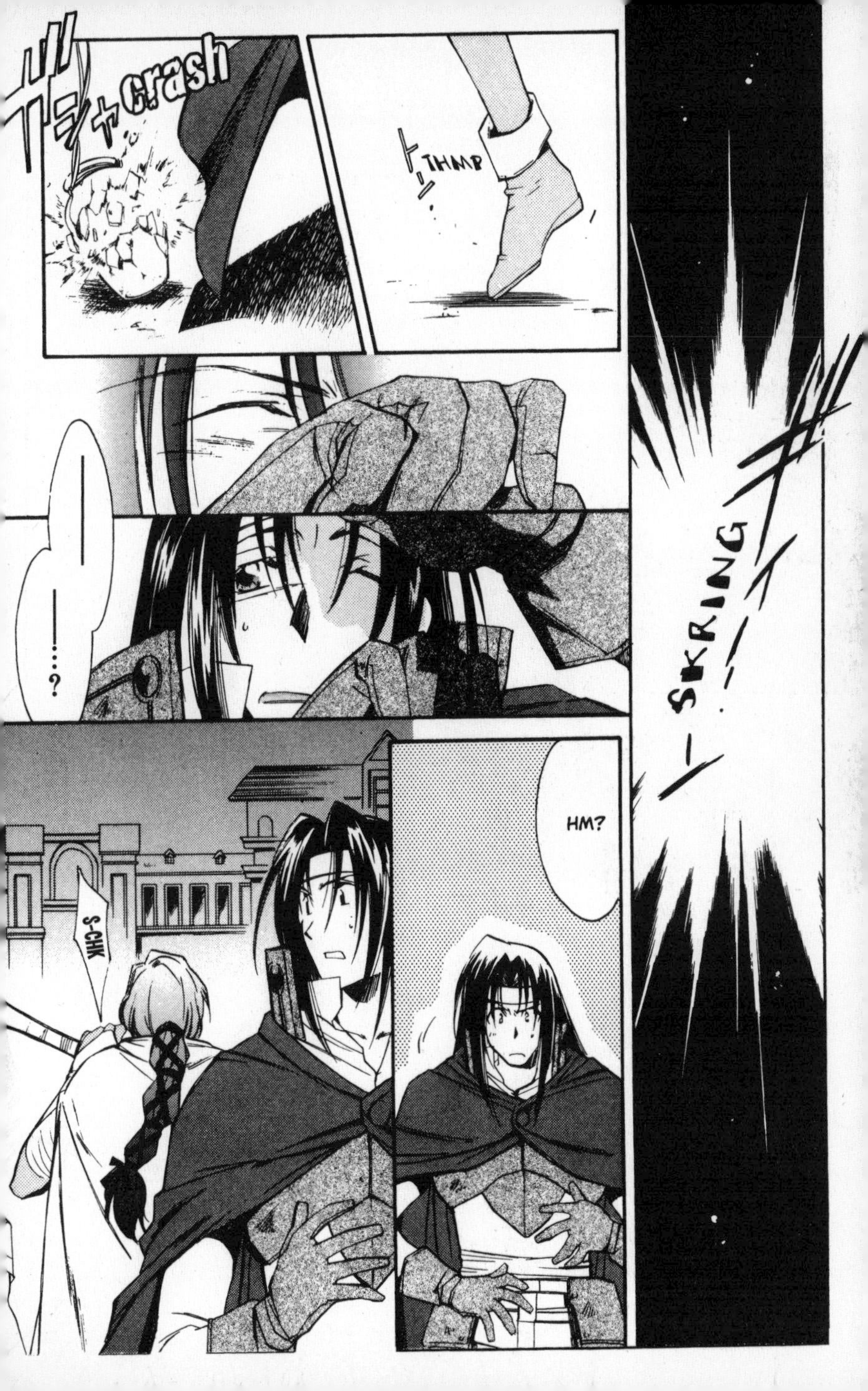
SKRING
THMP
crash
—— ....?
HM?
S-CHK

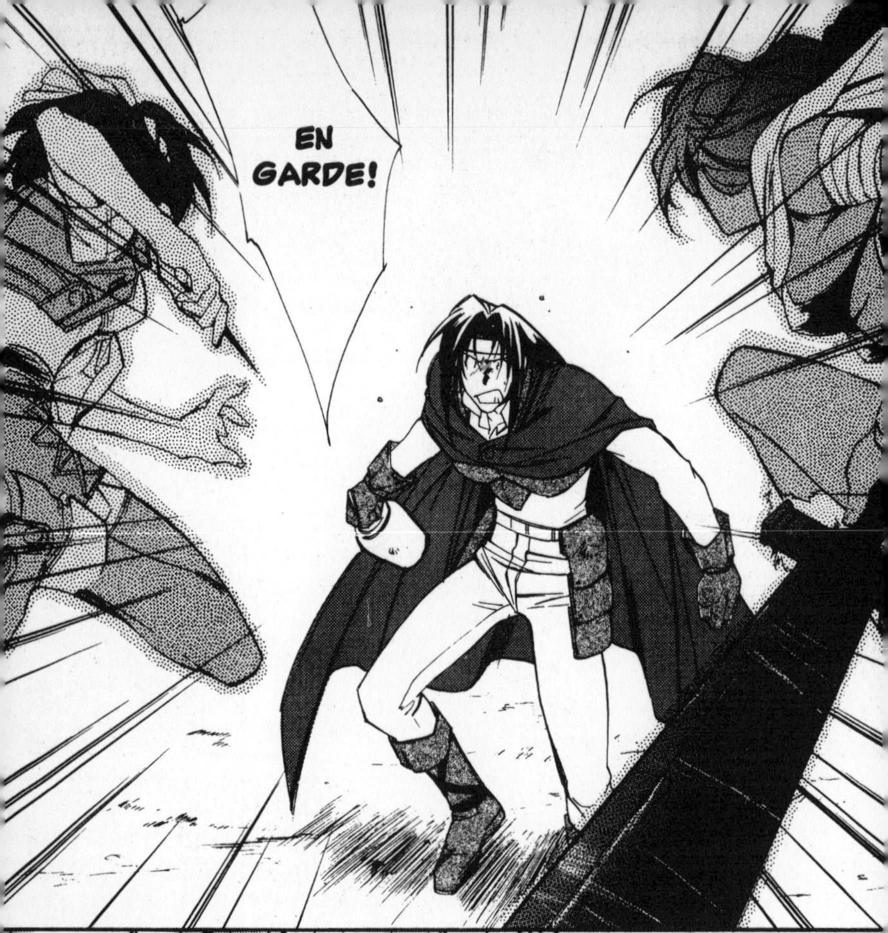
EN GARDE!

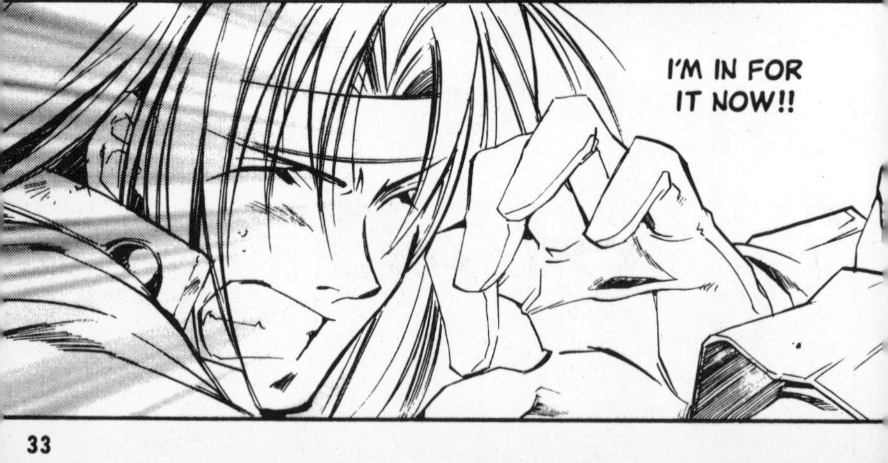
I'M IN FOR IT NOW!!

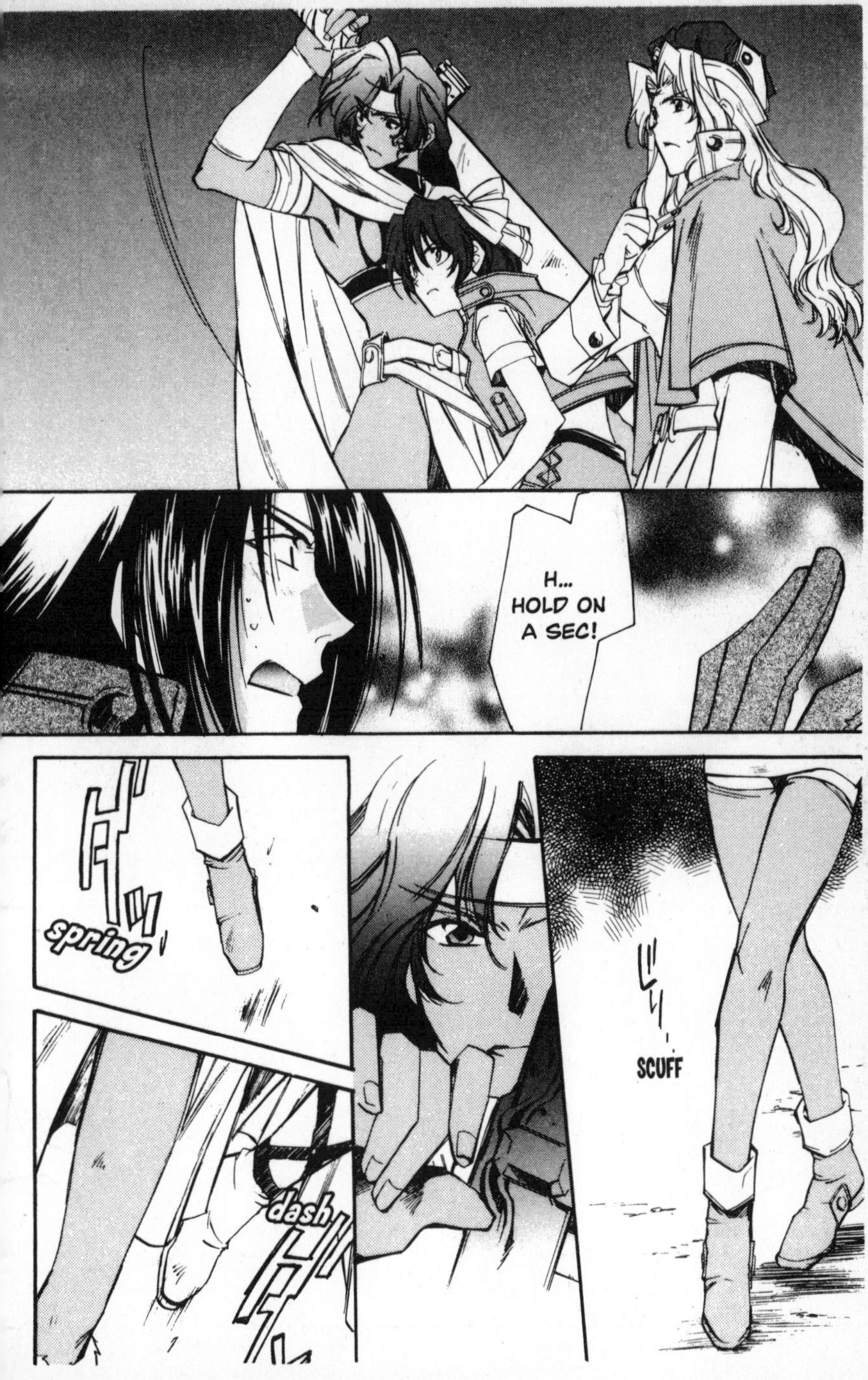
H...
HOLD ON
A SEC!
SCUFF
spring
dash

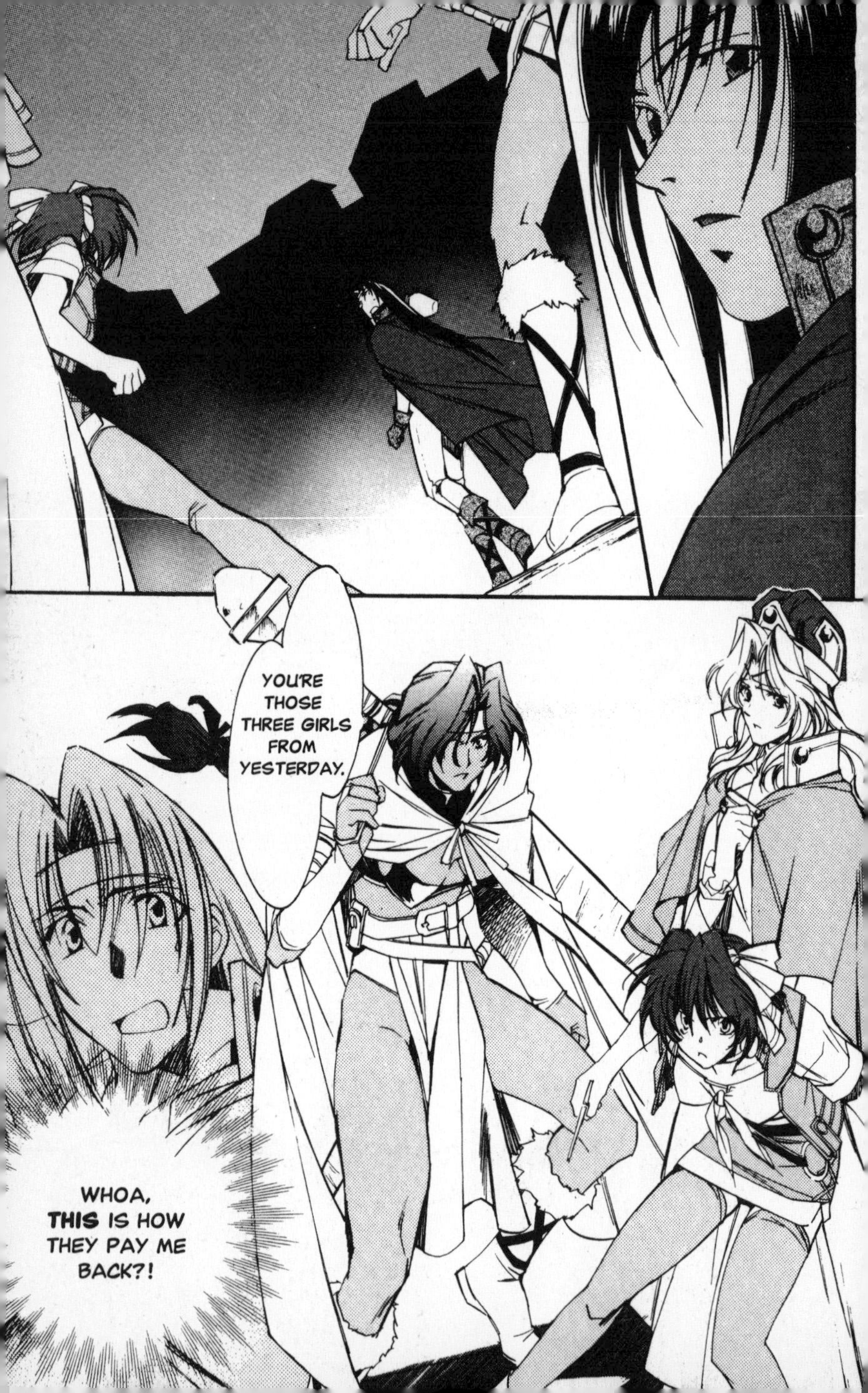
YOU'RE THOSE THREE GIRLS FROM YESTERDAY.
WHOA, **THIS** IS HOW THEY PAY ME BACK?!

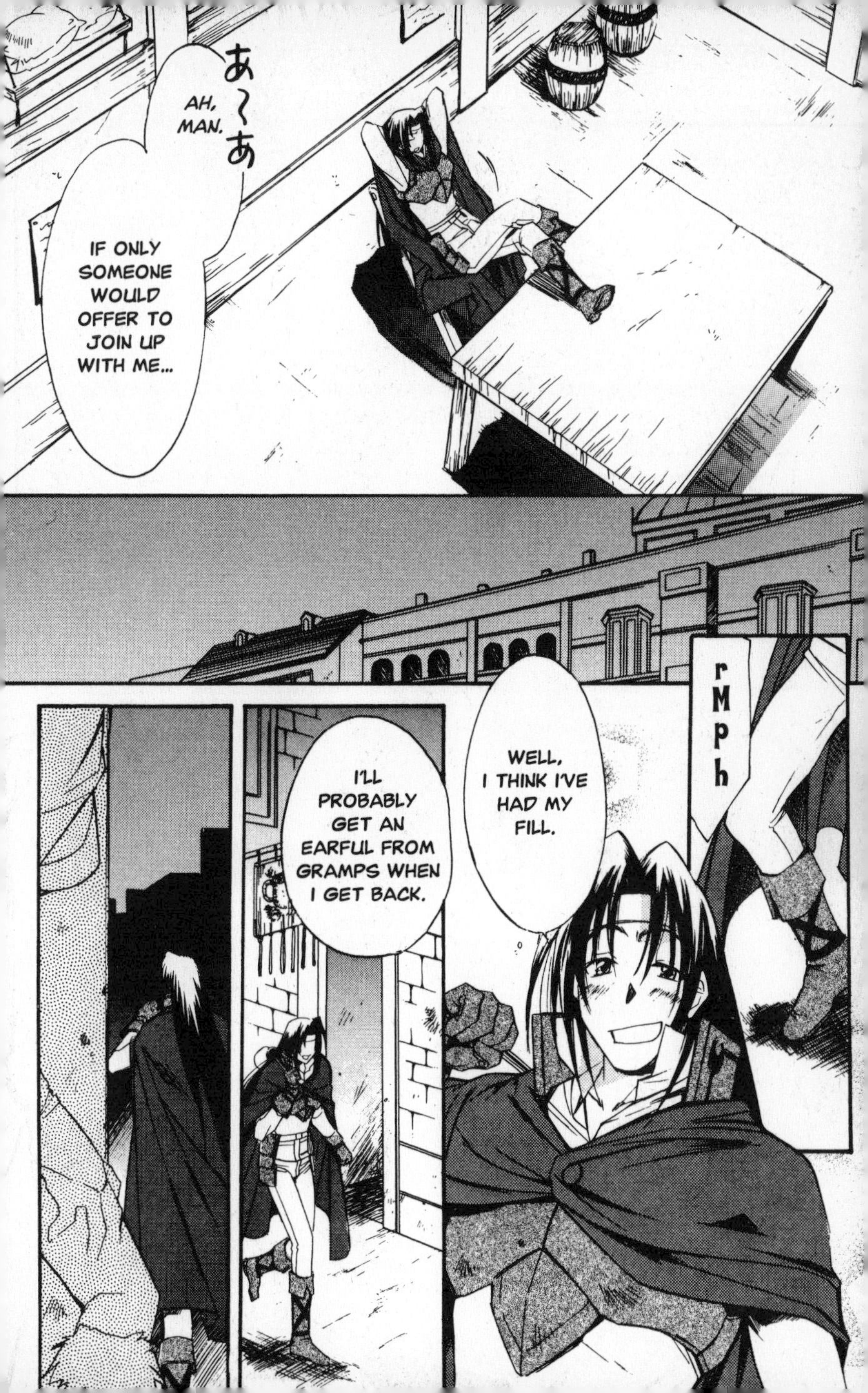
あ～あ
AH, MAN.
IF ONLY SOMEONE WOULD OFFER TO JOIN UP WITH ME...
rMPh
WELL, I THINK I'VE HAD MY FILL.
I'LL PROBABLY GET AN EARFUL FROM GRAMPS WHEN I GET BACK.

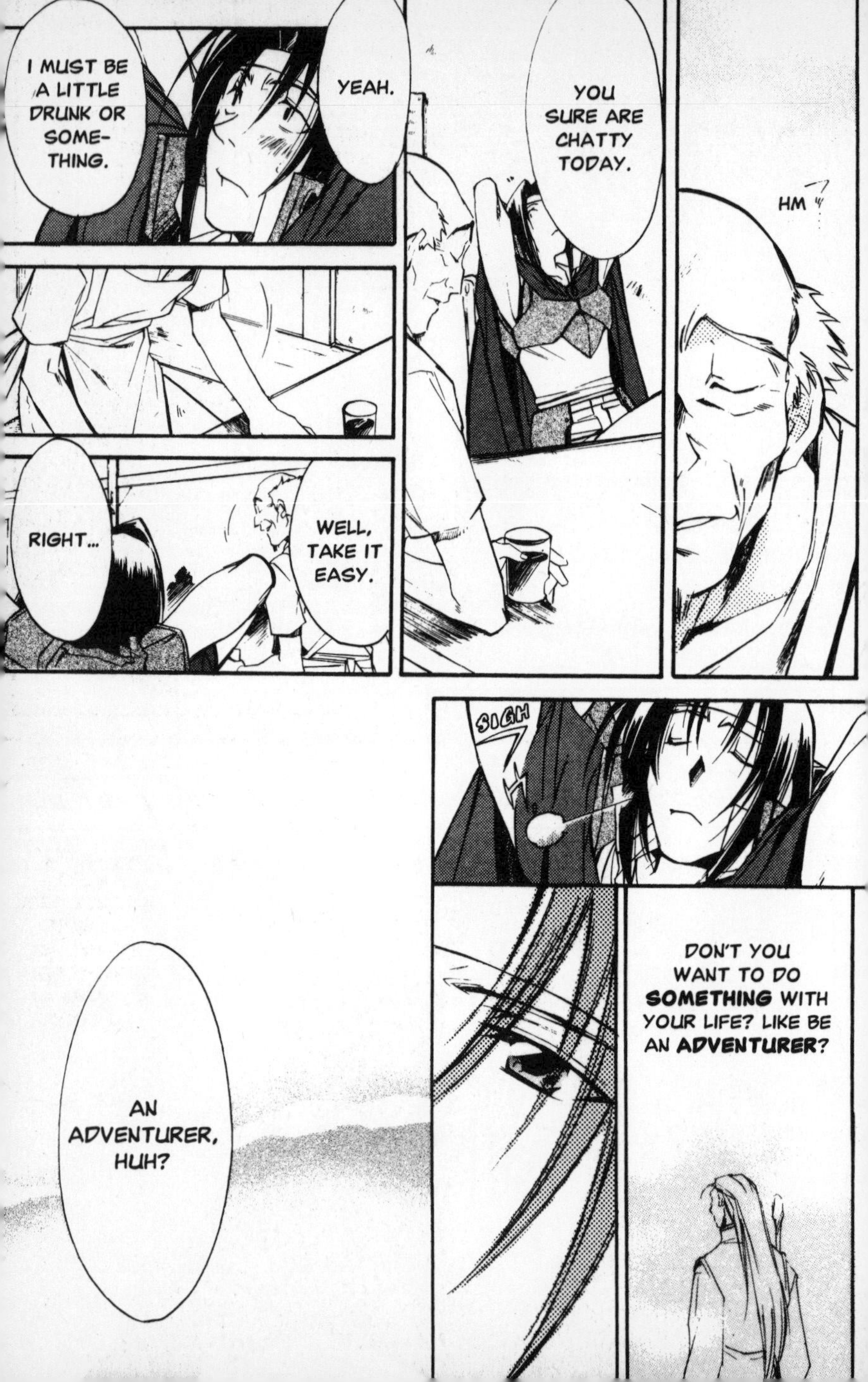
HM
YOU SURE ARE CHATTY TODAY.
YEAH.
I MUST BE A LITTLE DRUNK OR SOME-THING.
WELL, TAKE IT EASY.
RIGHT...
SIGH
DON'T YOU WANT TO DO **SOMETHING** WITH YOUR LIFE? LIKE BE AN **ADVENTURER**?
AN ADVENTURER, HUH?

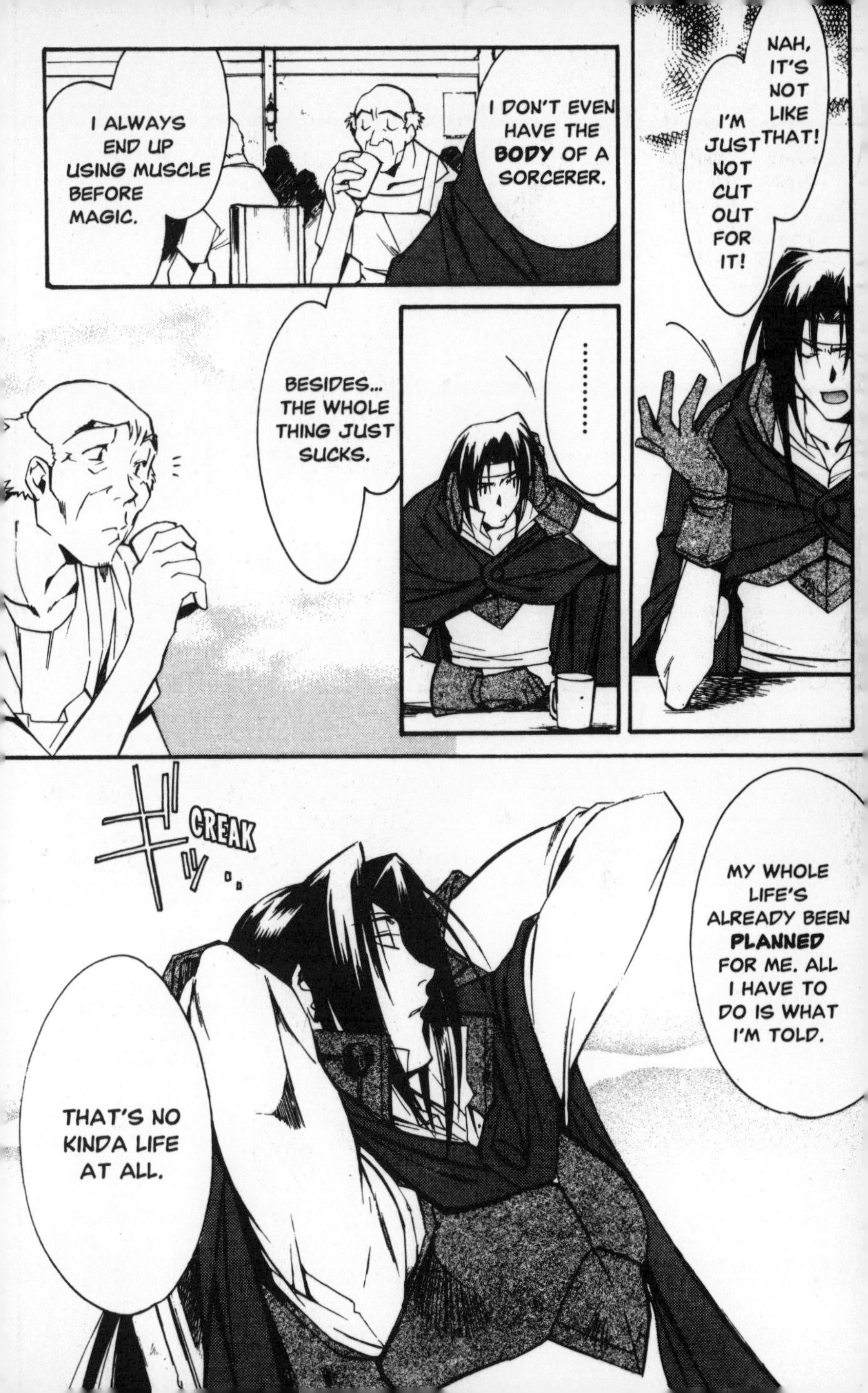
NAH, IT'S NOT LIKE THAT!
I'M JUST NOT CUT OUT FOR IT!
I DON'T EVEN HAVE THE **BODY** OF A SORCERER.
I ALWAYS END UP USING MUSCLE BEFORE MAGIC.
......
BESIDES... THE WHOLE THING JUST SUCKS.
MY WHOLE LIFE'S ALREADY BEEN **PLANNED** FOR ME. ALL I HAVE TO DO IS WHAT I'M TOLD.
CREAK
THAT'S NO KINDA LIFE AT ALL.

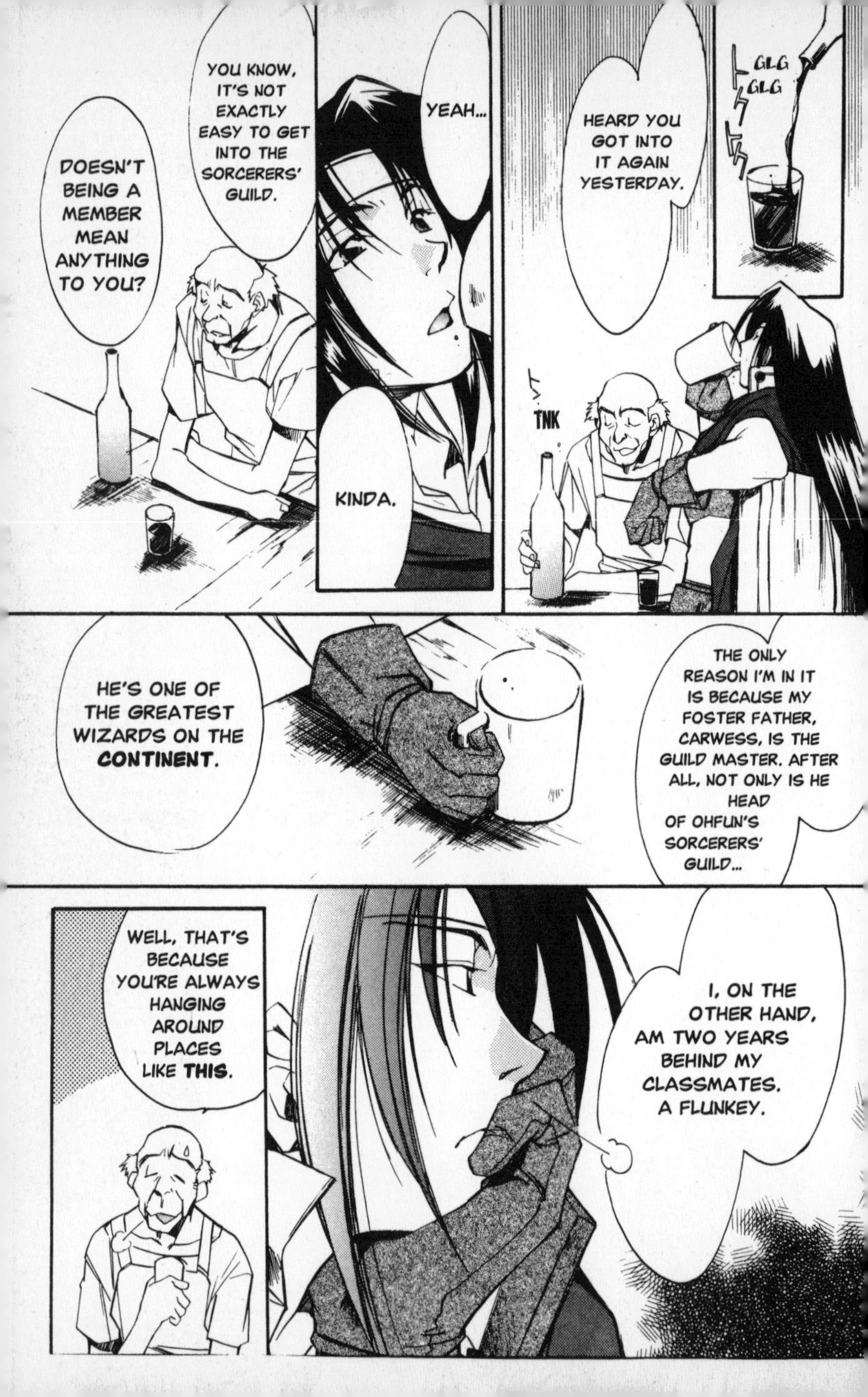
GLG GLG
HEARD YOU GOT INTO IT AGAIN YESTERDAY.
TNK
YEAH...
KINDA.
YOU KNOW, IT'S NOT EXACTLY EASY TO GET INTO THE SORCERERS' GUILD.
DOESN'T BEING A MEMBER MEAN ANYTHING TO YOU?
THE ONLY REASON I'M IN IT IS BECAUSE MY FOSTER FATHER, CARWESS, IS THE GUILD MASTER. AFTER ALL, NOT ONLY IS HE HEAD OF OHFUN'S SORCERERS' GUILD...
HE'S ONE OF THE GREATEST WIZARDS ON THE **CONTINENT**.
I, ON THE OTHER HAND, AM TWO YEARS BEHIND MY CLASSMATES. A FLUNKEY.
WELL, THAT'S BECAUSE YOU'RE ALWAYS HANGING AROUND PLACES LIKE **THIS**.

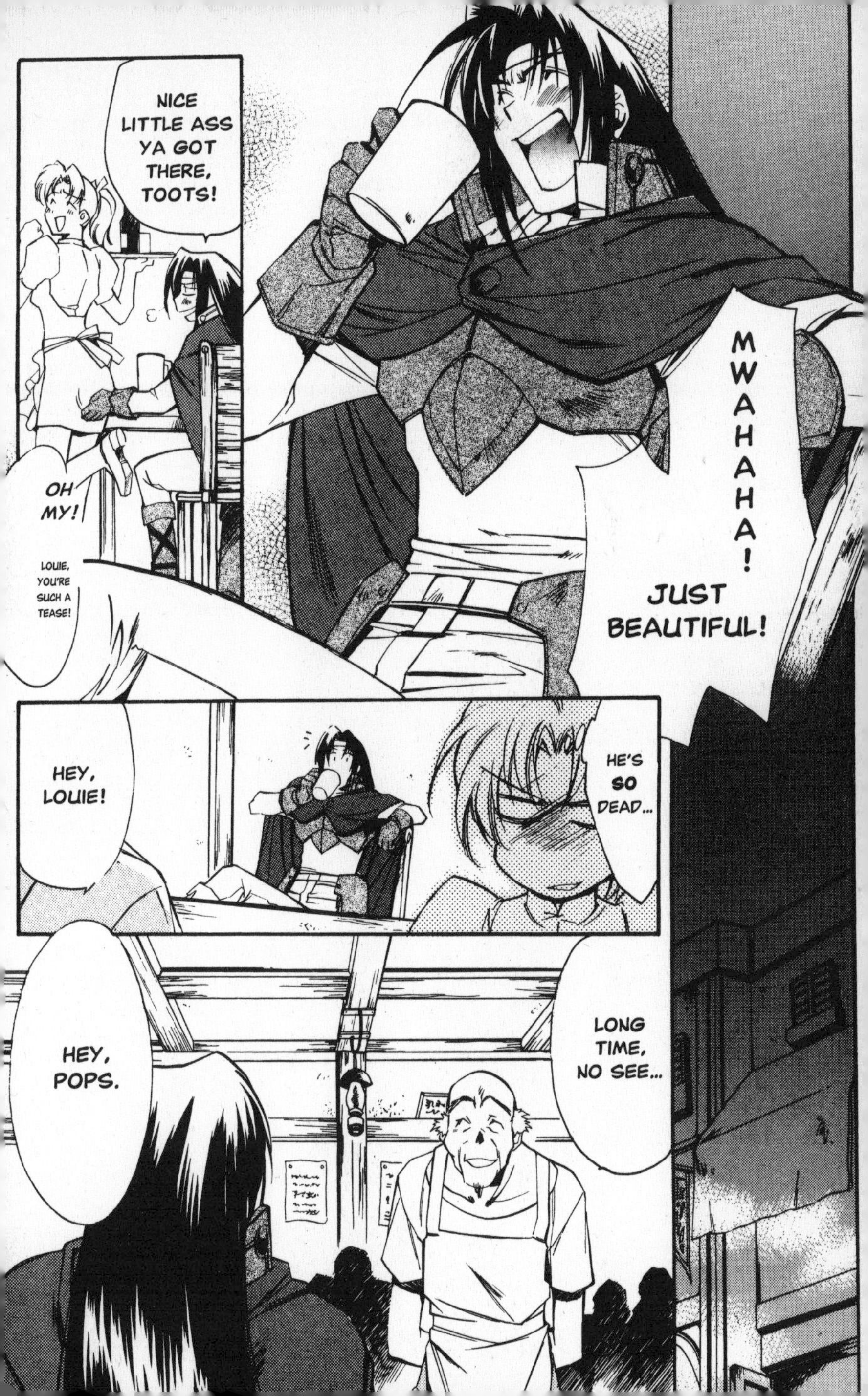
MWAHAHA!
JUST BEAUTIFUL!
NICE LITTLE ASS YA GOT THERE, TOOTS!
OH MY!
LOUIE, YOU'RE SUCH A TEASE!
HE'S SO DEAD...
HEY, LOUIE!
LONG TIME, NO SEE...
HEY, POPS.

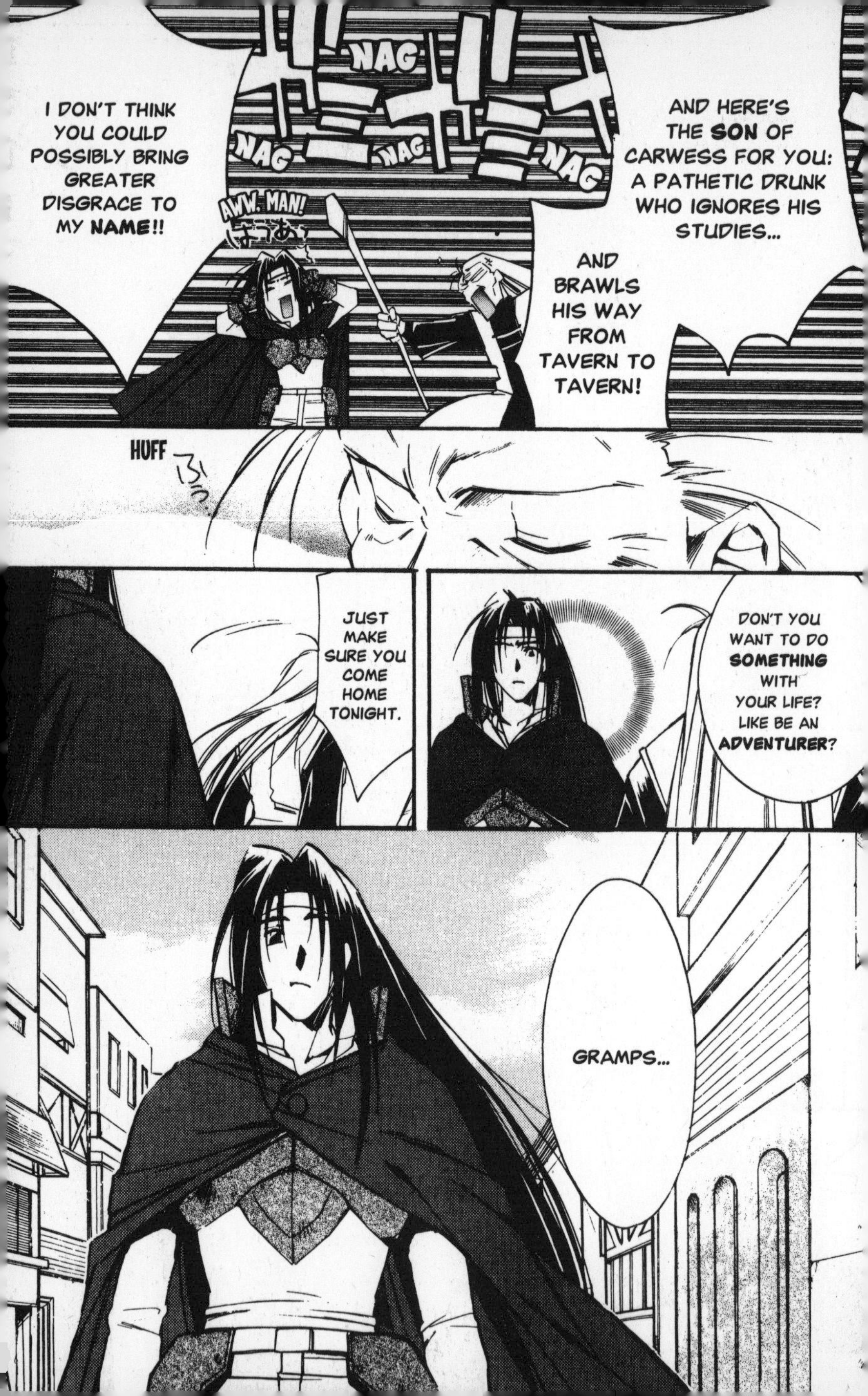
AND HERE'S THE SON OF CARWESS FOR YOU: A PATHETIC DRUNK WHO IGNORES HIS STUDIES...
AND BRAWLS HIS WAY FROM TAVERN TO TAVERN!
NAG
NAG
NAG
NAG
AWW, MAN!
I DON'T THINK YOU COULD POSSIBLY BRING GREATER DISGRACE TO MY NAME!!
HUFF
DON'T YOU WANT TO DO SOMETHING WITH YOUR LIFE? LIKE BE AN ADVENTURER?
JUST MAKE SURE YOU COME HOME TONIGHT.
GRAMPS...

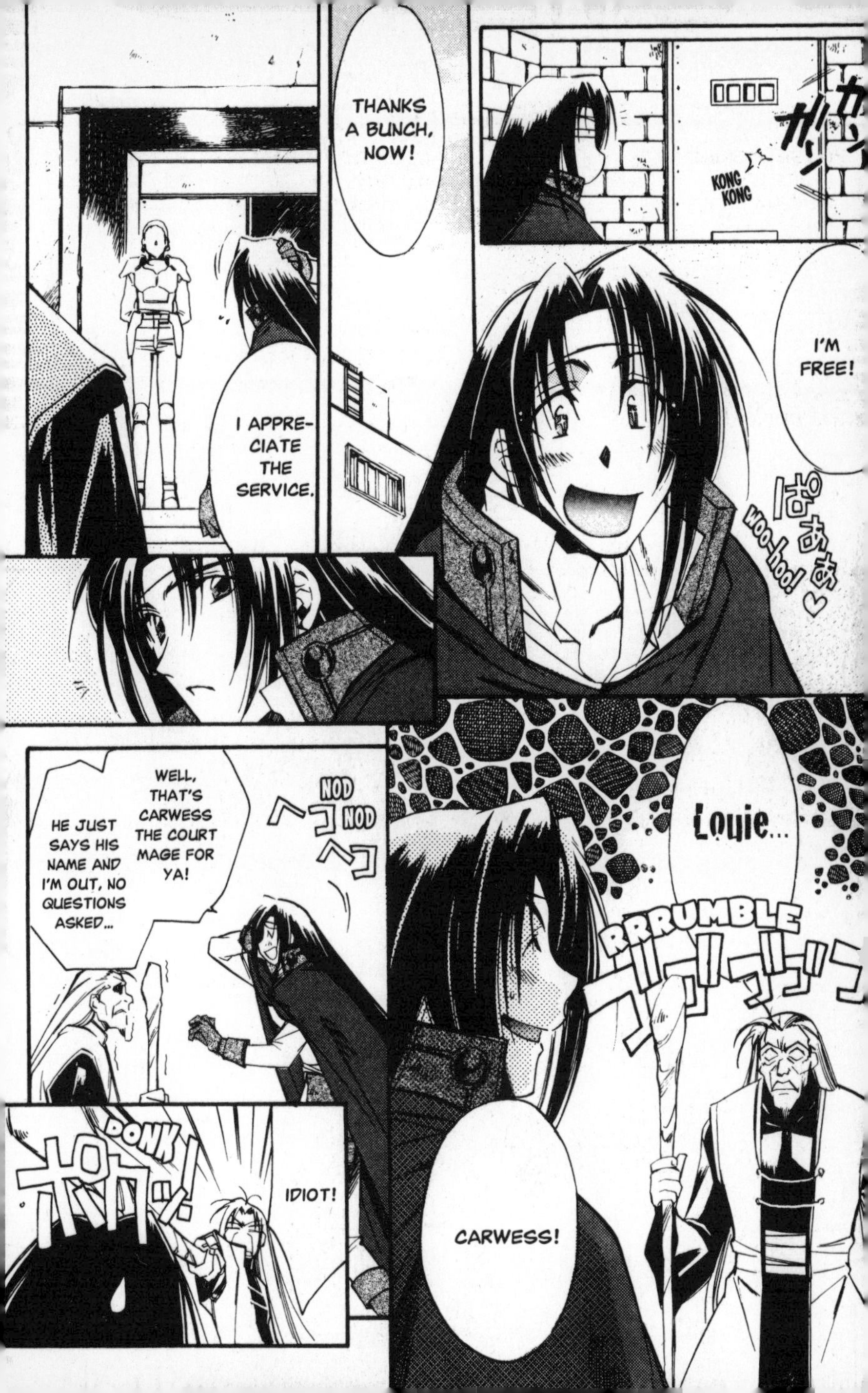
KONG KONG
I'M FREE!
ぱあぁ
woo-hoo!
THANKS A BUNCH, NOW!
I APPRECIATE THE SERVICE.
Louie...
RRRUMBLE
CARWESS!
WELL, THAT'S CARWESS THE COURT MAGE FOR YA!
HE JUST SAYS HIS NAME AND I'M OUT, NO QUESTIONS ASKED...
ヘコヘコ
NOD NOD
ポカッ!
DONK!
IDIOT!

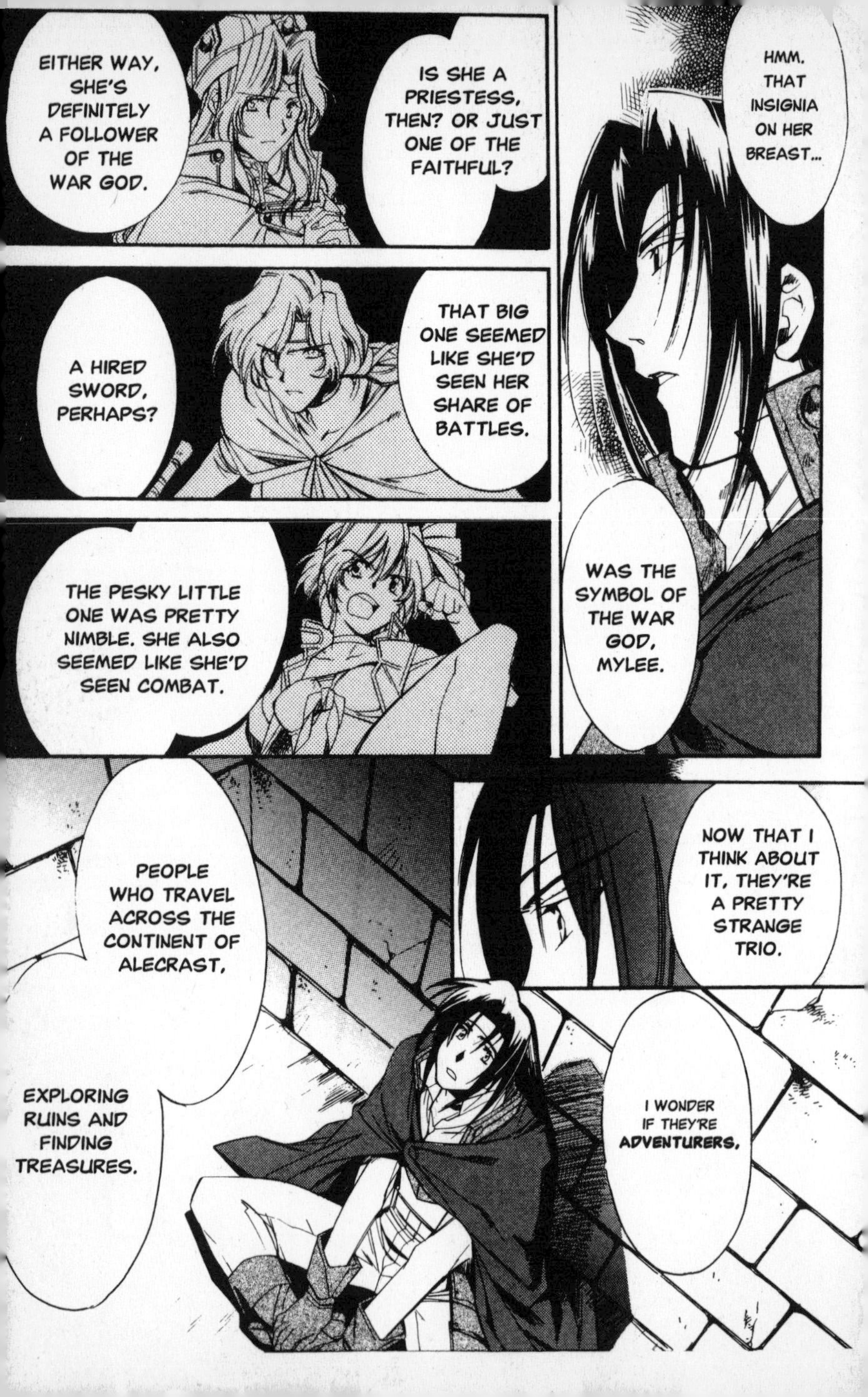
HMM. THAT INSIGNIA ON HER BREAST...
WAS THE SYMBOL OF THE WAR GOD, MYLEE.
IS SHE A PRIESTESS, THEN? OR JUST ONE OF THE FAITHFUL?
EITHER WAY, SHE'S DEFINITELY A FOLLOWER OF THE WAR GOD.
THAT BIG ONE SEEMED LIKE SHE'D SEEN HER SHARE OF BATTLES.
A HIRED SWORD, PERHAPS?
THE PESKY LITTLE ONE WAS PRETTY NIMBLE. SHE ALSO SEEMED LIKE SHE'D SEEN COMBAT.
NOW THAT I THINK ABOUT IT, THEY'RE A PRETTY STRANGE TRIO.
I WONDER IF THEY'RE **ADVENTURERS,**
PEOPLE WHO TRAVEL ACROSS THE CONTINENT OF ALECRAST,
EXPLORING RUINS AND FINDING TREASURES.

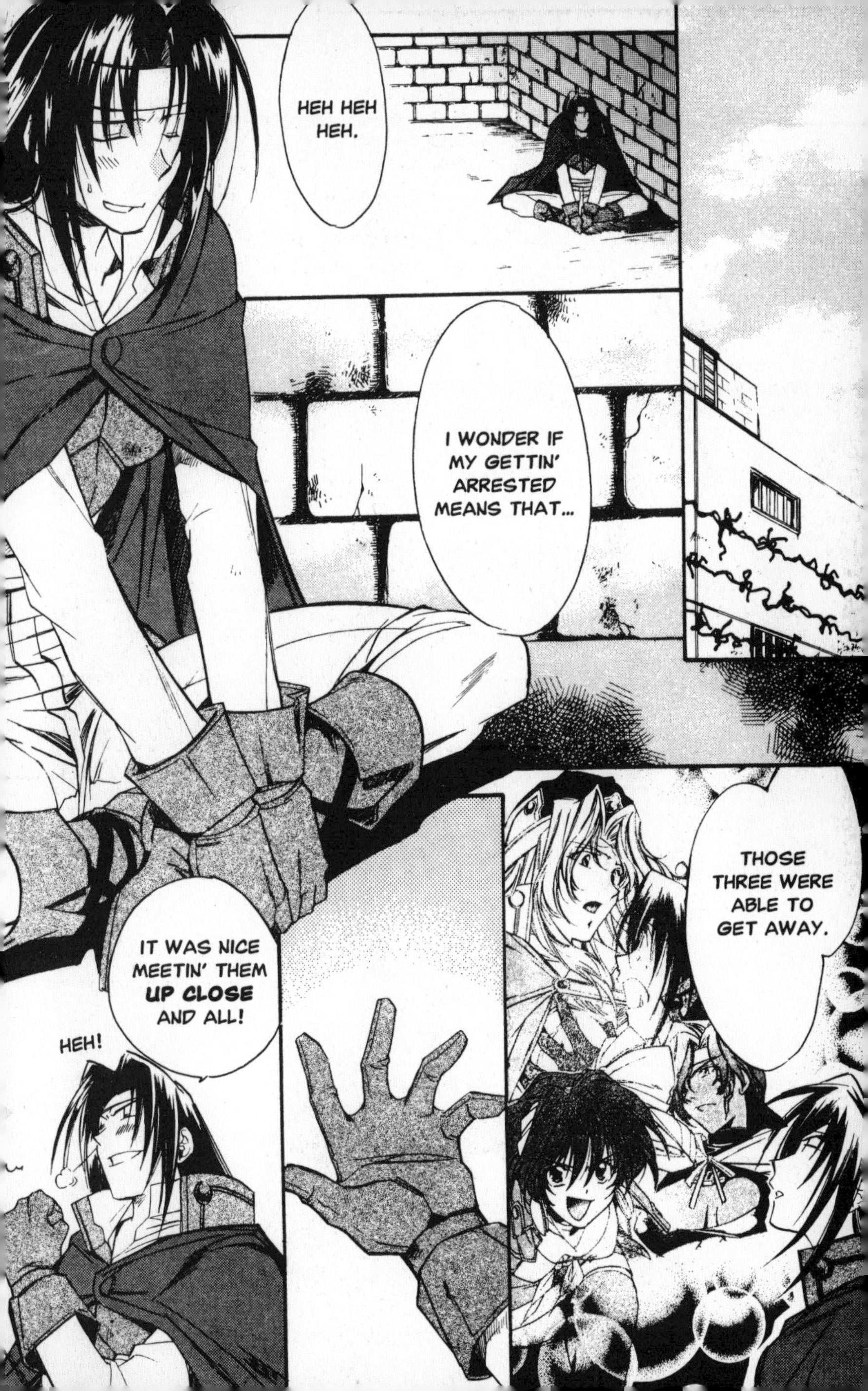
HEH HEH HEH.
I WONDER IF MY GETTIN' ARRESTED MEANS THAT...
THOSE THREE WERE ABLE TO GET AWAY.
IT WAS NICE MEETIN' THEM **UP CLOSE** AND ALL!
HEH!

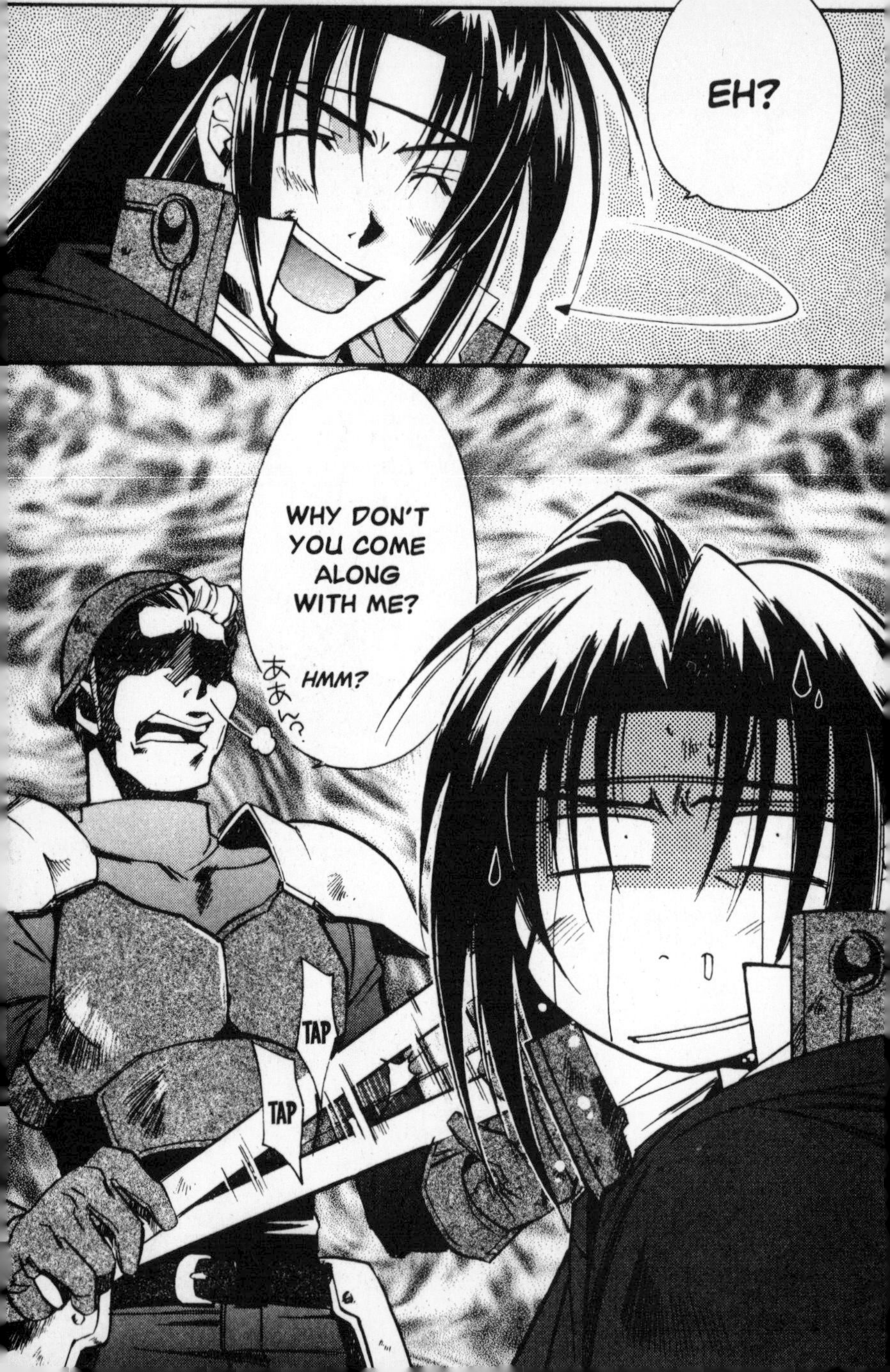
EH?
WHY DON'T YOU COME ALONG WITH ME?
HMM?
ああん?
TAP
TAP

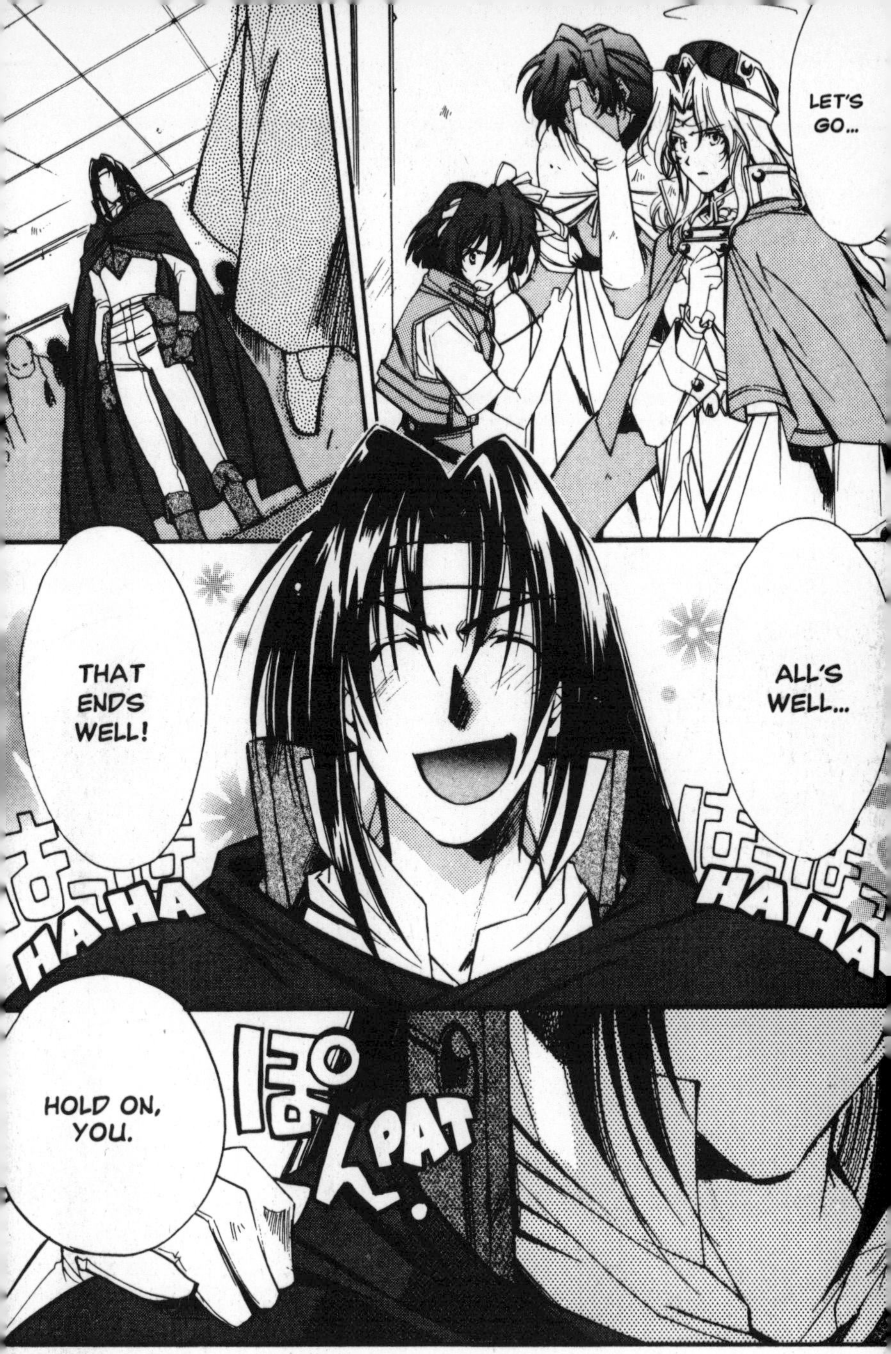
LET'S GO...
ALL'S WELL...
HA HA HA
THAT ENDS WELL!
HA HA HA
PAT
HOLD ON, YOU.

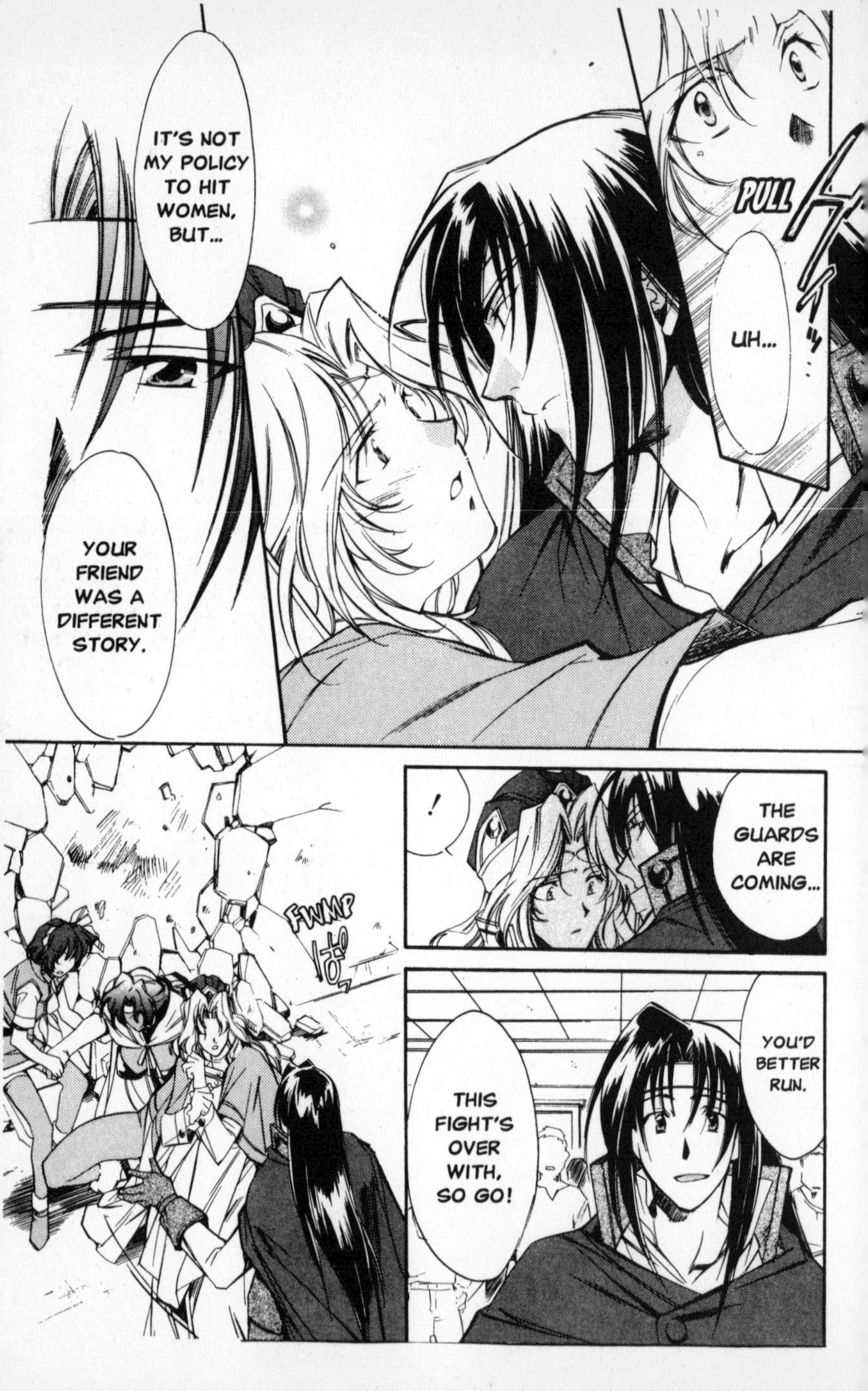
PULL
UH...
IT'S NOT MY POLICY TO HIT WOMEN, BUT...
YOUR FRIEND WAS A DIFFERENT STORY.
THE GUARDS ARE COMING...
!
YOU'D BETTER RUN.
THIS FIGHT'S OVER WITH, SO GO!
FWMP

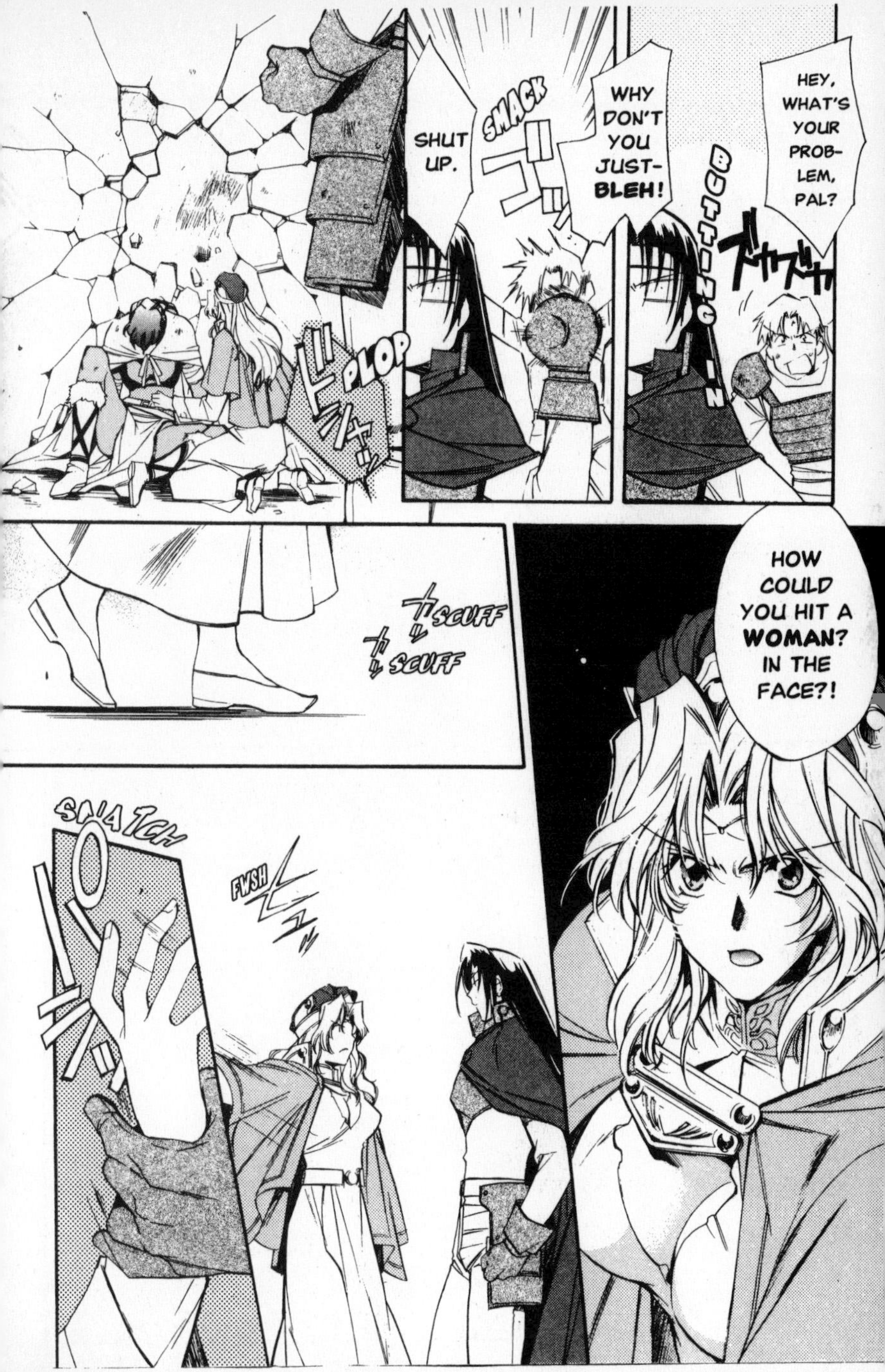
HEY, WHAT'S YOUR PROB-LEM, PAL?
BUTTING IN
WHY DON'T YOU JUST- **BLEH**!
SMACK
SHUT UP.
PLOP
HOW COULD YOU HIT A **WOMAN**? IN THE FACE?!
SCUFF
SCUFF
SNATCH
FWSH

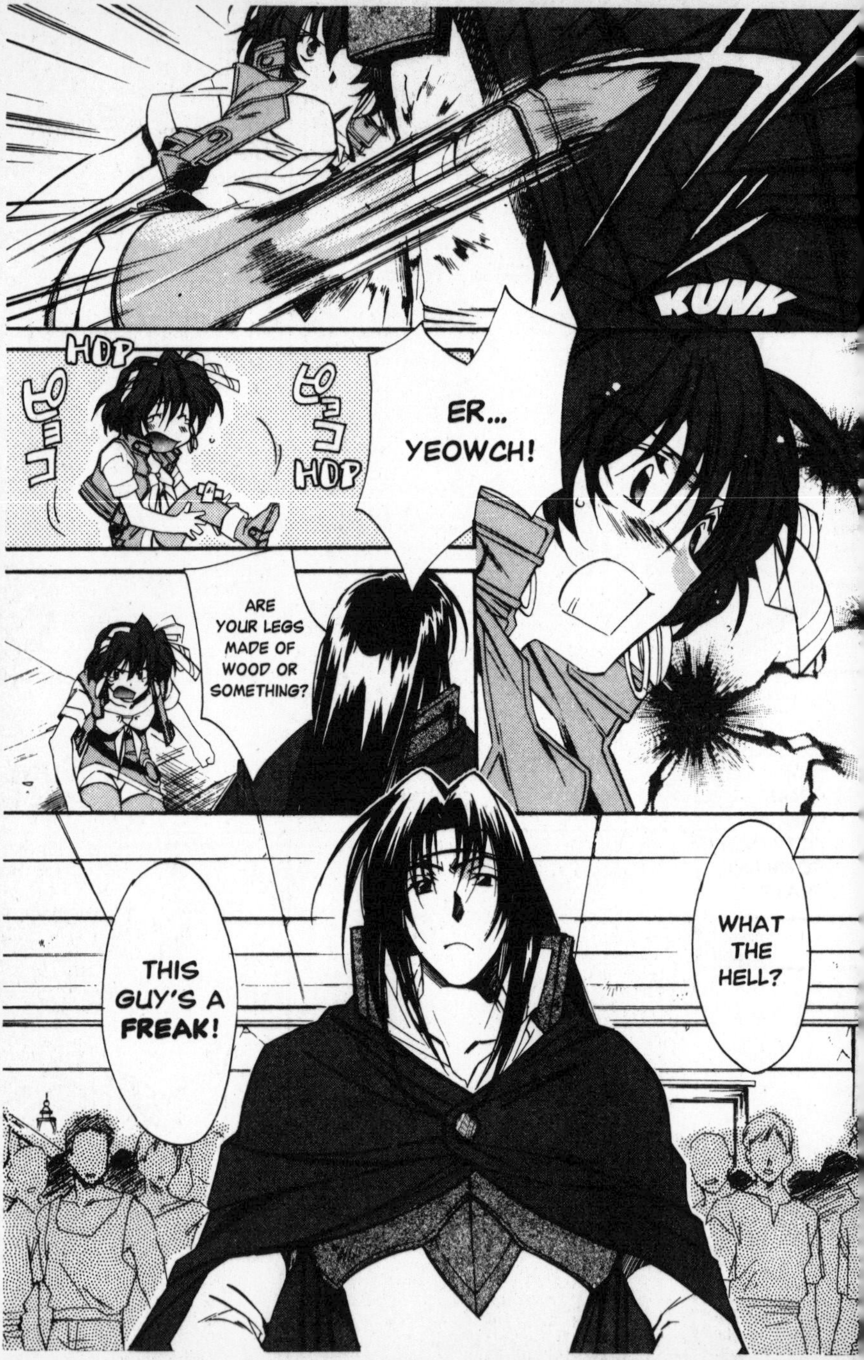
KUNK
ER...
YEOWCH!
ピョコ
HOP
ピョコ
HOP
ARE YOUR LEGS MADE OF WOOD OR SOMETHING?
WHAT THE HELL?
THIS GUY'S A FREAK!

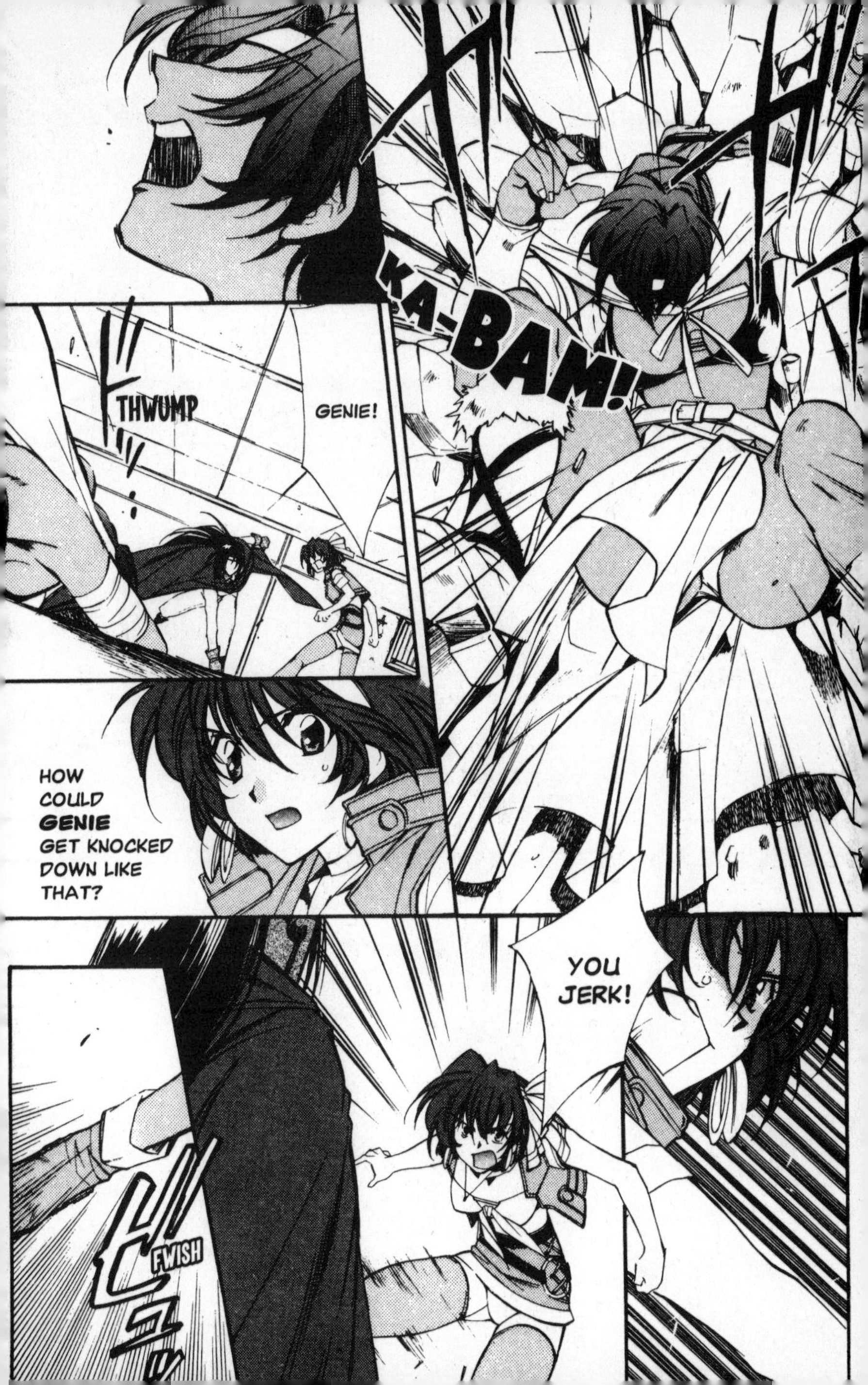
KA-BAM!
GENIE!
THWUMP
HOW COULD GENIE GET KNOCKED DOWN LIKE THAT?
YOU JERK!
FWISH

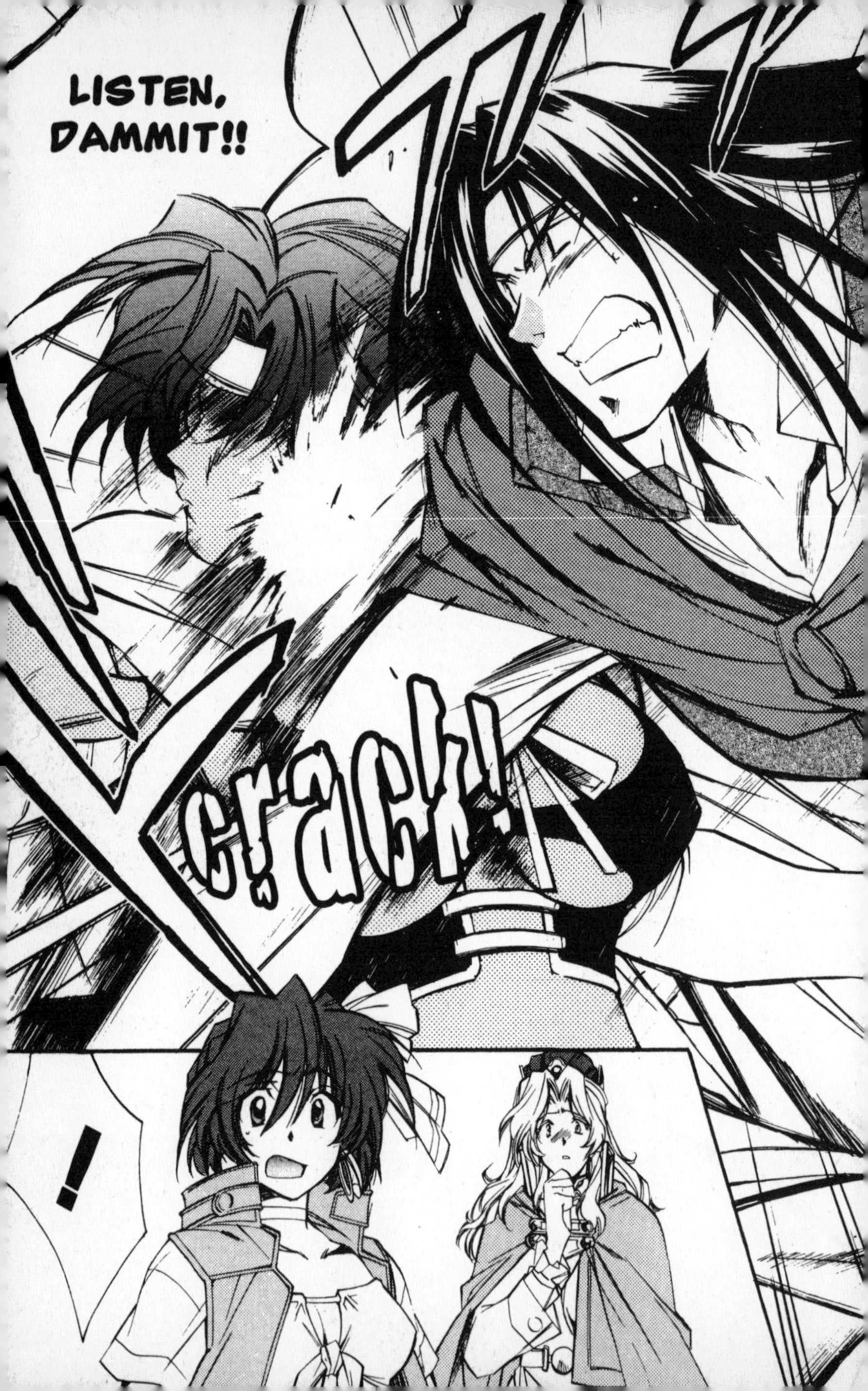
LISTEN, DAMMIT!!
CRACK!
!

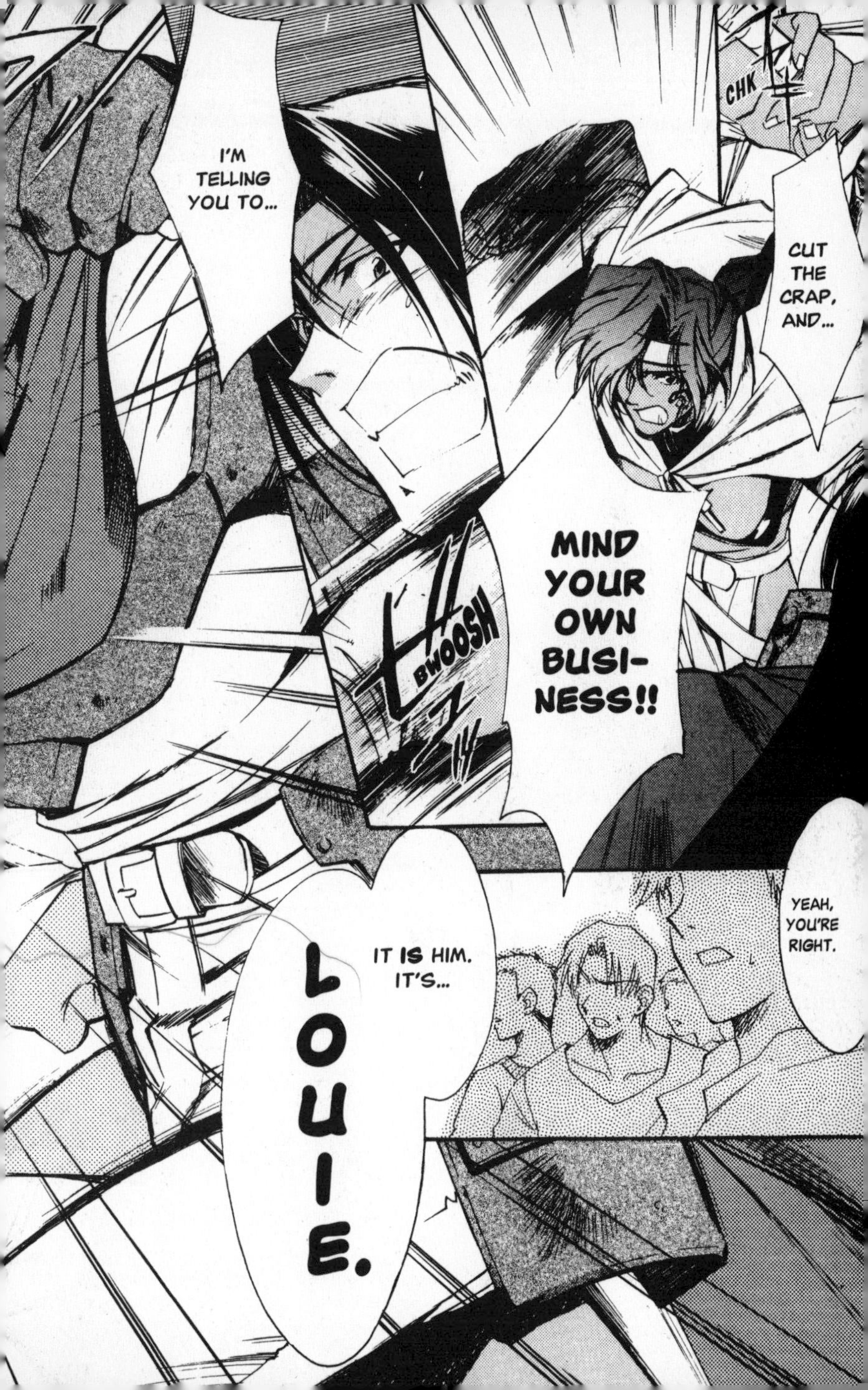
CHK
CUT THE CRAP, AND...
I'M TELLING YOU TO...
MIND YOUR OWN BUSI-NESS!!
BWOOSH
YEAH, YOU'RE RIGHT.
IT IS HIM. IT'S...
LOUIE.

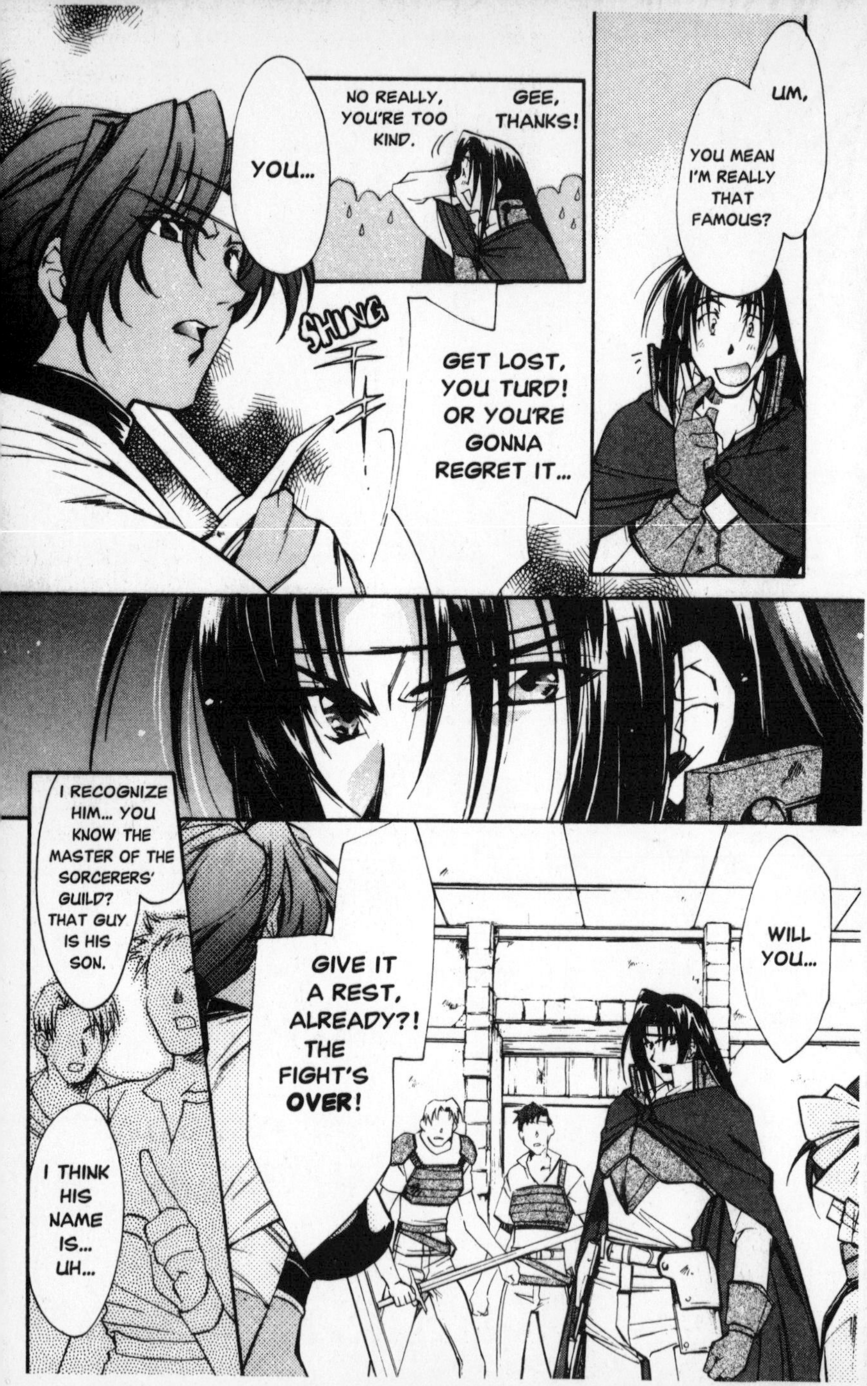
UM,
YOU MEAN I'M REALLY THAT FAMOUS?
GEE, THANKS!
NO REALLY, YOU'RE TOO KIND.
YOU...
SHING
GET LOST, YOU TURD! OR YOU'RE GONNA REGRET IT...
WILL YOU...
GIVE IT A REST, ALREADY?! THE FIGHT'S **OVER**!
I RECOGNIZE HIM... YOU KNOW THE MASTER OF THE SORCERERS' GUILD? THAT GUY IS HIS SON.
I THINK HIS NAME IS... UH...

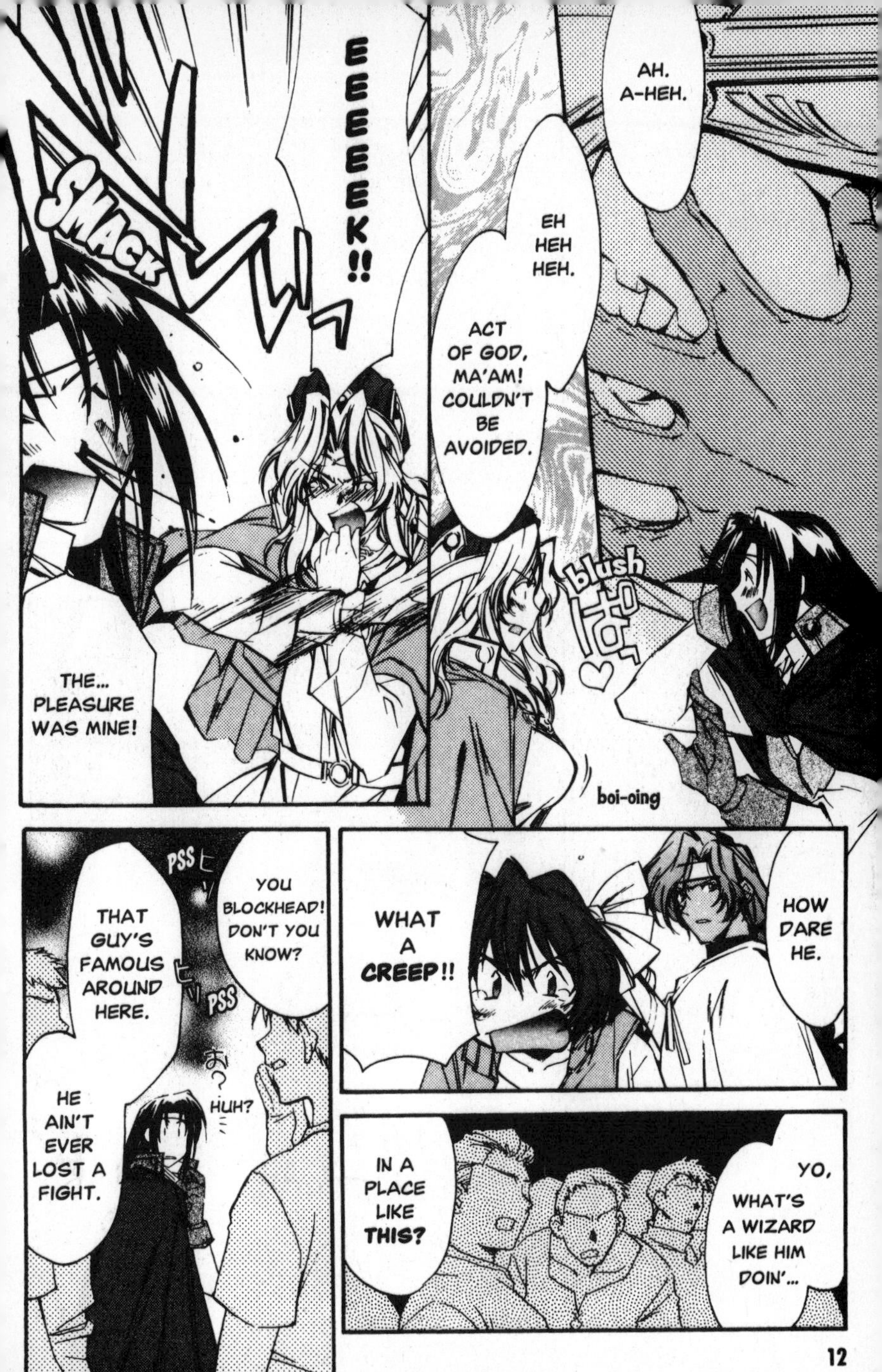
AH. A-HEH.
EH HEH HEH.
ACT OF GOD, MA'AM! COULDN'T BE AVOIDED.
blush
boi-oing
EEEEEEK!!
SMACK
THE... PLEASURE WAS MINE!
HOW DARE HE.
WHAT A CREEP!!
YO, WHAT'S A WIZARD LIKE HIM DOIN'...
IN A PLACE LIKE THIS?
YOU BLOCKHEAD! DON'T YOU KNOW?
PSS
THAT GUY'S FAMOUS AROUND HERE.
PSS
HUH?
HE AIN'T EVER LOST A FIGHT.

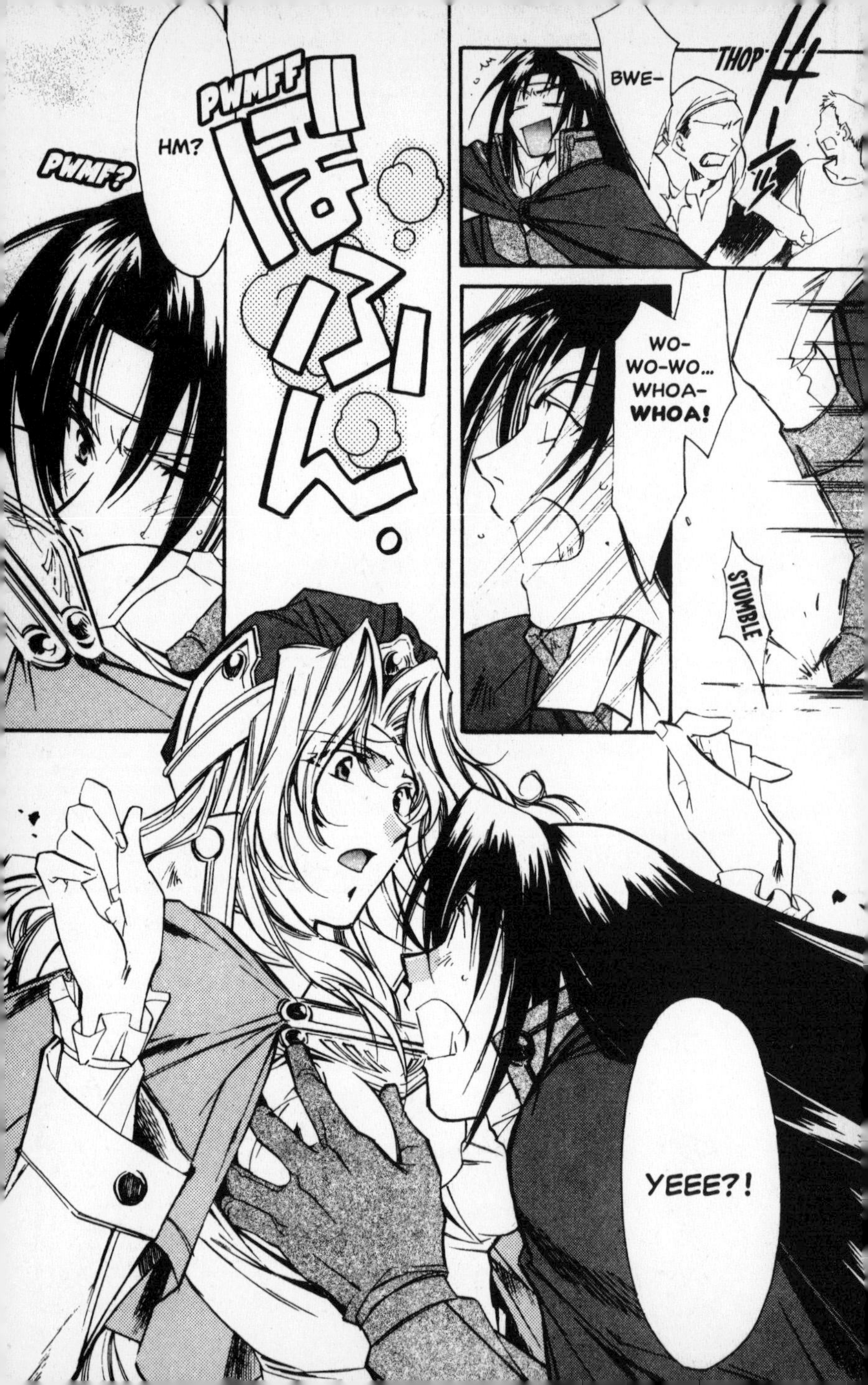
BWE-
THOP
WO-WO-WO... WHOA-WHOA!
STUMBLE
PWMFF
ぼふん。
HM?
PWMF?
YEEE?!

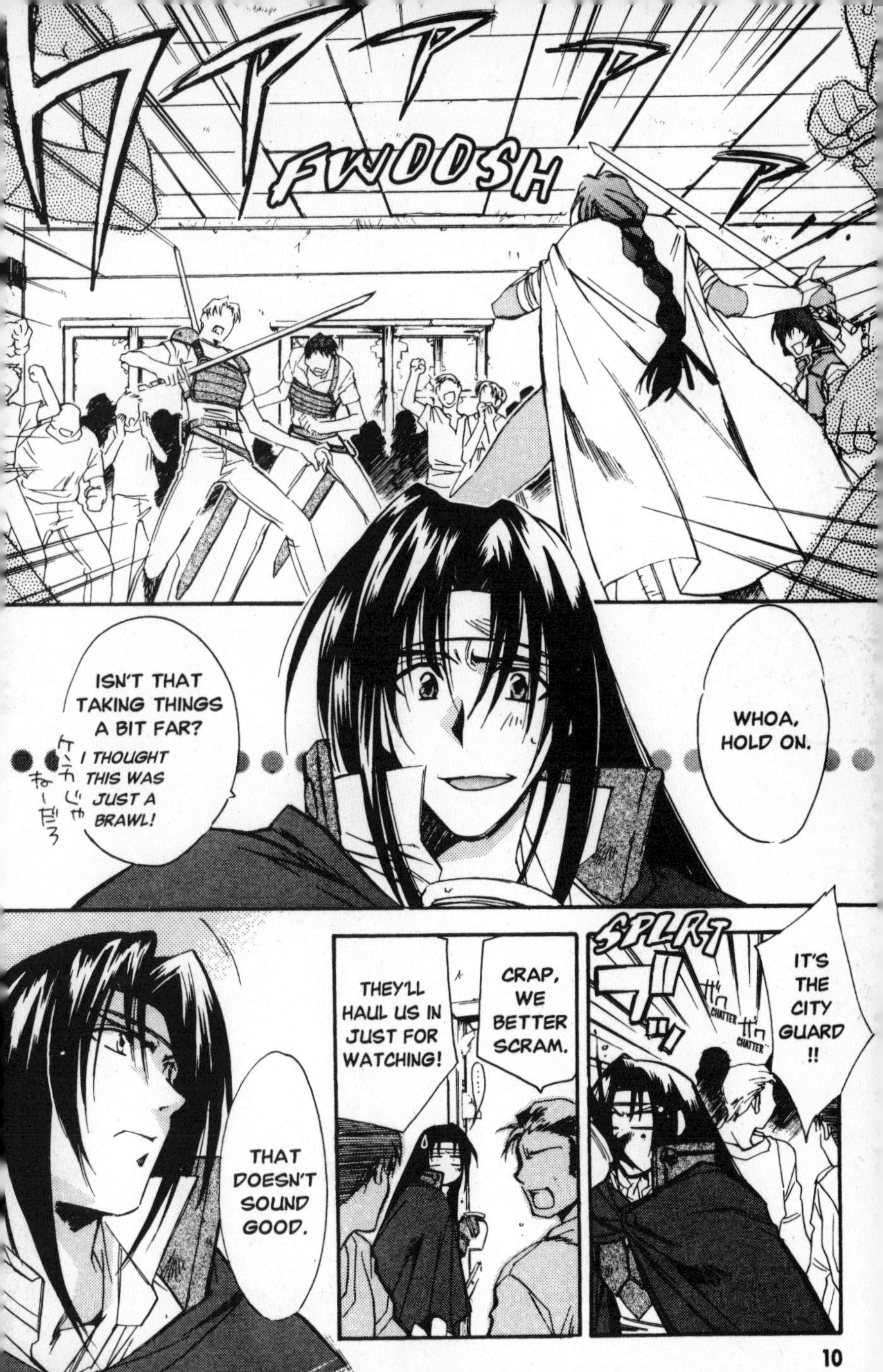
FWOOSH
WHOA, HOLD ON.
ISN'T THAT TAKING THINGS A BIT FAR?
I THOUGHT THIS WAS JUST A BRAWL!
ケンカじゃねーだろ
SPLRT
IT'S THE CITY GUARD!!
CHATTER
CHATTER
CRAP, WE BETTER SCRAM.
THEY'LL HAUL US IN JUST FOR WATCHING!
...
THAT DOESN'T SOUND GOOD.

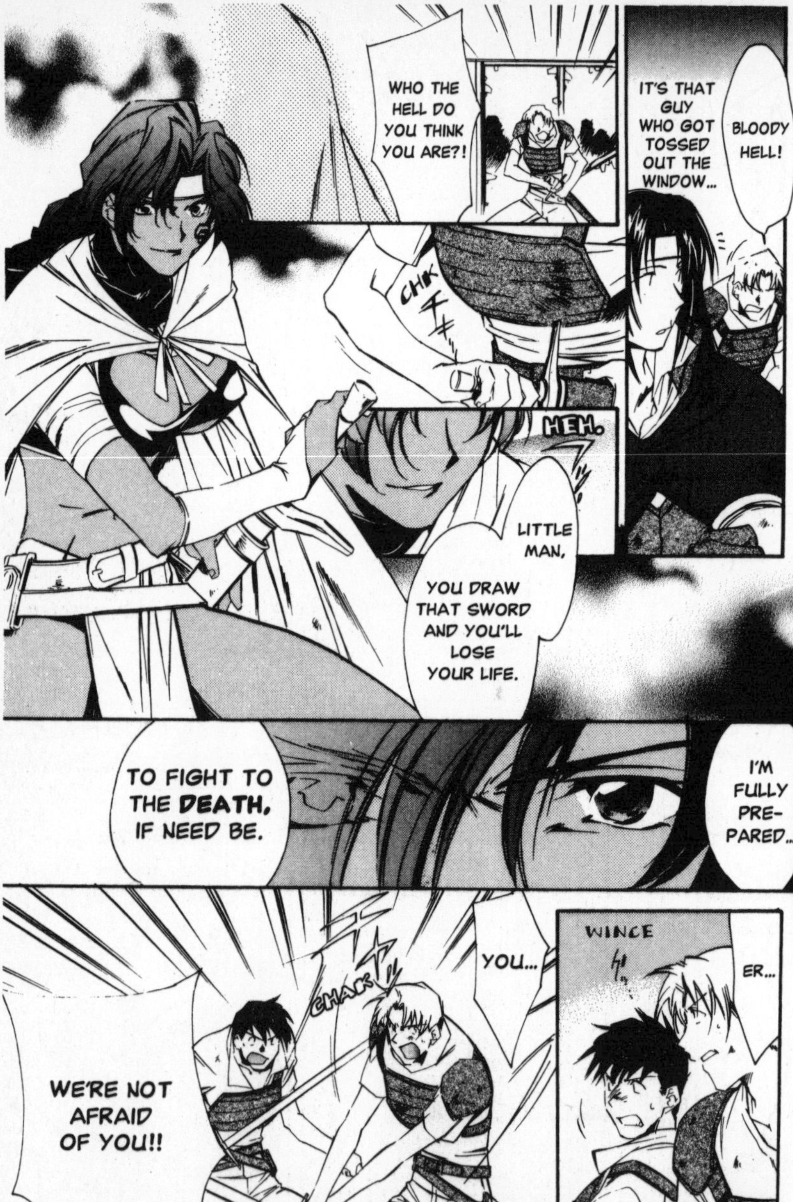
BLOODY HELL!
IT'S THAT GUY WHO GOT TOSSED OUT THE WINDOW...
WHO THE HELL DO YOU THINK YOU ARE?!
CHIK
HEH.
LITTLE MAN,
YOU DRAW THAT SWORD AND YOU'LL LOSE YOUR LIFE.
I'M FULLY PRE-PARED...
TO FIGHT TO THE **DEATH,** IF NEED BE.
ER...
WINCE
YOU...
CHAK
WE'RE NOT AFRAID OF YOU!!

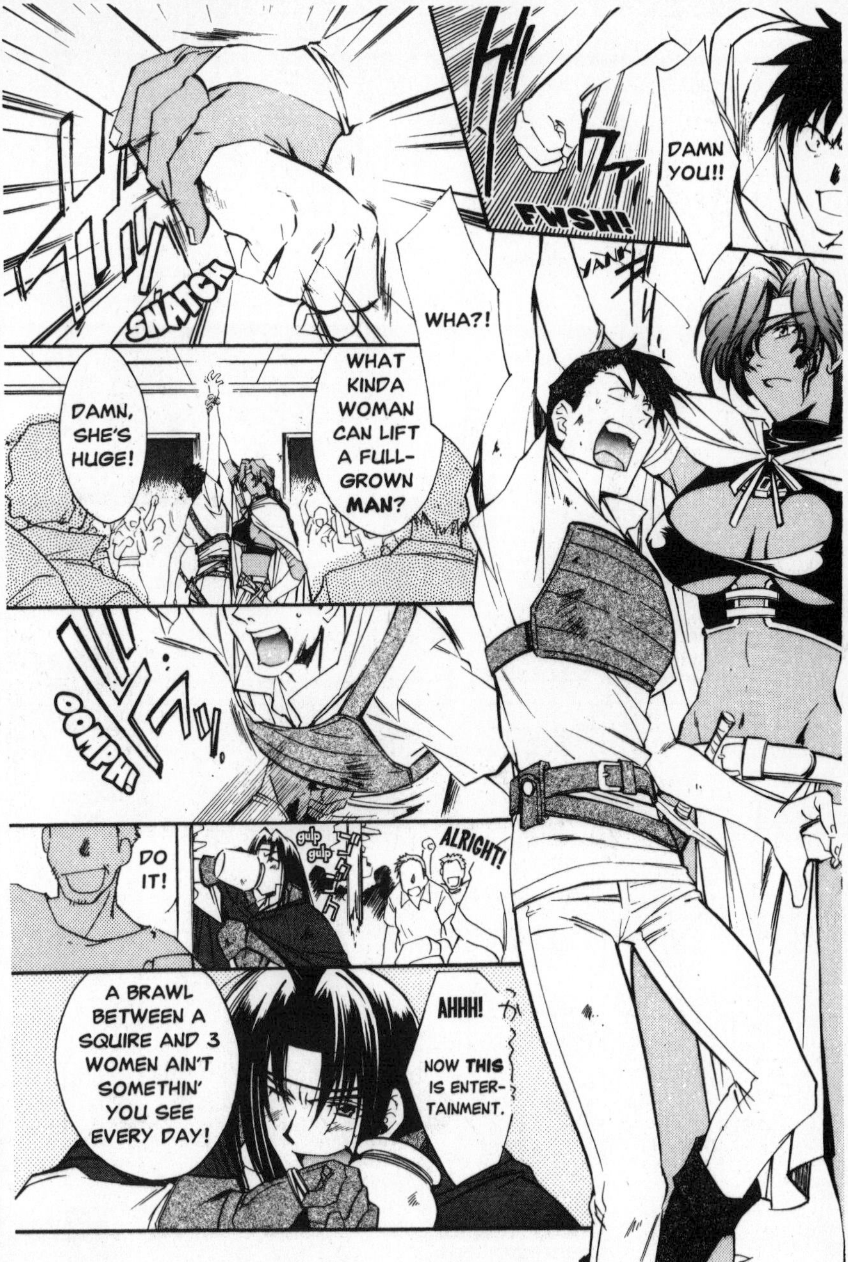
DAMN YOU!!
FWSH!
SNATCH
YANK
WHA?!
WHAT KINDA WOMAN CAN LIFT A FULL-GROWN MAN?
DAMN, SHE'S HUGE!
OOMPH!
ALRIGHT!
gulp gulp
DO IT!
AHHH!
NOW THIS IS ENTER-TAINMENT.
A BRAWL BETWEEN A SQUIRE AND 3 WOMEN AIN'T SOMETHIN' YOU SEE EVERY DAY!

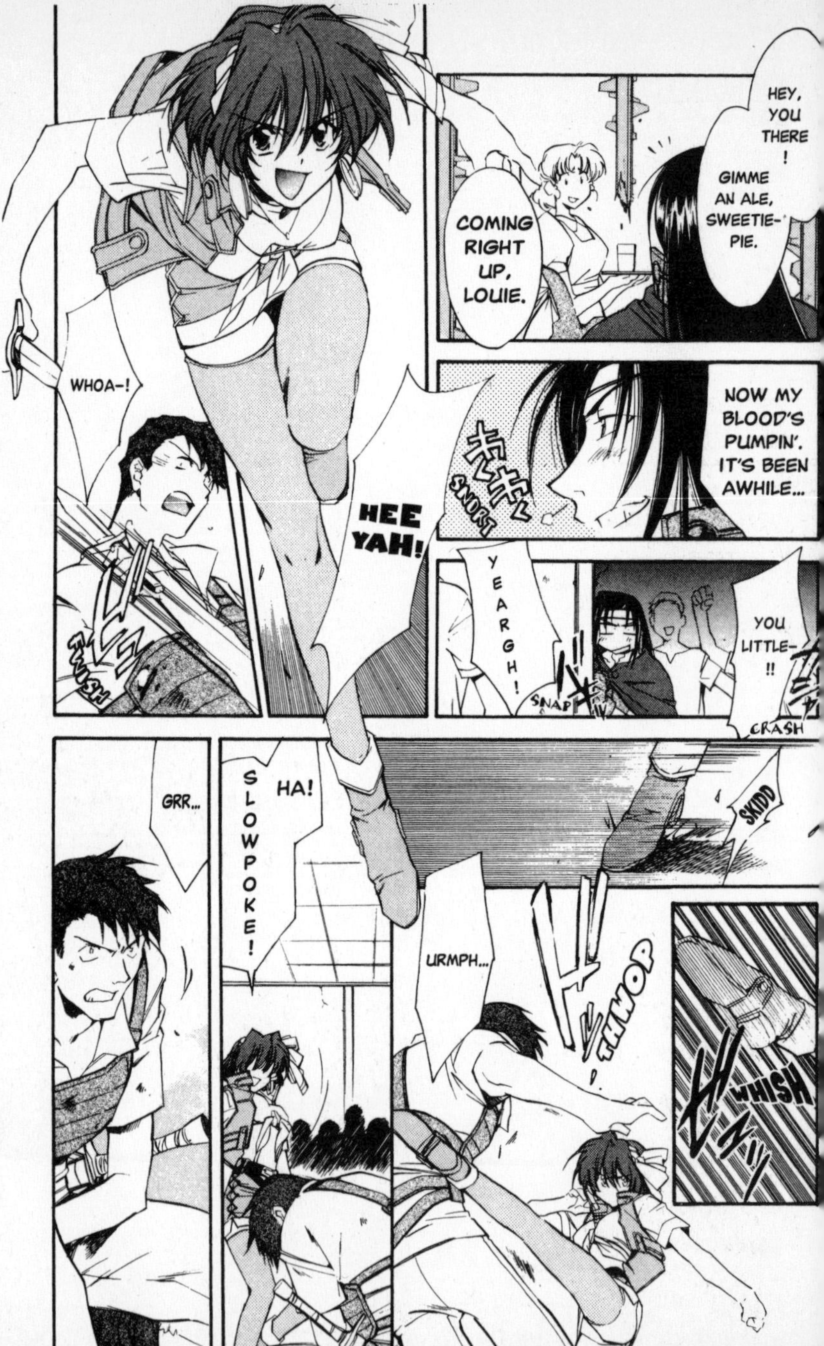
HEY, YOU THERE! GIMME AN ALE, SWEETIE-PIE.
COMING RIGHT UP, LOUIE.
NOW MY BLOOD'S PUMPIN'. IT'S BEEN AWHILE...
キレキレ
SNORT
YOU LITTLE-!!
CRASH
YEARGH!
SNAP
HEE YAH!
WHOA-!
FWISH
SKIDD
WHISH
THWOP
URMPH...
HA!
SLOWPOKE!
GRR...

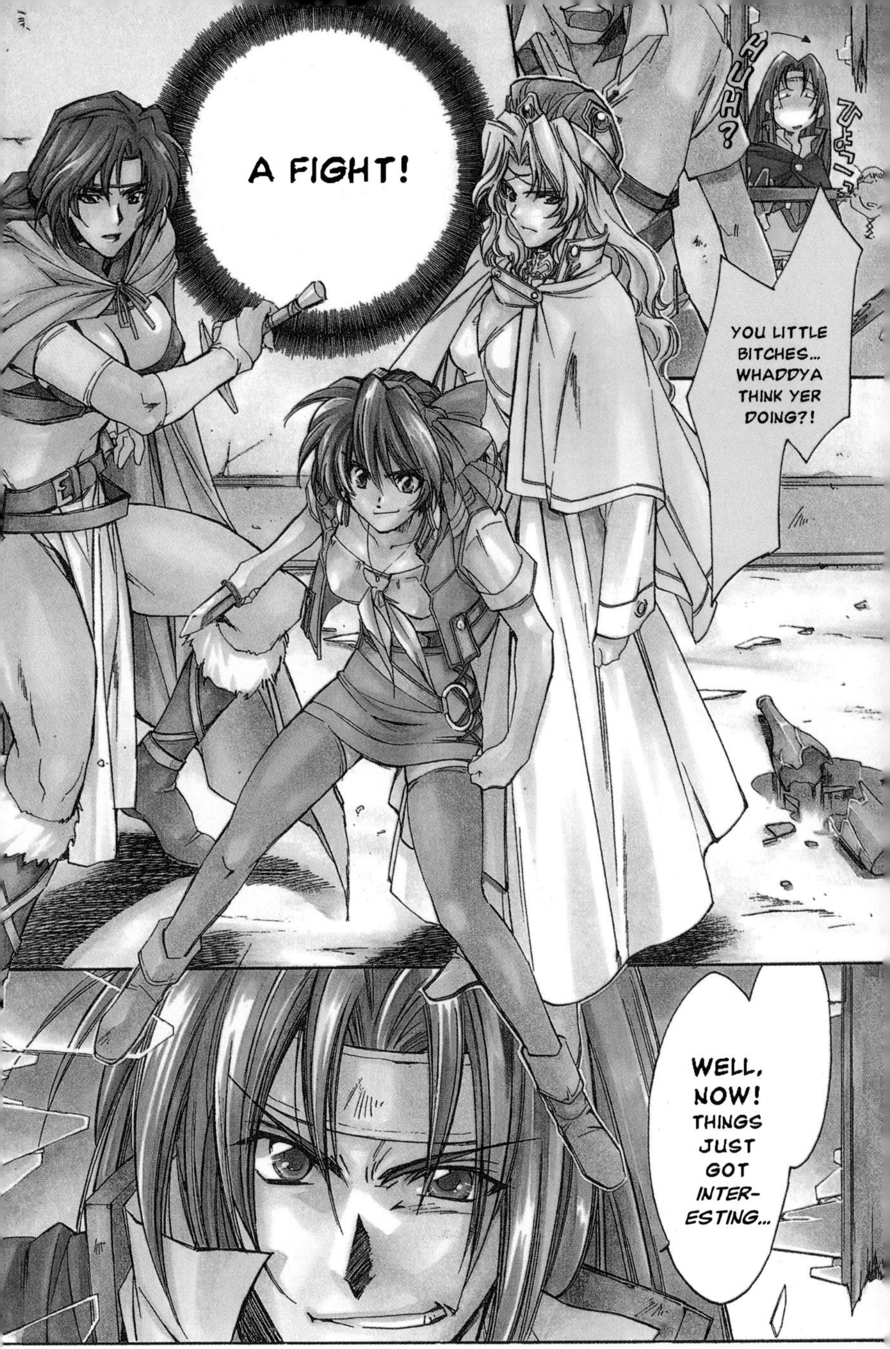
HUH?
YOU LITTLE BITCHES... WHADDYA THINK YER DOING?!
A FIGHT!
WELL, NOW! THINGS JUST GOT INTER-ESTING...

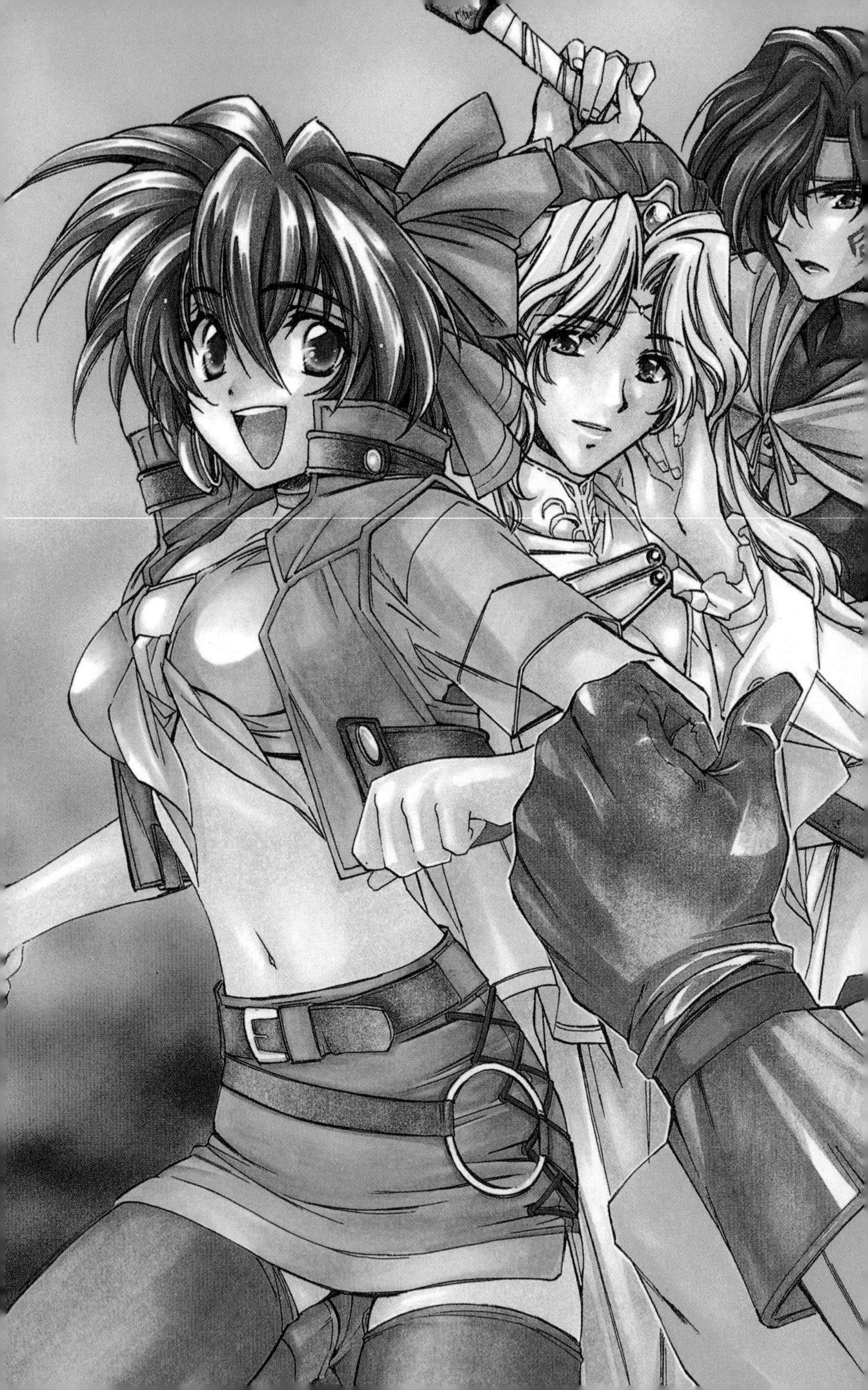

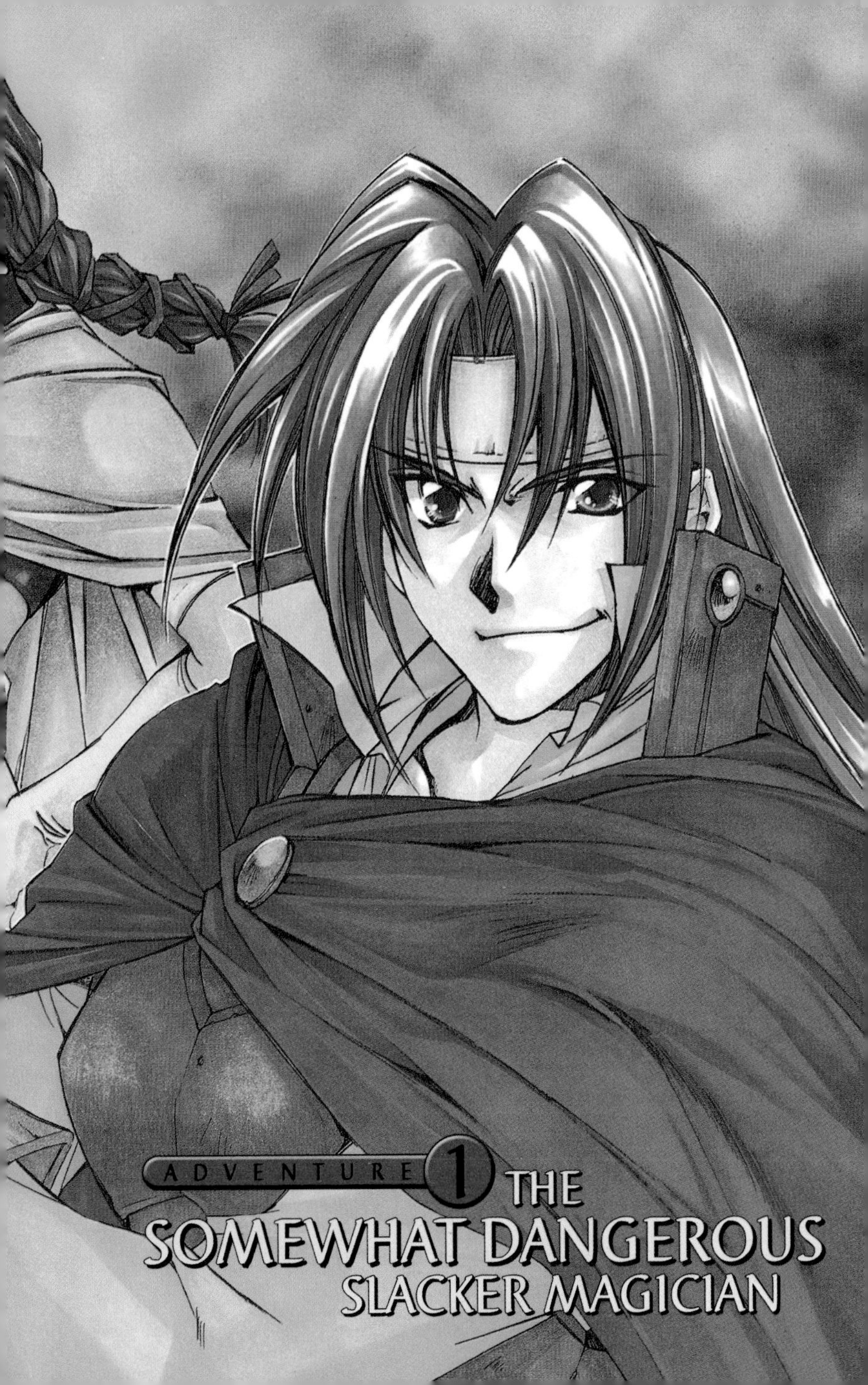
ADVENTURE 1
THE SOMEWHAT DANGEROUS SLACKER MAGICIAN

THE SOMEWHAT DANGEROUS SLACKER MAGICIAN

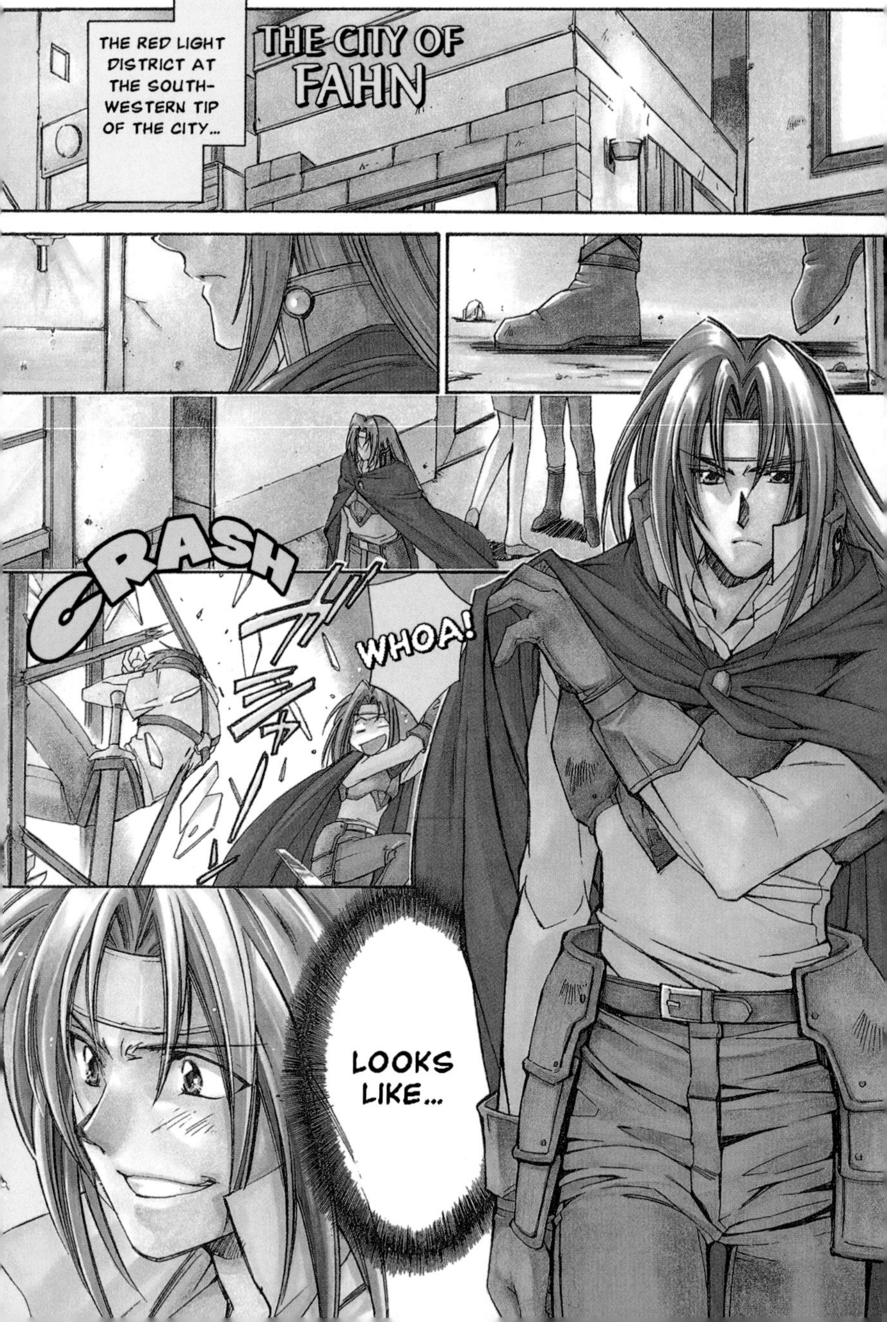
THE CITY OF FAHN
THE RED LIGHT DISTRICT AT THE SOUTH-WESTERN TIP OF THE CITY...
CRASH
WHOA!
LOOKS LIKE...

LOUIE the RUNE SOLDIER

CONTENTS

STORY RYOU MIZUNO · ART JUN SASAMEYUKI
CHARACTER DESIGNS MAMORU YOKOTA
OTHER DESIGNS and CG YASUMITSU SUETAKE

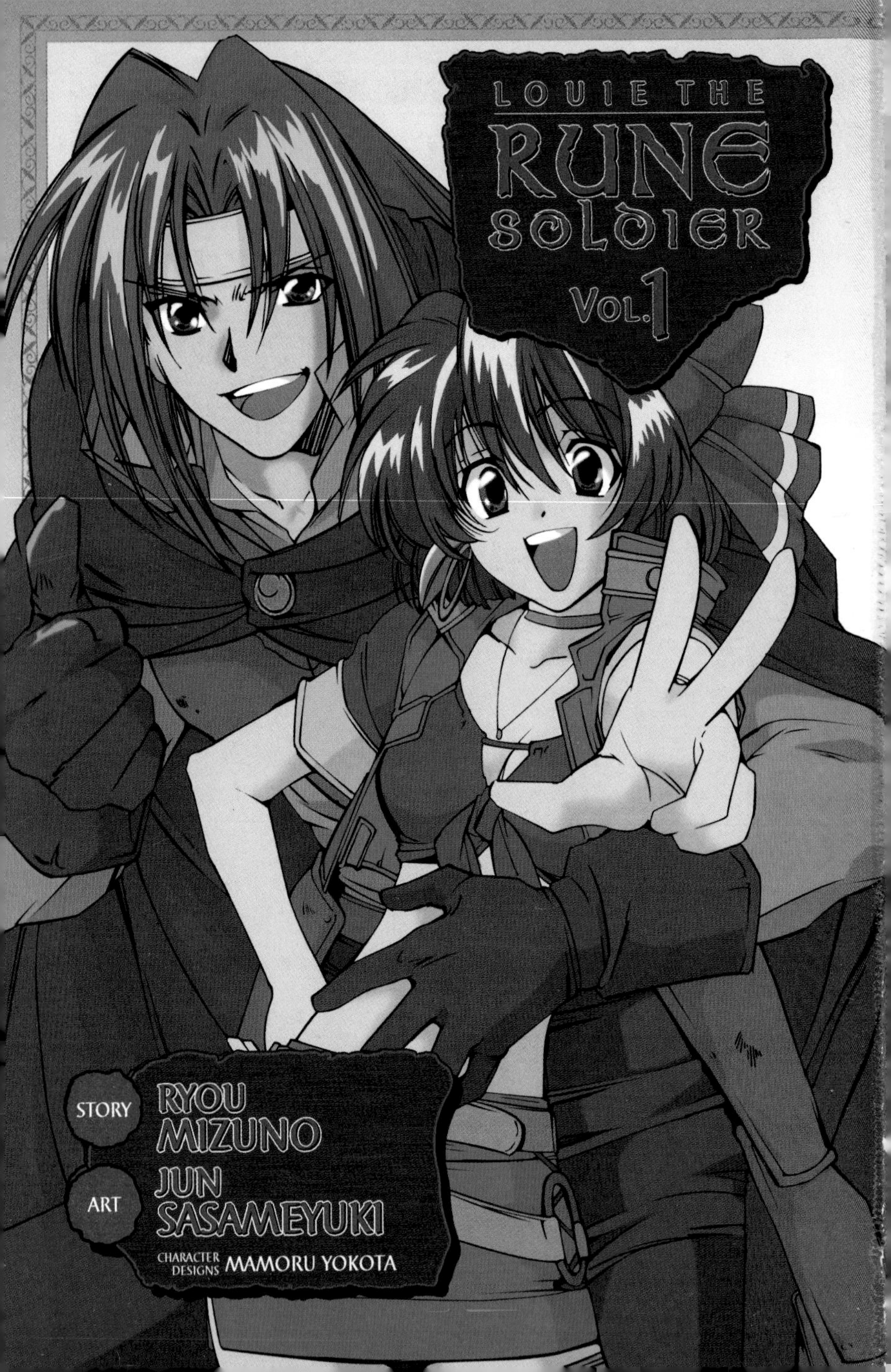
LOUIE THE
RUNE
SOLDIER
VOL.1
STORY
RYOU
MIZUNO
ART
JUN
SASAMEYUKI
CHARACTER DESIGNS
MAMORU YOKOTA